Spanish-English
English-Spanish
Dictionary

Cover Design 1994 - Carol-Ann McDonald

ISBN #1-884907-06-7

30059

NEW
WEBSTER'S
SPANISH-ENGLISH
ENGLISH-SPANISH
DICTIONARY

1994 EDITION

Paradise Press, Inc.

Miami, Florida

ENGLISH — SPANISH DICTIONARY

Spanish Grammar

Pronunciation: The Spanish alphabet consists of twenty-eight letters: a, b, c, ch, d, e, f, g, h, i, j, k, l, ll, m, n, ñ, o, p, q, r, rr, s, t, u, v, x, y, z (k and w are used only in words of foreign origin). Generally, they retain the same sound in every case, but there are some exceptions according to their place in the word or syllable. However, there are some general rules, fairly constant, which can be used as a reliable guide in the pronunciation of the Spanish language. Therefore, once these principles are mastered, there is no need to give the pronunciation of each work in this dictionary.

Vowels and diphthongs. The vowels are five in number and are pronounced as follows: *a* as in father (*casa* house, *vaca* cow), *e* as in met (*pelo* hair, *mesa* table), *i* as in police (*mina* mine, *pino* pine), *o* as in notary (*polo* pole, *cola* tail) and *u* as in moon (*nube* cloud, *uno* one).

Vowels may be divided into strong (*a, e, o*) or weak (*i, u*), on the basis of their sonority. The combination of a strong and a weak vowel or two weak vowels forms a diphthong; but in Spanish do not exist proper diphthongs, as met with in English (oo, ou) or in French (eu, eau), and each vowel of the diphthong should be distinctly pronounced.

Nevertheless, there are slight changes in some vowels when they form a diphthong: *i*, when first member of a diphthong, it is a semiconsonant and is pronounced like the English *y* in yes (*bien* well, *viento* wind); when it is the second member of a diphthong, it is a semivowel and has the English equivalent of *y* in they. (At the end of a word, the *i* becomes *y*: (*ley* law, *rey* king) . When *u* is the first member of a diphthong, it is a semiconsonant and is pronounced like the English *w* in wet (*bueno* good, *escuela* school); when it is the second member of a diphthong, it is a semivowel and has the English equivalents of *w* in few (*viuda* window) or like the *ou* in foul (*cauto* cautious). The Spanish diphthong *eu* has no equivalent in English, and in this case the *u* is pronounced distinctly, but shorter and closer than in English. In the syllables *que, qui, gue, gui*, the vowel *u* is generally silent.

Consonants. They have the following sounds:

b is softer than in English, it is a fricative, not an explosive.

c has two sounds: before *a, o, u*, or before a consonant, it is similar to the English *k*; before *e, i*, it has the sound of *th* in think, but in Spanish America it is pronounced like the *s* in sound.

ch is like the English *ch* in choose.

d is softer than in English, and the sound resembles that of *th* in though. At the end of a word, it is almost inaudible.

f is similar to the English *f*.

g, before *a, o, u*, or before a consonant, or after *n*, has the sound of the English *g* in gas; before *e, i*, it is pronounced like the Spanish *j*. In the combination *gue, gui*, the *u* is silent, being only a sign to indicate the *g* is not to be pronounced like the Spanish *j*, but like *g* in gas.

h is always silent.

j has no equivalent in English.. It is the German *ch* in ach; noch; it is a strongly aspirated English *h*.

l is similar to the English *l* in leave.

ll sounds like the English *ll* in brilliant, but in current speech is pronounced as *y*.

m is pronounced as in English.

n sounds as in English.

ñ sounds like *ny* in canyon.

p is similar to the English *p*.

q only occurs in the combinations *que, qui,* being an equivalent of the English *k*. As we have seen, in this case the *u* is silent.

r has two sounds; between two vowels has the sound of English *r* in caramel; when it begins a word or is preceded by *l, n or s*, it sounds like the Spanish *rr*.

rr has the same sound that *r*, with a strong trill.

s has the sound of English *ss* in essence.

t is more vigorous than the English *t*.

v is like the Spanish *b*.

x sounds like the *ks* between vowels and like *gs* before a consonant. In current speech, it is sometimes pronounced like the *s* in sound.

y sounds as in the English word year.

z is similar to the Spanish *c* before *e or i*, but in Spanish America is pronounced as the *s* in sound.

Accentuation. Words ending in a vowel, or in *s* or *n*, stress the next to the last syllable (*nadre* father, *dicen* they say, *nombres* names) words ending in a consonant other than *s* or *n* stress the last syllable (*papel* paper, *ciudad* city, *comer* to eat); words stressed in violation of the preceding rules must have the written accent on the stressed syllable (*café* coffee, *capitán* captain, *después* after, *árbol* tree, *lápiz* pencil, *último* last). An accent is also used to distinguish certain words that are written alike but have different meanings (*sí* yes, *si* if; *él* he, *el* the).

The Article: The article indicates the gender of nouns. There are two genders: masculine and feminine.

The masculine definite article is *el* the (plural) *los* the; the feminine definite article is *la* the (plural *las* the).

The indefinite article for masculine nouns is *un*; for feminine nouns, *una* (both *mena* a, an); the plural of this article, *unos, unas,* means several, any, a few, etc. Before feminine nouns beginning with *a* or *ha* and accented on the first syllable, the article *el* and *un* are used instead of *la* or *una*, respectively. However, if the stress is laid on any other syllable than the first, *la* and *una* are used.

The Noun: Nouns are either masculine or feminine. Names of male beings, and those terminating in *e, y, o,* or *u,* as well as the names of the days of the week, months, rivers, oceans, and mountains are masculine (*hombré* man, *muchacho* boy, *rey* king, *lunes* Monday, *enero* January, *Tajo* tagus, *Atlántico* Atlantic.)

Names of female beings, and those terminating in *a, ián, tad, dad* and *umbre*, as well as the names of the letters of the alphabet are feminine (*mujer* woman, *muchacha* girl, *estación* station, *amistad* friendship, *ciudad* city, *mechedumbre* crowd).

Formation of the feminine. Nouns ending in *o*, change *o* into *a* (*hijo* son, *hija* daughter); those ending in *án, ón,* or *or,* add *a* (*holgán* lazy man, *holgazana* lazy woman; *patrán* patron, *patrona* patroness; *pastor* shepherd, *pastora* shepherdess). Some nouns express the difference of gender by a different word (*poeta* poet, *poetize* poetess; *hombre* man, *mujer* woman).

Plural of nouns. Nouns ending in an unaccented vowel form the plural by adding *s* (*libro* book, *libros* books); nouns ending in an accented vowel or in a consonant (including the letter *y*) form the plural by adding *es* (*rubí* ruby, *rubíes* rubies; *canción* song, *canciones* songs; *rey* king, *reyes* kings). Nouns ending in *es* or *is* do not change in the plural (*lunes* Monday, *lunes* Mondays.) Nouns ending in *z* change the *z* to *c* before the plural ending *es* (*cruz* cross, *cruces* crosses).

The Adjective. The Spanish adjective agrees with the noun it qualifies (*hombre bueno* good man, *mujer buena* good woman; *hombres buenos* good men, *mujeres buenas* good women).

Plural of adjectives. They follow the same rules as nouns.

Formation of the feminine. Adjectives ending in *o* change *o* to *a* (*bueno, buena* good); adjectives ending in other vowels are invariable (*verde* green); adjectives ending in consonant are invariable (*fácil* easy) except those ending in *ón, án,* or, which add an *a.*

Adjectives denoting nationality add *a* to form the feminine (*francés, francesa* French).

Some adjectives (*alguno* someone, *ninguno* no one, *bueno* good, *malo* bad, and *santo* saint, the numerals *uno a, primero* first, *tercero* third, *postrer* last and *ciento* one hundred) undergo a slight variation when used before a masculine noun in the singular, and become, *algún, ningún, buen, mal, san, un, primer, tercer, postrer* and *cien.*

An adjective qualifying two nouns must be plural (*la hermana y la hija están felices* the sister and the daughter are happy); if the nouns are different genders, the adjective is put in the plural masculine (*el hombre y la mujer están contentos* the man and the woman are satisfied).

Position of adjectives. Adjectives are divided into two classes, limiting and descriptive. Limiting adjectives are the articles, demonstratives, possessives, numerals, and indefinites. They regularly precede the noun they modify (*la casa* the house, *esta casa* this house, *mi casa* my house, *dos casas* two houses, *ninguna casa* no house).

Descriptive adjectives may either precede or follow the noun according to well defined laws of usage. They precede when they denote an inherent or logical characteristic of the noun they modify (*la blanca nieve* the white snow); they follow when they denote a differentiating characteristic of the noun they modify (*la casa blanca* the white house).

Degrees of comparison. Adjectives form the comparative and superlative by means of the modifying adverb *mós* (more). While the comparative and superlative are identical in form, their difference in meaning Is made clear by the context of the sentence (*hermoso* beautiful, *más hermoso* more beautiful, *el más hermoso* the most beautiful, or *la más hermosa* feminine). After superlative expressions, *de* is equivalent to *in* (*Pedro es el alumno más alto de la clase* Peter is the tallest student in the class). In Spanish there is also an absolute superlative which is formed by the addition of the syllable *ísimo* for the masculine and *isima* for the feminine to the positive degree of the adjective (*santo* holy, *santísimo* very holy).

Some adjectives have an irregular comparison in addition to the regular one (*bueno* good, *mejor* better, *mejor* best; *malo* bad *peor* worse, *peor* worst; *grande* large, *mayor* larger, *mayor* largest, *pequeño* small, *menor* smaller, *menor* smallest, etc.)

The Pronoun. In Spanish, there are six kinds of pronouns: personal, demonstrative, possessive, interrogative, relative and indefinite.

Personal pronouns. They are as follows:

Singular	**Plural**
ti I me	*nosotros, nosotras* we
me me	*nos, nos* us
me me	*nosotros, nosotras* us
conmigo with me	*con nosotros, con nosotras* with us
tú thou	*vosotros, vosotras* you
te thee	*os, os* you
ti thee	*vosotros, vosotras* you
contigo with thee	*con vosotros, con vosotras* with you
usted you	*usted* you
a usted, le, la, se you	*a usted, los, las, se* you
a usted, le se, a él, sí you	*a ustedes, les, se, a ellos, sí* you
con usted, consigo with you	*con ustedes o consigo* with you
él he, it	*ellos* they
le, se; él, sí him, it	*los, se; ellos, sí* them
le, se, él, sí him, it	*les, se; ellos, sí* them
con él, consigo with him, with it	*con ellos, consigo* with them
ella she, it	*ellas* they
la, se; ella, sí her, it	*las, se; ellas, sí* them
le, se; ella, sí her, it	*les, se; ellas sí* them
con ella, consigo with her, with it	*con ellas, consigo* with them

Mí, tí, sí are always preceded by prepositions.

me, te, se, le, las, la, las, les are governed by verbs and never placed after prepositions.

Demonstrative pronouns. The following words are pronouns when used instead of a noun: *ésto* this, *ésta* this, *ésto* this, *éstos* these, *éstas* these, *ése* that, *ésa* that, *éso* that, *ésos* those, *ésas* those; *aquél* that, *aquélla* that, *aquéllo* that, *aquéllos* those, *aquéllas* those.

These same words, when followed by a noun, are demonstrative adjectives, but in this latter case they are used without the written accent.

Possessive pronouns. With the possessive pronouns, the first thing to decide is whether a stress is laid on them or not. If not, the short forms are used (adjectives):

Singular	**Plural**
mi, mis my	*nuestro, nuestra, nuestros, nuestras* our
tu, tus thy	*vuestro, vuestra, vuestros, vuestras* your
su, sus (de usted) your	*su, sus (de ustedes)* your
su, sus (de él) his	*su, sus (de ellos)* their
su, sus (de ella) her	*su, sus (de ellas)* their

If a stress is laid on the possessive pronoun, longer and more sonorous forms should be used, which always follow the noun. They are as follows:

Singular	**Plural**
mío, mía, míos, mías my	*nuestro, nuestra, nuestros, nuestras* ours
tuyo, tuya, tuyos, tuyas thy	*vuestro, vuestra, vuestros, vuestras* your
suyo, suya, suyos, suyas (de usted) your	*suyo, suya, suyos, suyas (de ustedes)* your
suyo, suya, suyos, suyas (de él) his	*suyo, suya, suyos, suyas (de ellos)* their
suyo, suya, suyos, suyas (de ella) her	*suyo, suya, suyos, suyas (de ellas)* theirs

Conjunctive and personal pronouns. These pronouns, called in Spanish pronombres complementos, are used as direct or indirect objects of the verb. They are called "conjunctive" because they are used in conjunction with the verb, and no other word can intervene. They generally precede the verb.

Accusative	Dative
me me	*me* to me
te thee	*te* to thee
le, lo you	*le* to you
le, lo him, it	*le* to him, to it
la he, it	*le* to her, to it
nos us	*nos* to us
os you	*os* to you
les, los you	*les* to you
los them	*les* to them
las them	*les* to them

Redundant personal pronouns. In view of the fact that the pronouns of the third person, *le, la, los, las, les,* have, respectively, more than one meaning, there is a possible ambiguity when the antecedent is not clearly established by the context. To avoid such ambiguity we use a redundant construction; for this purpose, we retain the ambiguous construction intact, and add to it the prepositional form of the pronoun (*le digo* I tell him, I tell her, I tell you: *le digo a él*).

The same thing happens with the possessive adjective *su, sus,* (*Juan lee su libro* John reads his book, John reads her book, John reads their book, John reads your book: *Juan lee su libro de ellos*).

Interrogative and relative pronouns. The interrogative pronouns differ only from the relative pronouns inasmuch as they have the written accent:

Interrogative	Relative Pronouns
quién, quiéns who?	*quien, quiens* who
cuál, cuáles, which?, what?	*cual, cuales* which, that
que what?	*que* that
cúyo, cuya, cuyos, cúyas, whose?	*cúyo, cuya, cuyos, cuyas,* whose?

With the exception of *quién, quiénes,* the forms of the interrogative pronouns serve also as interrogative adjectives.

Indefinite pronouns. They are: *alguien* (somebody, anybody) *nadie* (nobody), *alguno, alguna, algunos, algunas* (somebody some); *ninguno, ninguna, ningunos, ningunas* (nobody, none); *algo* (something); *nada* (nothing); *quienquiera, quiensequiera* (whoever).

The following indefinite adjectives may also be used as indefinite pronouns: *uno, una, unos, unas* (one, some); *cada* (each); *cada uno, cada una* (each one); *ambos, ambas* (both); *los demás, las demás* (the rest of); *cualquiera, cualesquiera* (whichever, whatever); *mucho, mucha, muchos, muchas* (much, many); *poco, poca, pocos, pocas* (little, few); *todo, toda, todos, todas* (all); *otro, otra, otros, otras* (another, other); *tanto, tanta, tantos, tantas* (so much, so many); *cuanto, cuanta, cuantos, cuantas* (as many, all that); *tal, tales* such a, such) *mismo, misma, mismos, mismas* (self, selves).

The Adverb. Adverbs modify verbs, adjectives, or other adverbs. They are either proper adverbs, as bien well, or formed from adjectives or participles by the addition of the termination *mente* to the feminine singular of adjectives. (The suffix *mente* is simply the feminine noun *mente* mind, intelligence. The feminine gender of this noun accounts for the use of the feminine form of the adjective.)

If the adjective ends in *o*, this *o* is changed into *a* before adding *mente* (*diestro* dexterous, *diestramente* dexterously); if the adjective does not end in *o*, *mente* is simply added to the termination (*fácil* easy, *fácilmente* easily). When the adjective has a written accent, this accent is retained In the adverbial compound (*último* last, *últimamente* lastly, recently).

If several adverbs ending in *mente* follow each other, this termination is, for the sake of euphony, added to the last only (*hablo correcta y rápiamente* I speak correctly and rapidly, instead of *correctamente y rápidamente*).

Adverbs form their comparative like adjectives.

The Preposition. The Spanish prepositions govern no particular case. They are simply placed before the noun. The most frequent are: *a* (at, to for) *ante, antes* (before), *con* (with), *contra* (against), *de* (of, from), *desde* (from), *en* (in, on, at), *entre* (between, among), *hacia* (towards), *hasta* (until), *para* (for, to), *por* (by, for, through), *según* (according), *sin* (without), *sobre* (on, upon), and *tras, detrars* (behind).

The Conjunction. Conjunctions are invariable, only *e* is used instead of *y* (and) when the following word begins by *i* of *hi*; *u* is employed instead of *o*, when the following word begins by *o* or *ho*).

The Verb. By the termination of the infinitive mood we distinguish three different forms of conjugation. The first conjugation, with the infinitive mood ending in *ar* (*amar* to love); the second conjugation, with the infinitive mood ending in *er* (*temer* to fear), and the third conjugation, with the infinitive mood ending in *ir* (*batir* to beat).

Compound tenses. These are formed by placing after the verb *haber* (to have), the past participle of the verb conjugated (*yo he amado* I have loved, *tú habís amado* you had loved, etc.).

Auxiliary verbs. We give the complete conjugation of verbs *haber* or *tener* (to have) and *ser* or *estar* (to be).

Irregular verbs. Irregular verbs can suffer a change either in their radical letters of in the terminations of the conjugations to which they belong, or in both. The total number of such verbs in the Spanish language is about eight hundred and eighty. To learn them, the student must master by heart six models or paradigms, which we cannot give here.

Abbreviations Used in This Dictionary

a.	adjective		(Med.)	Medicine
adj.	adjective		(Mil.)	Military
adv.	adverb		(Min.)	Mineralogy
(Agr.)	Agriculture		(Mit.)	Mythology
Am.	American		(Mús.)	Music
(An.)	Anatomy		(Náut.)	Nautical
(Arq.)	Architecture		(Pat.)	Pathology
(Aut.)	Automotive		*pl.*	plural
aux.	auxiliary		*pers.*	personal
art.	article		*poss.*	possessive participle
(Av.)	Aviation		*pp.*	past participle
(Biol.)	Biology		*prep.*	preposition
(Bot.)	Botany		*pron.*	pronoun
cnj.	conjunction		(Fis.)	Physiology
(Com.)	Commerce		(Fon.)	Phonetic
comp.	comparative		(Fot.)	Photography
dem.	demonstrative		(Fsl.)	Physiology
(Der.)	Legal		(Geom.)	Geometry
(dial.)	dialect		(Gram.)	Grammar
(Ecl.)	Ecclesiastical		(Hist.)	History
(Elec.)	Electric		(Hort.)	Horticulture
f.	feminine		(Qm.)	Chemistry
(fam.)	familiar		*ref.*	reflexive
(Far.)	Pharmaceutical		*s.*	substantive
(fig.)	figurative		*super.*	superlative
(Fil.)	Philosophy		*tr.*	transitive verb
imp.	imperative verb		(Tt.)	Theater
in.	intransitive		(var.)	variation
indef.	indefinite		(vulg.)	vulgar
inf.	infinitive		(Zool.)	Zoology
(Ingl.)	English			
int.	interrogative			
intr.	intransitive			
(Irl.)	Ireland			
m.	masculine			
(Mat.)	Mathematics			
(Mec.)	Mechanics			

A

a *art. indef.* un, una.
aback *adv.* detrás, atrás.
abandon *tr.* abandonar.
abandonment *s.* abandono.
abase *tr.* humillar, degradar.
abash *tr.* avergonzar.
abate *tr.* disminuir, reducir.
abbess *s.* abadesa.
abbey *s.* abadía, monasterio.
abbot *s.* abad, prior.
abbreviate *tr.* abreviar,
   abreviatura.
abdicate *tr.* e *in.* renunciar.
abdomen *s.* abdomen; vientre.
abduct *tr.* raptar, secuestrar,
   abducir; *Am.* plagiar.
abed *adv.* en cama.
abeyance *s.* suspensión;
   vacante.
abhor *tr.* aborrecer.
ability *s. (pl: -ties)* habilidad.
ablative *adj.* ablativo.
ablaze *adj.* brillante.
able *adj.* hábil, capaz.
ablution *s.* ablución, lavado.
abode *s.* domicilio, hogar.
abolish *tr.* abolir, angular.
aboriginal *adj. & s.* nativo.
abort *tr.* e *in.* abortrar.
abound *in.* abundar.
about *adv.* alredor de; *prep.* y
   adv. sobre.
above *adj & s.* antedicho,
   prep. sobre; *adv.* arriba.
abreast *adv.* al lado *(uno de
   otro)*, de frente.
abridge *tr.* abreviar;
   simplificar.
abrogate *tr.* abrogar.
abrupt *adj.* abrupto.
abscond *in.* evadirse.
absence *s.* ausencia.
absent *adj.* ausente.
absolution *s.* absolución.
absolve *tr.* perdonar.
absorb *tr.* absorber.

abstain *in.* abstenerse.
abstract *adj.* abstracto.
abstract *tr.* resumir.
absurd *adj.* absurdo.
abundant *adj.* abundante.
abuse *tr.* maltratar; abusar de.
abutment *s.* linde, confin.
abysm *s.* abismo.
academy *s. (pl: -mies)*
   academia, colegio.
accede *intr.* acceder.
accelerate *tr.* acelerar.
accent *s.* acento; *tr.* acentuar;
   -uate *tr.* acentuar.
accept *tr.* aceptar.
access *s.* acceso. ible *a.*
   accesible.
accessory *a.* accesorio.
accident *s.* accidente.
acclamation *s.* aclamación.
acclivity *s. (pl: -ties)* rampa.
accommodate *tr.* acomodar;
   -tion *s.* acomodación.
accompany *tr. (pret. y pp.
   -nied)* acompañar.
accomplish *tr.* realizar;
—ed *a.* realizado.
—ment *s.* realización.
accord *s.* acuerdo; *tr.*
   concordar.
according *a.* acorde.
account *s.* cuenta.
accountant *s.* contable.
accumulate *tr.* acumular;
—ion *s.* acumulación.
—ive *a.* acumulativo.
—or *s.* acumulador.
accuracy *s. (pl: -cies)*,
   precisión.
accusation *s.* acusación.
ace *s.* as, uno, unidad.
ache *s.* dolor continuo.
achieve *tr.* acabar;
—ment *s.* realización.
acid *a.* ácido.
acolyte *s.* acólito.
acorn *s.* (Bot.) bellota.
acquaint *tr.* informar.
acquiesce *int.* asentir.

acquiescence s. consentimiento.

acquire tr. adquirir;

—ment s. adquisición.

—ion s. adquisición.

acrobat s. acróbata, sonámbulo.

across adv. a través.

act s. acto, acción.

acting adj. interino.

actively adv. activamente.

actress s. actriz.

actual adj. verdadero.

acute adj. agudo, perspicaz.

ad s. anuncio.

adamant s. diamante.

adapt tr. adaptar.

adaptability s. (pl: -ties) adaptabilidad, facilidad.

add tr. añadir.

adder s. víbora.

addicted adj. aficionado a.

addle tr. e intr. vaciar.

address s. direccion.

adept adj. experto.

adequate adj. suficiente.

adhere intr. adherir (se).

adieu (pl: **adieus** o **adieux**) s. adiós.

adjective adj. y s. adjetivo.

adjudge tr. decretar.

adjunct adj. adjunto.

adjure tr. implorar.

adjust tr. ajustar.

adjustable adj. adaptable.

administer tr. administrar.

admirable adj. admirable.

admiral s. almirante.

admire tr. admirar.

admissible adj. admisible.

admittance s. admisión.

admixture s. mezcla.

admonish tr. advertir.

ado s. ruido.

adolescent s. adolescencia.

adore tr. adorar, idolatrar.

adorn tr. adornar.

adrift adv. a la deriva.

adroit adj. hábil, diestro.

adult adj. y s. adulto.

advance s. adelanto.

advance tr. adelantar.

advancing adj. progresivo.

adventure s. aventura; tr. aventurar, int. aventurarse.

adversary s. (pl: -ies) adversario.

adverse adj. adverso, contrario (viento).

advert intr. aludir.

advice s. consejo, aviso.

advise tr. aconsejar.

aerate tr. airear, ventilar.

aerial adj. aéreo.

afar adv. lejos.

affair s. asunto, aventura.

affect tr. impresionar.

affiliate tr. afiliar, adoptar.

affinity s. (pl: -ties) parentesco.

affirm tr. afirmar; intr. afirmarse.

afflict tr. afigir.

affluence s. afluencia.

afford tr. tener (dinero, etc.).

affranchise tr. emancipar.

affright tr. aterrar.

afoot adv. a pie, en marcha.

afraid adj. espantado, asustado.

afresh adv. otra vez, de nuevo.

after adj. siguiente; adv. después; pre. después de; según; cnj. después que.

afternoon s. tarde (refiriéndose a la tarde).

again adv. de nuevo, otra vez, aún; además, por otra parte; **again and** — repetidas veces; **now and** — de vez en cuando; **never** — nunca más. Con frecuencia equivale al prefijo re del castellano; **to send** — reenviar, volver a enviar.

against prep. contra; cerca de; en contraste con.

age s. edad.

A

agency *s. (pl:* -**cies**) agencia; medio.

aggrandize *tr.* agrandar, engrandecer.

aggravate *tr.* agravar; (fam.).

aggrieve *tr.* afligir.

aghast *adj.* horrorizado.

agile *adj.* ágil, hábil.

agitate *tr.* agitar; *intr.* agitar, hacer campaña.

aglow *adj.* y *adv.* fulgurante; encendido.

ago *adv.* hace, ha, pasado; **long time** — hace mucho tiempo.

agog *adj.* ansioso.

agony *s. (pl:* -**nies**) agonía, angustia.

agrarian *adj.* agrario.

agree *intr.* concordar, ponerse de acuerdo.

agreeable *adj.* agradable.

agreed *pp.* y *adj.* convenido.

agreement *s.* acuerdo.

aground *adj.* y *adv.* varado, encallado.

ague *s.* escalofrío.

ah *inj.* ¡ah!

aha *inj.* ¡ajá!

ahead *adv.* delante, al frente.

aid *s.* ayuda, auxilio; **in — of** a beneficio de; **first —** botiquín. *tr.* e *intr.* ayudar.

ail *tr.* inquietar; *int.* sufrir.

ailing *adj.* enfermizo, achacoso.

ailment *s.* enfermedad, achaque.

aim *s.* puntería.

ain't (Conv.) contracción de **am** y **not**, equivalente a **am not**, **is not**, **are not**.

air *s.* aire; ambiente.

airing *s.* ventilación; paseo para tomar el aire. **to take an —** dar una vuelta.

airless *adj.* sin aire.

airline *s.* línea aérea.

air mail *s.* correo aéreo; — **letter** *s.* carta por avión.

airplane *s.* avión.

airport *s.* aeropuerto.

airstrip *s.* pista *(de despegue o alterrizaje).*

airtight *adj.* hermético.

aisle *s.* pasillo.

ajar *adj.* entreabierto, entornado.

akin *adj.* emparentado; semejante.

alas *inj.* ¡ay!, ¡ay de mí!

albeit *conj.* aunque, bien que.

alderman *s. (pl:* -**men**) concejal.

ale *s.* cerveza inglesa.

alight (**alighted** o **alit**), apearse, bajar.

alike *adj.* semejante, parecido, igual.

aliment *s.* alimento; *tr.* alimentar.

alive *adj.* vivo, activo.

all *adj. indef.* todo, todos; todo el, todos los; *pron. indef.* todo; todos, todo el mundo; **not at**—nada, no hay de qué; **once and for —** de una vez para siempre; — **right** está bien; — **the better** tanto mejor; — **the worse** tanto peor; **in — en** resumidas cuentas.

allay *tr.* aliviar, calmar, mitigar.

allegiance *s.* lealtad, fidelidad.

allergy *s. (pl.* -**gies**) alergia.

alleviate *tr.* aliviar.

alley *s.* callejuela.

allocate *tr.* asignar, colocar.

allot *tr. (pret.* y *pp:* **alloted;** *ger: **alloting**) asignar, distribuír, adjudicar, fijar.*

allow *tr.* permitir; asignar, conceder.

alloy *tr.* alear, ligar; mezclar, adulterar.

allude *intr.* aludir, referirise a.

allure *tr.* seducir, atraer.

almighty *adj.* todopoderoso.

almost *adv.* casi; — **at any moment** de un momento a otro.

alms *s.* limosna.

aloft *adv.* arriba, en alto.

alone *adj.* solo, a solas.

along *prep.* a lo largo de; *adv.* a lo largo; adelante; conmigo, consigo.

alongside *prep.* junto a, a lo largo de.

aloof *adj.* apartado; reservado; *adv.* lejos, a distancia.

aloud *adv.* alto, con voz alta.

already *adv.* ya.

also *adv.* también, además.

alter *tr. alterar; intr.* alterarse.

although *cnj.* aunque, a pesar de que.

altogether *adv.* enteramente, por completo, en conjunto.

always *adv.* simpre, en todo tiempo.

amain *adv.* con fuerza, con violencia.

amaze *tr.* asombrar, pasmar.

amelioration *s.* mejora, reforma.

amend *tr.* enmendar, corregir; *intr.* enmendarse.

amid *prep.* en medio de, rodeado por.

amidst *prep.* en medio de.

amiss *adv.* erradamente, impropiamente, de más.

ammunition *s.* munición; *tr.* amunicionar.

among *prep.* entre, en el número de.

amongst *prep.* entre, en medio de.

amount *s.* cantidad, suma total; *intr.* ascender (*a cierta cantidad*), **to — to** ascender a, subir a.

ampleness *s.* amplitud.

amplitude *s.* amplitud.

amply *adv.* ampliamente, abundantemente.

amputate *tr.* amputar, cortar.

amuse *tr.* divertir, entretener.

amusing *adj.* divertido, entretenido.

an *art. indef.* var. de *adj.* (*ante sonido precedido de vocal*), un, una.

ancestral *adj.* ancestral, de los antepasados, hereditario; — **home** casa solariega.

and *cnj.* y, e; — **so on**, — **so forth** y así sucesivamente; (fam.) **bread — butter** pan con mantequilla; a, de (*con ciertos infinitivos*).

anew *adv.* nuevamente, de nuevo.

anger *s.* ira, cólera, furia; *tr.* airar, enfurecer, irritar.

angle *s.* ángulo; (fig.) punto de vista, anzuelo, caña de pescar; *intr.* pescar con caña; (fig.) intrigar; **to — for** echar el anzuelo a, intrigar por conseguir.

angler *s.* pescador de caña; (fig.) intrigante.

angrily *adv.* airadamente.

angry (*adj.* (comp. **-ier**; *superl.* **-iest**); enojado; **to become — with** enojarse con o contra.

anguish *s.* anguistia, congoja, tormento, ansia.

animadvert *tr.* advertir, observar; *intr.* advertir; **to — on** o **upon** censurar.

animosity *s.* (*pl:* **-ties**) animosidad, rencor.

ankle *s.* tobillo, talón.

annihilate *tr.* aniquilar, destruír.

announce *tr.* anunciar, avisar, pregonar.

annoy *tr.* molestar, fastidiar.

annoying *adj.* molesto, engorroso.

annual *adj.* anual, publicación anual.

annual *tr. (pret.* y *pp.* **-nulled**; *ger.* **-nulling**) anular, invalidar.
anoint *tr.* consagrar.
anon *prep.* pronto.
another *adj.* y *pron. indef.* otro, uno más; **one** — uno a otro.
answer *s.* respuesta; explicación, solución.
ant *s.* hormiga.
antecedent *s.* antecedente.
antelope *s.* (Zool.) antílope, gacela.
antenna *s. (pl:* **-nae**) antena; *(pl:* **-nas**) antena.
anthem *s.* himno; (Ecl.) antífona.
anthropoid *adj.* antropoide; (Zool.) antropoideo.
antibody *s. (pl:* **-dies**) anticuerpo.
antic *adj.* extraño.
anticipation *s.* previsión, anticipación.
anti-freeze *s.* anticongelante.
antipathetic *adj.* antipático.
antipoison *s.* contraveneno.
antique *adj.* antiguo; anticuado.
anti-Semitism *s.* antisemitisimo.
antler *s.* cornamenta.
anus *s.* (An.) ano.
any *adj. indef.* algún, cualquiera; — **place** en cualquier parte; **any time** alguna vez; **at** — **rate** pase lo que pase; *pron. indef.* alguno, cualquiera; *adv.* algo.
anybody *pron. indef.* alguno, alguien, cualquiera, quienquiera; **not** — ninguno, nadie.
anyhow *adv.* de cualquier modo.
anyone *pron. indef.* alguno.

anything *pron. indef.* algo, alguna cosa; — **but** todo menos.
anyway *adv.* de culaquier modo.
anywhere *adv.* dondequiera.
anywise *adv.* de cualquier modo.
apace *adv.* aprisa.
apartment *s.* apartamento, piso.
ape *s.* (Zool.) mono; (fig.) mona (*persona que imita a otras*).
aperient *adj.* y *s.* laxante.
apiece *adv.* cada uno, por cabeza.
apogee *s.* apogeo.
apologetic *adj.ÿ*
apoplexy *s. (pl:* **-xies**) (Med.) apoplejía.
apostasy *s. (pl:* **-sies**) — apostasía.
apostle *s.* apóstol.
apostrophe *s.* apóstrofe.
apothecary *s. (pl:* **-ies**) tobicario, droguera. **—'s shop** botica.
appalling *adj.* espantoso.
apparatus *s. (pl:* **-tus -tuses**) aparato.
apparel *s.* ropa, atavío; (Náut.) aparejo; *tr. (pret.* y *pp;* **-eled** o **-elled**) vestir, ataviar.
apparent *adj.* aparente.
apparition *s.* aparición.
appeal *s.* súplica.
appeal *intr.* ser atrayente.
appear *intr.* aparecer.
appease *tr.* apaciguar.
append *tr.* añadir.
appendage *s.* dependencia.
appertain *intr.* pertenecer.
applaud *tr.* e *intr.* aplaudir.
apple *s.* (Bot.) manzana niña, pupila (*del ojo*); **tree** *s.* manzano. **-sauce** *s.* salsa de manzana.
appliance *s.* instrumento.

applicant s. candidato.
applied adj. aplicado.
apply tr. intr (pret. y pp.
-**plied**) dirgirse a, concernir,
aplicar.
appoint tr. nombrar, amueblar.
apposite adj. oportuno.
appraise tr. tasar.
appreciation s. apreciación,
agradecimiento.
apprehend tr. aprehender.
apprentice s. aprendiz.
apprise tr. informar.
approach s. acercamiento,
entrada.
approaching adj. próximo.
approval s. aprobación.
approve tr. aprobar.
approximate tr. aproximar;
intr. aproximarse.
appurtenance s. pertenencia.
apricot albaricoque; — **tree**
albaricoquero.
April s. abril.
apron s. delantal.
apse s. (Arq.) ábside.
apt adj. apto.
Arab adj. árabe; s. árabe.
arable adj. arable — **land**
campiña.
arc s. acro — **ade** s. (Arq.)
arcada.
arch adj. astuto; travieso.
archaic adj. arcaico.
archbishop s. arzobispo.
arched ad. abovedado.
architect s. arquitecto.
archlike adj. en forma de arco.
archpriest s. arcipreste.
archway s. (Arq.) arcada,
pasaje abovedado.
ardent adj. ardiente.
are segunda persona del
singular y 1.ª, 2.ª y 3.ª del
plural del presente de
indicativo de **to be**.
arena s. arena.
argue tr. debatir.
argument s. argumento.

arise intr. (pret **arose**; pp.
arisen) levantarse; alzarse,
sublevarse.
arithmetic s. aritmética.
ark s. arca.
armament s. armamento;
fuerzas militares.
armature s. armadura; (Zool.)
coraza.
armless adj. manco.
armorial adj. heráldico.
arms s. pl. armas, milicia.
army s. (pl: -**mies**) ejército;
adj. militar, castrense, del
ejército.
around adv. alrededor.
arouse tr. despertar; mover.
arraign tr. acusar.
arrange tr. disponer.
array s. orden; batalla; adorno.
arrears s. pl. atraso,; dinero
por ganar.
arrest s. prisión.
arrive intr. llegar; tener éxito.
arrogate tr. arrogarse.
arrow s. flecha.
arson s. incendio
premeditado; provocado.
art s. arte; habilidad; **fine** —**s**
bellas artes; —**s and crafts**
artes y oficios.
artesian s. pozo artesiano.
artful adj. mañoso, artificial.
artificiality s. (pl: -**ties**) falta
de naturalidad.
artisan s. artesano.
artist s. artista.
artless adj. sencillo.
as conj. como, a semejanza
de, según.
asbestos s. uralita.
ascend tr. subir; **to** — **the
throne** subir al trono.
ascent s. ascensión,
promoción.
ascertain tr. averiguar.
ash s. ceniza; —**tray** cenicero.
ashore adv. en tierra, a tierra.
asparagus s. (Bot.) espárrago.
aspect s. aspecto.

A

asphalt *s.* asfalto.
aspiration *s.* aspiración, anhelo.
aspire *intr.* aspirar, pretender.
aspirin *s.* aspirina.
assail *tr.* asaltar.
assassin *s.* asesino.
assault *s.* asalto.
assay *s.* ensayo.
assemblage *s.* asamblea.
assert *tr.* afirmar.
assess *tr.* gravar.
assessment *s.* gravamen.
assign *tr.* asignar.
assist *tr.* asistir.
assort *tr.* ordenar.
assuage *tr.* aliviar.
assume *tr.* asumir,; adoptar; *intr.* imaginarse, dar por sentado.
assuming *adj.* presumido.
assurance *s.* aseguramiento.
assure *tr.* asegurar, garantizar.
astern *adv.* (Náut.) a popa.
astir *adv.* en movimiento.
astonish *tr.* asombrar.
astonishing *adj.* asombroso.
astound *tr.* pasmar.
astray *adv.* por mal camino.
astuteness *s.* astucia.
atom *s.* átomo.
atone *intr.* expiar; dar reparación.
atonement *s.* expiación.
attach *tr.* atar; pegar.
attack *s.* ataque, — **of fever** acceso de fiebre.
attain *tr.* lograr.
attainder *s.* muerte civil.
attempt *s.* tentativa; atentado.
attend *tr.* atender; asistir.
attenuate *tr.* atenuar.
attest *tr.* atestiguar.
attestor *s.* testigo.
attic *adj.* y *s.* ático.
attire *s.* atavío; *tr.* ataviar.
attorney *s.* procurador; abogado.
attrat *tr.* atraer; ganarse.

attune *tr.* afinar.
auburn *adj.* pardo, rojizo.
audience *s.* audiencia; auditorio.
audir *s.* (Com.) intervención,; *tr.* intervenir.
auditor *s.* oyente.
augment *tr.* aumentar.
August *s.* agosto.
aunt *s.* tía.
austere *adj.* austero.
authenticate *tr.* autorizar, autenticar, legalizar.
authority (*pl:* **-ties**) autoridad; autorización.
autobiography autobiografia.
autonomous *adj.* autónomo.
autonomy *s.* (*pl:* **-mies**) autonomía.
autumn *s.* otoño.
avail *s.* provecho; *tr.* beneficiar; *intr.* aprovechar.
available *adj.* disponible, útil.
available assets *s.* activo disponible.
avenge *tr.* vengar.
avenue *s.* avenida, alameda.
aver *tr* (*pret.* y *pp.* **averred**) afirmar.
averse *adj.* adverso, contrario.
avert *tr.* devisar, impedir.
aviary *s.* (*pl.* **-ries**) pajarera.
avid *adj.* ávido.
avoid *tr.* evitar.
avoidable *adj.* evitable.
avow *tr.* admitir, declarar.
await *tr.* aguardar, esperar.
awaken *tr.* e *intr.* despertar.
away *adj.* ausente.
awe *s.* miedo.
awesome *adj.* imponente.
awhile *adv.* algún tiempo.
awn *s.* (Bot.) arista.
ax(e) *s.* hacha.
axis *s.* (*pl:* **-axes**) eje.
axle *s.* eje.
azure *s.* azul.

B

babble *s.* charla, murmullo; *intr.* hablar por los codos.
babe *s.* nene, criatura.
baby *s.* (*pl:* **-bies**) nene, bebe; *adj.* infantil.
babyish *a.* infantil, pueril.
back *adv.* atrás, detrás; *s.* espalda, respaldo; **on one's —** postrado en cama; **full—** defense (*fútbol*): **with one's — to the wall** entre la espada y la pared; **to be —** estar de vuelta; **to go — and forth** ir y venir; **—in** allá por; *tr.* e *intr.* mover o moverse hacia atrás; encuadernar.
backbite (*pret:* **-bit**; *pp:* **-bit** o **-bitten**) *tr.* a, calumniar; *intr.* murmurar.
back-door *s.* puerta falsa.
background *s.* fondo.
backing *s.* apoyo, sostén.
backshop *s.* trastienda.
back street *s.* callejón.
backward *adj.* atrasado; *adv.* atrás; cada vez peor.
backwardness *s.* atraso, timidez.
bacon *s.* tocino con jamón.
bad *adj.* malo, falso.
badge *s.* insignia, divisa.
badminton *s.* juego de raqueta y pelota con plumas.
baffle *s.* confusión, pantalla acústica; *tr.* frustrar; *intr.* luchar en vano.
bag *s.* saco; rodillera (*del pantalón*); *tr.* (*pret.* y *pp.* **bagged**), embolsar.
baggage *s.* equipaje.
bagpipe *s.* gaita.
bail *s.* fianza; *tr.* (Der.) dar fianza (*por uno*).
bailiff *s.* alguacil, corchete.

bait *s.* cebar, carnada.
baize *s.* bayeta.
bake *tr.* cocer (*al horno*).
baker *s.* panadero.
balancing *s.* equilibrio.
balcony *s.* (*pl.* **-nies**) balcón; paraíso.
bald *adj.* calvo, desnudo.
bale *tr.* embalar, empaquetar.
balk *s.* lomo entre surcos; *tr.* evitar.
ball *s.* bola; baile; *tr.* **fancy —** baile de máscaras.
ballad *s.* (Mús.) balada.
ballot *s.* papeleta, cédula para botar; **— box** urna; *intr.* votar.
balm *s.* bálsamos.
ban *s.* prohibición; maldición.
banana *s.* (Bot.) plátano (*árbol y fruto*).
band *s.* banda; cuadrilla (*de ladrones*); anillo (*de puro*); banda (*de música*).
bandage *s.* venda.
bandit *s.* (*pl.* **-dits** o -*ditti*) bandido.
bane *s.* azote, castigo.
bang *s.* detonación, golpazo; *adv.* de repente.
bangle *s.* ajorca, pulsera.
banish *tr.* desterrar.
bank *s.* banco, banca.
banknote *s.* billete de banco.
bankrupt *adj.* y *s.* insolvente.
banner *s.* bandera.
bantam *adj.* pequeño.
baptism *s.* bautismo.
bar *s.* barra, reja; bar.
barbarian *adj.* y *s.* bárbaro.
barbed *adj.* armado de púas, punzante.
barber *s.* barbero.
bare *adj.* desnudo; raído.
barefoot *adj.* descalzo.
bareness *s.* desnudez.
bargain *s.* negocio, trato.
bark *s.* corteza; ladrido; tos.
barker *s.* labrador; descortezador.

B

barley *s.* (Bot.) cebada.
barm *s.* levadura *(de cerveza).*
barmaid *s.* camarera.
barman *s. (pl:* **-men)** camarero.
barn *s.* granero, pajar.
barrage *s.* presa de embalse.
barrel *s.* barril. tonel; cañon.
barren *adj.* estéril, árido, seco.
barring *prep.* excepto, salvo.
barrister *s.* abogado.
barter *s.* cambio, trueque; *tr.* trocar, cambiar.
baseless *adj.* infundado, sin base.
bashful *adj.* vergonzoso, tímido.
basin *s.* palangana, vasija.
basis *s. (pl:* **bases)** base, fundamento.
bask *tr.* asolear, calentar.
bass *s.* (Mús.) bajo; *adj.* (Mús.) bajo; (ict.).
bastion *s.* bastión, baluarte.
bat *s.* palo, raqueta.
batch *s.* cochura, hornada; coleción; lote; (fam.) soltero.
bath *s.* baño.
bathroom *s.* cuarto de baño.
bathtub *s.* bañera.
bathe *tr.* bañar; *instr.* bañarse.
bathing *s.* bañ0.
battalion *s.* batallón; *s. pl* **—s** tropas.
batten *s.* tabla; *tr.* enlistonar; engordar; *intr.* engordar.
battery *s. (pl:* **-ries)** batería.
battle *s.* batalla; *tr.* batallar con; *intr.* batallar, luchar.
bawdy *adj (comp* **-ier**; *superl.* **-iest)** obsceno.
bawl *s.* voces; *tr.* vocear; *intr.* gritar.
bay *s.* bahía; ladrido; pajar; trance; apuro; (Bot.) laurel.
beach *s.* playa, costa.
bead *s.* cuenta; perla; *s. pl.*
beam *s.* viga; rayo. *tr.* emitir; *intr.* brillar; sonreír con alegría.

bear *tr. (pret:* **bore**; *pp:* **borne)** cargar; sentir; permitir; parir, relatar.
bearings *s. pl.* armas.
beast *s.* bestia; animal.
beat *(pret:* **beat**; *pp:* **beaten** o **beat)** *tr.* golpear; *intr.* latir.
beating *s.* paliza.
beauteous *adj.* bello.
beautification beatificación.
beautiful *adj.* hermoso.
beautify *(pret.* y *pp.* **-fied)** *tr.* embellecer, hermosear.
becalm *tr.* serenar, calmar; *intr.* calmarse.
because *cnj.* porque; a causa de.
beckon *tr.* e *intr.* hacer señas; *s.* seña.
become *(pret.* **became**; *pp.* **become** *tr.* convenir; *intr.* cambiarse; convertirse en.
bed *s.* cama, lecho.
bedeck *tr.* adornar.
bedew *tr.* rociar.
bedim *(pret.* y *pp:* **bedimmed)** *tr.* oscurecer, deslumbrar.
bedizen *tr.* adornar, aderezar.
bedlam *s.* confusión, manicomio.
bedroom *s.* dormitorio.
bedside table *s.* mesita de noche.
bedspread *s.* sobrecama.
bee *s.* abeja.
beef *s. (pl:* **beeves** o **beefs)** carne vacuna.
beer *s.* cerveza.
beet *s.* (Bot.) remolacha.
beetle *s.* escarabajo.
befall *(pret.* **fell**; *pp.* **-fallen)** *tr.* acontecer a; *intr.* suceder.
befit *(pret.* y *pp:* **-fitted**; *ger.* **-fitting)** *tr.* convenir, venir bien.
befog *(prett.* y *pp:* **-fogged**; *ger.* **-fogging)** *tr.* oscurecer, confundir.

befool *tr.* engañar.
before *prep.* delante de; *adv.* antes.
befriend *tr.* amparar.
beg *(pret.* y *pp:* **begged**; *ger.* **begging)** *tr.* rogar.
beget *(pret.* **-got**; *pp:* **-gotten** o **got**; *ger.* **getting** *tr.* engendrar.
beggar *s.* mendig.
begging *adj.* mendigante.
begin *(pret.* **-gan**; *pp.* **-gun**; *ger.* **-ginning)** *tr.* empezar.
beginner *s.* principiante.
beginning *s.* principio.
begrudge *tr.* envidiar.
beguile *tr.* engañar.
behave *intr.* actuar.
behead *tr.* decapitar.
behind *s.* trasero, culp; *adv.* detrás.
behold *(pret.* y *pp.* **beheld)** *tr.* mirar; *inj.* ¡mirad!, ¡he aquí!
beholden *adj.* obligado.
behoof *s.* provecho.
behove *tr.* convenir. *intr.* ser necesario.
bekiss *tr.* cubrir de besos.
belabor *tr.* maltratar.
belfry *s.* *(pl.* **-fries)** campanario.
belief *s.* creencia, fe.
believe *tr.* creer; *intr.* creer *(en Dios).*
belittle *tr.* despreciar.
bell *s.* campana; timbre.
bellow *s.* bramido; *tr.* gritar; *intr.* bramar.
bellows *s. pl.* fuelles.
belly *s.* *(pl:* **-lies)** vientre.
belong *tr.* pertenecer.
beloved *adj.* amado.
below *adv.* abajo; *prep.* debajo de.
belt *s.* cinturón; zona; *tr.* ceñir, unir.
bemean *intr.* empequeñecer.
bemoan *tr.* deplorar.
bemuse *tr.* aturdir; confundir.
bench *s.* banco, asiento.

bend *s.* curva. *tr. (pret.* y *pp:* **bent)** encorvar; *intr.* encorvarse, inclinarse.
benighted *adj.* sorprendido por la noche.
benign *adj.* benigno.
bent *s.* pliegue; inclinación; *adj.* encorvado.
benumb *tr.* entorpecer.
bequeath *tr.* (Der.) legar.
berate *tr.* reñir.
bereave *tr. (pret.* y *pp:* **-reaved** o **-reft)** despojar.
beret *s.* boina.
berry *s.* *(pl:* **-ries)** baya.
berth *s.* litera; camarote.
beset *(pret.* y *pp:* **-set**; *ger.* **-setting)** acometer.
beside *adv.* cerca; *prep.* junto a.
besides *adv.* además; *prep.* además de, excepto.
besmirch *tr.* ensuciar.
bespatter *tr.* salpicar.
bespeak *tr. (pret.* **-spoke**; *pp:* **-spoken)** apalabrar; demostrar.
best *adj. superl.* de **good**, el mejor; *adv.* lo mejor.
bestir *tr. (pret.* y *pp:* **-stirred**; mover.
bestow *tr.* otorgar.
bestowal *s.* donativo.
bet *s.* apuesta; *tr.* e *intr. (pret.* y *pp:* **bet** o **betted)** apostar.
bethink *tr. (pret.* y *pp:* **-thought)** recapacitar; recordar.
betide *intr.* suceder; *tr.* presagiar.
betimes *adv.* pronto.
betray *tr.* traicionar.
betroth *tr.* desposar.
betrothal *s.* noviazgo.
betrothed *adj.* y *s.* prometido.
better *adj. (compar.* de **good)** major; *adv.* más; *tr.* mejorar.
betting apuesta.
between *adv.* en medio.
beverage *s.* bebida.

bevy *s. (pl.* **-ies**) bandada *(de pájaros)*; grupo *(de personas).*

bewail *tr.* e *intr.* lamentar.

beware *intr.* guardarse *(Es verbo defectivo. Se usa sólo en Inf. e imper.).*

bewilder *tr.* extraviar.

bewitch *tr.* hechizar.

beyond *adv.* lejos; *prep.* detrás de; *s.* el otro mundo.

bib *s.* babero.

bicameral *adj.* bicameral.

bid *s.* oferta; *tr. (pret.* **bade** *pp:* **bidden**) ordenar, proclamar, rogar, pujar *(subasta)*; **to — adieu** despedirse; **to — welcome** dar la bienvenida.

bidding *s.* mandata; invitación.

bide *tr. (pp.* **bided or bode**) esperar, soportar.

bier *s.* féretro.

big *adj.* grande; engreído; *adv.* (fam.) con jactancia.

bight *s.* codo.

bigot *s.* fanático.

bill *s.* cuenta; cartel, anuncio; proyecto do ley; (Com.) letra de cambio, giro.

billow *s.* oleada; *intr.* sublevarse; ondular.

bind *tr. (pret.* y *pp:* **bound**) atar, vendar, ceñir, encuadernar.

bird *s.* pájaro, ave; (fam.) chica; **— of pray** ave de rapiña; **— cage** jaula; **a — in the hand is worth two in the bush** más vale pájaro en mano que ciento volando.

birth *s.* nacimiento; **to give — to** dar a luz; **untimely —** aborto; **— certificate** partida de nacimiento; **— rate** natalidad; **— sin** pecado original.

biscuit *s.* bizcocho.

bisect *tr.* dividir en dos partes iguales; *intr.* impalmar.

bishop *s.* obispo; alfil *(pieza del juego de ajedrez).*

bit *s.* bocado, trozo.

bith *s.* perra; zorra; ramera.

bite *s.* mordedura; picadura; *tr. (pret.* **bit** y *pp:* **bit** o **bitten**) morder; satirizar.

bitter *adj.* amargo; *s.* amargura.

biweekly *adj.* quincenal.

blab *s.* hablador; *tr.* chismear.

black *adj.* negro; oscuro; **— market** estraperlo.

blackboard *s.* pizarra.

blacken *tr.* ennegrecer.

blackmail *s.* chantaje.

blacksmith herrero.

bladder *s.* vejiga.

blade *s.* hoja *(de espada)*; cuchilla; tallo *(de hierba).*

blame *s.* culpa; *tr.* acusar.

blanch *s.* blanca; *tr.* desteñir.

bland *adj.* blando.

blank *adj.* hueco; libre *(verso)*; en blanco *(limpio, no escrito)*; blanco; vacío.

blanket *s.* manta; *tr.* cubrir *(con manta).*

blast *s.* ráfaga; toque *(de trompeta, etc.).*

blasted *adj.* arruinado.

blather *s.* charla; *intr.* charlar.

blaze *s.* llama, incendio.

blazing en llamas.

blazon *s.* blasón; *tr.* adornar.

bleak *adj.* sombrío; triste.

bleed *tr. (pret.* y *pp:* **bled**) sangrar; *intr.* desangrar; sufrir.

blemish *s.* mancha, deshonora; *tr.* manchar.

blend *s.* mezcla; *tr.* mezclar.

blind *adj.* ciego; obscuro.

blindfold *adj.* vendado; *s.* venda; *tr.* vendar.

blister *s.* ampolla; herida.

blithe (ful) *adj.* gozoso.

blizzard *s.* ventisca.

B

block *s.* bloque *(Amér. cuadra)*; cubo, dado; (carp.) llave, cuña, horma.

blocked cerrado.

blockhead *s.* necio.

blockhouse *s.* fortaleza.

blond, blonde *s.* rubio; *adj.* rubio.

blood *s.* sangre; cólera.

blood pressure *s.* presión sanguinea.

blood vessel *s.* vaso.

blossom *s.* flor; brote; *intr.* florecer.

blot *s.* borrón, mancha.

blouse *s.* blusa.

blow *s.* soplo; golpe, contratiempo; — **with the fist** peñetazo; **at one** — de un golpe, de una vez; **at a single** — de un solo golpe; **without striking a** — sin dar golpe; (Mil.) explosion; *tr. (pret.* **blew**; *pp:* **blown**) soplar; tocar *(un silbato, la trompeta, etc.)* pregonar, publicar.

blow pipe *s.* soplete.

bludgeon *s.* palo, estaca.

blue *adj.* azul.

bluffing *s.* fanfarronada.

bluffness *s.* rudeza.

blunder *s.* disparate.

bluntly *adv.* sin rodeos.

blur *s.* mancha.

bluster *s.* ruido; *tr.* violentar con gritos.

blusterer fanfarrón; ráfaga *(viento)*.

board *s.* tabla, plancha.

board and lodging *s.* cuarto y comida *(pensión completa)*.

boarder huésped.

boarding house *s.* pensión.

—school *s.* internado.

—student (or pupil) *s.* alumno interno.

boat *s.* barco.

bob *s.* chelin. *s. p.* nombre abreviado de Robert; *tr.* menearse.

bobby *s.* policía *(popular)*.

bobtail *s.* cola cortada.

bob-white *s.* codorniz *(en los Estados Unidos de Norte)*; perdiz *(en los del Sur)*.

bode *tr.* presagiar.

bodied *adj.* corpóreo.

—s *adj.* incorpóreo.

body *s.* cuerpo.

bog *s.* pantano; *intr.* atascarse.

boggle *intr.* dudar.

boil *s.* ebullición.

boiler *s.* caldera.

boisterous *adj.* ruidoso.

bold *adj.* osado.

boldness *s.* osadía.

bolster *s.* almohadón; *tr.* apoyar.

bombard *tr.* bombardear; (fig.) asediar *(a preguntas, etc.)*.

bond *s.* enlace; contrato; fianza; *pl.* valores; *tr.* hipotecar.

bondage *s.* cautiverio.

bone *s.* hueso; espina *(de peces)*; barba de ballena.

boneless *adj.* sin hueso.

bonfire *s.* hoguera.

bonnet *s.* gorra; capó *(coche)*; *tr.* cubrir *(la cabeza)*.

bonny *s.* bonito, lindo.

bony *adj.* huesudo.

booby-prize *s.* premio de consolación.

book *s.* libro; *tr.* asentar en un libro; inscribir; anotar; sacar billetes *(coche, teatros, etc.)*.

booking office taquilla, despacho de billetes.

bookkeeping *s.* contabilidad.

booklet *s.* folleto.

bookseller *s.* librero.

book shop *s.* librería.

bookstall *s.* puesto para venta de libros.

boom s. estampido; prosperidad.

boost s. empujón (hacia arriba); alza (de precios).

boot s. bota; — **laces** cordones.

booth s. quiosco; cabina.

border s. frontera; tr. limitar; intr. confinar.

bore s. barreno. tr. agujerear; aburrir, dar la lata.

bored adj. aburrido.

born adj. nacido; **newly** — recién nacido; **to be** — nacer.

born, borne s. arroyo; meta; margen, límite.

borough s. burgo, villa, ciudad, barrio; **Municipal** — (Ingl.) corporación municipal.

borrowing s. préstamo.

bosom s. seno, pecho.

boss s. jefe; (fam.) amo, gallo, capataz, gerente; (fam.) cacique (en asuntos politicos); tr. regentar, dominar.

both adj. ambos.

bother s. incomodidad; tr. incomodar, molestar; intr. molestarse.

bottle s. botella; **water** — cantimplora; tr. embotellar.

bough s. rama.

boulder s. guijarro.

bound s. salto; límite; adj. atado, sujeto; obligado; pret. y pp. de **to bind**; tr. limitar; intr. saltar.

boundary s. límite.

bounder s. vulgar.

boundless adj. ilimitado.

bounteous adj. generoso.

bounty s. generosidad.

bow s. inclinación, reverencia; (Náut.) proa.

bow s. arco; nudo; ojo (de la llave); adj. arqueado; tr.

(Mús.) tocar con arco; intr. arquearse.

bower s. glorieta, músico de arco.

bowie-knife s. cuchillo de monte, machete.

bowl s. taza; **sugar** — azucarero.

bow-window s. ventana arqueada o saliente.

box s. caja; arca; palco; (Impr.) cajetín; (Mec.) cojinete del motor; (Dep.) boxeo; **letter** — buzón; **P.O.** — apartado de correos; —**car** (f.c.) furgón; tr. embalar; boxear.

Boxing Day s. día festivo después de Navidad en que se dan regalos a los empleados.

boy s. muchacho, chico; **the old** — el diablo; — **scout** explorador.

bra s. sostén, sujetador.

bracket s. puntal; escuadra; brazo de lámpara; tr. apuntalar, asegurar; pl. —**s** (Impr.) paréntesis.

braggart adj. y s. fanfarrón.

braid s. trenza.

brain s. (An.) cerebro; inteligencia.

brain-wave s. idea luminosa.

braise tr. dorar (la carne, cocerla a fuego lento).

brake s. freno; matorral.

branch s. rama; sucursal; adj. sucursal, dependiente; intr. ramificarse.

brand s. marca.

brandy s. coñac.

brand-new adj. flamante.

brass. s. latón; (fam.) descaro, desvergüenza.

brave adj. bravo; airoso; s. valiente; tr. desafiar, retar.

bravery s. bravura, valentía; pompa.

brawn s. músculo.

B

braze s. soldadura.
brazen adj. hecho de latón; bronceado.
breach s. abertura.
bread s. pan; **on — and water** a pan y agua; **— and butter** pan con mantequilla; **new —** pan tierno.
breadth s. anchura; adv. a lo ancho.
break s. interrupción; cambio repentino; fragmento; grieta; blanco (en los escritos).
breakable adj. frágil.
breakage s. fractura.
breakdown s. parada imprevista; avería.
breaker s. triturador.
breakfast s. desayuno.
breath s. respiración; soplo; susurro; **out of —** sin aliento; **to waste one's — on** gastar saliva en.
breathe tr. respirar; inspirar; suspirar, tomar aliento; **— one's last** exhalar el último suspiro.
breech s. trasero; (fam.) pantalones; **to wear the —** ponerse los pantalones.
breed s. raza; especie; intr. criarse; **to — disturbance** meter cizaña.
breeze s. brisa.
breezy adj. airoso; (fam.) ligero.
brethren s. pl. hermanos.
brew s. mezcla; intr. fabricar cerveza.
bribe s. soborno; tr. sobornar.
brick s. ladrillo; tr. enladrillar.
bridal adj. nupcial; s. boda.
bride s. novia; **the — and groom** los recién casados.
bridegroom s. novio.
bridesmaid s. madrina de boda; s. padrino de boda.
bridge s. puente; bridge (juego de naipes).

brief adj. breve; s. resumen.
briefless adj. (Amér.) de sabana.
brigant s. bandolero.
bright adj. brillante; transparente.
brilliant adj. genial; s. brillante (joya).
brim s. borde; ala (de sombrero).
brimstone s. azufre.
brindle adj. jaspeado, rayado.
bring tr. (pret. y pp. **brought**) traer (llevar consigo, conducir); traer (a la memoria, al pensamiento); traer (consecuencias); acarrear; llevar; aportar; **to — back** devolver; **to — down** derribar; (fig.); **to — forth** parir; dar fruto.
bringing up s. educacion.
briny adj. salado.
brisk s. vivo, animado; fuerte; tr. avivar, animar.
Britain s. Bretaña.
British adj. británico.
brittle adj. quebradizo.
broach s. mecha; brochure; asador.
broad adj. ancho; comprensivo.
broadcast s. difusión; adj. difundido; adv. por todas partes; tr. difundir, radiar.
broaden tr. ensanchar; intr. ensancharse.
broadish adj. algo ancho.
broadly adv. anchamente.
broad-minded adj. de amplias miras.
brochure s. folleto.
broil s. carne a la parrilla.
broiler s. parrilla, pollo asadero.
broke adj. (fam.) sin blanca; pret. de **to break**.
broken adj. quebrado; interrumpido.
broker s. (Com.) corredor.

bronco s. potro, caballo salvaje.

bronze s. bronce; tr. broncear; intr. broncearse.

brooch s. alfiler de pecho.

brood s. cría, camada; tr. empollar.

brooder s. incubadora.

brook s. arroyo; tr. sufrir.

broom s. escoba.

broth s. caldo.

brother s. hermano; —in-law cuñado; half— or step— medio hermano; foster — hermano de leche.

brotherlike adj. fraternal.

brow s. frente; ceja.

browbeat tr. intimidar; desconcertar.

browless adj. descarado.

brown adj. moreno; s. pardo; tr. ponerse moreno.

brown shirt s. camisa parda.

browse tr. comer; pacer; intr. pacer; hojear (un libro).

bruise s. magulladura, contusión; tr. magullar, contundir.

brush s. cepillo; pincel; choque.

brushwood s. matorral.

brusque adj. áspero.

bubble s. burbuja.

bubbler s. engañador.

bubbly adj. espumoso.

buck adj. (Zool.) cabrón; gamo; (U.S.) indio o negro adulto; tr. lavar (en la colada); int. cubrir (el macho a la hembra).

bucket s. cubo, balda.

buckle s. bucle; hebilla; tr. hebillar; hacer bucler; intr. ajustarse, apretar las hebillas.

buckler s. escudo; tr. defender.

bud s. vástago; capullo; intr. brotar; tr. (Agr.) injertar.

budge adj. pomposo; tr. mover; moverse.

budget s. presupuesto; mochila.

buff s. ante; color de ante.

buffer s. cojinete.

buffet s. bofetada; intr. abofetear.

buffet s. ambigú, cantina.

bug s. chinche, bicho.

buggy adj. chinchoso; s. calesa de cuatro ruedas.

bugle s. corneta; azabache.

build s. estructura.

builder s. arquitecto, aparejador, constructor; autor.

building s. edificio, construcción; fábrica; obra.

bulb s. (Bot.) cebolla.

bulk s. bulto, volumen; intr. abultar; in — (Com.) adj. granel.

bull s. toro; bula; (fig.) disparate; adj. robusto; tr. cubrir el toro a la vaca; —'s-eye tragaluz.

bulldog s. mastín, revólver de gran calibre.

bullfight s. corrida de toros.

bullfighter s. torero.

bullet s. bala; plomada de pescador.

bullock s. novillo, buey.

bullring s. plaza de toros, redondel.

bully s. matón; adj. magnífico; tr. intimidar; intr. bravear.

bulwart s. baluarte; fortaleza.

bum s. nalgas; (U.S.) holgazán.

bumble tr. chapucear; intr. zumbar.

bumblebee s. abejorro.

bump s. batacazo; golpe.

bumper s. tope; parachoques; copa o vaso lleno.

bun s. bollo; moño. (pelo).

B

bunch *s.* manojo; racimo; manada; *tr.* agrupar; *intr.* arracimarse.

bundle *s.* bulto, lío; haz *(de leña, hierba, etc.); tr.* atar; *intr.* escaparse precipitadamente.

bungalow *s.* bungalou *(casa de campo de un solo piso y con terrazas).*

bunk *s.* tarima, litera; *intr.* dormir en tarima.

bunker *s.* carbonera.

bunny *s.* conejito.

burden *s.* carga; estribillo; *tr.* cargar.

bureau *s.* cómoda; escritorio; oficina.

burg *s.* (fam.) pueblo, ciudad.

burglar *s.* ladrón.

burial *s.* entierro.

burn *s.* quemadura; (Esc.) arroyo; *tr. (pret. y pp.* **burned** o **burnt**) quemar; cocer *(ladrillos);* calcinar; (Qm.) oxidar; **to — out** quemar *(un motor, transformador, etc.);* fundir *(una bombilla).*

burnish *s.* bruñido; *tr.* bruñir; *intr.* tomar lustre.

burr *s.* erizo; fresa *(de torno).*

burrow *s.* madriguera.

bursar *s.* tesorero universitario.

burst *s.* explosión; reventón *(pret. y pp.* **burst**) *tr.* reventar; reventarse.

bury *tr.* enterrar.

bus *s.* ómnibus; autobús.

bush *s.* arbusto; matorral.

bushel *s.* medida de capacidad, fanega.

bushy *adj.* espeso; lanudo.

business *s.* negocio, asunto; — **district** barrio comercial; — **expert** perito mercantil; — **man** comerciante, hombre de negocios; — **trip** viaje de engocios.

bust *s.* busto; pecho de mujer; *tr.* arruinar; *intr.* fracasar.

bustle *s.* alboronto; *intr.* apresurarse.

busy *adj. (compar.* **-ier**; *superl.* **-iest**) ocupado; *tr.* ocupar.

but *s.* objeción; *adv.* sólo; *prep.* excepto; *cnj.* pero.

butcher *s.* carnicero; *tr.* matar *(reces).*

butler *s.* mayordomo.

butt *s.* culata; colilla.

butter *s.* mantequilla.

butterfly *s.* mariposa.

buttonhole *s.* ojal.

butress *s.* contrafuerte; apoyo.

buxom *adj.* rollizo.

buy *tr. (pret. y pp.* **bought**) comprar.

buyer *s.* comprador.

buzz *s.* susurro.

by *prep.* por; de; (Mat.) por *(para indicar multiplicaci–n;* para; a; cerca de, junto a, al lado de; — **chance** por casualidad; — **day** de dia; — **far** con mucho; — **law** en virtud de la ley, según la ley; — **then** para entonces, entonces.

bye-bye *s.* voz para arrullar a los niños; *inj.* ¡adiós! hasta luego.

by-election *s.* elección para cubrir una vacante.

bygone *adj.* pasado.

by-law, bye-law *s.* estatuto; reglamento; ley municipal.

by-pass *s.* desviación; *tr.* desviar.

bypath *s.* senda.

byre *s.* establo.

by-road *s.* camino apartado, atajo.

bystander *s.* espectador; *s. pl.* circunstantes.

by-street *s.* callejuela.

C

cab s. taximetro.
cabal s. cábala; tr. e intr.
　tramar.
cabbage s. (Bot.) col.
cabin s. cabaña; (Náut.)
　camarote; tr. apretar.
cabinet s. vitrina, escaparate;
　gabinete; adj. ministerial.
cache s. escondite; tr.
　esconder.
caddish adj. mal educado.
caddy s. bote, lata.
cage s. jaula; cárcel; tr.
　enjaular.
caisson s. cajón.
cake s. bollo, pastelillo;
　wedding — pastel de boda.
calculate tr. calcular.
caldron s. caldero.
calf s. (pl. calves) ternera;
　cuero.
call s. llamada; grito; visita;
　escala (de buque, de
　avión); invitación; tr. llamar;
　señalar; citar; convocar
　(una reunión, etc.); intr.
　pararse un rato; (Náut.
　hacer escala; exigir.
calling s. profesión, vocación.
callow adj. joven.
callowness s. inexperiencia.
calm s. calma.
calumniate tr. calumniar.
camera s. cámara fotorgráfica.
camisole s. camiseta de
　mujer.
camouflage s. disfraz; (Mil.)
　tr. enmascarar.
campaign s. veraneo.
compaigner s. veterano.
campus s. (pl. -es) campo,
　(U.S. patio o calustro de
　colegio.
can s. bote; envase; tr. (pret.
　y pp. canned) enlatar,
　envasar; canned goods

conservas; — opener
　abrelatas; aus. def. (pret.
　could) poder; saber; he —
　dance él sabe bailar.
candidate s. candidato,
　aspirante, opositor.
candle s. candela; vela.
candy s. bombón, dulce.
cane s. bastón; caña.
canine adj. canino, perruno;
　— tooth, colmillo.
canister s. bote, frasco.
canker s. llaga, úlcera.
cannon s. cañón; (Zool.)
　metatarso.
canny adj. (compar. -ier;
　superl. -iest) astuto.
cant s. lenguaje insincero;
　canto, esquina; inclinación;
　adj. inclinado; hipócrita; tr.
　inclinar, invertir; intr.
　inclinarse.
can't contracción (fam.) de
　can not.
canvas s. escrutinio,
　investigación.
canyon s. cañón, (paso entre
　montañas).
caoutchouc s. caucho.
cap s. gorr; cima; tapón;
　cápsula; (Arq.) capitel,
　cornisa; casquete.
capable adj. capaza,
　competente.
capacious adj. espacioso.
cape s. capa; cabo
　(geográfico).
capital adj. capital; magnífico;
　mayúscula (letra) s. capital
　(dinero); capital (ciudad);
　(Arq.) capitel.
capsize tr. e intr. volcar.
captious adj. criticón;
　insidioso.
capivating adj. fascinante.
captivate tr. cautivar.
captor, capturer s.
　capturador.
car s. coche.
carafe s. garrafa.

caramel *s.* caramelo.
carbide *s.* carburo.
carbine *s.* carabina.
carcass, carcase *s.* carróoa; cadáver *(de animal)*; esqueleto o armazón *(de una cosa)*.
card *s.* tarjeta; naipe; ficha; carnet.
cardboard *s.* cartón, carulina.
cardigan *s.* chaqueta de lana.
care *s.* cuidado, preocupación; **to have a —** andar con cuidado; **to take** **—** tener cuidado; cuidado, custodia; **I don't —** me tiene sin cuidado; *intr.* tener cuidado; preocuparse, tener interés.
career *s.* carrera.
careful *adj.* cuidado.
careless *adj.* descuidado.
caress *s.* caricia; *tr.* acariciar.
caretaker *s.* vigilante, conserje.
carnage *s.* carnicería.
carnation *s.* (Bot.) clavel.
carnival *s.* carnaval.
carob *s.* (Bot.) algarrobo.
carol *s.* canción; *tr.* cantar villancicos.
carousal *s.* festín.
carouse *intr.* juerguear, emborracharse; *s.* juerga.
carp *s.* carpa; *intr.* censurar, criticar.
carpenter *s.* carpintero; **stage** **—**; tramoyista.
carpet *s.* alfombra.
carriage *s.* carruage; transporte.
carriage-free *adj.* franco de porte.
carrier *s.* portador; empresa de transportes.
carrot *s.* (Bot.) zanahoria.
carroty *adj.* pelirrojo.
cart *s.* carretera; *tr.* acarrear.
carter *s.* carretero.

cartridge *s.* cartucho; carrete o rollo *(de película)*; repuesto *(de bolígrafo, etc.)*.
carve *tr.* tallar.
case *s.* caso, caja, funda; (Der.) pleito; (fam.) persona divertida.
casement *s.* puerta, ventana; marco *(de una ventana)*.
cash *s.* dinero contante; *tr.* hacer efectiva *(una letra)*; **to pay —** pagar al contado.
cashier *s.* cajero; *tr.* destituir.
casing *s.* cubierta; marco de puerta o ventana.
cask *s.* tonel; cuba.
casket *s.* ataúd.
casserole *s.* cacerola.
cassock *s.* sotana.
cast *s.* echada; forma, molde; tinte, matiz; pieza fundida; mirada bizco; (Tt.) reparto; *tr. (pret.* y *pp.* **cast)** echar; volver *(los ojos)*; fundir, vaciar.
castaway *s.* náufrago; *adj.* abandonado.
cast-iron *s.* hierro fundido *(colado)*.
castle *s.* castillo, torre *(ajedrez)*.
castor *s.* castor; vinagreras,; salero, vinagrera.
castor oil *s.* aceite de ricino.
cat *s.* gato, gata.
catarrh *s.* catarro.
catch *s.* cogida *(de la pelota)*; broche; botín; pestillo; pesca; trampa; **to — cold** coger un resfriado; **to —** **fire** encenderse; **to — up** asir, empuñar; coger al vuelo; cazar *(sorpreder a uno)*; *intr.* pegarse *(una enfermedad)*.
catch drain *s.* cuneta.
catching *adj.* contagioso; seductor.
categoric, -al *adj.* categórico.

cater *tr.* e *intr.* abastecer, proveer.
cattle *s.* (sin *pl.*) ganado.
cauf *s.* vivero de peces.
cauliflower *s.* (Bot.) coliflor.
cause *s.* causa; *tr.* causar.
causeway *s.* terraplén.
cavalcade *s.* cabalgata.
cavalier *s.* caballero, galán.
cave *s.* cueva; *intr.* hundirse.
cease *tr.* parar; *intr.* cesar.
cecils *s.* albóndigas de carne.
cede *tr.* ceder.
ceiling *s.* techo.
celebrate *tr.* e *intr.* celebrar.
celebrated *adj.* célebre, famoso.
celibacy *s.* celibato, soltería.
cell *s.* celda; célula.
cellar *s.* sótano, bodega.
cello *s.* violoncelo.
cement *s.* cemento; *tr.* revestir de cemento; unir con cemento; — **mill** fábrica de cemento; *intr.* unirse, pegarse.
cemetery *s. (pl:* -**ties**) cementerio.
censorship *s.* censura.
center *s.* centro; *tr.* centrar.
centimeter, centimetre *s.* centímetro.
centre *s.* centro; *tr.* concentrar; **to — upon**, versar sobre.
century *s. (pl:* -**ies**) siglo; centuria.
cereal *s.* y *adj.* cereal.
certain *adj.* cierto, postivo.
certify *tr.* certificar.
cessation *s.* cesación, paro.
cession *s.* cesión, traspaso.
cesspool *s.* pozo negro.
chafe *s.* frotamiento; *tr.* trotar.
chaffer *s.* regateo; *tr.* regatear, burlarse.
chagrin *tr.* disgustar; *s.* pesadumbre, disgusto.

chain *s.* cadena; **guard** —, grillo; — **mail**, cota de malla; *tr.* encadenar.
chair *s.* silla; cátedra *(universidad)*, presidencia; **arm** —, silón; **rocking** — mecedora; **to take the** — presidir la sesión.
chairman *s. (pl:* -**men**) presidente de una junta o sociedad.
chairmanship *s.* presidencia.
chalk *s.* yeso, tiza; — **for cheese** compra barata.
challenge *s.* desafío; *tr.* desafiar, exigir.
chamber *s.* cámara, alcoba; — **of Commerce** Cámara de Comercio.
chamber-maid *s.* camarera; doncella.
chamois *s.* (Zool.) gamuza, ante.
championship *s.* campeonato.
chancellor *s.* canciller; Rector *(universidad);* — **of Exchequer** Ministro de Hacienda.
change *s.* cambio; dinero suelto; mudanza; *tr.* cambiar; mudar; *intr.* corregirse, mudarse.
changeful *adj.* cambiante; voluble.
changeless *adj.* immutable.
channel *s.* cana; cauce; **irrigation** — acequia; **English** — Canal de la Mancha; **the usual —s** los trámites reglamentarios; *tr.* encauzar.
chant *s.* canción; *tr.* e *intr.* cantar.
chantry *s. (pl:* -**tries**) capilla; sepulcro enrejado.
chap *s.* mandíbula; grieta; muchacho, mozo; *tr.* agrietar; *intr.* agrietarse.
chapel *s.* capilla, ermita.

chaperon s. señora o señorita de compañia, tr. acompañar.
chaplain s. capellán.
chapter s. capítulo; **cachar** s. jornal; tarea al jornal; carbón de leña; intr. (pret. y pp. **charred**) hacer tareas a jornal; carbonizarse.
charcoal s. carbón vegetal.
charge s. carga; gasto; precio; mandato; comisión.
chargé d'affaires s. encargado de negocios.
charger s. cargador; caballo de batalla.
chariot s. carroza; carro militar.
charity s. caridad.
charm s. encanto; amuleto; tr. encantar.
charmer s. hechicero.
chart s. mapa, plano, carta.
charter s. escritura; fuero.
charwoman s. criada, asistenta.
chary adj. (compar **ier**; super. **iest**) cuidadoso; económico.
chase s. caza; encaje; tr. cazar; persequir; montar (piedras preciosas).
chasm s. hendidura.
chaste adj. casto.
chasten tr. castigar.
chastise tr. castigar.
chat s. conversación; intr. charlar.
chattels s. pl. bienes muebles.
chauffeur s. chófer.
cheap adj. barato; (fig.) **to go on the** — ir de gorra.
cheat s. trampa; engaño; tr. engañar; estafar.
check tr. moderar; detener; reñir; examinar; rechazar; facturar; comprobar; intr. pararse.
checkers s. pl. juego de damas; tr. cuadricular.

checkgirl s. guardarropa (persona encargada del guardarropa).
cheek s. mejilla.
cheeky adj. (fam.) descarado.
cheer s. alegría; aplauso; **what cheer?** ¿qué tal?; tr. alegrar; intr. alegrarse; — **up!** ¡ánimo!
cheerful adj. alegre.
cheerio inj. (fam.) ¡hola! ¡adiós!
cheery adj. (compar. **ier**; superl. **iest**) alegre.
cheese s. queso.
chef s. jefe de cocina.
chemist s. químico, farmacéutico; —**'s shop**, farmacia.
cherish tr. acariciar; abrigar (esperanzas).
cherry s. (pl: **-rries**) (Bot.) —**tree**, cerezo; cereza.
chess s. ajedrez.
chessboard s. tablero de ajedrez.
chest s. pecho; caja de caudales.
chestnut s. (Bot.) castaño; adj. castaño; marrón.
chew s. mascadura; tr. mascar.
chewing-gum s. chicle.
chicanery s. (pl: **-ries**) embuste.
chicken s. pollo; polluelo; cobarde; (fig.) jovencito; — **coop** galinero.
chickpea s. (Bot.) garbanzo.
chief s. jefe, caudillo; adj. principal.
chiffon s. tejido muy fino.
child s. (pl: **children**) niño; hijo; **to be with** — estar embarazada.
childbirth s. parto.
chill s. frialdad; resfriado; adj. frío; reservado; tr. helar, enfriar; desanimar; intr. escalofriarse.

chilly *adj.* frío.
chin *s.* barba.
chinese puzzle *s.* problema complicadísimo.
chink *s.* grieta; sonido del dinero; *tr.* hender; hacer sonar *(dinero); intr.* henderse, rajarse.
chip *s.* astilla; *tr.* cortar; **a —off the old block** de tal palo tal astilla.
chit *s.* chiquillo; *tr.* quitar los brotes; *intr.* brotar.
chock-full *adj.* colmado, lleno.
choice *s.* elección; *adj.* selecto.
choir *s.* coro.
choose *tr. (pret.* **chose;** *pp.* **chosen)** elegir; *intr.* optar.
chopper *s.* hacha.
chord *s.* (Mús.) acorde; cuerda.
christen *tr.* bautizar.
chronicler *s.* cronista, historiador.
chummy *adj.* (fam.) íntimo *(muy amigo).*
chunk *s.* pedazo grueso de algo.
chunky *adj. (compar* -ier; *superl.* -iest) rechoncho.
church *s. (pl:* -ches) iglesia.
churchyard *s.* cementerio.
cider *s.* sidra.
cigar *s.* cigarro, puro; —holder, boquilla.
cinder *s.* ceniza.
cipher *s.* cifra; cero.
circumvent *tr.* embaucar.
circus *s.* circo, redondel, arena.
cistern *s.* cisterna.
citadel *s.* ciudadela.
cite *tr.* citar, advertir.
citizen *s.* y *adj.* ciudadano.
city *s. (pl:* -ties) ciudad; **city** — City-Hall Ayuntamiento; **city fathers** concejales.
civilian *s.* hombre civil, paisano; *adj.* civil.

civility *s.* cortesía, atención.
clack *s.* ruido agudo y corto; *intr.* repiquetear.
claim *s.* demanda; reclamación; *tr.* demandar, reivindicar.
clairvoyant *adj.* y *s.* clarividente.
clamber *intr.* trepar.
clammy *adj.* frío, húmedo.
clamour *tr.* gritar; *s.* alboroto.
clamp *s.* empalmadura; tornillo de banco.
clan *s.* clan, familia.
clang *s.* sonido metálico.
clap *s.* golpe seco; aplauso; *tr.* golpear, aplaudir.
clash *s.* choque; *intr.* chocar, golpear.
clasp *s.* broche, hebilla; *tr.* abrochar.
class *s.* clase, categoría; *tr.* clasificar.
classmate *s.* compañero de clase.
clavicle *s.* (An.) clavícula.
claw *s.* (Zool.) uña; *tr.* agarrar, arañar.
clay *s.* arcilla.
clean *adj.* limpio; perfecto.
clear *adj.* claro; limpio; libre *(de culpa, deudas, estorbos, etc.);* neto; seguro, cierto; entero, — **track** vía libre; claro; absolutamente; — **through** de parte a parte; *tr.* aclarar; rebajar *(un terreno).*
clearness *s.* claridad.
cleft *s.* llave.
clench *s.* agarro; *tr.* agarrar; remachar.
clergy *s.* clero.
clerk *s.* dependiente *(de comercio);* oficinista; (Der.) escribano.
clever *adj.* inteligente; hábil.
click *s.* golpe suave; tecleo.
cliff *s.* precipicio; acantilado.

C

climax s. crisis; punto culminante.

climb s. subida; tr. e intr. trepar, subir.

clipping s. recorte; adj. (fam.) rápido.

clique s. pandilla, corrillo.

cloak s. capa, manto; disimulo; tr. disimular.

cloakroom s. guardarropa.

clock s. reloj de mesa o de pared.

clockmaker s. relojero.

clod s. tierra.

clog s. madreña; obstáculo.

cloister s. claustro; tr. enclaustrar.

closed chapter s. asunto concluído.

closeness s. cercanía; tacañería; reserva.

clot s. grumo; intr. coagularse.

cloth (pl. **cloths**) s. lienzo, paño; (pl. **clothes**) vestidos.

cloud s. nube; tr. anublar; intr. anublarse.

cloudless adj. sin nubes.

clove s. clavillo; — of garlic diente de ajo.

clover s. (Bot.) trébol; to live in — (fig.) vivir lujosamente.

clown s. payaso; intr. hacer el payaso.

cloy tr. e intr. empalagar.

club s. porra; club; intr. reunirse; pegar con un garrote.

clue s. guía, pista.

clump s. mata, grupo.

clumsy adj. tosco.

cluster s. racimo; enjambre; grupo; tr. agrupar.

clutter s. confusión; alboroto; tr. e intr. alborotar.

coach s. coche de viajeros; preceptor; tr. dar clases particulares.

coal s. carbón; tr. proveer de carbón.

coast s. (Náut.) costa; tr. costear; intr.0 navegar en cabotaje.

coat s. chaqueta, abrigo.

cobble s. guijarro; tr. empedrar; remendar; intr. remendar zapatos.

cobweb s. telaraña.

cock s. gallo; grifo.

cockle s. (Zool.) almeja; tr. arrugar.

cockpit s. cabina (de un avión).

cockroach s. cucaracha.

cocksure adj. completamente seguro; confiado.

cod s. abadejo, bacalao.

coddle tr. mimar.

codex s. pl. códice, s.

coffee s. café.

coffin s. ataúd.

cog s. diente.

cogent adj. fuerte.

cogitate tr. e intr. meditar.

cognate adj. semejante.

cohabit intr. cohabitar.

coif s. cofia.

coiffure s. peinado, tocado.

coil s. follo; tr. enrollar; intr. enrollarse.

coin s. moneda; tr. acuñarse.

coiner s. monedero, acuñador.

colander s. colador.

cold adj. frio; (fig.) indiferente.

collabroate tr. colaborar.

collaspe s. hundimiento; tr. aplastar; sufrir colapso.

collar s. cuello; collar.

collect tr. coger; coleccionar; cobrar; intr. acumularse; — on delivery contrarreembolso.

college s. colegio superior.

collide intr. chocar.

collie s. perro de pastor.

colliery s. mina de carbón.

colliflower s. coliflor.

collocate tr. colocar.

colloquial adj. familiar.

colonnade s. columnata.

color *s.* color; — **film** película en colores; **to call to the** —**s** llamar a filas; **to show one's** — declarar sus opiniones o proyectos; *tr.* colorear, colorear; *intr.* sonrojarse, encenderse.

colored *adj.* de color; colorado.

colorless *adj.* incoloro, pálido.

colt *s.* potro; mozuelo sin juicio; revólver.

column *s.* columna; **gossip** — crónica.

comb *s.* peine; *tr.* peinar; romper *(las olas)*.

combat *s.* combate; *tr.* combatir; *intr.* combatirse.

comedian *s.* cómico.

comely *adj.* gracioso.

come-off *s.* salida.

coming *adj.* venidero; *s.* advenimiento.

command *s.* mandato; *tr.* mandar, ordenar.

commanding *adj.* poderoso; autorizado.

commemorate *tr.* commemorar, celebrar.

commence *tr.* c *intr.* comenzar.

commend *tr.* alabar.

comment *s.* comentario; *intr.* comentar.

commiserate *tr.* compadecer; *intr.* compadecerse.

commit *tr.* y *pp.* -**mitted** confiar; cometer; **to** — **oneself** obligarse.

commodious *adj.* cómodo, holgado.

common *adj.* común, corriente, habitual; **in** — **with** de común con.

common place *adj.* común; *s.* cosa común u ordinaria.

commonwealth *s.* comunidad británica de naciones; estado *(de los Estados Unidos)*.

communicate *tr.* comunicar; contagiar; comulgar; *intr.* comunicarse, hacer saber, particpar.

commuter *s.* conmutador.

compact *tr.* comprimir, apretar; convenir, pactar; *intr.* unirse.

compare *tr.* comparar; cotejar *(textos)*.

compass *s.* brújula; compás; *tr.* circundar.

compeer *s.* compañero, colega.

compensate *tr.* compensar; indemnizar, reparar.

compete *intr.* competir, rivalizar.

compile *tr.* recopilar.

complain *intr.* quejarse, lamentarse; — **against**.

complaint *s.* enfermedad.

completion *s.* terminacion; ejecución.

complex *adj.* y *s.* complejo.

complexion *s.* complexión, color, estado.

compliance *s.* condescendencia.

compliant *adj.* condescendiente, dócil.

complicate *tr.* complicar, embrollar.

compliment *s.* alabanza; cumplimiento; *tr.* cumplimentar, saludar.

comportment *s.* conducta, comportamiento.

compose *tr.* componer; redactar; ordenar; *intr.* componer; componerse.

composer *s.* (Imp.) compositor; autor.

composure *s.* compostura.

compound *s.* y *adj.* compuesto; mezcla.

compound *tr.* componer; combinar; *intr.* componerse.

comprehend *tr.* comprender.

C

compress *s. (pl: -es)*
compresa; *tr.* comprimir.
comprise *tr.* comprehender;
abarcar.
compunction *s.*
arrepentimiento.
compute *tr.* e *intr.* computar,
calcular.
comrade *s.* camarada.
conceal *tr.* encubrir; esconder.
concede *tr.* conceder.
conceit *s.* orgullo; concepto.
concentrate *s.* sustancia
concentrada; *tr.* concentrar;
intr. concentrarse.
concern *s.* asunto; interés;
negocio; empresa; *tr.*
concernir, atañer.
concert *s.* concierto, convenio.
concert *tr.* e *intr.* concertar,
ajustar.
conciliate *tr.* conciliar,
granjear.
conclude *tr.* e *intr.* concluír;
acabar, decidir.
concoct *tr.* confeccionar;
tramar.
concrete *adj.* concreto; de
hormigón; *s.* hormigón.
concur *tr. (pret.* y *pp: -curred)*
concurrir, acordarse.
condemn *tr.* censurar;
condenar; expropiar.
condense *tr.* condensar;
abreviar; *intr.* condensarse.
condescend *intr.* dignarse.
condition *s.* condición,
calidad; estipulación,
calidad; estipulación; *tr.*
condicionar; acondicionar.
condole *tr.* condolerse,
deplorar.
conduce *intr.* conducir.
conduct *tr.* e *intr.* conducir,
comportarse; dirigir
(orquesta).
cone *s.* cono; *tr.* e *intr.* hacer
cómico.
confection *s.* confección;
confitura; *tr.* confeccionar.

confederacy *s. (pl: -ries)*
confederación; alianza.
confer *tr. (pret.* y *pp: -ferred)*
conferenciar, tratar; otorgar.
confess *tr.* confiar; *intr.*
confiarse.
confident *adj.* seguro; *s.*
confidente.
configurate *tr.* configurar.
confine *s.* confín; *tr.* confinar;
limitar; *intr.* lindar.
confirm *tr.* confirmar.
confiscate *tr.* confiscar,
decomisar.
conflict *tr.* combatir.
conform *tr.* e *intr.* conformar.
confound *tr.* confundir;
desconcertar; *intr.*
condenar.
confounded *adj.* maldito.
confront *tr.* confrontar con;
hacer frente a.
confuse *tr.* confundir,
desconcertar.
confutable *adj.* refutable.
confute *tr.* refutar; anular.
congest *tr.* congestionar;
apiñar.
conglomerate *tr.*
conglomerar, aglomerar;
intr. conglomerarse,
aglomerarse.
congratulate *tr.* congratular,
felicitar.
congregate *tr.* congregar,
reunir; *intr.* congregarse,
reunirse.
congress *s.* congreso
asamblea; (U.S.)
Parlamento.
conjecture *s.* conjetura;
suposición; *tr.* conjeturar,
sospechar.
conjoin *tr.* juntar; asociar; *intr.*
juntarse; asociarse.
conjugate *tr.* conjugar; *intr.*
conjugarse.
conjure *tr.* conjurar, adjurar;
intr. practicar por arte de
magia; — **away** exorcizar.

connect *tr.* conectar, unir, relacionar; *intr.* enlazarse, relacionarse.

connive *intr.* fingir, hacer la vista gorda.

connoisseur *s.* conocedor, perito.

conquer *tr.* e *intr.* conquistar, ganar.

conscienceless *adj.* sin conciencia.

conscientious *adj.* concienzudo, responsable.

conscious *adj.* consciente.

conscribe *tr.* reclutar.

conscrate *tr.* consagrar, dedicar.

consequent *adj.* consiguiente, lógico.

conserve *s.* conserva; *tr.* conservar, guardar.

consider *tr.* considerar, examinar; reconocer; opinar; darse cuenta de.

consign *tr.* consignar, enviar.

consist *intr.* consistir, constar de.

console *tr.* consolar, confortar.

consolidate *tr.* consolidar; *intr.* consolidarse.

consort *s.* consorte; cónyuge; *tr.* asociar, casar; *intr.* asociarse.

conspicuity *s.* claridad, evidencia.

conspire *tr.* maquinar, tramar; *intr.* conspirar.

constable *s.* policia; guardián, alguacil.

constabulary *s.* comisaría, policía.

constitute *tr.* constituír, componer.

constrain *tr.* constreñir; restringir, forzar; *intr.* contenerse.

constrict *tr.* apretar, constreñir.

construct *tr.* construir, edificar.

construe *tr.* interpretar; construir.

consult *tr.* consultar, considerar; *intr.* consultarse.

consume *tr.* consumir, acabar; desgastar.

consummate *tr.* consumar.

contact *tr.* ponerse en contacto con, contactar.

contagion *s.* contagio, contaminación.

contain *tr.* contener; *intr.* contenerse.

container *s.* envase, recipiente.

contemn *tr.* desacatar, despreciar.

contemplate *tr.* e *intr.* contemplar, meditar.

contempt *s.* descato, desprecio.

contemptuous *adj.* desdeñoso, despectivo.

contend *tr.* sostener; *intr.* contender, afirmar.

contest *s.* competencia, contienda.

contest *tr.* disputar; *intr.* competir.

continuance *s.* continuidad; permanencia.

continue *tr.* e *intr.* continuar, seguir, durar.

contort *tr.* retorcer.

contour *s.* contorno, perímetro.

contract *tr.* contraer; *intr.* contraerse.

contradict *tr.* contradecir.

contrast *tr.* hacer contrastar; *intr.* contrastar.

contravene *tr.* contravenir a; contradecir.

contribute *tr.* e *intr.* contribuir, poner.

contriet *adj.* contrito, arrepentido.

contrive *tr.* inventar; gestionar.

control *s.* gobierno; control.

controversy s. (pl: -sies)
controversia, disputa.
controvert tr. e intr.
controvertir, disputar.
conundrum s. adivinanza;
rompecabezas.
convalesce intr. convalecer.
convene tr. convocar; intr.
convenir, juntarse.
convenience s. comodidad,
conveniencia; **public —**
servicios públicos
(urinarios).
converge tr. e intr. convergir,
dirigirse hacia.
conversant adj. versado,
entendido; familiar; **to
become — with**
familiarizarse con.
converse adj. contrario;
inverso; s. conversación.
convert tr. convertir; intr.
convertirse, transformar.
convey tr. transportar,
conducir; expresar;
transferir.
conveyance s. transporte.
convict tr. (Der.) probar la
culpabilidad.
convince tr. convencer,
satisfacer.
convivial adj. jovial, sociable.
convoke tr. convocar, citar.
convulse tr. convulsionar;
agitar.
cook s. concinero (a); tr.
cocinar; cocer, guisar;
(fam.) falsear.
cooker s. cocina.
cooky s. pastelito de dulce.
cool adj. fresco; sereno; tr.
enfriar.
cop s. cumbre, cima; rollo de
hilos; agente de policia; tr.
(pret y pp: **copped**) coger,
arrestar.
cophouse s. caseta de
herramientas.
copier s. copista.
copiousness s. abundancia.

copper s. cobre; calderilla;
adj. cobrizo; tr. cubrir o
forrar con cobre.
copse s. matorral.
copulate tr. unir, juntar.
copy s. copia; imitación;
ejemplar (libro).
copyright s. propiedad
literaría; derechos de autor.
cord s. cuerda; tr. acordonar;
spinal — médula espinal.
core s. corazón, centro,
hueso, pepita; tr. quitar el
corazón o centro; quitar la
pepita de una fruta.
cork s. corcho, tapón.
corn s. maíz; grano; semilla.
corner s. ángulo, esquina,
rincón; tr. arrinconar,
acorralar.
cornet s. (Mús.) corneta.
corps s. cuerpo **army —**
cuerpo de ejército.
corpse s. cadáver.
corpulent adj. corpulento.
correct adj. correcto; exacto;
tr. corregir.
correctness s. corrección.
correspond intr.
corresponder; escribirse.
correspondent adj.
correspondiente; s.
corresponsal.
corridor s. pasillo.
corroborate tr. corroborar,
confirmar.
corrode tr. morder.
corrupt adj. corrompido; tr.
corromper; intr.
corromperse, seducir.
coruscate intr. brillar;
relampaguear.
cost s. costa, costo; (Der.)
costas; intr. (pret. y pp:
cost) costar; tr. valer.
costless adj. de balde, gratis.
costly adl. costoso, suntuoso.
costume s. traje.
cosy adj. (compar -**ier**; superl.
-**iest**) confortable.

cot s. catre; choza.

coterie s. grupo; confradía.

cottage s. cabaña, casa del campo.

cottager s. veraneante, morador de una choza.

cotton s. algodón *(tejidos)*.

cotton wool s. algodón *(empleado en curas)*.

cough s. tos; *intr.* toser.

council s. concilio; junta.

councillor, councilman s. concejal, consejero.

counsel s. consejo; consejero; *tr.* aconsejar; *intr.* aconsejarse.

count s. cuenta; cálculo; (Der.) cargo; *tr.* contar, numerar; **to — noese** contar las personas o cabezas presentes.

countenance s. semblante; serenidad; favor; **to lost —** turbarse; **to keep one's —** contenerse; *tr.* favorecer, aprobar.

counter s. contador *(persona o cosa)*; ficha; mostrador; *adj.* contrario; *tr.* oponerse a; *instr.* devolver un golpe.

counteract *tr.* contrariar.

counterfeit s. imitación; falsificación; *tr.* e *intr.* falsificar.

counterfoil s. talón *(cheque)*.

counterpane s. cubrecama.

counterpart s. copia.

countersign s. contraseña, consigna.

countess s. condesa.

countless *adj.* incontable.

country s. *(pl: -ies)* pals; patria; terruño, campo; *adj.* rústico.

county s. *(pl: -ties)* partido; provincia.

coup s. golpe; jugada brillante.

couple s. par; matrimonio; *tr.* juntar; conectar, casar; *intr.* juntarse.

courage s. valor; firmeza.

course s. curso; trayectoria; pista, cubierto *(comidas)*.

court s. corte; (Der.) tribunal; atrio, patio; pista *(tenis)*; *tr.* cortejar.

courtesy s. cortesía.

court martial s. consejo de guerra.

courtship s. cortejo; noviazgo.

cousin s. primo, prima.

covenant s. pacto, escritura de contrato; *tr.* e *intr.* pactar.

covering s. cubierta; techado.

covert s. escondrijo, asilo.

covet *tr.* e *intr.* codiciar.

cow s. vaca; *tr.* acobardar.

coward *adj.* y s. cobarde, gallina.

cowardice s. cobardía.

cowboy s. vaquero.

cower *intr.* agacharse.

coxcomb s. fanfarrón; cresta de gallo.

coxswian s. (Náut.) timonel, patrón.

coy *adj.* *(compar -ier; superl. -iest)* rectado; *tr.* acariciar, halagar.

cozy *adj.* *(compar. -ier superl. -iest)* cómodol sociable.

crab s. (Zool.) cangrejo; (fam.) persona de mal genio; *tr.* (fam.) criticar; *intr.* coger cangrejos.

crack s. grieta; prueba, resquebrajo.

crack *tr.* romper haciendo crujir; agrietar; *intr.* agrietarse.

cracker s. galleta.

crackle s. crujido; *intr.* crujir.

cradle s. cuna; *tr.* acunar; colgar *(el teléfono)*.

craft s. arte; oficio; embarcacion; **air—** avión.

crafty *adj.* *(compar -ier; superl. -iest)* **astuto, pícaro.**

crag s. peñasco.

cram *tr. (pret.* y *pp:*
crammed) embutir; hartar;
atracar; rellenar, empollar
(estudios antes de un
examen).
cramp *s.* grapa; calambre;
aprieto; *adj.* apretado; *tr.*
engrapar; apretar;
restringir; dar calambres.
crane *s.* grúa.
cranium *s.* cráneo.
crank *s.* biela; concepto;
(fam.) maniático; *adj.*
inestable; *intr.* acodar.
crash *s.* desplome; colisión;
intr. desplomarse; (Com.)
quebrar; *tr.* romper, mover.
crass *adj.* craso.
crave *tr.* ansiar; *intr.* suplicar.
crawl *s.* marcha lenta;
arrastre; *intr.* trepar;
arrastrarse.
crayon *s.* lápiz; *tr.* dibujar a
lápiz.
craze *s.* moda; manía, locura;
tr. enloquencer.
crazy *adj.* loco, insensato.
cream *s.* crema, nata; *tr.*
poner crema en; *intr.*
desnatar.
creamery *s.* mantequería;
lechería.
crease *s.* arruga; *tr.* arrugar;
intr. plegarse.
create *tr.* crear, criar; causar,
originar.
credit *s.* crédito; (Com.)
haber; saldo acreedor;
notable *(exámenes).*
creditable *adj.* honorable.
creed *s.* credo.
creek *s.* arroyo.
cremate *tr.* incinerar.
creole *adj.* y *s.* criollo.
crest *s.* cresta; *tr.* encrestarse.
crestfallen *adj.* cabizbajo.
crevice *s.* grieta.
crew *s.* equipo; (Náut.)
tripulación.
crib *s.* pesebre, cuna.

crick *s.* calambre, tortícolis.
cricket *s.* grillo.
crier *s.* pregonero.
crime *s.* crimen.
cripple *adj.* y *s.* lisiado, etc.;
tr. lisiar, baldar.
crisp *adj.* frágil; *tr.* encrespar;
intr. encresparse.
critic *s.* crítico; censor.
criticise, criticize *tr.* criticar;
intr. censurar.
croak *s.* graznido *(canto de la*
rana, del cuervo).
crockery *s.* loza, cacharros.
crony *s.* camarada.
crook *s.* gancho; *intr.*
encorvar.
crooked *adj.* encorvado.
crosier *s.* cayado, báculo de
obispo.
cross *s.* cruz; cruce; *adj.*
cruzado; de mal humor; *tr.*
cruzar; contrariar; hacer la
señal de la cruz.
cross-bar *s.* travesaño.
crossbred *adj.* cruzado *(de*
raza).
cross-examine *tr.* (Der.)
interrogar rigurosamente.
crossing *s.* crucer; travesía.
crosswise *adv.* en cruz; al
través; equivocadamente.
crossword *s.* crucigrama.
crouch *intr.* agacharse;
rebajarse.
crow *s.* grajo; canto *(del*
gallo); intr. cacarear.
crowbar *s.* palanca.
crowd *s.* gentío; vulgo; *tr.*
apiñar; **to — around**
arremolinarse.
crown *s.* coronilla *(cabeza),*
copa *(sombrero),* cima
(montaña); tr. coronar.
crown prince *s.* príncipe
heredero.
cruise *s.* excursión; crucero;
tr. e *intr.* navegar.
crumb *s.* miga; pan rallado.

crumble *tr.* desmenuzar; *intr.* desmoronarse.

crumpet *s.* bollo blando.

crunch *tr.* mascar.

crush *s.* estrujadura, apretura; *tr.* estrujar, aplastar; moler, prensar.

crust *s.* corteza.

cry *s. (pl.* **cries)** grito; lamento, llanto.

cryin *adj.* llorón.

cryptic, -al *adj.* secreto, escondido.

cub *s.* cachorro; ballenato.

cube *s.* cubo; *tr.* cubicar.

cuckoo *s.* cuclillo.

cuddle *s.* abrazo cariñoso; *tr.* abrazar con cariño.

cue *s.* señal; apunte; cola *(de personas que esperan)*; taco de billar; humor.

cuff *s.* puño; bofetda; *tr.* abofetear.

cuff links *s. pl* gemelos *(para los puños)*.

cull *tr.* entresacar.

cult *s.* culto, secta.

cultivate *tr.* cultivar.

culture *s.* cultura; cultivo; *tr.* cultivar, educar.

cumulate *tr.* acumular.

cunning *adj.* mañoso; astuto; *s.* astucia; (U.S.) gracioso, divertido, mono.

cup *s.* taza, copa; vino sagrado.

cupboard *s.* aparador.

cupidity *s.* codicia.

curate *s.* cura.

curb. *s.* freno.

curd *s.* cuajada; *tr.* cuajar; *intr.* cuajarse.

cure *s.* cura, remedio; *tr.* curar, remediar, salar ahumar; *intr.* curarse.

curfew *s.* queda, toque de queda.

curiosity *s. (pl.* **-ties)** curiosidad.

curious *adj.* curioso, preguntón, raro.

curling *s.* ensortijamiento, abarquillamiento.

curling iron *s.* rizador, maquinilla de rizar.

curly *adj.* encrespado; rizado.

currant *s.* uva pasa de corinto.

currency *s.* moneda corriente; valor corriente; **paper —** papel moneda.

current *adj.* corriente, común; admitido, en boga; *s.* corriente *(de aire, etc.)*.

current account *s.* cuenta corriente.

curry *s.* cari; *tr. (pret. y pp:* **-ried)** curtir.

curse *s.* maldición; maleficio; *tr.* maldecir; *intr.* blasfemar; echar pestes.

cursory *adj.* precipitado, de pasada, por encima.

curt *adj.* corto, conciso; brusco.

curtail *tr.* acortar; reducir; privar; escatimar.

curtain *s.* cortina; telón; *tr.* poner cortinas; **to draw a — over** correr un velo sobre.

curve *s.* curva; *adj.* curvo; *tr.* encorvar; *intr.* encorvarse.

cushion *s.* cojín; almohadón; amortiguador.

custard *s.* natillas. **caramel — flan.**

custody *s.* custodia; **in —** en prisión.

custom *s.* costumbre, hábito, uso.

customary habitual, común; *adj.* acostumbrado.

customs *s.* aduana; **customs clearance** despacho de aduanas; **customs declarations** declaración de aduana; **customs duties** derecho de aduana.

C

D

dab s. golpecito; tr. (pret. y pp.
  dabbed) golpear
  ligeramente.
dabble tr. salpicar; rociar; intr.
  chapotear.
dad s. (fam.) papá.
daft adj. chiflado.
dagger s. daga.
daily adj. diario; adv.
  diariamente; s. diario.
daintiness s. golosina.
dairy s. lechería.
dais s. estrado.
daisy s. margarita.
dale s. valle, cañada.
daily intr. juguetear; tardar.
dam s. presa; pantano; tr.
  embalsar.
damage s. daño; pérdida; tr.
  dañar, perjudicar.
dame s. dama, ama; (fam.) tía.
damn tr. condenar.
damp adj. húmedo; s.
  humedad; tr. humedecer;
  amortiguar; abatir,
  desanimar.
damsel s. señorita.
dance s. danza.
dandriff, dandruff s. caspa.
danger s. peligro.
dangle tr. e intr. colgar.
dapper adj. aseado.
daring adj. atrevido; s.
  atrevimiento.
dark s. oscuridad.
darken tr. oscurecer.
darling adj. y s. querido; **my
  — amor mío.
darnel s. cizaña.
dart s. dardo; tr. lanzar; intr.
  lanzarse.
dash s. colisión; tr. lanzar;
  intr. avanzar, arrojarse.
date s. fecha; **up to —** al día;
  (fam.) cita; (Bot.) dátil; tr. e
  intr. datar, fechar.

daughter s. hija; **god —**
  ahijada; **— in law** nuera.
daunt tr. espantar.
dawdle tr. malgastar (tiempo);
  intr. perder el tiempo.
dawn s. amanecer.
day s. día; **the — after
  tomorrow** pasado mañana;
  — off día de descanso;
  every other — cada dos
  días; adj. diurno.
daylight s. luz del día;
  publicidad.
dazzle tr. deslumbrar.
dead adj. muerto; (fam.)
  cansado; **— certainty**
  certeza absoluta; **— drunk**
  borracho perdido.
deadlock tr. estancar.
deaf adj. sordo.
deafen tr. ensordecer.
deafness s. sordera.
deal s. negocio; cantidad,
  porción; tabla de pinto; tr.
  (pret. y pp. **dealt**) repartir;
  intr. negociar.
dean s. decano; deán.
dear adj. querido; costoso.
dearth s. escasez.
death s. muerte.
debar tr. (pret. y pp. **-barred**)
  excluir; prohibir.
debark tr. e intr. desembarcar.
debase tr. rebajar, degradar,
  falsificar.
debauch s. libertinaje; tr.
  seducir.
debilitate tr. debilitar.
debit s. (Com.) debe; cargo;
  tr. (Com.) adeudar.
debouch intr. desembocar.
debris s. ruinas.
debunk tr. desbaratar.
decamp intr. largarse, tomas
  las de Villadiego.
decanter s. garrafa.
decay s. podredumbre; tr.
  pudrir; intr. pudrirse.
decease intr. fallecer.
deceit s. engaño.

deceptive adj. engañoso.
decide tr. e intr. decidir.
decipher tr. descifrar.
deck s. (Náut.) cubierta;
puente; tr. adornar.
declaim tr. e intr. declamar.
declare tr. e intr. declarar;
confesar.
declension s. declinación.
decode tr. descifrar.
decompose tr. descomponer;
intr. descomponerse.
decorate tr. decorar;
condecorar.
decoy s. reclamp; tr. atraer.
decrease s. reclamo; tr. atraer.
decrease s. disminución; tr. e
intr. disminuír.
decree s. decreto; ley; tr.
decretar.
decrepit adj. caduco.
decrown. tr. destronar.
decry tr. (pret. y pp. -cried)
desacreditar.
dedicate tr. dedicar.
deduct tr. deducir.
deed s. hecho; proeza; (Der.)
escritura.
deem tr. e intr. pensar,
considerar.
deep adj. profundo; serio;
absorto.
deepend tr. profundizar.
deep-freeze s. congeladora;
tr. congelar.
deeply adv. profundamente.
deer. s. ciervo.
deface tr. desfigurar.
defame tr. difamar.
default s. falta; (Der.)
rebeldía; tr. e intr. faltar;
dejar de cumplir.
defeat s. derrota; (Der.)
anulación; tr. derrotar,
vencer.
defend tr. defender.
defer tr. diferir; remitir; intr.
demorarse.
defiance s. desafio, reto.

deficiency s. deficiencia,
dâficit.
defile tr. manchar, deshonra;
intr. desfilar.
define tr. definir.
definite adj. definido.
deflate tr. desinflar.
deflect tr. desviar; intr.
apartarse.
deflower tr. violar.
deforest tr. talar bosques.
deform tr. deformar.
defraud tr. defraudar.
defray tr. costear.
defrost tr. deshelar.
deft s. ágil.
defy tr. desafiar; despreciar.
degenerate intr. degenerar.
degrade tr. degradar.
degree s. grado; categoría.
deity s. divinidad.
deject tr. abatir.
delay s. demora, retraso; tr.
dilatar, aplazar; intr.
retrasarse.
delegate y s. delegado; tr.
delegar.
delete tr. borrar, suprimir.
delft s. zanja.
deliberate tr. felexionar.
delicate adj. delicado; fino,
educado; enfermizo.
delight s. deleite; tr. deleitar;
encantar.
dell s. hondonada.
delude tr. engañar.
deluge s. inundación.
delve tr. e intr. cavar; ahondar.
demand s. requerimiento,
exigencia; (Com.) pedido,
solicitud; tr. demandar,
requerir, exigir, pedir.
demean tr. rebajar; intr.
portarse; rebajarse.
demise s. muerte; transmisión
de la corona; (Der.)
transmisión de dominio; tr.
arrendar; intr. morir.
demit tr. dimitir, renunciar.
demolish tr. demoler.

D

demon s. demonio; adj.
  endemoniado.
demonstrate tr. demostrar.
demoralize tr. desmoralizar.
demount tr. desmontar.
demur s. demora; objeción; tr.
  aplazar.
den s. caverna; antro.
denial s. negación.
denizen s. vecino; tr.
  avecindar; intr.
  naturalizarse.
denominate tr. denominar.
denote tr. indicar, significar.
denounce tr. denunciar;
  amenazar.
dent s. mella; diente; tr.
  abollar, mellar.
denture s. dentadura.
denude tr. desnudar; intr.
  depojarse.
denunciate tr. denunciar.
deny tr. negar; contradecir.
deodorant adj. y s.
  desodorante.
depart intr. partir, retirarse; tr.
  dejar, abandonar.
departed s. difunto; adj.
  difunto.
depend intr. depender, colgar.
depict tr. pintar.
depilate tr. depilar.
deplete tr. agotar.
deplore tr. deplorar.
deploy tr. (Mil.) desplegar.
depopulate tr. despoblar; intr.
  despoblarse.
deport tr. deportar.
deportment s.
  comportamiento, conducta.
depose tr. deponer; intr.
  testificar.
deposit s. depósito; señal; tr.
  depositar; intr. depositarse.
deprave tr. corromper,
  adulterar.
deprecate tr. desaprobar,
  censurar.
depress tr. deprimir.
deprive tr. privar, despojar.

depurate tr. depurar.
derrail intr. descarrilar.
derby s. sombrero hongo;
  derby (carrera de caballos).
deride tr. ridiculizar.
derisory adj. irrisorio.
derive tr. e intr. derivar.
derrick s. grúa.
descend tr. e intr. descender.
describe tr. describir, explicar.
descry tr. (pret. y pp.
  descried) descubrir, divisar.
descrate tr. profanar, violar.
deserve tr. merecer; intr.
  tener merecimientos.
designate adj. designado; tr.
  designar.
designer s. dibujante;
  proyectista.
desire s. deseo; tr. desear,
  ambicionar.
desist intr. desistir.
desk s. escritorio, pupitre.
desolate tr. desolar, arrasar.
despair s. desesperación; intr.
  desesperar.
despairins adj. desesperado,
  desesperante.
despicable adj. despreciable.
despise tr. despreciar.
despite s. insulto.
despoil tr. despojar.
despond s. abatimiento; tr.
  abatirse.
dessert s. postre.
destine tr. destinar, designar.
destitute adj. indigente.
destroy tr. destruir, invalidar.
desultory adj. deshilvanado,
  descosido; variable.
detach tr. separar; destacar.
detachment s. separación;
  imparcialidad; (Mil.)
  destacamento.
detail s. detalle; tr. detallar.
detain tr. detener.
detect tr. descubrir; detectar.
deteriorate tr. deteriorar; intr.
  deteriorarse.

determine *tr.* determinar; *intr.* decidirse.

detest *tr.* detestar.

dethrone etr. destronar.

detonate *tr.* e *intr.* detonar, estallar.

detour *s.* rodeo; *tr.* desviar.

detract *tr.* apartar; *intr.* menguar.

deuced *adj.* diabólico.

devalue *tr.* desvalorizar.

devastate *tr.* devastar.

develop *tr.* desenvolver, desarrollar; explotar *(una mina)*; revelar; *intr.* desarrollarse.

deviate *tr.* desviar; *intr.* desviarse.

device *s.* dispositivo; artificio.

devil *s.* demonio.

devise *tr.* proyectar, inventar.

devolve *tr.* transmitir.

devote *tr.* dedicar.

devout *adj.* devoto, piadoso.

dew *s.* rocio; *tr.* rociar.

diagnose *tr.* diagnosticar.

dial *s.* esfera; disco selector *teeâfono)*; *tr.* marcar, llamar.

dialogue *s.* diálogo; *tr.* e *intr.* dialogar.

diamond *s.* diamante.

dice *s. pl.* dados.

dictate *tr.* e *intr.* dictar; mandar.

dictatorship *s.* dictadura.

diction *s.* dicción, lenguaje.

dictume *s.* dictamen; sentencia.

die *s.* dado; troquel; *intr.* morir, acabar.

diet *s.* dieta; *intr.* estar a dieta.

differ *intr.* diferir.

diffidence *s.* timidez.

diffuse *adj.* difuso, extendido; *tr.* difundir, extender.

dig *s. tr.* cavar; escudriñar.

digest *tr.* diferir; asimilar.

digress *tr.* divagar.

dilapidate *tr.* dilapidar.

dilate *tr.* dilatar.

dilute *tr.* diluir; *int.* diluirse.

dim *adj.* oscuro.

diminish *tr.* disminuir.

din *s.* ruido, estrepito; *tr.* golpear con ruido.

dine *tr.* dar de comer, convidar.

dingy *adj. (comparativo* **-ier**; *superl.* **-iest**) sucio.

dining room *s.* comedor.

dinner *s.* comida, cena; — **jacket** smoking.

dint *s.* golpe; *tr.* abollar.

dip *s.* baño. *tr. (pret.* y *pp.* **dipped)** *tr.* sumergir.

direct *adj.* directo; abierto; exacto; *tr.* dirigir; ordenar.

directness *s.* franqueza.

dirt *s.* lodo; polvo.

disable *tr.* inhabilitar; *adj.* incapacitado.

disaccord *s.* desacuerdo.

disadvantage *s.* desventaja; *tr.* dañar.

disagree *intr.* disentir.

disagreement *s.* discrepancia.

disappear *intr.* desaparecer.

disappoint *tr.* decepcionar, defraudar; dejar plantado.

disapprove *tr.* e *intr.* desaprobar, rechazar.

disarm *tr.* e *intr.* desarmar.

disaster *s.* desastre, calamidad.

disavow *tr.* negar, repudiar.

disband *tr.* disolver; (Mil.) licenciar.

disbelief *s.* incredulidad.

disburse *tr.* desembolsar.

discard *s.* descarte; *tr.* descartar; despedir.

discern *tr.* e *intr.* discernir.

discipline *s.* disciplina; *tr.* disciplinar, educar.

disclose *tr.* descubrir; revelar.

discomfit *tr.* derrotar.

discompose *tr.* descomponer; agitar.

disconcert *tr.* desconcertar, confundir.

D

disconnect *tr.* desunir;
desconectar.

discount *tr.* descontar,
rebajar.

discourse *s.* discurso; *tr.*
discursear, discurrir.

discover *tr.* descubrir.

discredit *s.* descredito;
deshonra; *tr.* desacreditar.

discriminate *tr.* distinguir.

discuss *tr.* e *intr.* discutir,
debatir.

disdain *s.* desprecio; *tr.*
despreciar.

disease *s.* enfermedad; *tr.*
enfermar.

disembark *tr.* e *intr.*
desembarcar.

disentangle *tr.* desenredar.

disfigure *tr.* desfigurar.

disgrace *s.* deshonra; *tr.*
deshonrar; desacreditar.

disguise *s.* disfraz, máscara;
tr. disfrazar.

disgust *s.* repugnancia; *tr.*
repugnar.

dish *s.* (*pl.* **-shes**) plato;
vasija; *tr.* servir en un plato.

dishearten *tr.* abatir.

dishonor *s.* deshonra; *tr.*
deshonrar.

disincline *tr.* desinclinar;
indisponer.

disinfect *tr.* desinfectar.

disinherti *tr.* desheredar.

disintegrate *tr.* desintegrar,
disgregar.

disjoin *tr.* desunir.

disjoint *tr.* desarticular,
dislocar; *intr.* desarticularse.

dislike *s.* aversión, antipatía;
tr. no gastar.

dislocate *tr.* dislocar.

dislodge *tr.* desalojar.

dismal *adj.* triste, tetrico.

dismantle *tr.* desmantelar,
desarmar.

dismay *s.* desmallo; *tr.*
desanimar.

dismiss *tr.* despedir.

dismount *tr.* desmontar; *intr.*
desmontar, apearse.

disobey *tr.* e *intr.*
desobedecer.

disorder *s.* desorden, *tr.*
desordenar.

disorganize *tr.* desorganizar.

disown *tr.* repudiar.

disparage *tr.* menospreciar;
desacreditar.

dispatch *s.* despacho;
expedición. *tr.* despachar.

dispense *tr.* dispensar,
distribuir.

disperse *tr.* dispersar;
disgregar; *intr.* dispersarse.

dispirit *tr.* desalentar.

displace *tr.* dislocar.

display *s.* despliegue;
ostentación; *tr.* desplegar;
exhibir.

displeasing *adj.*
desagradable.

disport *s.* diversión; *tr.* divertir.

dispose *tr.* disponer;
componer; mover.

disposition *s.* disposición;
índole, genio.

dispossess *etr.* desposeer.

disproof *s.* refutación.

disprove *tr.* refutar.

dispute *s.* disputa, querella;
tr. discutir, pelear.

disquiet *s.* inquietud; *tr.*
inquietar.

disregard *s.* desatención;
desaire; *tr.* desatender.

disrepair *s.* desconcierto; mal
estado.

disrespect *s.* falta de respeto;
tr. desacatar, desairar.

disrupt *tr.* romper.

dissatisfaction *s.*
descontento.

dissect *tr.* disecar; analizar.

dissemble *tr.* disimular,
esconder; *intr.* ser hipócrita.

disseminate *tr.* diseminar,
propagar.

dissert *tr.* disertar.

dissimulate *tr.* e *intr.*
disimular.
dissipate *tr.* disipar;
desaparecer; *intr.* disiparse.
dissociate *tr.* disociar; *in.*
disociarse.
dissuade *tr.* disuadir.
distant *adj.* distante;
indiferente.
distate *s.* disgusto.
distasteful *adj.* desagradable.
distil *tr.* e *intr. (pret.* y *pp.*
-tilled) destilar.
distinguish *tr.* distinguir,
percibir.
distort *tr.* torcer, deformar.
distract *tr.* distraer.
distress *s.* pena; peligro; *tr.*
apenar.
distribute *tr.* distribuir, repartir.
distrust *s.* desconfianza; *tr.*
desconfiar.
distrustfulness *s.*
desconfianza, sospecha.
disturb *tr.* turbar, trastornar;
interrumpir.
disunite *tr.* desunir; *intr.*
desunirse.
disuse *s.* desuso.
disuse *tr.* desusar.
diteh *s.* zanja, acequia,
cuenta.
divagate *in.* divagar.
divan *s.* diván.
diver *s.* buzo; nadador.
diverge *in.* divergir.
divert *tr.* divertir; desviar.
divest *tr.* desnudar.
divide *tr.* e *in.* dividir.
divine *s.* teólogo; *adj.* divino.
divorce *s.* divorcio; *tr.*
divorciar.
divulge *tre.* divulgar, publicar.
do *tr. (pret.* **did;** *pp.* **done)**
hacer *(causar); (ejecutar);*
resolver; terminar, arreglar.
dock *s.* (Náut.) dársena,
muelle; (Der.) tribuna de los
acusados.

docker *s.* trabajador del
muelle, descargador.
dockyard *s.* astillero, arsenal.
doctor *s.* doctor; médico; *tr.*
doctorar; *intr.* (fam.)
practicar la medicina; tomar
medicinas.
dodder *intr.* temblar,
tambalearse.
dodge *s.* regate, movimiento
rápido; *intr.* regatear; *tr.*
evitar *(golpes, etc.);* evadir.
doer *s.* actor, agente.
doings *s. pl.* actos; conducta.
doleful *adj.* dolorido.
doll *s.* muñeca; *tr.* engalanar.
domain *s.* dominio; propiedad.
dome *s.* cúpula.
domesticate *tr.* domesticar;
amansar.
domicile *s.* domicilio; *tr.*
domiciliar.
domineer *tr.* e *intr.* dominar.
dominion *s.* dominio, señorío.
donate *tr.* donar, dar.
done *adj.* hecho, terminado;
(fam.) cansado.
donkey *s.* burro, asno.
doom *s.* destino, suerte;
ruina; *tr.* condenar a
muerte, desahuciar.
door *s.* puerta; entrada (fig.)
acceso; — **bolt** cerrojo.
doorkeeper *s.* portero.
doorway *s.* portal.
dop *s.* droga, narcótico; *tr.* e
intr. drogarse.
dormant *adj.* durmiente.
dose *s.* dosis; *tr.* dosificar.
dossier *s.* expediente.
dot *s.* señal.
dote *intr.* chochear.
doubt *s.* duda; **beyond** — sin
duda; *tr.* e *intr.* dudar.
doubtless *adj.* indudable.
dough *s.* masa, pasta.
dour *adj.* abatido, melancólico.
douse *tr.* zambullir.
dove *s.* paloma.

D

downfall s. caída, ruina; descenso.

downpour s. aguacero.

downright adj. absoluto.

dowry s. dote.

doze s. sueño ligero; intr. dormitar.

dozen s. docena.

dozy qdj. (comparar -ier; superl. -iest) adormecido.

drag s. rastra; rastreo; tr. arrastrar.

drake s. pato.

drape tr. cubrir, adornar.

draper s. tapicero.

draw s. empate; tablas (en damas y ajedrez).

drawback s. desventaja.

drawbridge s. puente levadizo o giratorio.

drawer s. cajón.

drawing s. dibujo; sorteo (en la lotería).

dread s. horror, temor; adj. espantoso, terrible; tr. e intr. temer.

dream s. sueño.

dreary adj. (compar. -ier; superl. -iest) triste.

dredge s. draga; tr. e intr. dragar, excavar, limpiar.

dregs s. pl. heces; restor, desperdicios.

drench s. mojadura; tr. mojar, saturar.

dress s. vestido, traje; hábito; tr. vestir de etiqueta; ataviar; peinar.

drill s. taladro.

drink s. bebida; **to take —** echar un trago; tr. (pret. **drank**; pp. **drunk**) beber.

drinking s. acción de beber.

drip s. goteo; intr. gotear; destilar.

drive s. calzada para coches; paseo en coche.

driver s. conductor, chofer.

drizzle s. llovizna.

droll adj. cómico.

drone s. zángano; tr. e intr. hablar monótonamente.

drop s. gota; pendiente, cuesta.

dropper s. cuentagotas.

dross s. escoria.

drought s. sequía.

drove s. manada; rebaño.

drown tr. apagar; intr. anegarse, ahogarse.

drudge s. yunque; esclavo del trabajo; tr. abrumar de trabajo.

drudgery s. afán; trabajo penoso.

drug s. droga; narcótico.

druggist s. droguero; farmacéutico.

drum s. tambor; cilindro.

drumstick s. palillo de tambor.

drunken adj. borracho.

drying s. secado.

dry celaning s. limpieza en seco.

dub s. jugador torpe; toque de tambor; tr. titular.

duck s. pago; (fam.) querida; tr. agachar (la cabeza); zambullir; intr. agacharse.

dudgeon s. resentimiento.

due adj. debido; pagadero.

duel s. duelp tr. combatir en el duelo.

dug s. teta.

dullars s. estúpido.

dumb adj. mudo.

dumbfound tr. pasmar.

dusk s. crepúsculo; adj. oscuro.

dust s. polvo; cenizas.

duster s. plumero, borrador.

dutiful adj. obediente.

duty s. (p. **duties**) obligación.

dwarf adj. y s. enano; tr. impedir el desarrollo de.

dwell intr. (pret. y pp. **dwelled** o **dwelt**) vivir.

dwelling s. vivienda.

dwindle tr. disminuír.

dye s. tinte; matiz.

E

each *adj.* cada, cada uno.
eager *adj.* ansioso, anhelante.
eagle *s.* águila —**eyed** ojo avizor.
ear *s.* oreja; oído; asa; espiga; —**ring** pendiente; —**drum** tímpano; **to turn a deaf —** hacerse el sordo; *m.* espigar.
earache *s.* dolor de oídos.
earl *s.* conde.
earliness *s.* prontitud.
early *adj. (compar.* -**ier**; *superl.* -**iest**) temprano; antiguo, próximo; *adv.* temprano; al principio.
earn *tr.* ganar.
earth *s.* tierra; mundo.
eathernware *s.* loza de barro.
earthquake *s.* terremoto.
ease *s.* alivio; comodidad; *tr.* tranquilizar; facilitar; *intr.* aliviarse.
East *s.* Este, Oriente, Levante.
Easter *s.* Pascua de Resurrección, Semana Santa.
easy *adj. (compar.* -**ier**; *superl.* -**iest**); facil, acomodado.
eatable *adj.* comestible.
eavesdrop *s.* gotera; *intr.* escuchar detrás de las puertas.
ebb-tide *s.* baja mar.
echo *s.* eco; *tr.* repetri; *intr.* resonar.
economy *s. (fl.* -**ies**) economía.
edge *s.* filo; margen; ángulo; *tr.* afilar; ribetear; *intr.* avanzar de lado.
edible *adj.* y *s.* comestible.
edition *s.* edición.
educate *tr.* educar, formar.
eerie *adj.* misterioso.

efface *tr.* borrar.
effectual *adj.* eficaz.
effemiate *tr.* afeminar; *adj.* afeminado.
effort *s.* esfuerzo, empeño.
egg *s.* huevo.
egtist *s.* egoista.
eider-down *s.* edredón.
eight *adj.* y *s.* ocho.
eighteen *adj.* y *s.* dieciocho.
eighty *adj.* y *s.* ochenta.
either *adv.* tampoco.
eject *tr.* expulsar.
eke *tr.* aumentar con dificultad.
elaborate *tr.* elaborar.
elapse *tr.* pasar.
elate *tr.* regocijar.
elbow *s.* codo.
elder *adj. (compar.* de **old**) mayor *(de edad); s.* mayor; anciano.
elect *tr.* elegir.
electrify *tr.* electrificar.
element *s.* elemento; (Qm.) cuerpo simple.
elevate *tr.* elevar.
eleven *adj.* y *s.* once.
elf *s. (pl.* -**elves**) duende.
elicit *tr.* sacar.
eliminate *tr.* eliminar.
elope *tr.* escaparse.
else *adj.* otro, diferente; **nobody —** nadie más; *adv.* de otro modo, en otra parte.
embalm *tr.* embalsamar.
embark *tr.* embarcar.
embarrass *tr.* desconcertar.
embarrassing *adj.* vergonzoso, desconcertante.
embassy *s. (pl.* -**sies**) embajada.
embellish *tr.* embellecer.
embezzle *tr.* desfalcar.
embitter *tr.* amargar.
emblem *tr.* simbolizar.
embosom *tr.* abrigar, proteger.
embrace *s.* abrazo; *tr.* abrazar.
embroidery *s.* bordado.

emerald *s.* esmeralda.
emerge *tr.* emerger.
emigrate *intr.* emigrar.
emit *tr. (pret.* y *pp.* -**mitted**)
  emitir.
emperor *s.* emperador.
emphasize *tr.* acentuar.
employ *s.* empleo *tr.* emplear.
employer *s.* patrón.
emptiness *s.* vacío.
empty *adj. (compar.* -**ies**;
  superl. -**iest**) vacíío; *tr.* e
  intr. (pret. y *pp.* -**tied**) vaciar.
enable *tr.* capacitar, permitir.
enact *tr.* decretar, establecer.
enact *tr.* decretar, establecer.
enactment *s.* promulgación
  (de una ley).
enamour *tr.* enamorar.
encage *tr.* enjaular.
encase *tr.* encerrar.
encircle *tr.* cercar.
enclose *tr.* incluir.
encore *s.* bis, repetición; *inj.*
  ¡que se repita!
encourage *tr.* animar.
encroach *tr.* invadir.
encumber *tr.* embarazar.
end *s.* fin; final.
endanger *tr.* poner en peligro.
endeavor *s.* esfuerzo; *intr.*
  esforzarse.
ending *s.* (Gram.) desinencia,
  terminación.
endow *tr.* dotar.
endurance *s.* aguante.
endure *tr.* aguantar; *intr.* durar.
energize *tr.* dar energía; *intr.*
  obrar con energía.
enfold *tr.* envolver, incluir.
engage *tr.* comprometer,
  apalabrar.
engender *tr.* engendrar.
engineer *s.* ingeniero; *tr.*
  dirigir con acierto.
England *s. p.* Inglaterra.
English *adj.* inglés.
engrave *tr.* grabar.
engross *tr.* absorber; copiar o
  transcribir caligrá ficamente.

enjoy *tr.* gozar de, disfrutar;
  divertirse.
enlarge *tr.* ensanchar.
enlighten *tr.* ilustrar.
enmity *s. (pl.* -**ties**) enemistad.
enough *adj., adv.* y *s.*
  bastante; *inj.* ¡basta!
enrapture *tr.* embelesar,
  arrebatar.
enrich *tr.* enriquecer.
enshroud *tr.* envolver.
ensue *intr.* seguir.
ensure *tr.* asegurar.
entangle *tr.* enredar.
enter *tr.* penetrar, en;
  matricular.
enterprise *s.* empresa.
entertain *tr.* entretener; recibir.
entice *tr.* inducir.
entity *s. (pl.* -**ties**) entidad.
entrance *s.* entrada.
entrance *tr.* encantar.
entreat *tr.* rogar.
entrust *tr.* confiar, encargar.
enumerate *tr.* detallar.
envelop *tr.* envolver, forrar.
envoy *s.* enviado.
enry *s.* envidia. *tr. (pert.* y *pp.*
  -**vied**) envidiar.
equestrian *adj.* ecuestre; *s.*
  jinete.
equip *tr. (pret.* y *pp.*
  equipped) equipar.
erase *tr.* borrar.
erect *adj.* erguido; *tr.* levantar,
  instalar.
erode *tr.* erosionar.
err *intr.* errar.
errand *s.* recado, mensaje.
erupt *tr.* arrojar *(lava, llamas);*
  intr. hacer erupción.
escalade *s.* (Mil.) escalada; *tr.*
  escalar.
escape *tr.* escapar a; *in.*
  escapar.
escort *s.* escolta.
essay *tr.* ensayar.
establish *tr.* establecer.
estate *s.* estado; hacienda.
esteem *tr.* estimar.

ethics *s.* ética.
eulogize *tr.* elogiar.
evacuate *tr.* evacuar.
evade *tr.* evadir.
evaluate *tr.* evaluar.
evaporate *tr.* evaporar.
eve *s.* víspera.
even *adj.* igual, llano.
evening *s.* tarde, atardecer, anochecer; velada.
evenness *s.* igualdad.
event *s.* suceso.
ever *adv.* siempre.
everlasting *adj.* eterno.
every *adj.* cada; todo; **— now and then** de vez en cuando, **— other day** cada dos días.
evict *tr.* desahuciar.
evil *adj.* malo; *s.* mal.
evoke *tr.* evocar.
evolve *tr.* desarrollar; *intr.* evolucionar.
ewe *s.* oveja.
exact *adj.* exacto; *tr.* exigir.
exam *s.* (fam.) examen.
exasperate *tr.* irritar; agravar, enconar.
excavate *tr.* excavar, zanjar.
exceed *tr.* exceder, superar; *intr.* excederse.
except *prep.* excepto; *tr.* exceptuar.
excerpt *s.* selección, cita.
excerpt *tr.* citar, escoger.
exchange *s.* cambio; Bolsa; *tr.* cambiar.
excite *tr.* excitar.
exclaim *tr.* e *in.* exclamar, gritar.
exclude *tr.* excluír.
excuse *tr.* discu.par.
execute *tr.* ejecutar.
executive *adj.* 4 ejecutivo; jefe del estado; poder ejecutivo.
exercise *s.* ejercicio, práctica.
exert *tr.* ejercer.
exhaust *s.* escape; *tr.* agotar; escapar.
exhausting *adj.* agotador.

exhilarate *tr.* alegrar.
exile *s.* desiterro; *tr.* desterrar, espatriar.
exist *in.* existir; vivir.
exit *s.* (*pl.* **exeunt**) salida.
expand *tr.* extender.
expect *tr.* esperar, aguardar.
expedient *adj.* conveniente.
expense *s.* gasto.
expensive *adj.* caro.
explain *tr.* explicar.
explanation *adj.* explicación.
explode *tr.* e *intr.* volar, refutar.
exploit *s.* hazaña.
explore *tr.* explorar, sondear.
export *s.* exportación; *tr.* e *in.* exportar.
expose *tr.* exponer.
expostulate *tr.* protestar.
expound *tr.* exponer, explicar.
extempore *adj.* improvisado.
extend *tr.* extender.
exterior *adj.* externo.
extinct *adj.* extinguido.
extinction *s.* extinción, abolición.
extol *tr.* exaltar.
extort *tr.* arrancar.
extreme *adj.* y *s.* extremo.
extremity *s.* (*pl.* **-ties**) extremidad.
exude *tr.* e *intr.* sudar.
eye *s.* ojo; **—** ojo por ojo; **one-eyed** tuerto; **to keep an — on** vigilar; **with the naked —** a simple vista; *tr.* (*pret.* y *pp.* **eyed**) mirar, clavar la mirada en.
eyebrow *s.* ceja.
eyelash *s.* pestaña.
eyelid *s.* párpado.
eyesight vista.
eyestrain *s.* irritación o can sancio de lo ojos.
eyetooth *s.* (*pl.* **eyeteeth**) colmillo.
eyewitness *s.* testigo presencial.

E

F

fable s. fábula.
fabric s. fábrica; tela o género.
fabricate tr. fabricar.
facade s. fachada.
face s. cara; faz.
facetious adj. chistoso.
facilitate tr. facilitar.
fact s. hecho; in fact de
hecho.
fade tr. marchitar, desteñir.
fail s. suspenso; tr. faltar a.
failing s. falta.
failure s. fracaso.
fair adj. justo; lega; hermoso;
rubio; s. mercado, feria.
fairy s. hada.
faith s. fe.
fake s. (fam.) falsificación;
impostor; tr. (fam.) falsificar.
fallacious adj. falaz.
fallacy s. (pl. -cies) error.
falsify tr. falsificar.
falter s. vacilación.
familiar adj. y s. conocedor,
íntimo.
family s. familia, raza.
famine s. hambre.
famous adj. famoso.
fan s. abanico; ventilador; tr.
(pret. y pp. fanned) aventar.
fancied adj. imaginario.
fancy s. fantasía.
fang s. colmillo (de las fieras);
dientes (de reptil; de
tenedor, etc.).
far adj. lejano; largo; adv.
lejos, a distancia.
farce s. farsa, sainete.
farcical adj. absurdo.
fare s. precio del billete; intr.
acontecer, irle a uno (bien o
mal).
farewell s. despedida, adiós.
farm s. granja, cortijo; tr.
labrar o cultivar.
farmyard s. corral de granja.

farther adv. más lejos.
farthing s. cuarto de penique.
fashion s. forma, uso, estilo.
fast s. ayuno; cable; adj.
fuerte; rápido; adv.
rápidamente; in. ayunar.
fasten tr. afirmar; atar; in.
fijarse.
fastening s. asegurador;
cerradura.
fat adj. (compar. -tter; superl.
-ttest) gordo; fértil; s. grasa.
father s. padre; tr. engendrar;
adoptar como hijo.
fatherland s. madre patria.
fathom tr. sondear.
fatness s. gordura.
fatten tr. e in. engordar,
alimentar.
faucet s. grifo.
fault s. falta; culpa; avería.
favor s. favor, servicio, tr.
ayudar, apoyar.
favored adj. favorito.
fear s. temor, miedo; tr. temer,
recelar.
fearless adj. intrépido.
feasible adj. factible.
feast s. fiesta; tr. festejar.
feat s. hazaña.
feather s. pluma, vanidad;
feathers; s. p. alas.
February s. febrero.
fee s. honorarios; tr. pagar.
feed s. alimento, pienso; tr.
(pret. y pp. fed) alimentar.
feel s. sensación; tino, tr.
(pret. y pp. felt) palpar;
sentir; in. hallarse.
feet s. pl. de foot pies.
feign tr. e in. fingir.
fell s. tala (de árboles); adj.
cruel; tr. talar, derribar.
fellow s. compañero; socio;
— countryman
compatriota.
felon adj. cruel; s. (Der.) reo.
female s. hembra.
fen s. pantano.

fence *s.* valla; traficante; guía; *tr.* cercar.

fend *tr.* parar, apartar; *in.* rechazar; defenderse.

ferment *tr.* e *in.* fermentar, venirse.

ferry *s.* balsa, transbordador; *tr.* cruzar el río en barco.

fester *s.* úlcera.

fetch *tr.* acción de ir a buscar; *tr.* traer, ir por.

fetus *s.* feto.

feud *s.* riña.

fever *s.* fiebre; *tr.* causar calentura.

few *adj.* y *pron. indef.* pocos, algunos.

fiancé *s.* novio.

fiancée *s.* novia.

fib *s.* embuste; *intr.* mentir.

fiber *s.* fibra.

fickle *adj.* inconstante.

fiddle *s.* (fam.) violín.

fidget *s.* persona agitada; *tr.* agitar; *in.* agitarse.

field *s.* campo, tierra laborable.

fiend *s.* diablo.

fierce *adj.* fiero; cruel.

fifteen *adj.* y *s.* quince.

fifty *adj.* y *s.* cincuenta.

fifty-fifth *adj.* y *adv.* mitad y mitad, a medias.

fig *s.* higo.

fight *s.* lucha.

filch *tr.* birlar, hurtar.

file *s.* ima, fila; archivo; *tr.* limar, archivar.

fill *s.* abundancia; *tr.* llenar.

film *s.* película; *tr.* filmar.

filter *s.* filtro; *tr.* e *in.* filtrar.

fin *s.* aleta de los peces.

find *s.* hallazgo; *tr. (pret.* y *pp.* found) hallar, descubrir.

fine *adj.* fino; *s.* multa; *tr.* multar; — arts *s. pl.* bellas artes.

finery *s.* vestido de gala.

finish *s.* fin, término; conclusión; *tr.* acabar, rematar, aniquilar; *in.* finalizar.

fir *s.* (Bot.) abeto.

fire *s.* fuego; incendio,; *tr.* encender; calentar el horno; iluminar.

fireworks *s.* fuegos artificiales.

firm *adj.* firme; *s.* firma, entidad, empresa.

first *adj.* primero; *adv.* primeramente; *s.* primero; — aid primeros auxilios.

firth *s.* estuario.

fish *s.* pez, pescador; *tr.* pescar; — hook anzuelo.

fist *s.* puño; *tr.* empuñar, dar puñetazos.

fit *s.* ajuste; encaje; *tr.* ajustar; encajar.

fitfulness *s.* capricho.

fitting *adj.* apropiado; *s.* prueba; *pl.* accesorios.

five *adj.* y *s.* cinco.

fix *s.* apuro, aprieto; *tr. (pret.* y *pp.* fixed o fixt) fijar; reparar.

fixed *adj.* fijo.

flag *s.* bandera, insignia.

flagrant *adj.* escandaloso.

flake *s.* escama, copo *(de nieve)*.

flame *s.* llama; *in.* llamear.

flange *s.* pestaña; *tr.* rebordear.

flank *s.* costado; *tr.* flanquear, orillar; *in.* lindar con.

flannel *s.* franela.

flap *s.* falda.

flask *s.* frasco.

flatness *s.* planicie.

flatten *tr.* allanar; desalentar; *intr.* aplanarse.

flavor *s.* aroma, sabor; *tr.* saborear, condimentar.

flaw *s.* defecto; ráfaga; *tr.* agrietar; *intr.* ajarse.

flea *s.* pulga.

flee *tr.* e *intr.* huír.

fleece *s.* lana.

fleet *adj.* veloz.

flemish *adj.* flamenco.
flesh *s.* carne.
fleshpot *s.* olla.
flight *s.* fuga.
flimsy *adj. (compar.* **-ier**; *superl.* **-iest**) débil.
fling *s.* tiro; baile escocés muy rápido; *tr.* tirar, arrojar; *in.* arrojarse, lanzarse.
flirt *s.* coqueta; *in.* flirtear.
flock *s.* manada, rebaño; *tr.* reunirse.
flood *s.* inundación.
floor *s.* piso; *tr.* enlosar.
florist *s.* florista.
flour *s.* harina.
flout *s.* mofa; *tr.* e *in.* mofarse.
flow *s.* flujo; *in.* fluir, correr.
flower *s.* flor.
flowing *adj.* fluído; *s.* manatial.
flu *s.* gripe.
fluent *adj.* afluente; líquido; abundante.
fluff *s.* plumón.
flurry *s.* agitación; *tr.* agitar, confundir.
fluster *s.* aturdimiento; *tr.* confundir.
flute *s.* flauta.
flutter *s.* tumulto; *tr.* agitar.
fly *s. (pl.* **-flies**) mosca, braqueta; **on the — al vuelo.
flying *adj.* volador.
foal *s.* potro, buche.
foam *s.* espuma.
foe *s.* enemigo.
fog *s.* niebla, confusión.
foil *s.* chapa metálica; rastro, pista.
fold *s.* pliegue; *tr.* plegar, doblar.
folding *adj.* plegable.
folk *s.* gente, pueblo,; *adj.* popular.
follow *tr.* seguir, suceder, copiar.
folly *s.* locura, disparate.
forment *tr.* fomentar.
fond *adj.* aficionado.

fondle *tr.* acariciar.
food *s.* alimento.
food *s.* tonto, idiota; *tr.* engañar, embaucar.
foolhardy *adj.* temerario.
footmark *s.* huella.
footpath *s.* camino para peatones.
orbear *s.* antepasado.
forbid *tr. (pret.* **forbade**; *pp.* **forbidden** prohibir.
forceps *s.* pinzas, tenazas.
fore *adj.* anterior; *adv.* anteriormente; *s.* delantera; proa.
forearm *s.* antebrazo.
forecast *tr.* pronosticar, calcular.
forefather *s.* antepasado.
forego *tr. (pret.* **forewent**; *pp.* foregone) ir adelante; renunciar.
foreground *s.* primer plano.
forehead *s.* frente.
foreman *s. (pl.* **-men**) capataz.
foremost *adj.* delantero; *adv.* primero.
forenoon *s.* mañana.
foresay *tr. (pret.* y *pp.* **foresaid**) pronosticar.
foresee *tr. (pret.* **foresaw**; *pp.* **foreseen**) prever.
forest *s.* bosque.
forestall *tr.* impedir.
forewarn *tr.* prevenir.
foreword *s.* advertencia; prólogo.
forfeit *s.* multa; *tr.* perder el derecho a.
forge *s.* fragua; *tr.* fraguar.
forgery *s. (pl.* **-ries**) falsificación.
forget *tr. (pret.* **forgot**; *pp.* **forgotten**) olvidar.
forgive *tr. (pret.* **forgave**; *pp.* **forgiven**) perdonar.
form *s.* forma; banco *(de asiento); tr.* formar; *in.* formarse.

formal *adj.* formal;
ceremonioso, solemne.
formulate *tr.* formular.
forsake *tr. (pret.* **forsook**; *pp.*
forsaken) abandonar.
forsooth *adv.* ciertamente.
fort *s.* fuerte, castillo.
fortify *tr. (pret. y pp.* **-fied)**
fortificar; reforzar.
fortnight *s.* quincena.
foster *adj.* adoptivo; *tr.*
adoptar; mimar; criar.
found *tr.* fundar; fundir.
fount *s.* fuente.
fountain *s.* fuente; **fountain
pen** pluma estilográfica.
four *adj. y s.* cuatro; **to go on
all —s** andar a gatas.
fourteen *adj. y s.* catorce.
fowl *s.* ave; carne de ave; *in.*
cazar aves de corral.
fox *s.* zorro.
foxy *adj. (compar.* **-ier**; *superl.*
-iest) astuto.
frame *s.* estructura;
armadura; *tr.* formar;
ajustar.
franchise *s.* franquicia,
privilegio.
frank *adj.* franco, sincero.
frankness *adj.* franqueza,
sinceridad.
fraud *s.* fruade, engaño.
freak *s.* capricho.
freckle *s.* peca.
free *adj.* libre; independiente;
gratis, franco.
freedom *s.* libertad.
freeholder *s.* dueño absoluto
de una finca.
freeze *s.* helada; *tr.* helfar.
freight *s.* carga, flete.
French *adj. y s.* francés,
idioma francés.
frequent *tr.* frecuentar.
fresh *adj.* fresco, reciente.
freshen *tr.* refrescar; *in.*
refrescarse.
fretful *adj.* irritable;
impaciente.

friar *s.* fraile.
frigate *s.* fragata.
fright *s.* susto; miedo.
frighten *tr.* asustar; espantar;
in. asustarse.
fringe *s.* franja.
fritter *tr.* desmenuzar;
esparcir.
frizzle *s.* rizo; *tr.* rizar;
ensortijar.
fro *adv.* atrás.
frock *s.* vestido; blusa, bata.
frog *s.* rana.
frolic *s.* travesura; *in.*
juguetear; divertirse.
from *prep.* de; desde.
front *s.* frente; fachada; *adj.*
delantero.
frugality *s. (pl.* **-ties)**
parquedad; escasez.
fruit *s.* fruta; resultado; —
basket frutero; — **knife**
cuchillo de postre; — **stone**
cuesco de fruta.
fry *s. (pl.* **fries)** fritada, fritura;
tr. freír.
frying pan *s.* sartén.
fuel *s.* combustible.
fulfill *tr.* cumplir.
full *adj.* lleno, completo.
fulsome *adj.* de mal gusto.
fumble *tr.* manosear;
balbucear.
fun *s.* broma.
fund *s.* fondo, capital; *tr.*
consolidar una deuda.
funny *adj. (compar.* **-ier**;
superl. **-iest)** cómico,
divertido.
fur *s.* piel; *tr.* cubrir o forrar
con pieles.
furnace *s.* horno.
furnish *tr.* amueblar; proveer.
furniture *s.* ajuar, mobilario.
furrier *s.* peletero.
fuse *s.* fusible; *tr.* fusionar; *in.*
fusionarse.
fuss *s.* alboroto, ajetreo.

F

G

gag s. mordaza; tr. amordazar; (Mec.) taco.

gage s. prenda, fianza; tr. medir, calcular.

gaiety s. (pl. -ties) alegría; diversión.

gain s. ganancia, ventaja; tr. ganar; alcanzar; conquistar.

gait s. paso, andar.

gale s. viento fuerte, explosión; temporal.

gall s. hiel; rencor; rozadura; tr. rozar.

gallantry s. (pl. -tries) gallardía, nobleza.

gallery s. (pl. -ries) galería; balcón corrido.

gallon s. galón (medidal); (U.S.) ,78 litros — (Ingl.) 4,5 litros.

gallows s. horca.

gamble tr. jugar; in. jugar, especular.

game s. juego; caza; deporte.

gang s. pandilla.

gap s. boquete; tr. hacer brecha en, desgarrar.

gape s. abertura; intr. bostezar.

garb s. vestidura; aspecto; tr. vestir.

garbage s. basura.

garden s. jardín; huerto.

garish adj. charro, chillón.

garland s. guirnalda; corona.

garlic s. (Bot.) ajo.

garment s. prenda de vestir; tr. vestir.

garnish s. adorno; tr. adornar.

garret s. desván, buhardilla.

gas s. gas; — **cooker** cocina de gas; — **fire** estufa de gas.

gash s. herida; incisión; tr. acuchillar.

gate s. puerta, verja.

gather s. frunce; tr. fruncir; reunir, amontonar.

gauge s. calibre; medida; tr. medir; calcular.

gay adj. alegre.

gaze s. mirada fija; tr. mirar.

gear s. utensilios; marcha (coche) engranaje; tr. engranar, encajar, conectar.

gender s. (Gram.) género; (fam.) sexo.

gent (contr. de **gentlman**) s. caballero; **gents** para señores.

gentle adj. suave, honrado.

gentleman s. (pl. -men) caballero, señor.

gentlewoman s. señora, dama.

germ s. germen, brote.

get tr. (pret. **got**; pp. **got**, **gotten**) obtener, adquirir, proporcionar, engendrar, entender; in. volverse, ponerse, hacerse; estar, hallarse; meterse, introducirse.

ghastly adj. (compar. -ier; superl. -iest) horrible.

ghetto s. judería (barrio de judíos).

giant adj. y s. gigante.

gibbet s. horca; tr. ahorcar.

gibe s. burla; intr. mofarse.

giddiness s. vértigo.

gift s. dote; regalo; tr. dotar; obsequiar.

gild tr. dorar; dar lustre.

gilt adj. y s. dorado.

gin s. ginebra; trampa, grúa.

girdle s. corsé, faja, cinturón.

girl s. muchacha, niña; **girl friend** novia.

give tr. (pret. **gave**; pp. **given**) dar; entregar, conceder; aplicar, dedicar, describir; ofrecer, representar (una obra de teatro).

given adj. dado; aficionado.

glad adj. alegre.

glance *s.* vistazo; alusión breve; *in.* lanzar una mirada.

gland *s.* glándula; bellota.

glare *s.* resplandor, mirada feroz, superficie lisa y brillante *(helada)*; *tr.* expresar indignación con la mirada; *in.* deslumbrar.

glaring *adj.* brillante.

glass *s.* vidrio, vaso; *s. pl.* **glasses** anteojos, gafas; poner cristales a; **— cut** vidrio tallado; **ground —** vidrio esmerilado; **looking —** espejo; **hour—, sand—** reloj de arena; **— case** vitrina; **—ware** vajilla de cristal; cristalería.

gleam *s.* brillo; *intr.* destellar, resplandecer.

glider *s.* aeroplano sin motor.

glitter *s.* brillo, resplandor; *in.* brillar, resplandecer.

gloom *s.* oscuridad, tinieblas.

gloss *s.* brillo; apariencia falsa; *tr.* abrillantar, glosar.

glove *s.* guante.

glow *s.* resplandor; esplendor; viveza de color *(mejillas, etc.)*; animación; *tr.* encender; *in.* estar candente.

glue *s.* cola; *tr.* encolar.

gnaw *tr.* roer.

go *s.* curso, energía; éxito; **to have a —** intentarlo; **it's a —** es un trato hecho; **it's all the —** está muy de moda; **on the —** en continuo movimiento; *in.* *(pret.* **went**; *pp.* **gone**) *in.* andar, dirigirse, circular; transcurrir; venderse; **to — about** andar de un sitio para otro.

goal *s.* meta, objeto, fin, gol.

goalkeeper *s.* portero, guardameta.

goat *s.* cabra; macho cabrío.

goatee *s.* perilla.

goblet *s.* copa *(para licor)*.

god *s.* dios; *n. p.* Dios; **willing — ** Dios mediante; **for God's sake** por el amor de Dios.

godchild *s. (pl.* **godchildren** ahijado, ahijada.

godfather *s.* padrino.

godmother *s.* madrina, comadre.

godson *s.* abrigado.

gold *s.* oro; dinero.

gone *adj.* agotado; débil; arruinado.

good *adj.* bueno, sano; conveniente, apto, útil, adecuado; verdadero.

goodbye *s.* adiós.

good evening *s.* buenas tardes, buenas noches.

gorge *s.* garganta, desfiladero.

gospel *s.* evangelio.

gossip *s.* murmuración.

gourmet *s.* gastrónomo.

gout *s.* (Pat.) gota.

govern *str.* e *intr.* gobernar.

gown *s.* vestido; *tr.* vestir con toga.

grade *s.* grado; calidad; escalón; **at —** a nivel; *tr.* graduar; clasificar.

grain *s.* grano, cereal.

grammar *s.* gramática; **— school** (Ingl.) Colegio de Segunda Enseñanza.

granary *s. (pl.* **-ries**) granero.

grand *adj.* grande.

grandad *s.* abuelo.

grandchild *s. (pl.* **-children**) nieto, nieta.

granddaughter *s.* nieta.

grandfather *s.* abuelo.

grandma *s.* abuela.

grandmother *s.* abuela; **great — ** bisabuela.

G

H

habit s. hábito; costumbre.
hack s. corte, hacha; tos seca; tr. cortar, acuchillar.
hackney s. caballo de silla; coche de alquiler; adj. de alquiler; tr. gastar; embotar.
haft s. mango, puño.
haggle s. regateo; in. regatear.
hail s. llamada; granizo; tr. granizar; aclamar, saludar; llamar (con voces); in. granizar.
hair s. pelo; vello; cabellos.
hairbrush s. cepillo de cabeza.
haircut s. corte de pelo.
hairdresser s. peluquero, peinador (a).
hairless adj. calvo.
hairlock s. rizo.
hairline s. raya.
hairpin s. horquilla para el pelo.
hake s. merluza.
halcyon adj. sereno, tranquilo.
half s. (pl. halves) mitad, medio; adj. medio a medias.
hall s. vestíbulo.
hallo s. inj. ¡hola! ¡oiga!
halt adj. cojo; s. alto, parado; tr. parar, detener; in. hacer alto; cojear, tartamudear.
ham s. jamón.
hamlet s. caserío.
hammer s. martillo.
hand s. mano; mano de obra, aguja (reloj); adj. de mano; manual; —bag bolso de señora; —writing carácter de la letra; —shake apretón de manos; to be—in glove with ser uña y carne con; short— taquigrafía; tr. entregar, dar; poner en manos de.

handicraft s. destreza o habilidad manual, mano de obra.
handiwork s. trabajo manual.
handkerchief s. pañuelo.
handle s. asa; puño; tr. tocar; manejar.
handmaid(en) s. asistenta.
handsome adj. hermoso; elegante; liberal.
handy adj. (compar. -ier; superl. -iest) manual, manejable.
hangman s. ejecutor de la justicia.
haphazard adj. casual; s. casualidad, accidente.
happen in. acontecer.
happy adj. (compar. -ppier; superl. -ppiest) feliz, dichoso, contento.
harass tr. acosar; fatigar, cansar.
harbour s. puerto; adj. portuario.
hard adj. duro; difícil; adv. duramente; fuertemente, difícilmente.
harden tr. endurecer; curtir; in. endurecerse; consolidarse.
hardiness s. ánimo, valor.
hardship s. apuro, penalidad, estrechez; injusticia.
hardware s. quincalla; ferretería.
hare s. (Zool.) liebre.
harm s. daño; perjuicio; tr. dañar; perjudicar.
harmless adj. inofensivo.
harry tr. (pret. y pp. -ried) acosar; atormentar.
harsh adj. áspero.
hart s. ciervo.
harvest s. cosecha; tr. cosechar.
haste s. prisa.
hasten tr. apresurar; in. apresurarse, darse prisa.
hat s. sombrero.

hate *s.* odio, aversión; *tr.* odiar.
haul *s.* tirón; trayecto; ganancia; *tr.* acarrear, transportar; *in.* tirar; retirarse.
haunch *s.* cadera.
have *tr. (pret. y pp.* **had)** haber *(v. auxiliar),* tener; tomar *(comidas);* (fam.) llevar ventaja; **to—on** llevar puesto *(prenda de vestir);* **to—to** tener que.
havoc *s.* destrucción; *tr.* destruir.
haystack *s.* pajar.
hazard *s.* peligro; riesgo; *tr.* arriesgar.
haze *s.* confusión; niebla; *in.* nublarse.
hazel *s.* (Bot.) avellano.
he *pron. pers.* (3.ª *pers. sing. masc.)* él; *pron. indef.* aquel que, el que; como prefijo ante un nombre de mamífero o ave designa su sexo masculino; **hebear** oso; **he-fox** zorro.
head *s.* cabeza; encabezamiento, título; *adj.* delantero; más alto; *tr.* acaudillar, dirigir.
headstone *s.* lápida.
heal *tr.* curar; cicatrizar.
health *s.* salud, sanidad.
heap *s.* montón; *tr.* amontonar.
hear *tr. e in. (pret. y pp.* **heard)** oír; decir.
hearing *s.* audiencia; audición; oído *(sentido);* (Der.) vista.
hearsay *s.* rumor.
heart *s.* corazón; *by —* de momoria; **to get the —** of profundizar.
hearten *tr.* animar.
heartfelt *adj.* cordial.
hearth *s.* chimenea, brasero.
hearty cordial, robusto.

heat *s.* calor; ardor; *tr.* calentar; *in.* calentarse; excitarse.
heater *s.* estufa; radiador.
heave *s.* esfuerzo; *tr. (pret. y pp.* **heaved** o **hove)** levantar.
heaven *s.* cielo, paraíso.
heaviness *s.* densidad.
hedge *s.* cercado.
heed *s.* atención.
heedful *adj.* atento, cuidadoso.
heel *s.* (An.) talón, calcañal.
heifer *s.* novilla.
height *s.* altura.
heighten *tr.* elevar.
heir *s.* heredero.
hell *s.* infierno.
help *s.* ayuda, socorro; *inj.* ¡socorro!; *tr.* ayudar.
helpful *adj.* útil.
helpmate *s.* compañero.
hem *s.* borde; dobladillo; *tr.* poner bastilla.
hemp *s.* (Bot.) cáñamo.
hen *s.* gallina.
hence *adv.* desde, de aquí que.
henceforward *adv.* de aquí en adelante.
her *adj.* su *(de ella);* *pron.* la; ella.
herald *s.* heraldo; precursor; *tr.* anunciar.
herb *s.* hierba.
herd *s.* manada, *tr.* reunir en manada, ir en manada.
hersman *s.* pastor.
here *adv.* aquí; acá.
herein *adv.* aquí dentro.
heretofore *adv.* hasta ahora.
hereupon *adv.* sobre esto.
herewith *adv.* con esto; de este modo.
hers *pron. poss.* el suyo.
herself *pron.* ella misma.
hesitate *intr.* vacilar.

H

hew *tr. (pret.* **hewed** *pp.*
hewed o *hewn)* cortar;
labrar *(piedra).*

hibernate *in.* (Biol.); invernar.

hiccup *s.* hipo; *tr.* decir con
hipo.

hick *adj. y s.* (vulg.)
campesino.

hickory *s.(pl.* **-ries)** (Bot.)
nuez dura; nogal americano.

hide *s.* cuero; *tr. (pret.* **hid;**
pp. **hidden** o **hid)**
esconder; encubrir; *in.*
esconderse, ocultarse.

hideous *adj.* feo.

hiding *s.* escondite; (fam.)
paliza.

hi-fi *adj.* de alta fidelidad.

higgle *intr.* regatear.

high *adj.* alto.

highly *adv.* sumamente; en
sumo grado.

highness *s.* altura.

highwayman *s.* bandido.

hiker *s.* (fam.) caminante.

hill *s.* colina; *tr.* amontonar.

hilt *s.* puño.

him *pron. pers. m.* él; le, lo, a
él.

himself *pron. pers. reflex. m.*
él, él mismo, se, sí mismo;
by— solo, por sí mismo.

hinder *tr.* impedir.

hindrance *s.* estorbo.

hint *s.* insinuación; *tr.* apuntar;
in. echar indirectas.

hip *s.* (An.) cadera.

hire *s.* alquiler; jornal; *tr.*
alquilar, asalariar.

his *adj. poss. m.* su, sus (de
él); *pron. poss. m.* el suyo,
el de él, suyo.

hiss *s.* silbido; *tr.* silbar.

hit *s.* golpe; éxito; *tr.* (3pret. y
pp. **hit)** golpear, acertar;
censurar.

hither *adv.* acá.

hitherto *adv.* hasta aquí.

hoard *s.* cúmulo; depósito; *tr.*
atesorar.

hoarse *adj.* ronco.

hoax *s.* engaño; *tr.* engañar.

hobble *s.* cojera; *in.* cojear.

hobby *s.(pl.* **-bies)** tema;
afición.

hobgoblin *s.* duende.

hog *s.* (Zool.) cerdo.

hogshead *s.* pipa, bocoy,
medida de capacidad
equivalente a 63 galones
nortamericanos (238,5
litros).

hoist *s.* grúa; *tr.* alzar; colgar.

hold *s.* asa, mango; sujeción;
autoridad.

holding *s.* posesión.

hole *s.* agujero.

holiday *s.* día de fiesta; *adj.*
festivo, de fiesta; **s**
vacaciones.

holiness *s.* santidad.

hollow *adj.* hueco; alhuecado;
s. cavidad; hoyo.

holy *adj.* santo, sagrado.

home *s.* hogar, domicilio;
suelo, patria chica; *adj.*
casero; nativo; *adv.* en
casa; —**land** patria, país
natal; **Home Office**
Ministerio del Interior o de
la Gobernación —**rule**
autonomía; —**work**
deberes *(escuela).*

homestead *s.* heredad; casa
solariega.

honest *adj.* honrado.

honey *s.* miel; dulzura; (fam.)
querido; *tr.* endulzar con
miel.

honeymoon *s.* luna de miel.

hood *s.* capucha; **Little Red
Riding** — Caperucita Roja.

hoodwink *tr.* vendar los ojos
a.

hook *s.* gancho; *tr.*
enganchar; pescar.

hoot *s.* grito; *tr.* silbar; *in.*
resoplar.

hop *s.* brinco; *in.* brincar.

hope *s.* esperanza, confianza; *tr. e in.* esperar.
hopeful *adj.* esperanzado.
horde *s.* multitud.
horizon *s.* horizonte.
horn *s.* cuerno.
hornet *s.* avispón, moscardó)n.
horse *s.* caballo; **—laugh** risotada; **racing** — caballo de carrera.
horseman *s.* jinete.
horsepower *s.* caballo de vapor; fuerza motriz.
hose *s.* media; calcetín; manga.
host *s.* patrón, huésped, hostia, forma.
hostel *s.* hostería, albergue.
hostess *s.* ama, dueña, patrona; (Av.) azafata.
hot *adj.* caliente; apasionado; violento; reciente, fresco.
hot dog *s.* salchicha, perritos calientes.
hound *s.* podenco; perro; *tr.* cazar con perros.
hour *s.* hora; momento.
house *s.* casa, residencia, edificio; (Com.) casa de comercio; *adj.* casero; *tr.* alojar; **full** — o **—full** (tt.) lleno, no hay billetes *(entradas)*; **boarding— pensión;** *public* — **cantina.**
household *s.* familia.
housekeeper *s.* ama de llaves.
housing *s.* albergue.
hovel *s.* covertizo; cabaña; *tr.* abrigar en cabaña.
hover *tr.* cubrir con las alas; *in.* revolotear.
how *cnj. int. y adv.* cómo, de qué modo; à cómo; cuánto.
however *cnj.* sin embargo; *adv.* como sea.
howl *s.* chillido; *tr.* decir a gritos; *intr.* chillar.

huddle *s.* pelotón, confusión; (fig.) reunión secreta; *tr. e in.* amontonar.
hue *s.* tinte, matiz.
huff *s.* enfado; *tr.* encolerizar; *intr.* hincharse.
hug *s.* abrazo.
huge *adj.* enorme.
hull *s.* casco; cáscara.
human *adj.* humano.
humble *adj.* humilde; *tr.* humillar.
humbug *s.* farsa, camelo.
humid *adj.* húmedo.
humor *s.* humor, carácter; *tr.* mimar.
hump *s.* joroba; *tr.* encorvar; **humpbacked** jorobado.
hundred *adj.* cien, ciento; *s.* cien, ciento, centenar.
hunger *s.* hambre.
hungry *adj. (compar.* **-ier**; *superl.* **-iest**) hambriento, deseoso.
hunt *s.* caza; *tr.* cazar; buscar; perseguir.
hurdle *s.* cañizo; *in.* saltar vallas.
hurl *s.* lanzamiento; *tr. e in.* tirar, lanzar, arrojar.
hurried *adj.* hecho de prisa, precipitado.
hurry *s.* prisa, premura; *tr. (pret. y pp.* **-ried)** activar; *in.* correr.
hurt *s.* daño; herida; *tr. (pret. y pp.* **hurt)** dañar.
husband *s.* marido; *tr.* ahorrar.
husbandry *s. (pl.* **-ries)** agricultura, labranza.
hush *inj.* ¡silencio!; *s.* quietud; *tr.* apaciguar, acallar; *in.* estar quieto.
husk *s.* cáscara, pellejo.
hustle *s.* prisa; *tr.* apresurar; mezclar; *in.* apresurarse.
hut *s.* choza.
hydrant *s.* boca de agua.
hyphen *s.* guión (-).

H

I

I *pron. pers.* Yo.
ice *s.* hielo; capa de azúcar;
  adj. de hielo; glacial; *tr.*
  cubrir con capa de azúcar.
icebox *s.* nevera.
icecream *s.* mantecado.
icy *adj.* helado, glacial.
identity *s.(pl.* **-ties**) identidad;
  — **card** carnet de identidad.
idle *adj.* ocioso; *tr.* gastar
  ociosamente; *in.* holgar.
idol *s.* ídolo.
if *s.* hipótesis; *cnj. cond.* si, en
  caso que; **as** — como si.
ignite *tr.* encender; *in.*
  encenderse.
ill *adj.* enfermo, doliente; *adv.*
  mal.
illiterate *adj.* ignorante.
illness *s.* enfermedad.
illuminate *tr.* iluminar.
illumine *tr.* iluminar, alumbrar;
  in. iluminarse.
illustrate *tr.* ilustrar.
illustrious *adj.* ilustr, célebre.
image *s.* imagen; símbolo.
imagine *tr. e in.* imaginar,
  pensar, discurrir, suponer.
imbibe *tr.* beber, chupar; *intr.*
  beber.
imitate *tr.* imitar, copiar.
immerse *tr.* inmergir,
  sumergir.
immovable *adj.* inmóvil,
  inmovible; (Der.) inmueble.
imp *s.* diablillo, duende.
impar *tr.* deteriorar, dañar.
impart *tr.* hacer saber;
  comunicar.
impeach *tr.* acusár;
  desacreditar.
impeachment *s.* juicio;
  acusación.
impede *tr.* impedir, dificultar.
impel *tr. (pret. y pp.* **-pelled**)
  impulsar, empujar.

imperfect *adj.* imperfecto;
  defectuoso.
imperil *tr. (pret. y pp.* **-iled** o
  -illed) exponer; arriesgar.
impersonate *tr.* personificar.
impish *adj.* endiablado,
  travieso.
implement *s.* instrumento,
  herramienta.
implicate *tr.* implicar.
implore *tr.* implorar, rogar.
import *s.* importación; —
  duties derechos de entrada.
import *tr.* importar.
importune *tr.* importunar,
  porfiar.
impose *tr.* imponer; *in.*
  imponerse.
imposture *s.* impostura,
  engaño.
impoverish *tr.* empobrecer.
impregnate *tr.* impregnar;
  imbuir.
impress *s.* impresión, señal,
  marca; huella; divisa, lema.
imprison *tr.* aprisionar.
impromptu *s.* improvisación;
  adv. de improviso.
improper *adj.* impropio.
improve *tr.* perfeccionar;
  reformar, (Com.) subir los
  precios; *in.* avanzar,
  progresar.
impudent *adj.* descarado,
  impúdico.
impugn *tr.* impugnar,
  rechazar.
impute *tr.* imputar, atribuir.
in *adv.* dentro; hacia adentro;
  prep. en; dentro de; sobre;
  entre.
inaccuracy *s. (pl.* **-cies**)
  inexactitud.
inaccurate *adj.* inexacto.
inactive *adj.* inactivo.
inadequacy *s.* insuficiencia.
in as much *cnj.* por cuanto,
  en cuanto; puesto que, ya
  que.
inaugurate *tr.* inaugurar.

inauspicious *adj.* impropicio.
inborn *adj.* innato, nativo.
incapable *adj.* incapaz.
incarnate *tr.* encarnar.
incautious *adj.* incauto.
inch *s.* pulgada; (fig.) pizca.
incite *tr.* incitar, animar.
incline *s.* declive, pendiente;
 tr. inclinar; *in.* inclinarse.
include *tr.* incluir,
 comprender, englobar.
income *s.* ingresos.
inconvenience *s.*
 inconveniencia; *tr.* molestar.
incorporate *tr.* incorporar;
 intr. incorporarse.
incorrect *adj.* incorrecto, falso.
incorrupt *adj.* incorrupto.
increase *s.* aumento,
 incremento.
increase *tr.* aumentar,
 incrementar.
increasing *adj.* creciente; *s.*
 acrecimiento.
incubate *tr. e in.* incubar.
inculpate *tr.* inculpar.
incur *tr.* incurrir en.
indebted *adj.* adeudado.
indeed *adv.* verdaderamente,
 en realidad.
indefatigable *adj.* infatigable.
indemnify *tr.* indemnizar.
index *s.* (*pl* **indices**) índice,
 exponente.
indicate *tr.* indicar, señalar.
indict *tr.* (Der.) procesar.
indigenous *adj.* indígena,
 innato.
indispose *tr.* indisponer.
individual *adj.* invididual,
 sólo, único; *s.* individuo.
indolent *adj.* indolente,
 holgazán.
indoor *adj.* interior.
indoors *adv.* dentro.
indorse *tr.* endosar.
induce *tr.* inducir, mover.
inducement *s.* incentivo,
 estímulo.
induct *tr.* introducir.

indult *s.* dispensa.
inequality *s.* (*pl.* **-ties**)
 desigualdad.
inert *adj.* inerte, flojo.
inexhaustible *adj.* inagotable.
inexpensive *adj.* barato.
infant *s.* infante, criatura; *adj.*
 infantil; — **school** escuela
 de párvulos.
infatuate *tr.* apasionar, cegar;
 adj. apasionado.
infect *tr.* infectar.
infer (*tr. pret. y pp.* **-ferred**)
 inferir, deducir.
infernal *adj.* infernal.
infest *tr.* infestar.
infiltrate *tr.* infiltrar.
infirm *adj.* enfermizo; inválido.
inflame *tr.* inflamar.
inflate *tr.* inflar.
inflect *tr.* torcer; modular;
 (Gram.) declinar.
inflict *tr.* infligir.
inform *adj.* informe; *tr.*
 informar, avisar.
infuriate *tr.* enfurecer.
ingot *s.* lingote.
ingraftment *s.* injerto.
ingrain *tr.* fijar, impregnar.
ingratiate *tr.* hacer aceptable.
inhabit *tr.* habitar.
inherit *tr. e in.* heredar.
inimical *adj.* enemigo.
initiate *tr.* comenzar.
inject *tr.* inyectar.
injunction *s.* mandato,
 precepto.
injure *tr.* injuriar.
ink *s.* tinta; **ink-pot** tintero.
inkling *s.* sospecha.
inkstand *s.* tintero.
inland *adj.* interior, del país,
 regional.
inlet *s.* estuario, ría.
inmate *s.* inquilino; preso.
inmost *adj.* interior.
inn *s.* posado, mesón.
inner *adj.* interno.
innkeeper *s.* posadero.
innovate *tr.* innovar.

I

input *s.* (Mec.) fuerza necesaria.
inquest *s.* encuesta.
inquire *tr.* inquirir.
insert *tr.* insertar, introducir.
inshore *adj.* cercano a la orilla.
inside *s.* interior, de dentro; forro; *adv.* dentro; *adj.* interno.
insight *s.* penetración.
insinuate *tr.* insinuar, indicar.
insist *in.* insistir, exigir.
inspect *tr.* inspeccionar, reconocer.
inspire *tr. e intr.* inspirar, sugerir.
install *tr.* instalar, colocar.
instant *adj.* inmediato; *s.* instante.
instead *adv.* en cambio.
institute *s.* instituto, establecimiento; *tr.* instituir.
instruct *tr.* instruir, educar.
insulate *tr.* aislar.
insult *tr.* insultar, ofender.
insure *tr.* asegurar o garantizar.
intact *adj.* intacto.
integrate *tr.* integrar.
intellect *in* intelecto.
intend *tr.* pensar, intentar.
intensify *tr.* intensificar.
inter *tr.* (pret. y pp. **-terred**) enterrar.
intercalate *tr.* intercalar.
intercede *intr.* interceder.
intercept *tr.* interceptar, atajar.
intercourse *s.* intercambio, comercio.
interdict *tr.* prohibir, vedar.
interest *s.* interés, beneficio; *tr.* interesar.
interlude *s.* intérvalo, intermedio.
interment *s.* entierro, funeral.
intermission *s.* intermisión, pausa.
interplay *s.* interacción.
interpose *tr. e in.* interponer.
interpret *tr.* interpretar.

interrupt *tr.* interrumpir, estorbar.
intersect *tr.* entrecortar, cruzarse.
into *prep.* en, dentro.
intoxicate *tr.* intoxicar.
introduce *tr.* introducir, insertar.
intrude *in.* entremeterse; estorbar.
inundate *tr.* inundar, abrumar.
inure *tr.* acostumbrar.
invade *tr.* invadir.
invalidate *tr.* invalidar, anular.
invective *s.* invectiva; *adj.* ofensivo, injurioso.
inveigle *tr.* engatusar, seducir.
invent *tr.* inventar, descubrir.
inventor *s.* inventor, autor.
invest *tr.* investir.
investigate *tr.* investigar, explorar.
investment *s.* inversión (de dinero)4; cerco.
invidious *adj.* injusto, abominable.
invigorate *tr.* vigorizar.
invite *tr.* invitar, brindar.
invoke *tr.* invocar.
involve *tr.* envolver, comprometer.
inward *adj.* interno.
irksome *adj.* fastidioso, cansado.
irradicate *tr.* arraigar.
irrelevant *adj.* impertinente.
irrigate *tr.* irrigar, regar.
irritate *tr.* irritar.
island *s.* isla; *adj.* isleño.
isolate *tr.* aislar, incomunicar.
it *pron. neutro* (pl. **-they**) él, ella; le, la, lo.
itch *s.* picor; prurito; (Med.) sarna; *tr.* picar.
item *s.* item; artículo.
its *adj. pose. neutro* su; *pron. poss. neutro* el suyo.
itself *pron. refl.* mismo; sí mismo; (solo para cosas).
ivory *s.* marfil.

J

jack *s.* individuo; marinero; sota *(naipe)*; (Mec.) gato; *tr.* alzar con gato.

Jack *n.p.* de John, Juanito.

jackass *s.* asno.

jacket *s.* chaqueta, cazadora.

jackknife *s.* navaja de bolsillo.

jade *s.* mujeruela, picarona; *adj.* verde; *tr.* cansar, embotar.

jag *s.* diente, púa; **to have a—on** (vulg.) estar borracho.

jail *s.* cárcel; *tr.* encarcelar; **—bird** preso.

janitor *s.* portero.

January *s.* enero.

jar *s.* jarro; sonido discordante; *tr. e in.* chocar.

jaw *s.* mandíbula; (vulg.) chismes; *tr.* (vulg.) reñir; *in.* charlar.

jeans *s. pl.* pantalones o guardapolvos.

jeer *s.* mofa, burla.

jeopardize *tr.* arriesgar, exponer.

jerk *s.* tirón, sacudida; *tr.* mover de un tirón; *intr.* moverse a tirones.

jest *s.* broma; *intr.* bromear.

jet *s.* chorro; surtidor; **— plane** (Av.) avión de propulsión a chorro; *tr.* *(pret. y pp.* **jetted)** echar, arrojar *(en chorro)*; *intr.* brotar en chorro.

Jew *adj. y s.* judío.

job *s.* trabajo, tarea.

jog *s.* empujoncito; *tr.* empujar.

join *s. tr.* juntar, unir.

joint *s.* empalme; grieta; *adj.* común, mutuo; colectivo; *tr.* articular; unir, juntar; **—heir** coheredero;**— owner** copropietario; **— stock** capital social; **— stock company** compañía por acciones, sociedad anónima.

joke *s.* broma; *tr.* burlarse de; *in.* bromear.

joker *s.* bromista, comodín *(naipe).*

jolt *s.* traqueteo; golpe; *tr.* sacudir; *intr.* dar saltos.

journal *s.* diario, periódico.

journey *s.* viaje; *in.* viajar.

joy *s.* alegría.

judge *s.* juez, magistrado; *tr. e in.* juzgar, censurar.

jog *s.* jarra; (vulg.) chirona, cárcel; *tr. (pret. y pp.* **jugged)** (vulg.) encarcelar; *in.* cantar.

juggle *s.* juego de manos; *intr.* hacer juegos de manos; hacer trampas.

juice *s.* jugo, zumo; (vulg.) electricidad, gasolina.

juicy *adj. (compar.* **-ier**; *superl.* **-iest**) jugoso, zumoso.

juke box *s.* tocadiscos que funciona con tragamonedas.

July *s.* julio *(mes).*

jumble *s.* mezcla; *tr.* emburujar, revolver.

jump *s.* salto; subida repentina de precios; *tr.* saltar, brincar; *intr.* saltar.

June *s.* junio.

junior *adj.* juvenil; más joven; *s.* joven.

juror *s.* jurado *(individuo).*

jury *s.* jurado *(cuerpo e institución)*; **— box** tribuna del jurado; **—man** miembro del jurado.

just *adj.* justo.

justify *tr. (pret. y pp.* **-fied)** justificar, probar.

K

keel *s.* quilla; *tr.* volcar.
keen *adj.* agudo, afilado.
keep *s.* manutención, subsistencia; torre; **to earn one's** — (fam.) ganarse la vida; *tr.* (*pret. y pp.* **kept**) guardar; tener; mantenerse firme en (su puesto).
keeper *s.* encargado; guarda.
keeping *s.* custodia, cuidado.
ken *s.* alcance de la vista o del saber.
kennel *s.* perrera.
kerb *s.* bordillo de las aceras.
kerchief *s.* pañuelo.
kernel *s.* grano; almendra.
kettle *s.* caldera, olla; cafetera, tetera.
key *s.* llave; clavija; *adj.* principal, fundamental.
kick *s.* puntapié; coz.
kid *s.* (Zool.) cabrito, chivo; (fam.) niños, chicos; *tr.* (*pret. y pp.* **kidded**) *intr.* bromear.
kidnap *tr.* (*pret. y pp.* **-naped** o **-napped**) *secuestrar, raptar.*
kidnapper *s.* secuestrador, raptor de niños.
kidnapping *s.* secuestro.
kidney *s.* (An.) riñon; especie.
kill *s. tr.* matar, destruír.
killing *s.* matanza; caza; éxito arrolador; *adj.* destructivo; irresistible.
kiln *s.* horno.
kilt *s.* falda escocesa.
kin *adj.* pariente.
kind *adj.* bueno; amable; *s.* género, especie, clase.
kindergarten *s.* jardín de la infancia.
kindle *tr.* encender; *in.* encenderse.

king *s.* rey; **—size** de tamaño largo (cigarillo).
kingdom *s.* reino, monarquía.
kipper *s.* sardinas ahumadas.
kiss *s.* beso; dulce, merengue; roce, ligero contacto; *tr.* besar; *intr.* besar.
kit *s.* equipaje (fig.).
kitchen *s.* cocina.
knack *s.* costumbre.
knapsack *s.* mochila.
knavish *adj.* bribón.
knead *tr.* amasar.
knee *s.* (An.) rodilla.
kneel *in.* (*pret. y pp.* **knelt** o **kneeled**) *arrodilarse.*
knickers *s. p.* calzones cortos; bragas.
knife *s.* (*pl.* **knives**) *s.* cuchillo; *tr.* acuchillar.
knight *s.* caballero (de una orden); caballo (de ajedrez).
knitting *s.* trabajo de punto.
knob *s.* bulto.
knock *s.* golpe; censura, criticar, censurar.
knoll *s.* toque de campanas.
knot *s.* nudo; *tr.* (*pret. y pp.* knotted) **anudar**; *intr.* anudarse.
know *tr. e intr.* (*pret.* **knew**; *pp.* known) **saber, conocer, entender.**
know-how *s.* destreza.
knur *s.* nudo de la madera.

L

lab *s.* (fam.) laboratorio.
label *s.* rótulo, etiqueta; *tr.* rotular.
labor *s.* labor, trabajo.
laboratory *s.* laboratorio, taller.
laborer *s.* trabajador, obrero.
lac *s.* laca, barniz.
lace *s.* encaje, puntilla; *tr.* atar, enlazar; *in.* apretarse.
lack *s.* carencia, falta; *tr.* necesitar.
lad *s.* muchacho, chico.
ladder *s.* escalera de mano.
ladle *s.* cucharón, cazo.
lady *s.* (*pl.* **-dies**) señora, señorita, dama.
ladylike *adj.* afeminado.
ladyship *s.* señoría (*persona, título*).
lag *adj.* rezagado; *s.* retraso; *tr.* revestir.
lager *s.* cerveza reposada.
lagoon *s.* laguna.
lake *s.* lago, laguna.
lamb *s.* cordero.
lame *adj.* cojo; débil pobre; *tr.* cojear.
lamp *s.* lámpara (fig.) astro; **street** — farola; —1shade pantalla.
lampholder *s.* portalámparas.
land *s.* tierra; país; *adj.* terrestre; *tr.* desembarcar; *in.* saltar a tierra; apearse.
landholder *s.* terrateniente.
landing *s.* aterrizaje; desembarcos.
landlady *s.* (*pl.* **-dies**) propietaria, ama.
landlord *s.* propietario, dueño.
landscape *s.* paisaje.
language *s.* lenguaje.
lank *adj.* largo, flaco.
lap *s.* falda, seno.
lapel *s.* solapa.

lapse *s.* lapso; caída *in.* recaer; (Der.) caducar.
larceny *s.* (*pl.* **-nies**) robo.
larder *s.* despensa.
large *adj.* grande, abultado.
lark *s.* alondra; (fam.) parranda.
lash *s.* látigo; *tr.* fustigar.
lass *s.* muchacha (fig.) novia.
lasso *s.* lazo.
last *adj.* último, postrero, final; *s.* última (*persona o cosa*); *in.* durar; — **night** anoche; **at long** — a la postre.
latch *s.* picaporte, pestillo.
late *adj.* tardío, lejano; avanzado; difunto; *adv.* tarde; **of** — recientemente.
latent *adj.* latente.
later *adj. y adv. compar.* de **late** más tarde.
latest *superl.* de **late**, el último, el más reciente.
lather *s.* espuma de jabón; *tr.* enjabonar; *in.* echar espuma.
lattice *tr.* enrejar; *s.* enrejado; celosía.
laud *s.* alabanza; *tr.* alabar.
laugh *s.* risa; *in.* reír, reírse.
launch *s.* botadura (*de un buque*); *tr.* botar (*un buque*).
laundry *s.* (*pl.* **-ries**) lavadero; (fam.) ropa lavada o por lavar.
lavatory *s.*(*pl.* **-ries**) lavado; **water**, retrete.
lavish *adj.* pródigo, gastador; *tr.* prodigar, malgastar.
law *s.* ley; derecho.
lawful *adj.* legítimo.
lawless *adj.* ilegal.
lawn *s.* césped.
lay *adj.* (pret. de **to lie**); *tr.* (pret. y pp. **laid**); poner, depositar; (fig.) enterrar; tender (*un cable*); extender; aplicar; cubrir, trazar (*un plan*); poner (*la mesa*);

imponer (castigos); apostar; presentar.

layer s. lecho; gallina ponedora.

laying s. capa; tendido (de un cable); instalación.

layman s. (pl. -men) lego, seglar.

laziness s. pereza.

lazy adj. (compar. -ier; superl. -iest) perezoso.

lead s. primacia, primer lugar.

lead s. plomo; — box caja de lápices.

leader s. líder, caudillo; guía; (Mús.) director; artículo de fondo; **leaders** s. pl. puntos suspensivos.

leadership s. dirección.

leading adj. director.

leaf s. (pl. **leaves**) hoja (de libro); hoja, pétalo (de planta, flor).

league s. liga; tr. e in. asociar.

leak s. gotera; fuga; tr. dejar escapar, dejar salir (agua); intr. tener fugas o escapes (una tubería); filtrarse; **to — out** divulgarse.

lean s. carne magra; inclinación; tr. e in. (pret. y pp. **leaned** o **leant**) inclinar.

leanness s. flaqueza; pobreza.

leap s. salto; tr. (pret. y pp. **leaped** o **leapt**) saltar, brincar.

learn tr. (pret. y pp. **learned** o **learnt**) aprender; oír decir.

learned adj. docto; culto.

learner s. aprendiz.

lease s. arrendamiento; tr. arrendar.

least adj. (superl. **little**) más pequeño; adv. menos; **not in the —** de ningún modo.

leather s. cuero.

leave s. licencia; despedida; **by your —** con permiso de Vd.; **to take —** despedirse; tr. (pret. y pp. **left**) dejar.

lecherous adj. lujurioso.

lecture s. conferencia, discurso; tr. dar lecciones a; in. dar una conferencia.

ledge s. repisa.

ledger s. losa; (Com.) libro mayor; traviesa de andamio.

lee s. mirada de reojo.

lees s. pl. heces, sedimento.

left adj. izquierdo; s. izquierda (mano).

leg s. pierna.

legate s. legado, embajador.

legend s. leyenda, letrero.

legislate tr. legislar.

leisure s. ocio; adj. desocupado.

lemonade s. limonada, gaseosa.

lend tr. (pret. y pp. **lent**) prestar.

lending s. prestación, préstamo.

length s. largo; **full —** de cuerpo entero.

lengthen tr. alargar.

leniency s. (pl. -cies) clemencia.

lens s. lente.

Lent s. Cuaresma.

leper s. leproso.

less adj. compar. de **little** menor; adv. menos.

lessen tr. disminuir, reducir.

lesser adj. compar. **little**, menor.

lesson s. lección, enseñanza; tr. intruir.

lest cnj. no sea que.

let tr. (pret. y pp. **let**) permitir; conceder; arrendar; pasar o salir; sacar (sangre); s. estorbo; **to — alone** dejar solo; **to — down** dejar; **to — known** hacer saber; **to — loose** soltar; **to — off** disparar; **to — slip** soltar.

letter s. carta; letra; tr. rotular.

lettuce s. (Bot.) lechuga.

level *s.* nivel; llanura; *adj.*
llano; *tr. (pret. y pp.,* **-eled** o
-elled) igualar; apuntar *(un
arma)*; —**crossing** *s.* paso
a nivel.

lever *s.* palanca, manivela;
hand — palanca de mano;
tr. e intr. apalancar.

lewd *adj.* lascivo.

liability *s.(pl.* **-ties**) riesgo;
deuda; responsabilidad.

liable *adj.* sujeto, responsable.

liaison *s.* enlace.

liar *s.* mentiroso.

liberate *tr.* libertad.

liberty *s. (pl.* **-ties**) libertad.

librarian *s.* bibliotecario.

library *s. (pl.* **-ies**) biblioteca.

lid *s.* tapa; (An.) párpado.

lie *s.* mentir; *in. (pret.* **lay** *pp.*
lain) mentir; *intr.* tenderse,
echarse.

lieutenant *s.* teniente.

life *s. (pl.* **lives**) vida; **to bring
to** — reanimar; **to come to**
— volver a la vida; **to take
one's** — **in one's hand**
jugarse la vida; **for** — para
toda la vida.

lifelike *adj.* natural, vivo.

lifeless *adj.* muerto.

lifelong *adj.* de toda la vida; *s.*
toda la vida; *adv.* durante
toda la vida.

lift *s.* elevación; alzar,
levantar; (Ingl.) ascensor;
tr. limpiar.

light *s.* luz; **to bring to** —
sacar a luz; farol; fuego
(para encender); *adj.*
luminoso; — **wave** onda
luminosa; *tr. (pret. y pp.* **lit**)
encender; alumbrar; *in.*
encendeer, apearse.

lighten *tr.* aligerar; iluminar;
in. regocijarse; iluminarse.

lighter *s.* encendedor; lancha.

lightning *s.* relámpago.

like *adj.* igual, parecido,
semejante; **to look** — **rain**
parece que va a llover; *adv.
prep., conj.* como, del
mismo modo que; *tr.*
querer, tener simpatía a,
gustar de.

likely *adj.* probable.

likeness *s.* semejanza.

liking *s.* gusto.

limb *s.* miembro *(extremidad)*;
miembro *(de una
communidad)*; rama *(de
árbol)*.

lime *s.* cal.

limp *s.* cojera.

line *s.* línea; verso; cuerda;
dotted — línea de punto;
to come into — alinearse;
(fig.) de acuerdo,
dispuesto; *tr.* rayar;
delinear.

lineage *s.* línaje, raza.

liner *s.* trsatlántico.

ling *s.* bacallao.

linger *intr.* demorar, ir
despacio.

lining *s.* forro.

link *s.* eslabón; *tr.* enlazar.

linnet *s.* jilguero.

lion *s.* león.

lioness *s.* leona.

lip *s.* labio; *tr.* besar; susurrar.

liquid *adj.* líquido.

liquidate *tr.* liquidar.

liquor *s.* licor.

list *s.* lista; *tr.* registrar.

listen *intr.* escuchar, oír.

lithe *adj.* flexible.

litre *s.* litro.

litter *s.* litera.

little *adj. (compar.* **less**;
superl. **least**) pequeño,
poco.

live *adj.* vivo; de actualidad.

live *in.* vivir, existir; habitar; *tr.*
lleva *(tal vida)*; vivir *(una
aventura, etc.)*.

liver (An.) hígado.

livestock *s.* ganado.

living *s.* modo de vivir; *adj.*
vivo, animado; **everything**

L

— (fam.) todo bicho viviente; — **room** cuarto de estar.

lizard *s.* (Zool.) lagarto.

load *s.* carga.

loaf *s. (pl.* **loaves)** hogaza de pan; **small** — bollo, panecillo; **—s and fishes** ganancias.

loan *s.* préstamo; *tr. e intr.* prestar.

loathe *tr.* aborrecer.

lobby *s. (pl.* **-bies)** salón de entrada, vestíbulo.

lobster *s.* (Zool.) langosta.

locate *tr.* poner; establecer.

lock *s.* cerradura; rizo; **—s** cabellos; *tr. e in.* cerrar con llave; encerrarse.

locust *s.* langosta; cigarra.

lodge *s.* casa de campo; logia *(de masones)*; *tr.* alojar; *in.* alojarse.

log *s.* leño, tronco; *tr.* cortar troncos; *in.* extraer madera.

loin *s.* lomo; solomillo.

loll *tr.* colgar; *intr.* colgar.

loneliness *.s* soledad.

long *adj.* largo, extenso; **in the — run** a la larga; **so —** hasta pronto; — **range** a largo plazo; *adv.* mucho; **before —** en breve; **as — as, so — as** mientras; *intr.* **(for, after, to)** ansiar, anhelar.

longing *s.* deseo.

look *s.* mirada, semblante; *tr.* mirar; expresar o indicar con la mirada; **to — up** buscar *(en un diccionario, etc.)*; *in.* mirar; parecer; **to — forward** mirar al porvenir.

lookout *s.* vigilancia.

loony *adj. (compar.* **-ier**; *superl.* **-iest)** y *s.* (vulg.) loco.

loop *s.* lazo; presilla; *tr.* enlazar.

loose *adj.* flojo; a granel; *s.* relajamiento; *tr.* soltar.

loosen *tr.* desatar; *in.* desatarse.

loot *s.* botín; *tr. e in.* saquear.

lop *s. tr.* podar; *in.* colgar.

lord *s.* señor; lod, título.

lose *tr. (pret. y pp.* **lost)** perder.

lost *adj.* perdido.

lot *s.* solar; *tr.* dividir echando suertes.

loud *adj.* alto; fuerte; llamativo; *adv.* en alta voz; — **speaker** altavoz.

lounge *s.* salón de tertulia; *tr.* gastar ociosamente; *in.* pasear perezosamente.

lovable *adj.* amable.

love *s.* amor; (fam.) preciosidad; *tr.* amar, querer.

lover *s.* amante, novio.

low *adj.* bajo; común; *s.* mugido; *adv.* bajo; *intr.* mugir, berrear.

lower *tr.* bajar; abatir.

lower *intr.* fruncir el ceño.

loyal *adj.* leal, fiel.

luck *s.* suerte, azar.

lucky *adj. (compar.* **-ier**; *superl.* **-iest)** afortunado, feliz.

ludicrous *adj.* absurdo.

luggage *s.* equipaje.

lullaby *s.* nana.

lumber *s.* madera de construcción; *tr.* amontonar trastos viejos; *intr.* cortar y madera.

lunch *s.* alumuerzo, merienda.

lung *s.* (An.) pulmón.

lure *s.* cebo.

lush *adj.* jugoso.

lust *s.* codicia; luguria; *intr.* codiciar.

lusty *adj. (compar.* **-ier**; *superl.* **-iest)** robusto.

luxury *s.* lujo.

lying *s.* mentira.

M

mace s. maza.
machine s. máquina, aparato;
  —**gun** ametralladora.
mackintosh s. impermeable.
mad adj. (compar. **madder**;
  superl. **maddest**) loco; tr.
  enloquecer.
madam s. señora.
madden tr. enloquecer.
made adj. hecho fabricado.
madhouse s. manicomio.
magazine s. revista; almacén.
magic adj. mágico; s. magia.
magistrate s. magistrado.
magnet s. imán.
magnify tr. (pret. y pp. **-fied**)
  amplificar.
mahogany s. (bot.) caoba.
maid s. criada; virgen.
mail s. correo,
  correspondencia; tr. enviar
  por correo.
maim tr. mutilar.
main s. océano, alta mar; adj.
  principal.
mainland s. tierra firme.
mainly adv. mayormente.
maintain tr. mantener.
maize s. (bot.) maíz.
majesty s. majestad.
major adj. mayor.
majority adj. mayoría.
maker s. fabricante.
makeshift adj. provisional.
make-up s. composición,
  maquillaje.
maladroit adj. torpe.
malady s. (pl. **-dies**) mal,
  enfermedad.
male s. varón, macho; adj.
  masculino.
malefactor s. malhechor.
malice s. malicia.
malign adj. maligno; tr.
  calumniar.
mall s. alameda.

malpractice s. inmoralidad.
malt s. malta.
maltreat tr. maltratar.
mammal s. (Zool.) mamífero.
man s. (pl. **men**) hombre;
  merchant — buque
  mercante; tr. tripular.
manacle s. manilla;
  manacles s. pl. esposas;
  (fig.) estorbo; tr. esposar.
manage tr. manejar.
management s. manejo.
manager s. gerente,
  entrenador (fúbol).
manequin, manikin s.
  maniquí.
manful adj. varonil.
manger s. pesebre.
mangy adj. (compar. **-ier**;
  superl. **-iest**) sarnoso.
manhood s. masculinidad.
manifest adj. y s. manifiesto;
  tr. manifestar.
manifold adj. múltiple.
mankind s. humanidad; s.
  sexo masculino.
manliness s. valentía.
manly adj. varonil.
mannerly adj. cortés.
maneuver s. maniobra; tr.
  maniobrar.
manor s. feudo.
manslaughter s. homicidio.
mantle s. manto; tr. tapar,
  envolver; in. extenderse.
manure s. estiércol, abono; tr.
  abonar.
many adj. muchos; **too** —
  demasiados.
map s. mapa.
mar tr. (pret. y pp. **marred**)
  estropear.
marble s. mármol.
march s. marcha; s. marzo; tr.
  e in. poner en marcha.
mare s. yegua.
margin s. margarina.
mark s. marca; huella; tr.
  marcar; calificar (un
  examen).

M

market *s.* mercado; bolsa;
intr. comercial.
marmalade *s.* mermelada de
naranja.
marriage *s.* matrimonio, boda.
married *adj.* casado.
marrow *s.* (An.) médula,
esencia.
marry *tr.* casar; *in.* casarse.
marsh *s.* pantano.
marshal *s.* maestro de
ceremonias.
mart *s.* emporio.
marvel(l)ous *adj.* maravilloso.
marzipan *s.* mazapán.
mash *s.* masa; *tr.* amasar.
mask *s.* máscara; *tr.*
enmascarar.
mason *s.* albañil.
masonry *s.* masonería.
mass *s.* masa, gran cantidad;
misa; **to hear** — oír misa;
the — **s** la gente, la
multitud; *tr.* juntar en masas.
massage *s.* masaje; *tr.* dar
masaje.
massif *s.* macizo.
mast *s.* (Naút.) mástil.
master *s.* patrón; amo; *tr.*
dominar.
masterly *adj.* magistral; *adv.*
magistralmente.
masterwork *s.* obra maestra.
mastery *s.* maestría.
masticate *tr.* masticar.
mat *s.* estera; *adj.* mate; *tr.*
(pret. y pp.) **matted**
enmarañar.
match *s.* cerilla; compañero;
tr. hermanar; *in.* pegar,
hacer juego.
matchless *adj.* sin igual.
mate *s.* compañero, socio.
matins *s.* oración matinal.
matter *s.* cuestión, asunto; *tr.*
importar.
mattress *s.* colchón; **spring**
— sommier.
mature *adj.* maduro; *tr.*
madurar.

maudlin *adj.* sentimental.
mauve *adj.* de color malva.
maxim *s.* máxima, sentencia.
may *intr. (pret.* **might**); poder
(de autorización), permiso;
it — **be** puede ser.
May *s.* mayo *(mes)*; (fig.)
juventud, primavera.
maybe *adv.* quizá.
mayor *s.* alcalde.
maze *s.* laberinto, confusión.
me *pron. pers.* me; mí; **with**
— conmigo.
mead *s.* pradera.
meal *s.* comida; harina.
meaning *s.* significado; *adj.*
significativo.
meantime *adv.* mientras
tanto; *s.* interín.
measles *s.* (Pat.) sarampión.
measure *s.* medida,
dimensión.
meat *s.* carne; **cold** — carne
fiambre; **roast** — asado;
stewed — estofado;
minced — picadillo.
medal *s.* medalla.
meddle *intr.* entremeterse.
medical *adj.* médico,
medicinal.
medicine *s.* medicina;
medicamento.
meditate *tr. e intr.* meditar,
considerar.
medium *s.(pl.* **media**) medio,
intermediario; *adj.* mediano.
medley *s.* mescolanza.
meek *adj.* manso.
meet *s. tr. (pret. y pp.* **met**)
encontrar; entrevistarse
con; ir a recibir; *in.* unirse.
meeting *s.* reunión.
mellow *adj.* maduro; *tr.*
madurar.
melody *s.* (pl. **-dies**) melodía,
canción.
melt *s.tr.* derretir; disolver
(azúcar); *intr.* derretirse.
membership *s.* asociación.
men *s. pl.* de **man** hombres.

menace s. amenaza; *tr. e intr.*
 amenazar.
mend s. *tr.* remendar.
mention s. mención; *tr.*
 mencionar, hablar de.
menu s. menú, lista de platos.
merciful *adj.* misericordioso.
merciless *adj.* despiadado.
mercy s. *(pl.* **cies)** gracia,
 perdón.
mere *adj.* solo; s. lago.
merge *tr.* fusionar.
merit s. mérito; *tr.* merecer.
mermaid s. sirena.
merrily *adv.* alegremente.
merriment s. alegría.
mesh s. malla; *tr.* enredar;
 engranar; *in.* enredarse.
mesmerise *tr.* hipnotizar.
mess s. revoltijo; *tr.* dar
 rancho.
message s. mensaje.
messy *adj. (compar.* **-ier**;
 superl. **-iest)** sucio.
meter s. metro; medidor.
method s. método.
mettle s. ánimo.
mew s. maullido.
mewl *intr.* lloriquear.
mice *pl.* de **mouse** ratones.
mid *adj.* medio; *pre.* entre.
middleman s. intermediario.
midnight s. medianoche; *adj.*
 de media noche.
midway s. medio camino.
midwife s. comadrona.
mien s. porte.
might s. fuerza.
mighty *adj.* fuerte.
migrate *intr.* emigrar.
mike s. (vulg.) micrófono; *n. p.*
 diminutivo de Michael.
mile s. milla (1.609 m.).
milk s. leche; *tr.* ordeñar.
milky *adj. (compar.* **-ier**;
 superl. **-iest)** lechoso.
mill s. molino; taller; *tr.* moler;
 triturar.
mince s. *tr.* desmenuzar;
 picar.

mind s. mente, espíritu; *tr.*
 notar, observar; *intr.*
 atender, preocuparse.
minded *adj.* inclinado,
 dispuesto.
mindful *adj.* atento.
mine *adj. poss.* mi; *pron. poss*
 mío; s. mina; *tr.* extraer.
miner s. minero; (Mil.).
mineral *adj. y s.* mineral.
mingle *tr.* mezclar; *intr.*
 mezclarse.
miniature s. miniatura; *adj.*
 miniatura.
minimize *tr.* reducir al mínimo.
minion s. válido, faborito; *adj.*
 lindo.
minister s. ministro.
ministry s. *(pl.* **-tries)**
 ministerio; sacerdocio.
mink s. (Zool.) visión.
minority s. *(pl.* **-ties)** minoría;
 adj. minoritario.
minster s. monasterio;
 basílica, catedral.
mint s. (Bot.) menta; casa de
 moneda; *tr.* acuñar.
minute *adj.* diminuto;
 minutes s. *pl.* acta; *tr.*
 levantar acta de.
mirage s. espejismo.
mire s. lodo, cieno.
mirror s. espejo; *tr.* reflejar.
mirth s. alegria, risa.
misadventure s. desventura.
miscalculate *tr. e intr.*
 calcular mal.
miscarriage s. aborto.
miscarry *intr. (pret. y pp.*
 -ried) malograrse.
mischance s. desgracia.
mischief s. daño; malicia.
misdeed s. fechoría.
misdemeanor s. mala
 conducta.
misdirect *tr.* dirigir
 equivocademente.
misdoer s. criminal.
misdoing s. maldad.
miser s. avaro, tacaño.

M

miserly *adj.* mísero.
misfortune *s.* desventura.
misgiving *s.* duda.
misgovern *tr.* desgobernar.
misguide *tr.* dirigir mal.
mishandle *tr.* manejar mal.
mishap *s.* accidente.
mislay *tr. (pret. y pp.* **-laid)**
traspapelar. perder.
misplace *tr.* colocar mal.
misprint *s.* errata de
imprenta; *tr.* imprimir con
erratas.
misshape *tr.* deformar.
missing *adj.* desaparecido.
misspend *tr.* malgastar.
mist *s.* niebla; llovizna.
mistake *s.* error; *tr.* interpretar
mal; *in.* equivocarse.
mister *s.* señor.
mistletoe *s.* (Bot.) muérdago.
mistress *s.* señora; ama de
casa; (vulg.) amada.
mistrust *s.* desconfianza; *intr.*
sospechar.
misunderstand *tr. e intr.*
entender mal.
misunderstanding *s.* mal
entendido, equivocación.
misusage *s.* abuso.
misuse *s.* abuso; *tr.* usar mal.
mitigate *tr.* mitigar.
mix *s.* mezcla; *tr.* mezclar;
intr. mezclarse; asociarse.
moan *s.* gemido, lamento; *tr.*
lamentar; *in.* lamentarse.
moat *s.* foso.
mob *s.* gentío; *tr.* promover
alborotos.
mobilise *tr.* movilizar.
mock *s.* mofa, burla; *adj.*
fingido, simulado.
mock-up *s.* maqueta.
mode *s.* moda; forma.
model *s.* modelo; *adj.* modelo,
ejemplar; *tr.* modelar.
moderate *tr.* moderar; *in.*
moderarse.
modern *adj. y s.* moderno.
modify *tr.* modificar, cambiar.

moist *adj.* húmedo, jugoso.
moisten *tr.* humedecer.
molest *tr.* molestar.
mollify *tr.* ablandar.
molten *adj.* derretido.
moment *.s* momento; ocasión.
money *s.* dinero, plata capital,
riqueza.
mongrel *adj. y s.* mestizo,
cruzado.
monk *s.* monje.
monopolize *tr.* monopolizar.
monotony *s.* monotonía.
monster *s.* monstruo; *adj.*
monstruoso.
month *s.* mes.
monthly *adj.* mensual; *s.*
revista mensual; *adv.*
mensualmente.
monument *s.* monumento.
mood *s.* (Gram.) modo;
humor.
moodily *adv.*
caprichosamente.
moon *s.* luna; **full** — luna
llena.
mop *s.* estropajo; *tr.* fregar.
mope *s.* apático, abatido.
moral *adj.* mora; *s.* moraleja;
pl. honestidad.
moralize *tr.* moralizar.
morass *s.* pantano, marisma.
moreover *adv.* además,
también.
morning *s.* la mañana; *adj.* de
la mañana.
morose *adj.* moroso.
morsel *s.* pedazo.
mortal *adj.* mortal; *s.* ser
humano.
mortar *s.* mortero, hormigón.
mortgage *s.* hipoteca; *tr.*
hipotecar.
mortify *tr. (pret. ypp.* **-fied)**
mortificar; *intr.* mortificarse.
mortuary *adj.* mortuorio,
funerario; *s.* (*pl.* **-ries)**
depósito de cadáveres.
mosaic *s. y adj.* mosaico,
encaje.

mosque *s.* mezquito.
mosquito *s. (pl. -toes* o *-tos)* mosquito; *adj.* de mosquito.
most *adj.* más; la mayor parte; *adv.* más; *s.* los más.
moth *s. (pl.* moths) polilla; (fig.) anticuado.
mother *s.* madre; *adj.* meterno.
motherhood *s.* meternidad.
motif *s.* motivo, asunto.
motionless *s.* inmóvil.
mottle *s.* mancha; *tr.* motear, jaspear.
motto *s.* lema, divisa.
mould *s.* molde; moldura; mantillo; *tr.* moldear; *intr.* enmohecerse.
moulding *s.* moldura.
mound *s.* montón de tierra; *tr.* amontonar.
mountain *s.* montaña.
Mr. *s.* señor.
Mrs. *s.* señora.
mourn *tr.* lamentar, llorar.
mournful *adj.* dolorido, triste.
mourning *s.* lamento; luto.
mousetrap *s.* ratonera, trampa.
mousseline *s.* muselina *(tejido).*
mouth *s.* boca; desembocadura *(de un río); tragante; mueca.*
mouthful *s.* bocado.
mouthpiece *adj.* boquilla; (fig.) portavoz.
movable *adj.* movible; *s.* mueble.
move *.s* movimiento; gestión; *tr.* mover; *intr.* moverse; mudarse.
movie *s.* cine; *pl.* movies películas.
mow *s.tr.* segar, cortar la hierba.
much *adj.* mucho; *adv.* mucho; casi; how —? ¿cuánto?; *s.* mucho; to

make — of tener en mucho, dar importancia a.
mucous *s.* moco.
mud *s.* barro, lodo; *tr.* embarrar.
muddle *s.* confusión; *tr.* confundir.
mudguard *s.* guardabarros.
muffle *s.* amortiguador de sonido; *tr.* amortiguar.
mummy *s. (pl. -mies)* momia; *s. dim.* de mamma mamá.
munch *tr.* mascar.
mural *adj.* mural; *s.* pintura mural.
murder *s.* asesinato; *tr.* asesinar.
murky *adj.* lóbrego.
murmur *s.* murmullo; *tr. e in.* susurrar; murmurar.
muse *s.* musa; *intr.* meditar.
museum *s.* museo.
mushroom *s.* (Bot.) seta.
music *s.* música; — hall salón de variedades; — stand atril.
musing *s.* (Zool.) mejillón.
mussy *adj.* (fam.) desaliñado; desordenado.
must *v. defectivo,* deber, tener que.
muster *s.* asamblea; reunión; *tr.* juntar, reunir.
mute *adj.* mudo; *s.* mudo.
mutilate *tr.* mutilar.
mutineer *s.* amotinado; *intr.* amotinarse.
mutiny *s. (pl. -nies)* motín; *intr. (pret. y pp.* nied) amotinarse.
mutter *s.* murmullo; *tr. e intr.* murmurar.
my *adj. poss.* mi, mis.
myrrh *s.* mirra.
myself *pron. pers.* yo mismo; mí, mismo, a mí, me.
mystery *s. (pl. -ies)* misterio; (tt.) auto drama.
myth *s.* mito; fábula.

M

N

nag *s.* jaca; *intr.* regañar.
nail *s.* uña; clavo; —1clippers cortauñas; *tr.* clavar.
naive *adj.* cándido, ingenuo.
naked *adj.* desnudo.
name *s.* nombre, fama; **by —** de nombre; **Christian —** nombre de bautismo o de pila; **full —** nombre y apellido; **surname** apellido; **nick —** mote; *tr.* llamar; nombrar.
nameless *adj.* anónimo.
namely *adv.* es decir.
nap *s.* lanilla, borrar; *intr.* dormitar, echar la siesta; **after-dinner —** siesta.
nape *s.* nuca.
napkin *s.* servilleta; pañal.
narrow *adj.* estrecho; minucioso; *tr.* estrechar, disminuir, escoger.
nastiness *s.* suciedad.
nasty *adj.* sucio, asqueroso.
national *adj. y s.* nacional; — **anthem** himno nacional.
naturalize *tr.* naturalizar, habituar.
nature *s.* naturaleza; modo de ser.
naught *s.* nada; cero.
naughty *adj.* desobediente, travieso.
navigate *tr. e intr.* navegar.
navy *s.* (*pl.* **-ies**) marina de guerra, armada; — **blue** azul marino.
nay *s.* no, voto en contra; *adv.* no, de ningún modo.
neap *adj.* ínfimo.
near *adj.* próximo; *adv.* cerca; *prep.* cerca de; *tr.* acercarse a.
nearly *adv.* casi, cercanamente.

neat *adj.* pulcro, limpio; *s.* res vacuna.
necessitate *tr.* necesitar.
neck *s.* cuello, mástil.
necklace *s.* collar.
necktie *s.* corbata.
need *s.* necesidad; *tr.* necesitar.
needle *s.* aguja.
needlewoman *s.* costurera.
needy *adj.* (*compar.* **-ier**; *superl.* **-iest**) necesitado, pobre.
ne'er *adv.* var. de **never** nunca.
negative *adj.* negativo; *s.* negativa; *tr.* denegar.
neglect *s.* negligencia; *tr.* descuidar.
negotiate *tr. e intr.* negociar.
negro *s.* (*pl.* **-groes**) negro; (*hombre*) *adj.* negro.
neigh *s.* relincho; *intr.* relinchar.
neighbor *s.* vecino; prójimo.
neighboring *adj.* cercano.
neither *pron. indef.* ningún; *adj. indef.* ninguno; *cnj.* ni.
nephew *s.* sobrino.
nerve *s.* nervio.
nest *s.* nido; *intr.* anidar.
nestle *in.* recostarse.
net *s.* red; malla; *adj.* neto.
network *s.* malla.
neuter *adj.* neutro.
never *adv.* nunca.
nevertheless *adv.* sin embargo.
new *adj.* nuevo.
newborn *adj.* recién nacido.
newcomer *s.* recién llegado.
newly *adv.* nuevamente.
newness *s.* novedad.
news *s.* noticias, novedades; — **boy** vendedor de periódicos.
newspaper *s.* periódico.
next *adj.* próximo, inmediato.
nib *s.* pico (*de ave*); pluma.
nice *adj.* bonito, guapo.

nickel *s.* (Qm.) níquel.
niece *s.* sobrina.
night *s.* noche; **good —** buenas noches.
nightingale *s.* ruiseñor.
nightly *adj.* nocturno; *adv.* por la noche.
nightmare *s.* pesadilla.
nil *s.* nada.
nimble *adj.* ágil, ligero.
nine *adj. y s.* nueve; **to the nines** a la perfección.
ninth *adj.* noveno, nono.
nip *s.* pellizco, mordisco; *tr.* pellizcar; mordiscar; (vulg.) coger, robar.
nipple *s.* (An.) pezón; tetilla *(del biberón).*
no *adv.* no.
noble *adj. y s.* noble.
nobody *s.* nadie; *pron. indef.* ninguno.
nod *s.* reverencia; cabezada *(del que duerme sentado).*
noise *s.* ruido; *tr.* divulgar.
noiseless *adj.* silencioso.
nomad *adj. y s.* nómada.
nominate *tr.* nominar.
none *pron. indef.* ninguno, nadie.
nonsense *s.* tontería, bobada.
nonstop *adj.* directo, sin parada; *adv.* sin parar.
nook *s.* rincón.
noon *s.* mediodía.
noose *s.* lazo o nudo corredizo.
nor *cnj.* ni, tampoco.
normalize *tr.* normalizar.
north *s.* norte; *adj.* del norte, septentrional; *adv.* al norte.
nose *s.* nariz; pico o boca de cafetera; *tr.* oler, olfatear.
nosey *adj.* (fig.) curioso.
nostalgia *s.* nostalgia.
nostril *s.* nariz.
not *adv.* no.
notch *s.* muesca, paso, desfiladero (U.S.); *tr.* hacer muescas en, entallar.

note *s.* nota, apunte; signo; *tr.* notar; marcar.
notebook *s.* libro de notas, agenda.
nothing *s.* nada; *pron. indef.* nada; *adv.* de ninguna manera.
notify *tr.* notificar, comunicar.
notwithstanding *adv.* no obstante; *prep.* a pesar de; *cnj.* a pesar de que.
nought *s.* nada, cero.
noun *s.* nombre, sustantivo.
nourish *tr.* nutrir, abrigar.
novel *s.* novela; *adj.* nuevo.
novelty *s.* novedad; innovación.
November *s.* noviembre.
novice *s.* novicio, principiante.
now *adv.* ahora, actualmente.
nowadays *s.* actualidad; *adv.* hoy en día.
nowhere *adv.* en ninguna parte.
nude *adj.* desnudo.
nudge *s.* codazo ligero; *tr.* empujar ligeramente con el codo.
nuissance *s.* molestia, estorbo.
null *adj.* nulo; *tr.* anular.
nullify *tr.* (*pret. y pp.* **-fied**) anular, invalida.
numb *adj.* entorpecido; *tr.* adormecer.
number *s.* número; *adj.* de número; *tr.* numerar.
nun *s.* monja, religiosa.
nurse *s.* ama, nodriza; *tr.* criar, cuidar *(a un enfermo).*
nursery *s.* (*pl.* **-ies**) crianza; cuarto de los niños; (Agr.) semillero.
nurture *s.* crianza, educación; *tr.* nutrir, alimentar.
nut *s.* (Bot.) nuez; (Mec.) tuerca; (vulg.) cabeza, chola.
nutcracker *s.* cascanueces.
nutmeg *s.* nuez moscada.

N

O

oafish *adj.* idiota.
oar *s.* remo; *intr.* remar.
oat *s.* (Bot.) avena.
oath *s.* juramento.
oatmeal *s.* harina de avena.
obdurate *adj.* obstinado; duro.
obseisance *s.* obediencia,
　homenaje.
obey *tr. e intr.* obedecer.
obfuscate *tr.* ofuscar.
object *s.* objecto, materia;
　(Gram.) complemento.
object *tr. e in.* objetar.
oblige *tr.* obligar; complacer.
obliging *adj.* complaceinte.
oblique *adj.* oblícuo.
obliterate *tr.* obliterar.
oblivion *s.* olvido.
obnoxious *adj.* detestable.
obscurity *s. (pl. -ties)*
　oscuridad; olivido.
obsequious *adj.* obsequioso,
　servicial, zalamero.
observance *s.* observancia.
observe *tr.* observar; guardar,
　celebrar.
obsolete *adj.* anticuado.
obstruct *tr.* obstruír, atascar.
obtain *tr.* obtener, adquirir; *in.*
　prevalecer.
obtuse *adj.* obtuso, romo.
obviate *tr.* obviar, impedir.
occasion *tr.* ocasionar; dar
　lugar a; *s.* ocasión.
occident *s.* occidente, oeste.
occult *adj.* oculto; secreto.
occupy *tr.* ocupar, dar
　ocupación.
o'clock contración de of the
　clock *adv.* por el reloj; it is
　five — son las cinco.
October *s.* octubre.
octopus *s.* pulpo.
odorous *adj.* oloroso.
odor *s.* olor, fragancia.

o'er *adv. y. prep.* var de over
　sobre; por encima de.
of *prep.* de.
off *adv.* lejos, a distancia,
　fuera; *adj.* apartado,
　alejado; *inj.*
offend *tr. e intr.* ofender.
offer *s.* oferta; *tr.* ofrecer; *intr.*
　hacer una ofrenda.
offhand, offhanded *adj.*
　hecho de improviso; brusco.
offing *s.* (Náut.) alta mar.
offshoot *s.* vástago; ramal.
offspring *s.* sucesión.
often *adj.* a menudo; not —
　pocas veces.
oilskin *s.* impermeable.
ointment *s.* ungüento.
O.K. *abrev.* de all correct
　está bien.
old *adj.* viejo; añejo; de edad;
　usado.
olive *s.* aceituna; *adj.* de oliva;
　— grove olivar.
omelet(-te) *s.* tortilla.
omen *s.* agüero.
omit *tr.* omitir.
omphalic *adj.* umbilical.
one *adj.* uno, una; primero;
　único; *pron.* uno, una; *s.*
　uno, la unidad.
onerous *adj.* oneroso,
　molesto.
oneself *pron.* uno mismo.
one-way *adj.* de una sola
　dirección.
onion *s.* (Bot.) cebolla.
onlooker *s.* mirón, espectador.
only *adj.* solo, unico; *adv.*
　solo, solamente.
onset *s.* arremetido,
　embestida.
onshore *adj.* de tierra; *adv.*
　hacia la tierra.
onward *adj.* hacia adelante;
　adv. hacia adelante.
ooze *s.* rezumo; cieno; *tr.*
　rezumar; *in.* rezumarse;
　fluir.

opener s. abridor; **tinopener**
abrelatas.

opening s. abertura, apertura.

operate tr. actuar; efectuar;
in. operar; funcionar.

opponent adj. oponente; s.
opositor.

opportune adj. oportuno.

oppose tr. oponer; objetar.

opposite adj. opuesto; s. lo
contrario; prep. en frente de.

oppress tr. oprimir.

oppugn tr. opugnar, combatir.

optician s. óptico.

optional adj. optativo,
facultativo.

or cnj. o, u; de otro modo.

orange s. naranja, color de
naranja.

oration s. oración, discurso.

orator s. orador.

oratory s. (pl. -ries) oratoria,
capilla; oratoria.

orb s. orbe; círculo.

orbit s. órbita.

orchard s. huerto.

orchestra s. orquesta.

ordain tr. ordenar.

ordinary adj. ordinario, usual;
out of the — extraordinario.

ordinance s. (Mil.) artillería,
cañones.

ore s. (Min.) mina, mineral.

organ s. órgano.

organise tr. organizar.

orient s. oriente; tr. orientar;
intr. orientarse.

orientate tr. orientar; intr.
orientarse.

original adj. original; s.
original.

ornate adj. ornado; florido.

orphan adj. y s. huérfano;
(Amér.) gaucho.

ostrich s. avestruz.

other adj. y pron. indef. otro;
the — one el otro; **every —
day** cada dos días.

otherwise eadj. diferente;
adv. de otro modo.

ought aud. defectivo deber
(moralmente), ser
necesario.

our adj. poss. nuestro, -a, -os,
-as.

ours pron. poss. nuestro, -a,
-os, -as.

ourselves pron. reflex.
nosotros mismos; nos.

oust tr. desahuciar.

outbid tr. pujar, ofrecer más
que.

outbreak s. tumulto, motin.

outcast adj. desterrado; s.
paria.

outclass tr. ser superior a.

outcry s. grito; griterío.

outdoor adj. al aire libre.

outer adj. exterior.

outfit s. equipo; menesteres;
tr. equipar, habilitar.

outing s. excursión, paseo.

outlander s. extranjero.

outlast tr. durar más que.

outlaw s. bandido; tr.
proscribir.

outlay s. desembolso; tr.
desembolsar.

outlet s. salida.

outline s. contorno; perfil; tr.
perfilar, delinear.

outlive tr. sobrevivir a.

outlook s. perspectiva;
aspecto.

outlying adj. remoto.

outmatch tr. aventajar.

outnumber tr. excederse en
número.

output s. producción,
rendimiento.

outrage s. atrocidad, ultraje;
tr. maltratar, violentar,
violar.

outright adv. enteramente.

outrun tr. aventajar, dejar
atrás.

outset s. principio,
inauguración.

O

outside *adj.* exterior; ajeno; *s.* exterior; *adv.* fuera; *prep.* fuera de.

outsider *s.* forastero; intruso.

outskirts *s. pl.* cercanías, suburbios.

outstand *intr.* sobresalir.

outstanding *adj.* saliente; notable.

outward *adj.* exterior, externo; *adv.* exteriormente.

outwear *tr.* gastar; consumir.

outweigh *tr.* pesar más que.

oval *adj.* oval; *s.* óvalo.

oven *s.* horno, hornillo.

over *adv.* encima, por encima.

overall *s.* mono, guardapolvo.

overawe *tr.* intimidar.

overbalance *s.* exceso de *(peso o valor); tr. e in.* preponderar.

overbear *tr.* dominar; derribar; *in.* dar dermasiados frutos.

overbearing *adj.* dominador.

overburden *tr.* cargar excesivamente.

overcast *adj.* nublado; *tr.* nublar, oscurecer

overcharge *s.* cargo excesivo; *tr.* recargar.

overcoat *s.* abrigo.

overcome *tr.* vencer; superar.

overdo *tr.* exagerar; agobiar; *in.* excederse en el trabajo.

overfeed *tr.* sobrealimentar.

overflow *s.* desbordamiento; inundación; *tr.* inundar; *in.* rebasar, desbordarse.

overgrown *adj.* demasiado desarrollado.

overhand *s.* proyección *tr.* sobresalir por; *intr. estar colgando.*

overhaul *tr.* examinar; *s.* revisión.

overhead *adv.* por encima.

overhear *tr.* aír por casualidad.

overheat *tr.* recalentar.

overjoy *s.* alboroto; *tr.* alborozar.

overland *adj. y adv.* por tierra.

overlay *s.* cubierta; *tr.* cubrir; abrumar.

overleaf *adv.* al dorso.

overlook *tr.* vigilar; pasar por alto; cuidar de.

overlord *s.* jefe supremo.

overnight *adj.* de noche; *adv.* toda la noche.

overpass *s.* viaducto; paso elevado; *tr.* atravesar; exceder; pasar por alto.

overpower *tr.* dominar.

override *tr.* recorrer; fatigar.

overrule *tr.* anular, revocar.

overrun *tr.* cubrir enteramente; infectar.

oversea *adj.* de ultramar; *adv.* ultramar.

oversee *tr.* dirigir, revisar.

overseer *s.* director, inspector.

overshadow *tr.* sombrear.

oversight *s.* inadvertencia, omisión.

oversleep *intr.* dormir demasiado.

overstate *tr.* exagerar.

overstep *tr.* exceder, pasar.

overt *adj.* abierto, manifesto.

overtake *tr.* alcanzar; sobrepasar.

overthrow *s.* derrocamiento; *tr.* derrocar; trastornar.

overtop *tr.* descollar sobre, exceder en.

overturn *s.* vuelco; *tr.* volcar; derrocar; *in.* volcar.

overwhelm *tr.* abrumar.

overwork *s.* exceso de trabajo.

overwrought *adj.* abrumado de trabajo.

owe *tr.* deber, adeudar.

owl *s.* buho, lechuza.

own *adj.* propio, particular; *intr.* confesar.

owner *s.* dueño, propietario.

ownership *s.* posesión.

oyster *s.* (Zool.) ostra.

P

pa s. (fam.) papá.
pace s. paso; tr. medir a pasos; marcar el paso; in. andar; ampliar.
pacify tr. pacificar, calmar.
pack s. lío; paquete; manada; baraja; tr. empaquetar; conservar en latas; apretar; in. hacer la maleta.
package tr. empaquetar; s. paquete.
packet s. paquete; tr. empaquetar.
pack-mule s. mula de carga.
pack s. pacto, convenio; tr. pactar.
pad s. cojinete, almohadilla; postizo, caderillas; tr. rellenar, forrar.
padding s. relleno; guata.
paddle intr. remar.
paddock s. dehesa; cercado para caballos.
padlock s. candado; tr. cerrar con candado.
page s. página; paje; tr. paginar.
pageant s. espectáculo público; representación al aire libre.
paid adj. pagado, asalariado.
pail s. cubo, balde.
pain s. dolor, sufrimiento; tr. doler.
painless adj. sin dolor; sin penas.
paint s. pintura; tr. pintar; in. ser pintor; pintarse.
painting s. pintura; cuadro.
pair s. par; pareja; tr. e in. emparejar.
pajamas s. pl. pijama (EE.UU.)
pal s. (volg.) compañero.
palate s. paladar.
pale adj. pálido; in. palidecer.

paling s. estaca.
palliate tr. paliar, encubrir.
palm s. palma; tr. esconder en la palma de la mano, manipular.
palpitate intr. palpitar.
palsy s. (Pat.) parálisis; tr. paralizar.
paltry adj. (comparativo -ier; superlativo -iest) vil, ruin.
pamper tr. mimar, atracar.
pamphlet s. folleto.
pan s. cazuela, cazo.
pane s. cristal.
pang s. dolor agudo.
pannier s. serón, cesta grande.
pansy s. (pl. -sies) (Bot.) pensamiento, suspiro.
pant s. palpitación; **pants** s. pl. (fam.) calzoncillos, pantalones; intr. palpitar, anhelar.
pantaloon s. bufón; pantalón.
pantry s. (pl. -tries) despensa, repostería.
panzer adj. (Mil.) blindado.
paper s. papel; documento; periódico; adj. de papel; tr. empapelar.
par s. paridad; par; adj. a la par.
parable s. parábola.
parachute s. paracaídas.
parade s. desfile, cabalgata; in. desfilar; pasearse.
paradise s. paraíso.
paragraph s. párrafo; artículo corto.
parallel adj. paralelo; s. paralela; tr. paralelizar.
paralyze tr. paralizar.
paramount adj. superior.
paramour s. amante.
parapet s. parapeto.
parasite s. parásito; gorrón.
parasol s. quitasol, sombrilla.
parcel s. paquete, lío; pl. (Der.) demarcación; tr. empaquetar; parcelar.

P

parch *tr.* tostar; abrasar.
parchesi, parchisi *s.* parchís.
parchment *s.* pergamino.
pardon *s.* perdón, indulto; *tr.* perdonar, dispensar.
pare *tr.* mondar.
parent *s.* padre o madre.
parentage *s.* parentela.
parish *s.* parroquia.
parishioner *s.* parroquiano.
park *s.* parque, jardín; *tr.* paparcar.
parley *s.* parlamento; *intr.* parlamentar.
parlour *s.* sala; locutorio.
parody *s.(pl.* **-dies)** parodia; *tr.* parodiar.
parole *s.* palabra de honor; régimen de libertad provisional.
parry *s. (pl.* **-ries)** parada; *tr.* rechazar.
parsley *s.* (Bot.) perejil.
parson *s.* cura, sacerdote, pastor.
partake *tr.* compartir; comer, beber; *intr.* participar.
participate *tr. e intr.* participar.
particle *s.* partícula.
parting *s.* partida; punto de partida; *adj.* de partida.
partisan *adj. y s.* partidario.
partition *s.* partición; *tr.* repartir.
partly *adv.* en parte.
partner *s.* compañero; cónyuge.
partnership *s.* asociación.
partridge *s.* (Zool.) perdiz.
passable *adj.* pasable.
passenger *s.* pasajero.
passer-by *s.* transeúnte.
passionate *adj.* apasionado.
Passover *s.* Pascua de los judíos.
passport *s.* pasaporte.
password *s.* santo y seña.
paste *s.* pasta, engrudo; *tr.* pegar, empastar.
pastime *s.* pasatiempo.

pastry *s. (pl.* **-tries)** pastelería.
pasture *s.* pasto; dehesa; *tr.* pastorear, pastar.
pat *adj.* bueno, apto, exacto; *adv.* oportunamente; *tr.* dar golpecitos.
patch *s.* parche; remiendo; *tr.* remendar.
patent *s.* patente; *adj.* patentado; *tr.* patentar.
path *s.* senda, sendero, vereda.
pathless *adj.* intransitable.
patience *s.* paciencia.
patient *adj. y s.* paciente, resignado.
patrol *s.* patrulla; ronda; *tr. e intr.* rondar; patrullar.
patron *s.* patrono; patrocinador; *adj.* patrocinador.
patronage *s.* patrocinio, protección.
pattern *s.* patrón, modelo; *tr.* modelar.
pauper *s.* pobre.
pave *tr.* empedrar, pavimentar.
pavilion *s.* pabellón, quiosco.
paw *s.* pata; *tr.* patear, sobar.
pawn *s.* peón; *tr.* dar en prenda, empeñar.
pay *s.* salario, sueldo; *tr. (pret. y pp.* **paid)** pagar.
pea *s.* (Bot.) guisante; **peanut** cacahuete.
peace *s.* paz, descanso.
peaceful *adj.* pacífico, tranquilo.
peach *s.* melocotón.
peak *s.* cumbre, pico, cima.
peal *s.* estruendo fragor; *tr. e intr.* repicar; resonar; vocear.
pear *s.* pera.
pearl *s.* perla, margarita.
peasant *adj. y s.* campesino, labrador.
peat *s.* turba.
pebble *s.* guijarro, china.

peck *s.* picotazo; *tr.* picotear; picar.
pedagogy *s.* pedagogía.
pedestal *s.* pedestal.
pedestrian *adj.* pedrestre; *s.* peatón.
pedigree *s.* árbol genealógico.
pedlar *s.* revendedor.
peel *s.* peil, cáscara; *tr. e in.* pelar, mondar.
peerage *s.* dignidad de par.
peevishness *s.* mal humor, desagrado.
peg *s.* clavija, pinza.
pellmell *adv.* confusamente.
pelt *s.* cuero, piel.
penal *adj.* penal.
penalise *adj.* penar, castigar.
penalty *s.* (*pl.* **-ties**) pena, sanción.
penance *s.* penitencia.
pence *s. pl.* peniques.
pencil *s.* lápiz; (fig.) pincel.
pencil-sharpener *s.* sacapuntas.
pend *intr.* estar pendiente de.
pending *adj.* indeciso.
penetrate *tr. e intr.* penetrar; conmover.
penetrating *adj.* penetrante.
penguin *s.* (Zool.) pingüino.
penitence *s.* penitencia.
penknife *s.* cortaplumas.
pennant *s.* banderín, insignia.
penniless *adj.* pobre; sin blanca.
penny *s.* penique; centavo (*de dólar*); cantidad pequeña; *adj.* de penique, de poco valor.
pension *s.* pensión, retiro; *tr.* jubilar.
pensive *adj.* pensativo, triste.
pent *adj.* acorralado, encerrado.
penury *s.* penuria, escasez.
people *s.* pueblo, gente; *tr.* poblar.
peppermint *s.* (Bot.) menta.
per *prep.* por.

perambulate *tr.* recorrer, transitar por.
perceive *tr.* percibir, conocer.
perch *s.* percha; *tr.* colocar en un sitio alto; *intr.* encaramarse.
perchance *adv.* por ventura.
peremptory *adj.* perentorio; autoritario.
perennial *adj.* perenne.
perfect *adj.* perfecto.
perfect *tr.* perfeccionar.
perforate *tr.* perforar, taladrar.
perform *tr.* efectuar, ejecutar; *intr.* actuar.
performance *s.* funcionamiento; actuación.
performer *s.* ejecutante; actor; músico.
perfume *tr.* perfumar, embalsamar.
perhaps *adv.* quizá, acaso, tal vez.
perilous *adj.* peligroso.
period *s.* período, época.
periodical *adj.* periódico; *s.* periódico.
perish *intr.* perecer, sucumbir.
perjure *intr.* perjurar.
permanent *adj.* permanente estable.
permeate *tr. e intr.* penetrar, calar, atravesar.
permit *tr.* permitir, consentir.
perpetrate *tr.* perpetrar, cometer.
perpetual *adj.* perpetuo.
perpetuity *s.* perpetuidad.
perplex *tr.* dejar perplejo, confundir.
persecute *tr.* perseguir, acosar.
persevere *intr.* perseverar, persistir.
perservering *adj.* perseverante.
persist *intr.* persistir, porfiar.
persistence *s.* persistencia, insistencia.

P

person s. persona; **no —** nadie; **in —** en persona, personalmente; **— in change** encargado.

personal adj. personal, en persona; s. pl. bienes o cosas de uso personal.

personality s. (pl. **-ties**) personalidad.

personalise tr. personalizar.

personify tr. personificar.

personnel s. personal (empleados).

perspicacious adj. perspicaz, sutil.

perspire tr. e intr. transpirar, sudar.

persuade tr. persuadir.

pert adj. atrevido, insolente.

pertain intr. pertenecer.

pertinent adj. pertinente.

pertness s. frescura, impertinencia.

perturb tr. perturbar.

peruse tr. leer.

pervade tr. penetrar, esparcirse por.

pervet tr. pervertir; intr. caer en el error.

pest s. peste; (fig.) plaga.

pester tr. molestar, importunar.

petal s. (Bot.) pétalo.

petard s. petardo.

Peter n. p. Pedro.

petition s. petición, solicitud; tr. suplicar; solicitar.

petrify tr. petrificar; intr. petrificarse.

petrol s. gasolina; **— station** gasolinera.

petticoat s. enaguas; falda; mujer; adj. de mujer.

petty adj. pequeño, menor.

pew s. banco de iglesia.

phantom s. fantasma; coco.

pheasant s. (Zool.) faisán.

phone s. teléfono; tr. e intr. telefonear.

phonetics s. fonética.

photo s. (pl. **-tos**) foto, retrato; abrev. de **photograph**.

physical adj. físico, natural.

physician s. físico, médico.

physique s. físico (de una persona), presencia.

piano s. (pl. **-os**) piano.

picklock s. ganzúa; ladrón nocturno.

picnic s. jira campestre, día de campo; intr. ir de merienda.

picture s. pintura, cuadro; tr. dibujar; pintar.

pie s. pastel, torta, empanada.

piece s. pedazo, retazo; pieza.

pier s. estribo; muelle; rompeolas.

pierce tr. agujerear; taladrar.

piercing adj. penetrante, agudo.

piety s. piedad, religiosidad.

pig s. (Zool.) cerdo, cochino.

pigeon s. paloma, pichón.

piggy adj. glotón.

pigheaded adj. cabezudo, terco.

pigtail s. trenza, coleta.

pilchard s. aguja (pez).

pile s. pila, montón, mole; tr. pailar, amontonar.

pilfer tr. e intr. ratear, sisar.

pilgrim s. pegregino.

pill s. píldora.

pillage s. pillaje, robo; tr. e intr. saquear, robar.

pillar s. pilar, poste; **— box** buzón.

pillow s. almohada, cojín.

pilot s. piloto; tr. pilotar; **— lamp** lámpara piloto de comprobación.

pimple s. grano, pupa.

pin s. alfiler; clavija; tr. prender; sujetar.

pincers s. pinzas.

pine s. (Bot.) pino.

ping s. silbido de bala, zumbido.

pink *adj.* sonrosado; *s.* (Bot.) clavel.

pinky *adj.* (*comparativo* -ier; *superlativo* -iest) rosado.

pioneer *s.* explorador; promotor; *intr.* explorar.

pipe *s.* caño; conducto.

piping *s.* cañería, tubería.

piquant *adj.* picante, áspero.

pique *tr.* picar, provocar; excitar.

piracy *s.* (*pl.* -cies) piratería.

pirate *s.* pirate; *tr.* robar; plagiar.

pistol *s.* pistola, revólver; *tr.* tirar con pistola.

piston *s.* pistón, émbolo.

pit *s.* hoyo; abismo; foso.

pitch *s.* pez, alquitrán; tiro; grado de inclinación; paso de rosca; *tr.* embrear; lanzar; *intr.* inclinarse.

pitcher *s.* cántaro, jarro.

pitiless *adj.* despiadado, inhumano.

pity *s.* (*pl.* -ties) piedad, misericordia, lástima; *tr.* apiadarse de, compadecer.

pivot *s.* espiga, pívote, eje de rotación.

placard *s.* cartel; edicto.

place *s.* sitio, lugar; local; distrito; decimal; *tr.* poner, colocar; acordarse bien de.

placid *adj.* plácido, sosegado.

plague *s.* plaga; peste; *tr.* plagar; apestar; infectar.

plain *adj.* llano; claro; sincero; feo; *s.* llano, llanura.

plaintiff *s.* (Der.) demandante.

plait *s.* trenza; pliegue; *tr.* trenzar; plegar.

plan *s.* plan, proyecto; *tr.* planear, proyectar; *intr.* hacer proyectos.

plane *adj.* plano; *s.* plano; (Av.) avión; *tr.* allanar igualar.

plank *s.* tablón.

plant *s.* planta; equipo; instalación, taller; *tr.* plantar, sembrar.

plaster *s.* emplasto; yeso; *tr.* emplastar; enyesar.

plastic *adj.* plástico; *s.* plástico.

plate *s.* plato; vajilla; cubierto.

plateau *s.* meseta, altiplanicie.

platinum *s.* platino.

platitude *s.* trivialidad, vulgaridad.

player *s.* actor, jugador.

plea *s.* súplica, ruego; argumento.

plead *tr.* alegar; defender en juicio; *intr.* abogar; suplicar.

pleasant *adj.* agradable, simpático.

please *tr. e intr.* gustar; agradar; por favor.

pleasure *s.* placer, deleite.

pleat *s.* pliegue; *tr.* plegar, arrugar.

pledge *s.* promesa; voto; fianza; *tr.* prometer; brindar por.

pleintiful *adj.* abundante.

plenty *s.* copia, profusión.

pliable *adj.* flexible, dócil.

pliers *s. pl.* alicates, pinzas.

plough *s.* arado; *tr. e intr.* arar; surcar.

pluck *s.* ánimo, valor, coraje; *tr.* dar un tirón; pelar.

plug *s.* taco; boca de agua; (Elec.) enchufe; (Aut.) bujía; *tr.* tapar.

plum *s.* (Bot.) ciruela.

plumb *s.* plomada; *adj.* vertical; *tr.* aplomar.

plumber *s.* fontanero.

plunder *s.* robo; botín; *tr.* saquear, pillar.

plunge *s.* zambullida; *intr.* zambullirse.

plus *s.* más (*signo*); *adj.* más.

ply *s.* capa; cordón, cable; *tr.* manejar, ejercer; *intr.* avanzar.

P

p.m. después del mediodía *(post meridian).* (**P.M.**) Primer Ministro.

pneumatic *adj.* neumático.

poacher *s.* cazador o pescador furtivo.

pocket *s.* bolsillo; saco; *tr.* embolsar.

poem *s.* poema.

poet *s.* poeta.

poignant *adj.* picante.

point *s.* punta; pico; gracia *(del chiste); tr.* aguzar; sacar punta a; *intr.* apuntar.

pointed *adj.* agudo, puntiagudo.

pointer *s.* indicador; manecilla *(de reloj);* fiel *(de balanza).*

poise *s.* equilibrio, serenidad; *tr.* equilibrar; *intr.* equilibrarse.

poison *s.* veneno; *tr.* envenenar; corromper.

poke *s.* empuje, codazo; *tr.* atizar; *intr.* husmear, fisgar.

pole *s.* poste, asta.

police *s.* policía; guardia; **revenue frontier —** carabinero.

policy *s. (pl.* -**cies**) política, plan de acción; póliza *(de seguros);* lotería (U.S.).

polish *s.* pulimento; cultura; elegancia; *tr.* pulir.

polished *adj.* fino, refinado, galante; culto.

polite *s.* culto; cortés, político.

poll *s.* votación; encuesta; *tr.* empadronar; obtener *(votos).*

pollute *tr.* corromper.

pollution *s.* contaminación, corrupión.

pomade *s.* pomada.

pommel *s.* pomo, *tr.* cascar.

pomp *s.* pompa, ceremonia.

pond *s.* estanque; pantano.

ponder *tr. e in.* ponderar; meditar.

poniard *s.* puñal; *tr.* apuñalar.

pony *s.(pl.* -**nies**) jaca, caballito.

poodle *s.* perro de lanas.

pool *s.* charco; balsa; *tr.* mancomunar, pagar a escote.

poor *adj.* pobre, necesitado.

pope *s.* papa.

poplar *s.* álamo, chopo.

poppy *s. (pl.* -**pies**) (Bot.) amapola.

populate *tr.* poblar.

population *s.* población, vecindario.

porcelain *s.* porcelana.

porch *s.* porche; portal.

pore *s.* pore; *intr.* reflexionar.

pork *s.* carne de cerdo.

porous *adj.* poroso.

port *s.* puerto; vino de Oporto.

portable *adj.* portátil.

portcullis *s.* rastrillo.

portend *tr.* presagiar.

portent *s.* prestigio.

portentous *adj.* portentoso, extraordinario.

porter *s.* portero, conserje.

portly *adj.* corpulento.

portrait *s.* retrato.

pose *s.* pose, postura; *tr.* colocar en cierta postura.

possess *tr.* poseer; reunir.

possible *adj.* posible, permitido.

postage *s.* franqueo.

poster *s.* cartel, letrero.

posterior *adj.* —posterior; *s.* nalgas, trasero.

postpone *tr.* aplazar.

postscript *s.* postdata.

pot *s.* pote, puchero.

potato *s. (pl.* -**toes**) patata; **sweet —** batata.

potent *adj.* potente.

pothole *s.* bache, hoyo.

pouch *s.* bolsa; cartuchera.

poultry *s.* aves de corral.

pounce *s.* arenilla, *tr.* espolvorear con grasilla o arenilla.

pound s. arenilla, tr.
espolvorear con grasilla o
arenilla.

pound s. libra (peso); libra
esterlina; tr. golpear.

poundage s. impuesto.

pour tr. verter, derramar; intr.
fluir; llover torrencialmente.

poverty s. pobreza.

powder s. polvo, polvos de
tocador; tr. pulverizar
empolvar; intr. empolvarse.

powder-blue s. azul pálido.

power s. poder; (fig.) energía;
tr. accionar.

powerless adj. impotente.

practice s. práctica; tr.
practicar.

practitioner s. profesional;
médico o abogado.

prairie s. pradera, llanura.

praise s. alabanza; tr. alabar.

pram s. cochecito de niño.

prattle s. charla, intr. charlar.

pray tr. rogar; intr. rezar.

prayer s. oración.

preach tr. e intr. predicar,
sermonear; tr. predicar.

precede tr. e intr. preceder.

precinct s. recinto.

precious adj. precioso;
querido.

precipice s. precipicio.

precipitate tr. precipitar.

precise adj. preciso.

preclude tr.. excluir.

precocious adj. precoz.

predict tr. predecir.

predominate intr. predominar.

prefer tr. preferir; promover.

preferment s. ascenso,
promoción.

pregnancy s. preñez,
embarazo.

prejudice s. prejuicio,
preocupación; tr. prevenir.

prelate s. prelado.

prelude s. preludio; tr. e intr.
preludiar.

premier adj. primero;
principal; s. jefe del estado.

prentice s. aprendiz.

prepare tr. preparar, prevenir;
intr. prepararse, disponerse.

preponderance intr.
preponderar.

prepossess tr. predisponer.

prepossessing adj.
simpático, agradable.

preposterous adj. absurdo.

prerequisite adj. previamente
necesario; s. requisito
previo.

prerogative adj. privilegiado;
s. prerrogativa.

presage s. presagio; tr.
presagiar.

presbiter s. presbítero,
sacerdote.

prescind intr. prescindir.

prescribe tr. e intr. prescribir.

present adj. presente; s.
regalo.

present tr. presentar.

preserve s. conserva; tr.
preservar; conservar.

preside intr. presidir,
gobernar.

pressing adj. apremiante.

prestige s. prestigio.

presume tr. presumir.

pretence s. pretensión.

pretend tr. aparentar.

pretty adj. (compar. -ier;
superl. -iest) bonito; bello.

prevail intr. estar en boga o
de moda.

prevaricate intr. engañar.

prevent tr. impedir; evitar; intr.
obstar.

preview s. inspección previa;
avance; tr. ver o
inspeccionar de antemano.

prey s. presa, botín; intr.
cazar.

price s. precio, valor; tr.
apreciar; valorar.

priceless adj. inapreciable.

P

prick s. pinchazo. tr. pinchar, picar.

prickle s. pincho, púa; intr. sentir una punzada, sentir picazón.

pride s. orgullo; soberbia; tr. enorgullecer.

priest s. sacerdote; cura.

priggish adj. pedante.

prim adj. estirado.

prime adj. primero; básico; primario.

primeval adj. primitivo, original.

princess s. princesa.

principle s. principio, causa; fundamento.

printed matter s. impresos.

printing s. impresión; edición; imprenta.

prisoner s. preso.

privacy s. (pl. -cies) aislamiento; habitación privada.

private adj. privado, particular; clandestino; s. soldado raso.

privy s. (pl. -ies) excusado, retrete.

prize s. premio; botín; adj. premiado; tr. apreciar.

probation s. prueba, ensayo.

probe s. sonda; exploración; tr. sondar; sondear.

procedure s. procedimiento.

proceed intr. proceder, avanzar.

proceeds s. pl. resultado, réditos.

proclaim tr. proclamar.

procrastinate tr. diferir; intr. tardar, no decidirse.

procreate tr. procrear.

procure tr. lograr, obtener.

prod s. empuje; tr. pinchar.

prodigal adj. pródigo; s. pródigo.

prodigious adj. prodigioso.

produce tr. producir; presentar al público.

producer s. productor.

production s. producción.

profane adj. profano; s. profano; tr. profanar.

profess tr. e intr. profesar.

proffer s. oferta, propuesta; tr. ofrecer.

proficiency s. pericia, destreza.

proficient adj. perito, hábil; s. perito.

profile s. perfil, contorno; tr. perfilar.

profit s. provecho, beneficio; tr. servir, aprovechar; intr. aprovecharse.

profitable adj. provechoso.

profiteer s. usurero.

progeny s. (-nies) prole, linaje.

progress s. progreso.

prohibit tr. prohibir, privar.

project s. proyecto, plan.

project tr. proyectar; arrojar, despedir; intr. salir fuera.

proliferate tr. (Biol.) multiplicar; tr. proliferar.

prolix adj. difuso, prolijo.

prolong tr. prolongar.

promenade s. paseo, vuelta.

promise s. promesa; tr. e intr. prometer.

promising adj. prometedor.

promote tr. promover.

prompt adj. pronto, puntual; tr. incitar, mover.

prone adj. inclinado.

proneness s. postración; disposición.

prong s. púa, punta; gajo.

pronoun s. pronombre.

pronounce tr. pronunciar.

proof s. prueba; evidencia.

propagate tr. e in. propagar.

propel tr. propulsar.

proper adj. propio.

properness s. propiedad.

property s. (pl. -ties) propiedad; adj. de propiedad.

prophecy *tr. e intr.* profetizar.
proposal *s.* oferta;
declaración.
propose *tr.* proponer; *intr.*
declararse.
propound *tr.* proponer.
propriety *s.* corrección.
prosaic, -al *adj.* prosaico.
proscribe *tr.* proscribir.
prosecute *tr.* (Der.) procesar.
prosecutor *s.* fiscal.
prospect *s.* perspectiva.
prospect *tr.* explotar; *intr.*
prometer.
prospecting *s.* sondeo.
prosper *tr. e intr.* prosperar.
prostitute *s.* prostituta; *tr.*
vender, prostituir; *intr.*
prostituirse.
protect *tr.* proteger.
protest *s.* protesta.
protest *tr.e intr.* protestar.
protestant *adj. y s.*
protestante; (Amér.) canuto.
proud *adj.* orgulloso.
prove *tr.* probar.
provide *tr.* proporcionar;
suministrar.
provided *cnj.* a condición de
que.
provoke *tr.* provocar, indignar.
prow *s.* (Náut.) proa.
prowess *s.* proeza.
prowl *tr. e intr.* rondar.
proxy *s.* (*pl.* **-xies**) poder;
apoderado, delegado.
prudent *adj.* sensato,
prudente.
prune *s.* ciruela pasa; *tr.*
mondar, podar.
psalm *s.* salmo.
pub *s.* taberna.
public *s.* públicar; editar.
publisher *s.* editor.
pucker *s.* arruga; *tr.* plegar
mal.
puffy *s. adj.* hinchado.
pull *s.* tirón, estirón; *tr.* tirar;
coger, abatir; *intr.* tirar con
esfuerzo.

pulley *s.* (Mec.) polea.
pullman *s.* coche-cama.
pulpit *s.* púlpito.
pulsate *intr.* pulsar.
pulse *s.* pulso, latido.
pulverize *tr.* pulverizar.
pump *s.* bomba; *adj.* de
bomba; *tr.* impeler.
pumpkin *s.* (Bot.) calabaza.
pun *s.* equívoco.
punch *s.* puñetazo.
punctual *adj.* puntual.
puncture *s.* pinchazo; *tr.*
pinchar.
pungent *adj.* picante.
punish *tr.* castigar.
pupil *s.* alumno.
puppet *s.* títere, muñeco;
(fig.) maniquí.
puppy *s.* (*pl.* **-ies**) cachorro.
purchase *s.* compra,
adquisición; *tr.* comprar,
adquirir.
pure *adj.* puro, limpio.
purée *s.* puré.
purge *tr.* purgar.
purify *tr.* purificar.
purple *s.* púrpurar; *adj.*
purpúreo.
purport *s.* significado, idea
principal; *tr.* significar.
purpose *s.* intención, objeto,
fin.
purse *s.* bolsa.
pursue *tr.* perseguir;
continuar.
pursuer *s.* seguidor.
pursuit *s.* seguimiento; *adj.*
de prosecución, de caza.
purvey *tr.* proveer, abastecer.
push *s.* empujón; embestida;
tr. empujar.
pushing *adj.* emprendedor,
activo.
put *adj.* puesto; *tr.* poner;
proponer; imponer.
puzzle *s.* enigma; acertijo; *tr.*
confundir, desconcertar,
embrollar; *int.* estar
perplejo o confuso.

P

Q

quack s. charlatán, curandero.
quadrille s. cuadrilla.
quaff s. trago grande; tr. e
  intr. beber a grandes tragos.
quail s. codorniz; intr.
  acobardarse.
quaint adj. curioso, raro.
quake s. temblor; intr. temblar.
qualified adj. calificado, apto.
qualify tr. calificar; capacitar;
  intr. capacitarse.
qualm s. escrúpulo, duda.
quarantine s. cuarentena.
quarrel s. disputa, riña; cincel;
  intr. disputar, reñir.
quart s. cuarto de galón.
quarter adj. cuarto; s. cuarto;
  trimestre; —s morada,
  vivienda; tr. descuartizar;
  hospedar; intr. alojarse,
  hospedarse.
quarterly adj. trimestral.
quartz s. cuarzo.
quash tr. sofocar, aplastar.
quaver s. temblor, vibración;
  intr. temblar, vibrar.
quay s. muelle,
  desembarcadero.
queen s. reina.
queer adj. curioso, raro.
quell tr. sofocar.
quench tr. extinguir.
query s. (pl. -ries) pregunta;
  intr. hacer preguntas.
quest s. búsqueda; tr. e intr.
  buscar, averiguar.
question s. cuestión;
  pregunta; tr. e intr.
  pregunta, examinar.
queue s. cola o fila; intr. hacer
  cola.
quibbling s. juego de
  palabras.
quick adj. rápido.
quicken tr. acelerar.
quicklime s. cal viva.

quickly adv. rápidamente.
quicksand s. arena movediza.
quiet adj. tranquilo;
  silencioso; adv.
  silenciosamente; tr. calmar;
  m. reposarse.
quill s. pluma de ave.
quilt s. cobertor.
quince s. (Bot.) membrillo.
quip s. sutileza.
quit adj. libre, sin
  obligaciones; dejar (libre);
  intr. irse.
quite adv. completamente.
quiver s. temblor,
  estremecimiento; intr.
  temblar.
quotation s. cotización.
quote tr. cotizar.

R

rabble s. chusma; multitud.
rabid adj. rabioso, violento.
rabies s. rabia, hidrofobia.
race s. raza, casta; tr. correr,
  desafiar; — **ground** campo
  de carrera; —1horse
  caballo de carreras.
rack s. estante; percha; tr.
  atormentar, torturar.
racket s. raqueta, pala.
radiate adj. radiado; tr. radiar;
  intr. radiar, centellear.
radical adj. radical,
  fundamental.
radio s. radio; — **station**
  emisora.
raffle s. rifa, lotería; tr. rifar,
  sortear.
raft s. balsa.
rag s. trapo, harapo; adj. de
  trapo; — **doll** muñeca de

trapos; *tr.* romper, hacer jirones.

rage *s.* rabia, ardor, entusiasmo; *intr.* rabiar, encolerizarse.

ragged *adj.* andrajoso, harapiento.

raid *s.* invasión, ataque inesperado; *tr.* atacar por sorpresa.

rail *s.* carril, raíl; *tr.* poner barrera o barandilla; *intr.* quejarse amargamente.

railing *s.* barandilla, pasamano.

railroad *s.* ferrocarril, *adj.* ferroviario.

railway *s.* ferrocarril; *adj.* ferroviario.

rain *s.* lluvia; *intr.* llover.

rainbow *s.* arco iris.

raincoat *s.* impermeable.

rainfall *s.* aguacero.

rainstorm *s.* tempestad de lluvia.

raise *s.* aumento, alza *(de precios, salarios, etcétera)*; *tr.* levantar, subir, exaltar, promover.

raisin *s.* pasa *(uva seca)*.

rake *s.* rastro, rastrillo; calavera; *tr.* rastrillar; raspar.

rally *s. (pl.* **-lies**) reunión popular, reunión política; *tr.* reunir.

ram *s.* carnero; *tr.* atacar.

ramble *s.* paseo, excursión; *intr. pasear; divagar.*

rampant *adj.* exuberante, excesivo.

rampart *s.* terraplén; muralla.

ranch *s.* hacienda, rancho.

rancor *s.* rencor.

random *s.* azar, acaso; *adj.* casual.

range *s.* fila; viaje; *intr.* alinearse; variar.

rank *s.* fila; (Mil.) grado; rango; *adj.* exuberante; denso; *tr.* alinear, ordenar; *intr.* formar o marchar en filas.

ransack *tr.* registrar, explotar.

ransom *s.* rescate; *tr.* rescatar.

rap *s.* manotón; censura; *tr. e intr.* golpear; *tr.* criticar duramente.

rape *s.* rapto; violación; *tr.* raptar; violar.

rapier *s.* estoque, espadín.

rapport *s.* relación; informe.

rapture *s.* rapto; arrebato.

rarefy *tr.* enrarecer; *intr.* enrarecerse.

rascal *s.* bribón, canalla.

rash *adj.* aventurero; *s.* brote.

rasp *s.* ronquido; ronquera; *tr.* raspar.

rat *s.* rata.

rate *s.* cantidad, grado; *tr.* valuar, estimar.

ratepayer *s.* contribuyente.

rather *adv.* bastante, mejor, más; *inj.* ¡claro!, ¡ya lo creo!

ratify *tr.* ratificar.

ration *s.* ración *tr.* racionar.

rattle *s.* carraca; sonajero; *tr.* traquetear; decir, proferir rápidamente; *intr.* repiquetear.

ravage *s.* estrago; *tr.* destruír.

rave *intr.* desvariar, delirar.

raven *s.* cuervo.

ravenous *adj.* voraz, hambriento.

ravine *s.* hondonada, barranco.

ravish *tr.* encantar.

ray *s.* rayo *(de luz)*; *tr.* irradiar; *intr.* radiar.

raze *tr.* arrasar, asolar.

razor *s.* navaja de afeitar.

reach *s.* alcance; extensión; *tr.* alargar, extender.

react *intr.* reaccionar.

read *adj.* leído, instruído.

read *tr.* leer; interpretar.

readable *adj.* legible, ameno.

R

reader *s.* lector;
conferenciante.
reading *adj.* lector; para leer;
s. lectura.
ready *adj.* listo, preparado.
reaffirm *tr.* reafirmar.
real *adj.* real, verdadero.
reality *s.* realidad.
realize *tr.* comprender, ver.
really *adv.* realmente.
realm *s.* reino, país.
reap *tr. e in.* segar.
rear *adj.* posterior; trasero; *tr.*
levantar; elevar; criar,
educar; *intr.* empinarse.
rearmost *adj.* último.
reason *s.* razón,
entendimiento; *tr. e in.*
razonar.
rebate *s.* descuento; *tr.*
descontar; *intr.* hacer una
rebaja.
rebel *intr.* rebelarse,
sublevarse.
rebuff *s.* desaire, rechazo; *tr.*
rechazar.
rebuild *tr.* reconstruír.
rebuke *s.* represión,
reproche.
recall *s.* llamada o aviso; *tr.*
hacer volver; revocar.
recede *intr.* retroceder, recular.
receipt *s.* abono, recibo.
receive *tr.* recibir; tomar.
recent *adj.* reciente, moderno.
recess *s.* intermisión, tregua;
s. hora de recreo.
recipe *s.* fórmula, receta.
recite *tr.* recitar.
reckless *adj.* descuidado.
reckon *tr.* considerar; calcular.
reckoning *s.* cómputo, cuenta.
reclaim *tr.* reclamar; ganar
terreno al mar.
recline *tr.* reclinar; *intr.*
reclinarse.
recluse *adj.* retirado, solitario;
s. ermitaño.
recognise *tr.* reconocer.

recoil *s.* retroceso, reculada;
intr. recular, retroceder.
recollect *tr. e intr.* recordar.
reconcile *tr.* reconciliar.
reconnoiter *tr. e intr.* (Mil.)
reconocer.
recount *tr.* contar de nuevo.
recount *tr.* referir.
recover *tr.* recuperar.
recreate *tr.* recrear, divertir.
recruit *s.* recluta; *tr.* reclutar;
abastecer.
rectify *tr.* rectificar.
recur *intr.* volver a ocurrir,
repetirse.
red *adj.* rojo; revolucionario.
redden *tr.* enrojecer; *intr.*
ruborizarse.
redeem *tr.* redimir.
redoubtable *adj.* formidable.
redress *tr.* enderezar, reparar.
redskin *s.* piel roja, indio.
reduce *tr.* reducir.
re-echo *intr.* resonar.
reel *s.* carrete; *tr.* devanar,
enrollar.
re-elect *tr.* reelegir.
re-enforce *tr.* reforzar.
reenlist *tr.* reengranchar.
re-establish *tr.* restablecer.
refer *tr.* referir, dirigir; *intr.*
aludir; recurrir a.
referee *s.* árbitro; *tr. e intr.*
arbitrar.
refill *tr.* rellenar.
refine *tr.* refinar, purificar.
reflect *tr.* reflejar; repercutir;
intr. reflexionar.
reflection *s.* reflexión; reflejo,
imagen.
refrain *s.* estribillo; (fig.)
cantinela; *tr.* refrenar,
contener.
refresh *tr.* refrescar; reanimar.
refresher course *s.* curso de
repaso.
refund *s.* reembolso; *tr.*
reembolsar, devolver.
refuse *s.* basura, desecho.
refuse *tr.* rehusar, rechazar.

refute *tr.* refutar.
regain *tr.* recobrar.
regale *tr.* regalar; recrear.
regard *s.* mirada;
consideración; *tr.* mirar,
contemplar, respetar.
regardless *adj.* descuidado,
desatento.
regiment *s.* (Mil.) regimiento;
pl. informe militar.
register *s.* registro *(libro)*;
archivo; inscripción; *adj.* de
registro; *tr.* registrar,
inscribir.
regret *s.* pesar, pena; *intr.*
sentir, lamentar.
regretful *adj.* pesaroso.
regrettable *adj.* lamentable.
regulate *tr.* regular, ajustar.
rehearse *tr.* ensayar.
reign *s.* reino,; reinado, *intr.*
reinar.
reimburse *tr.* reembolsar,
indemnizar.
rein *s.* rienda.
reindeer *s.* (Zool.) reno.
reiterate *tr.* reiterar, repetir.
reject *tr.* rechazar.
rejoice *tr.* elegrar, regocijar.
rejoin *tr.* reunirse con; *tr. e
intr.* responder.
rejoinder *s.* respuesta.
relapse *s.* recaída; *intr.* recaer.
relate *tr.* relatar, referir; *intr.*
relacionarse.
relative *adj.* relativo; *s.*
pariente.
relax *tr.* relajar, soltar; *intr.*
relajarse; esparcirse.
relaxation *s.* relajación,
aflojamiento.
relay *s.* relevo; parada; *adj.*
de relevos; *tr.* relevar,
mudar.
release *s.* liveración; alivio; *tr.*
libertar, soltar.
relent *intr.* ablandarse,
aplacarse.
relevant *adj.* pertinente.
reliable *adj.* fidedigno, veraz.

reliance *s.* confianza.
relic *s.* reliquia, vestigio.
relief *s.* ayuda, auxilio.
relieve *tr.* relevar, auxiliar.
relinquish *tr.* abandonar,
dejar.
relish *s.* buen sabor, gusto; *tr.*
saborear, paladear.
reload *tr.* recargar.
reluctance *s.* aversión,
repugnancia.
remain *intr.* quedar, sobrar.
remark *s.* observación, nota;
tr. observar, notar.
remedy *s.* (*pl.* **-dies**) remedio,
medicamento; *tr.* remediar,
curar.
remember *tr.* recordar,
acordarse de.
remind *tr.* acordar, recordar.
remiss *adj.* remiso,
descuidado.
remit *tr.* (*pret. y pp.* **-mitted**)
remitir, restituir.
remittance *s.* remesa, envío,
giro.
remonstrance *s.* protesta,
amonestación.
remonstrate *intr.* protestar,
censurar.
remorseless *adj.* implacable.
removal *s.* traslado, mudanza.
remove *s. tr.* traslada, extraer;
intr. mudarse, cambiar de
domicilio.
Renaissance *s.* Renacimiento.
rend *tr.* desgarrar.
render *s.* pago; primera capa
de enlucido; *tr.* rendir.
rendezvous *s.* cita.
renegade *adj. y s.* renegado.
renew *tr.* renovar; *intr.*
renovarse.
renounce *tr.* renunciar,
abdicar.
renovate *tr.* renovar.
rent *s.* renta, arrendamiento;
tr. alquilar; *intr.* alquilarse.
reopen *tr.* reabrir, reanudar.

R

repair *s.* reparación, reparo; *tr.* reparar, restaurar.
repast *s.* comida, comilona.
repay *tr.* reembolsar; compensar.
repayment *s.* reembolso.
repeat *s.* repetición; *tr. e intr.* repetir.
repeatedly *adv.* repetidamente.
repel *tr.* repeler, repulsar.
repent *tr.* arrepentirse de.
repetition *s.* repetición, vuelta.
replace *tr.* reemplazar, substituir.
replenish *tr.* llenar, henchir.
reply *s.* *(pl. -plies)* respuesta; *tr. e intr.* repsonder, contestar.
repose *s.* reposo; *tr.* descansar; *intr.* descansar.
represent *tr.* representar, simbolizar.
repress *tr.* reprimir, contener.
reprive *s.* suspensión; indulto; *tr.* suspender la ejecución de.
reprint *s.* reimpresión; tirada aparte; *tr.* reimprimir.
reprisal *s.* represalia.
reproduce *tr.* reproducir.
reprove *tr.* reprobar, censurar.
repudiate *tr.* repudiar, reachazar.
repulse *s.* rechazo; repulsa; *tr.* repulsar, rechazar.
reputable *adj.* de buena reputatión.
reputation *s.* reputación, fama.
repute *tr.* reputar, juzgar.
request *s.* petición, ruego.
require *tr.* requerir, pedir.
requiste *adj.* necesario, preciso; *s.* requisito.
requite *tr.* corresponder, pagar.
rescind *tr.* rescindir.
rescue *s.* rescate; liberación; *tr.* rescatar; libertar.

resell *tr.* revender.
resemble *tr.* asemejarse a.
resent *tr.* resentirse de.
resentful *adj.* resentido.
reserve *s.* reserva, silencio. *tr.* reservar, retirar.
reservoir *s.* depósito, estanque.
reshuffle *s.* recomposición; *tr.* revolver otra vez.
reside *intr.* residir.
residence *s.* residencia, domicilio.
residue *s.* residuo, resto, sobrante.
resign *tr.* renunciar, dimitir.
resilient *adj.* elástico.
resist *tr. e intr.* resistir, oponerse.
resolute *adj.* resuelto.
resolve *s.* resolución; *tr.* resolver.
resolved *adj.* resuelto.
resonant *adj.* resonante.
resort *s.* concurrencia; recreo; *intr.* acudir, frecuentar.
resound *tr.* hacer resonar; *intr.* resonar.
resounding *adj.* sonoro.
respect *s.* respecto; atención; *tr.* respetar, estimar.
respectful *adj.* respetuoso.
respecting *prep.* con respecto a.
respiration *s.* respiración.
respite *s.* respiro; tregua; *tr.* dar tregua a.
resplendent *adj.* resplandeciente.
respond *intr.* responder, contestar.
responsible *adj.* responsable, solvente.
rest *s.* descanso; reposo; *tr.* descansar; parar; *intr.* descansar; residir.
restitute *tr.* restituir.
restive *adj.* intranquilo; alborotado.

restlessness *s.*
  intranquilidad, desasosiego.
restock *tr.* reaprovisionar;
  repoblar.
restoration *s.* restauración.
restore *tr.* restaurar; instaurar.
restrain *tr.* refrenar; aprisionar.
restraint *s.* limitación,
  restricción.
restrict *tr.* restringir, limitar.
result *s.* resultado; *intr.*
  resultar.
resume *tr.* reasumir.
resurge *intr.* resurgir.
resurrect *in.* resucitar.
retail *s.* venta al por menor.
retain *tr.* retener, guardar.
retainer *s.* dependiente;
  partidario.
retaliate *intr.* vengarse.
retaliation *s.* venganza.
retard *tr.* retardar, retrasar.
retention *s.* retención.
reticence *s.* reserva.
retinue *s.* sequito.
retire *tr.* retirar; jubilar.
retirement *s.* retiro; jubilación.
retiring *adj.* retraído.
retort *s.* retorta; *tr.* rebatir;
  intr. replicar.
retrace *tr.* repasar.
retract *tr. e in.* retractar;
  retraer.
retreat *s.* retirada; retiro,
  retraimiento.
retrieve *s.* recuperación;
  cobra [en la caza]; *tr.*
  reparar; desquitarse de.
retrocede *tr.* hacer
  retrocesión de.
return *s.* retorno; devolución;
  respuesta; ganancia; *tr.*
  volver, devolver; responder;
  intr. regresar.
reunite *tr. e in.* reunir, juntar.
revalue *tr.* revalorizar.
reveal *tr.* revelar.
reveille *s.* (Mil.) toque de
  diana.
revel *s.* regocijo.

revenge *s.* venganza; *tr.*
  vengar; *intr.* vengarse.
revenue *s.* renta, rédito.
reverberate *tr.* reflejar.
revere *tr.* reverenciar.
reverend *adj.* reverendo,
  venerable; *s.* (fam.) clérigo;
  most — reverendísimo.
reverent *adj.* reverente.
reverie *s.* ensueño.
reverse *adj.* invertido, inverso;
  opuesto; *s.* revés; contrario;
  tr. invertir, trastrocar.
revert *intr.* volver atrás.
review *s.* revista; reseña; *tr.*
  revisar.
revile *tr.* ultrajar.
revise *tr.* revisar; corregir.
revive *tr.* reanimar; resucitar,
  restablecer.
revivify *tr.* hacer revivir; *intr.*
  reanimarse.
revoke *tr.* revocar, retirar.
revolt *s.* rebelión,
  sublevación; *intr.* rebelarse.
revolutionize *tr.* revolucionar.
revolve *tr.* revolver; dar
  vueltas; *intr.* girar.
revolver *s.* revólver.
revolving *adj.* giratorio.
revue *s.* (Tt.) revista.
reward *s.* premio,
  recompensa; *tr.* premiar.
rhetoric *s.* retórica.
rheum(a) *s.* (Pat.) reuma.
rhyme *.s* rima; *tr. e intr.* rimar.
ribald *adj.* obsceno, blasfemo.
ribbon *s.* cinta.
rice *s.* (Bost.) arroz.
rich *adj.* rico, acomodado;
  azucarado; *s. pl.* riqueza.
richness *s.* riqueza, opulencia.
rickety *adj.* (Pat.) raquítico.
rid *tr.* librar, desembarazar.
riddle *s.* enigma, misterio; *tr.*
  adivinar; descifrar.
ride *s.* paseo a caballo o en
  coche; *tr. e intr.* montar.

R

rider s. jinete, caballero;
ciclista; cláusula añadida a
un proyecto de ley.

ridge s. espinazo.

ridicule s. ridículo; tr.
ridiculizar.

riding s. cabalgata, paseo a
caballo o en coche.

rife adj. frecuente; abundante.

rifle s. rifle, fusil, carabina; tr.
hurtar, despojar.

rift s. raja, abertura; tr. rajar,
dividir; intr. rajarse, partirse.

rigging s. aparejo; avíos.

rightabout face s. media
vuelta a la derecha.

righteous adj. recto, justo.

rightful adj. justo; legitimo.

rightly adv. rectamente,
derechamente.

rigid adj. rigido, tieso.

rigour s. rigor, dureza.

rill s. arroyuelo, riachuelo; intr.
correr formando un
arroyuelo.

rim s. canto, borde.

rind s. corteza; peladura.

ring s. anillo,sortija; redondel;
ring, cuadrilátero; círculo; tr.
sonar; repicar; anunciar;
intr. sonar, tañer, resonar.

ringing adj. resonante; s.
toque.

rinse tr. enjuagar, aclarar.

riot s. tumulto; desenfreno;
motin; intr. armar alboroto.

rioter s. alboratador.

rip s. rasgadura; tr. rasgar,
romper.

ripe adj. maduro, sazonado.

ripen tr. madurar, sazonar.

riposte s. respuesta; réplica;
intr. responder.

ripple s. rizo, ondulación; tr.
ondular, rizar; intr. rizarse,
agitarse.

rising adj. ascendiente;
naciente; s. subida,
ascensión, levantamiento.

risk s. riesgo; tr. arriesgar,
aventurar.

risky adj. arriesgado,
peligroso.

rite s. rito.

rival s. rival, competidor; tr.
competir, emular.

rivalry s. rivalidad,
competencia.

rive tr. rajar, hender; intr.
rajarse.

river s. rio; adj. fluvial.

rivulet s. riachuelo, arroyo.

roach s. (Zool.) cucaracha.

road s. carretera; camino.

roadhouse s. posada en el
camino, parador.

roadside s. borde del camino.

roadway s. calzada.

roam intr. rodar, vagar.

roar s. rugido, bramido; intr.
rugir, bramar; hacer
estruendo; alborotar.

roast s. asado; carne para
asar; tr. asar; tostar.

roaster s. asador; tostador;
cocinero que asa.

rob tr. robar, saquear.

robe s. repaje, traje talar; s.
pl. vestido (de mujer); tr. e
investirse de gala.

robust adj. robusto.

rock s. roca, peña; tr. mecer,
acunar.

rocker s. mecedora.

rocket s. cohete; intr. subir o
elevarse como un cohete.

rod s. vara; varilla, bastón.

rodent adj. y s. (Zool.) roedor.

rogue s. pícaro, bribón.

roguish adj. bellaco, pícaro.

roisterer s. fanfarrón.

role s. papel (en el teatro,
etc.).

roller skate s. patín de ruedas.

rolling adj. rodante; girante; s.
rodadura; balanceo.

Roman adj. y s. romano; s.
latín.

romance *adj.* romance; *s.* romance; novela, historia.
romantic, -al *adj.* romántico; encantado; sentimental.
rood *s.* cruz, crucifijo.
roof *s.* techo, tejado; bóveda.
roofless *adj.* sin techo; desamparado.
rook *s.* grajo.
room *s.* habitación, cuarto; ocasión; espacio, sitio.
roomy *adj.* amplio, espacioso.
rooster *s.* gallo.
root *s.* raíz; origen; *tr.* plantar firmemente.
rope *s.* cuerda, soga; *tr.* atar.
rosace *s.* rosetón.
rosary *s.* rosario.
rose *s.* rosa; (Bot.) rosal.
rosebud *s.* (Bot.) capullo.
rostrum *s.* tribuna.
rosy *adj.* sonrosado; florido, risueño.
rot *s.* podredumbre; tontería; *intr.* pudrirse, corromperse.
rotate *tr.* hacer girar; alternar; *intr.* girar, rodar.
rote *s.* rutina.
rotten *adj.* podrido.
rotund *adj.* redondo de cuerpo.
rouge *s.* arrebol; *tr.* pintar, dar de colorete.
roughly *adv.* ásperamente; aproximadamente.
roughness *s.* aspereza, tosquedad.
rouse *tr.* despertar, provocar; *intr.* despertar.
rout *s.* rota, derrota; séquito; *tr.* derrotar, poner en fuga.
route *s.* ruta, itinerario.
rover *s.* vagabundo; veleta.
row *s.* riña, pelotera; alboroto, bullicio; *intr.* pelearse.
row *s.* fila, línea; *intr.* remar, bogar.
royal *adj.* real, regio; magnífico.

royalty *s.* realeza; derechos de autor.
rubber *s.* goma, caucho.
rubbish *s.* basura, desperdicios; disparate.
rubdown *s.* masaje.
ruby *s.* (*pl.* -bies) rubí
ruck *tr.* arrugar.
rudder *s.* timón.
rude *adj.* rudo; tosco.
rudiment *s.* rudimento; *pl.* raciones.
rug *s.* alfombra; felpudo.
ruin *s.* ruina; destrucción; *tr.* arruinar; estropear.
rule *s.* regla, precepto, ley; autoridad; *tr.* gobernar, dirigir; contener.
rum *s.* ron, aguardiente.
rumble *s.* rumor, retumbo; *tr.* pronunciar con un sonido sordo; *intr.* retumbar.
ruminant *adj. y s.* rumiante.
ruminate *tr. e intr.* rumiar, masticar.
rummage *s.* búsqueda.
rummy *adj.* raro, extraño.
rumor *s.* rumor, decir, fábula; *tr.* rumorear.
rump *s.* anca, nalga.
rumpus *s.* alboroto, bulla.
runaway *adj.* desbocado; *s.* fugitivo.
rung *s.* peldaño, travesaño; barrote.
runner *s.* corredor; mensajero.
runner-up *s.* subcampeón.
running *s.* carrera, corrida.
rupee *s.* rupia (*moneda*).
rupture *s.* ruptura; *tr.* romper, quebrar, fracturar.
ruse *s.* ardid, astucia; estafa.
rust *s.* orín, herrumbre, moho; *tr.* enmohecer.
rustic *adj. y s.* rústico, rural, agreste; labriego, paleto.
rustle *s.* susurro, crujido; *tr.* hacer susurrar o crujir.
rusty *adj.* oxidado, mohoso.
ruthless *adj.* despiadado.

R

S

sabbath s. día de descanso.
sabotage s. sabataje; tr. sabotear.
sabre s. sable; tr. acuchillar.
sacrament s. sacramento.
sacred adj. sagrado.
sacrifice s. sacrificio; inmoloción; tr. e intr. sacrificar, inmolar.
sad adj. triste, mustio.
sadden tr. entristecer.
saddle s. silla (de montar); sillín.
sadistic adj. sádico.
sadness s. tristeza.
safe adj. seguro; s. arca, caja de caudales.
safeguard s. salvaguardia; carta de seguridad; tr. proteger.
safety s. seguridad, resguardo.
saffron s. (Bot.) azafrán.
sagacious adj. sagaz.
sage s. (Bot.) salvia; adj. sabio, cuerdo.
sail s. (Náut.) vela, paseo o excursión en barco.
sailing s. navegación; barco de vela.
sailor s. marinero.
saint s. y adj. santo, santa.
sake s. causa, motivo.
salad s. ensalada.
salary s. salario, sueldo.
sale s. venta; salida.
saliva s. saliva.
sallow adj. pálido.
sally s. salida; excursión; intr. hacer una salida.
saloon s. salón, (U.S.) taberna o bar de lujo.
salt s. (Qm.) sal; pl. sales; tr. salar; sazonar.

salute s. saludo; tr. e intr. saludar; intr. (Mil.) cuadrarse.
salvage s. salvamento; tr. salvar.
salve s. ungüento, pomada; tr. curar con ungüentos.
same adj. mismo, igual; adv. **the** — del mismo modo.
sameness s. igualdad, identidad.
sanctify tr. santificar.
sanction s. sanción, ratificación; tr. sancionar, ratificar, aprobar.
sanctuary s. (pl. **-ries**) santuario, templo; asilo.
sand s. arena; adj. de arena; — **hill** duna.
sandal s. sandalia.
sandwich s. emparedado, bocadillo.
sandy adj. arenoso.
sane adj. sano.
sangfroid s. sangre fría.
sanguine adj. colorado, rubicundo.
sanitary adj. sanitario; higiénico.
sap s. savia; vigor; tr. extraer la savia de; minar.
sash s. faja, ceñidor; (carp.) marco de ventana.
satchel s. saco de mano, maletín.
sate tr. saciar.
satiate adj. saciado, harto; tr. saciar; hartar.
satin s. raso.
satirize tr. satirizar.
satisfy tr. satisfacer; contentar.
satuarte tr. saturar.
Saturday s. sábado.
sauce s. salsa, condimento; tr. aderezar, sazonar.
saucepan s. cacerola.
saucer s. platillo.
sauciness s. descaro, gracia.
saunter s. paseo; intr. pasear.
sausage s. embutido.

savage *adj.* salvaje; inculto.
savanna(h) *s.* sabana, pampa.
save *prep.* salvo, excepto; *tr.* salvar, librar.
saving *adj.* ahorrativo, económico; *s.* ahorro, economía.
savor *s.* sabor, gusto; *tr.* sabotear.
savory *adj.* apetitoso.
saw *s.* sierra; refrán; *tr. e intr.* serrar.
sawdust *s.* serrín.
Saxon *adj. y s.* sajón; anglosajón.
say *s.* dicho, afirmación; *tr.* decir, recitar.
saying *s.* dicho, aserto, relato.
scab *s.* (Med:) costra, postilla.
scabbard *s.* vaina.
scabies *s.* (Med.) sarna.
scaffold *s.* andamio; tablado; *tr.* construir andamios.
scaffolding *s.* andamiaje.
scald *tr.* escaldar; abrasar, quemar.
scalpel *s.* bisturí.
scamp *s.* golfo, bribón; *tr.* chapucear.
scamper *s.* fuga precipitada; *intr.* huir.
scan *tr.* repasar, escudriñar.
scandal *s.* escándalo.
scandalize *tr.* escandalizar.
scant *adj.* escaso, corto; *tr.* escatimar, reducir.
scanty *adj.* escaso, limitado.
scapegrace *s.* pícaro; *adj.* incorregible.
scar *s.* cicatriz.
scarcely *adv.* apenas.
scarceness *s.* escasez, penuria.
scare *s.* susto; pánico; *tr.* asustar, alarmar.
scarecrow *s.* espantapájaros.
scarf *s.* pañuelo *(para la cabeza o el cuello)*; bufanda.

scatter *tr.* dispersar, poner en fuga; *intr.* desparramarse.
scatterbrained *s. y adj.* ligero de cascos.
scavenger *s.* basurero.
scene *s.* escena; escenario.
scenery *s.* escenario, paisaje, (Tt.) decorado.
scent *s.* olfato; olor; *tr.* oler, olfatear, husmear; sospechar.
schedule *s.* lista, catálogo; *tr.* catalogar, planear.
scheme *s.* esquema; *tr.* proyectar, idear, trazar; *intr.* formar planes.
schism *s.* cisma.
scholar *s.* escolar, alumno, colegial.
scholarship *s.* saber, ciencia; educación literaria.
school *s.* escuela; clase, día de clase.
schooling *s.* instrucción, enseñanza.
science *s.* ciencia, sabiduría.
scintillate *intr.* centellear, chispear; *tr.* lanzar.
scion *s.* vástago, renuevo.
scission *s.* corte, división.
scissors *s. pl.* tijeras.
scoff *s.* mofa, burla; *intr.* mofarse de.
scold *s.* regañón; *tr. e intr.* regañar.
scone *s.* especie de bizcocho.
scooter *s.* patinete; embarcación de motor.
scope *s.* alcance *(de un arma)*.
scorbutus *s.* escorbuto.
scorch *tr.* chamuscar, abrasar.
scorching *adj.* ardiente, abrasador.
scorn *s.* desdén, desprecio; *tr.* desdeñar, despreciar.
scorpion *s.* (Zool.) escorpión, alacrán.
Scot *s.* escocés.
scoundrel *s.* granuja, bribón.

S

scour *tr.* fregar, restregar; limpiar.

scourge *s.* látigo, azote; *tr.* azotar; castigar.

scowl *s.* ceño, sobrecejo; *intr.* mirar con ceño.

scrabble *s.* garabatos, borrón; *tr. e intr.* garabatear, emborronar.

scraggy *adj.* desigual.

scramble *s.* lucha, contienda; *intr.* trpar, gatear.

scrape *s.* raspadura; aprieto, apuro; *tr.* raspar, rascar.

scraper *s.* raspador.

scratch *s.* arañazo, rasguño; *tr.* arañar, rasguñar.

scream *s.* chillido, grito; *intr.* chillar.

screen *s.* pantalla; biombo, mampara; *tr.* ocultar, encubrir, tapar.

screw *s.* tornillo, rosca; tuerca; espiral; *tr.* atornillar, apretar.

scribble *s.* escrito desmañado; *tr.* escribir de prisa.

Scripture *s.* Sagrada Escritura, Biblia.

scroll *s.* rollo; escrito.

scrub *s.* fregado; *tr.* fregar.

scrubby *adj.* desmirriado, bajo.

scruff *s.* pescuezo, nuca.

scruple *s.* escrúpulo; *intr.* tener escrúpulo.

scrutinise *tr.* escrutar, escudriñar.

scuffle *s.* lucha, riña; *intr.* luchar.

sculptor *s.* escultor.

sculpture *s.* escultura; *tr.* esculpir.

scum *s.* espuma; escoria; *tr.* espumar.

scurf *s.* caspa.

scurrilous *adj.* chabacano.

scurvy *s.* (*pl.* **-ies**) escorbuto.

scutcheon *s.* escudo de armas.

scuttle *s.* escotillón, trampa; cubo del carbón.

scythe *s.* guadaña.

sea *s.* mar, océano; *adj.* marino, del mar, marítimo.

seal *s.* sello; sigilo, (Zool.) foca; *tr.* sellar, precintar; lacrar.

sealskin *s.* piel de foca.

seam *s.* costura; grieta; *tr.* coser.

seaplane *s.* hidroplano.

search *s.* busca, búsqueda, investigación, *tr e intr.* busca; examinar, registrar.

searching *adj.* escrutador.

seashore *s.* playa, costa.

seaside *s.* playa, costa.

seasickness *s.* mareo.

seasonal *adj.* estacional; de temporada.

seasoning *s.* condimento, aliño.

seaward *adv.* hacia el mar.

secede *intr.* separarse.

secluded *adj.* retirado.

seclusion *s.* retraimíento, apartmiento.

secrecy *s.* secreto.

secretariat *s.* secretaría.

secretary *s.* (*pl.* **-ries**) secretario; ministro del Gobierno.

secrete *tr.* esconder, ocultar.

secretion *s.* segregación.

secretive *adj.* callado.

sect *s.* secta, grupo.

section *s.* sección trozo; *tr.* seccionar.

secularize *tr.* secularizar; *intr.* secularizarse.

secure *adj.* seguro; tranquilo; *tr.* asegurar.

sedate *adj.* sereno, ecuánime.

sediment *s.* sedimento.

sedition *s.* sedición.

seduce *tr.* seducir, camelar.

seducer *s.* seductor.

see *tr.* ver.
seed *s.* (Bot.) semillar, simiente.
seeing *s.* vista, acción de ver; *adj.* vidente.
seek *tr.* buscar; inquirir; pedir; ambicionar.
seem *intr.* parecer.
seeming *adj.* aparente, fingido.
seep *tr.* colar, pasar.
seer *s.* profeta, vidente.
seesaw *s.* columpio de tabla; balanceo.
seethe *intr.* hervir.
seether *s.* olla, caldera.
seize *tr.* coger, tomar; *intr.* atascarse.
seizer *s.* agarrador.
seizure *s.* captura, detención.
seldom *adv.* raramente.
select *adj.* selecto, escogido; *tr.* escoger, elegir.
self *adj.* mismo, idéntico; uniforme *(color)*.
selfish *adj.* interesado, egoísta.
selfishness *s.* egoísmo, amor propio.
sell *s.* (fam.) engaño, estafa; *tr.* vender, enajenar.
semblance *s.* semejanza; aspecto, forma.
semicolon *s.* punto y coma.
seminary *s.* (pl. -ries) semillero, plantel.
senate *s.* senado.
send *tr.* enviar, mandar, expedir; lanzar, despedir.
sender *s.* remitente; (Elec.) transmisor.
senior *adj.* mayor, de mayor edad, primero, padre.
sensational *adj.* sensacional; efectista.
sense *s.* sentido, juicio.
senseless *adj.* insensible, inerte.
sensibility *s.* sensibilidad.
sensitive *adj.* sensitivo.

sensuous *adj.* voluptuoso, sensible.
sentient *adj.* sensible; sensitivo; *s.* ser sensible.
sentinel *s.* centinela.
sentry *s.* (pl. -tries) (Mil.) centinela; — box garantía.
separate *tr.* separar; despegar, desprender; *intr.* separarse.
separatist *s.* desidente.
September *s.* Septiembre.
sepulcher, sepulchre *s.* sepulcro, tumba.
sequel *s.* secuela, conclusion.
sequence *s.* serie, sucesión.
sequestrate *tr.* secuestrar.
serene *adj.* sereno, claro.
serf *s.* ciervo, esclavo.
serfdom *s.* servidumbre.
sergeant *s.* (Mil.) sargento; escudero.
serial *adj.* de serie, en serie.
series *s.* serie, sucesión, progresión.
serious *adj.* serio, formal.
serpent *s.* (Zool.) serpiente.
serrate(d) *adj.* dentellado, serrado.
serried *adj.* apretado, apiñado.
serry *tr.* apiñar.
serum *s.* suero.
servant *s.* sirviente, criado.
service *s.* servicio.
serviceable *adj.* servible; útil.
servile *adj.* servil, bajo; *s.* esclavo.
servitude *s.* servidumbre, trabajo forzado.
session *s.* junta, sesión.
setback *s.* revés, contrariedad.
settee *s.* banco, sofá.
setting *s.* puesta, ocaso; fraguado; *adj.* poniente.
settle *s.* escaño, banco; *tr.* colocar, asentar; *intr.* posarse, asentarse.
settled *adj.* fijado, establecido.

S

settlement s. establecimiento; colonización.

settler s. poblador, colono.

seven adj. y s. siete.

seventeen adj. y s. diecisiete.

seventy adj. y s. setenta.

sever tr. separar, dividir.

several adj. varios; pron. indef. algunos.

severe adj. severo, grave.

sew tr. e intr. coser.

sewage s. aguas de alcantarilla.

sewer s. colector, alcantarilla; tr. alcantarillar, desaguar.

sewing s. costura.

sex s. sexo, naturaleza.

sexless adj. asexual, neutro.

sexton s. sacristán; enterrador.

shabby adj. (compar. -ier; superl. -iest) raído, gastado; andrajoso.

shack s. cabaña, choza.

shadow s. sombra, oscuridad; tr. sombrear, oscurecer.

shaft s. astil; asta; (Arq.) aguja; chimenea; (Mec.) eje, árbol; pozo.

shaky adj. trémulo, tembloroso.

shallow adj. bajo, poco, profundo.

sham s. simulación, farsa; adj. fingido, simulado; tr. e intr. fingir.

shame s. vergüenza, bochorno; tr. avergonzar, abochornar.

shamefaced adj. tímido, vergonzoso.

shamrock s. (Bot.) trébol.

shapeless adj. deforme.

share s. parte, porción; interés; tr. dividir, distribuir; intr. participar, tomar parte.

shareholder s. (Com.) accionista.

shark s. (Zool.) tiburón; usurero; intr. estafar.

sharp adj. agudo, cortante.

sharpen tr. afilar, aguzar.

shawl s. chal, toquilla.

she pron. pers. ella.

shear tr. cortar, esquilar.

sheath s. vaina, funda.

shed s. covertizo, refugio; tr. verter, derramar.

sheen s. lustre, brillo.

sheep s. (Zool.) oveja; ovejas; rebaño, congregación de fieles.

sheet s. hoja, lámina.

shelf s. estante; anaquel.

shell s. (Zool.) concha, caparazón; tr. descascarar, desvainar.

shellfish s. marisco.

shelter s. resguardo, protección; tr. resguardar, proteger.

shepherd s. pastor, ovejero; adj. de pastor; tr. pastorear.

sherry s. vino de Jerez.

shield s. escudo adarga; tr. escudar, resguardar.

shilling s. chelín.

shin s. espinilla.

shine s. brillo, resplandor; intr. brillar, resplandecer; tr.

ship s. (Náut.) buque, barco, nave; tr. embarcar; enviar.

shipwreck s. naufragio, desastre; tr. hacer naufragar.

shirk tr. eludir, evitar.

shirt s. camisa (de hombre).

shiver s. temblor, escalofrío, tiritón; intr. temblar; tr. hacer temblar.

shoal s. bajo; muchedumbre; banco (de peces); adj. poco profundo.

shoe s. zapato, bota; tr. calzar; herrar.

shoemaker s. zapatero.

shoot s. (Bot.) vástago, pimpollo; tr. herir o matar; disparar; intr. tirar, disparar.

shooting s. caza con escopeta.

shop s. tienda, comercio; *intr.* ir de compras.

shopwindow s. escaparate; vidriera.

shore s. orilla, costa, playa.

short *adj.* corto, pequeño; *adv.* brevemente; secamente.

shortage s. escasez.

shorten *tr.* acortar, reducir.

shorthand s. taquigrafía.

shortly *adv.* en breve.

shoulder s. hombro; codo; *intr.* echarse sobre las espaldas.

shout s. grito, exclamación; *tr. e intr.* gritar, vocear.

shove s. empujón; *tr. e intr.* empujar.

shovel s. pala; *tr.* mover con palas.

show s. presentación, exhibición; *tr.* mostrar, enseñar; *intr.* mostrarse, aparecer.

shower s. el que muestra o exhibe.

shower s. chubasco, chaparrón; *tr.* regar, mojar; *intr.* llover, caer chubascos.

showy *adj.* vistoso, ostentoso.

shred s. tira, trozo largo; *tr.* hacer tiras.

shrewish *adj.* regañón.

shrill *adj.* agudo, penetrante; *tr e intr.* chillar.

shrine s. urna, relicario.

shrivel *tr.* arrugar, fruncir; *intr.* arrugarse.

shroud s. mortaja, sudario; *tr.* amortajar.

shrub s. arbusto.

shrug *tr e in.* encoger los hombros.

shuck s. cáscara, exterior; *tr.* descascarar.

shun *tr.* huir, rehuir.

shut *adj.* cerrado; *tr.* cerrar.

shy *adj.* timido, vergonzoso,cauteloso; *intr.* hacerse a un lado, retroceder.

sick *adj.* enfermo, indispuesto.

sicken *tr.* enfermar, cansar.

sickliness s. indisposición.

sideboard s. aparador, bufete.

sidelong *adj.* oblicuo, inclinado.

sidewalk s. acera, andén.

sideward *adv.* de lado.

siege s. sitio, asedio.

sieve s. tamiz; *tr.* cerner; criba.

sift *tr.* cerner, cribar; examinar minuciosamente.

sigh s. suspiro; *intr.* suspirar.

sight s. vista; vislumbre; *tr.* avistar, vislumbrar.

sightless *adj.* ciego.

sign s. signo; señal; *tr.* firmar, suscribir.

signalize *tr.* señalar, distinguir.

signature s. firma, rúbrica.

signify *tr.* significar; indicar.

silence s. silencio; *tr.* imponer silencio a, hacer callar.

silk s. seda; *pl.* sedería, géneros de seda.

sill s. umbral de puerta.

silliness s. tontería.

silver s. plata; *adj.* de plata; *tr.* platear; blanquear.

silversmith *sm.* joyero.

simmer *tr.* hacer cocer a fuego lento; *intr.* hervir con poco fuego.

simp s. bobo, mentecato.

simper s. sonrisa tonta.

simple *adj.* simple, sencillo; s. simple, simplón.

simplify *tr.* simplificar.

sin s. pecado, culpa; *intr.* pecar; *tr.* cometer *(un pecado)*.

since *prep.* desde, después de; *adv.* desde entonces; *cnj.* desde que.

sinew s. (An.) tendón; energía; *tr.* fortalecer.

S

sing *tr. e intr.* cantar; *intr.* murmurar; sumbar.

singe *s.* chamusco; *tr.* chamuscar.

singer *s.* cantante.

single *adj.* sólo, único; soltero; *tr.* singularizar, escoger.

singsong *s.* cadencia uniforme; *adj.* monótono.

sinister *adj.* izquierdo, siniestro.

sinless *adj.* puro, libre de pecado.

sinner *s.* pecador.

sinous *adj.* sinuoso; tortuoso.

sir *s.* señor, caballero.

sire *s.* señor, padre, abuelo.

siren *s.* (Ant.), (Fís.) (fig.) sirena.

sirloin *s.* solomillo.

sister *s.* hermana; sor.

sisterhood *s.* hermandad, comunidad de monjas.

sit *tr.* sentar; empollar *(huevos)*; cabalgar; *intr.* sentarse.

site *s.* sitio, lugar.

sitting *s.* asentada, sentada.

situate *tr.* situar.

six *adj. y s.* seis; —o'clock las seis.

sixpence *s.* moneda de medio chelín.

sixteen *adj. y s.* dieciséis.

sixty *adj. y s.* sesenta.

size *s.* medida, tamaño; talla; *tr.* disponer o clasificar según tamaño.

skate *s.* patín; *intr.* patinar.

skeleton *s.* esqueleto, osamenta.

sketch *s.* boceto, esbozo; *tr.* esbozar.

skew *adj.* oblicuo, inclinado; *s.* oblicuidad; *tr.* sesgar, torcer; *intr.* tomar una dirección oblicua.

skid non — antideslizante; *intr.* patinar.

skill *s.* conocimiento práctico.

skilled *adj.* práctico.

skillful *adj.* hábil, mañoso.

skimpy *adj.* escaso, tacaño.

skip *s.* salto, brinco; *intr.* saltar, brincar.

skipper *s.* saltador, patrón.

skirt *s.* falda, saya; faldón; *tr e intr.* bordear, ladear; *tr.* escapar por poco a.

skit *s.* parodia; *intr.* asustarse; *tr.* denigrar, ridiculizar.

skulk *intr.* esconderse, andar escondido, *tr. . intr.* huir del cumplimiento del deber.

skull *s.* cráneo; calavera; cerebro.

sky *s.* cielo, firmamento.

skylark *s.* alondra.

slab *s.* tabla, plancha, losa; *tr.* cubrir de losas.

slack *adj.* flojo, débil, poco firme.

slacken *tr.* aflojar relajar.

slag *s.* escoria.

slake *tr.* apagar, extinguir.

slam *s.* portazo; *tr.* cerrar de golpe.

slander *s.* calumnia; *tr.* calumniar.

slang *s.* lenguaje vulgar.

slant *s.* sesgo, inclinación.

slap *s.* palmada, manotazo; *tr.* pegar, abofetear.

slash *s.* cuchillada; *tr.* acuchillar.

slate *s.* pizarra.

slaughter *s.* muerte, matanza; *tr.* matar, haver una carnicería.

slave *s.* esclavo; *tr.* esclavizar.

slavish *tr.* matar.

sledge *s.* trineo.

sleek *adj.* liso; *tr.* pulir.

sleep *s.* sueño; *intr.* dormir.

sleeper *s.* durmiente; traviesa; (U.S.) (f.c.) coche-cama.

sleet *s.* agua de nieve.

sleeve *s.* manga.

sleight *s.* destreza, habilidad.

slender *adj.* delgado, tenue.
slice *s.* rebanada, tajada; *tr.* rebanar.
slide *s.* deslizamiento; *intr.* resbalar, deslizarse.
slight *adj.* ligero, leve; pequeño; *tr.* despreciar, menospreciar.
slim *adj.* delgado, esbelto; *tr.* ponerse a régimen para adelgazar.
slimy *adj.* viscoso, limoso.
slipper *s.* zapatilla.
slit *s.* abertura, estrecha; *tr.* hender, rajar.
sloop *s.* (Náut.) balandro.
slop *s.* cuesta, ladera; 2*intr.* inclinarse; *tr.* inclinar.
slot *s.* hendedura, abertura.
sloth *s.* pereza, galbana.
sloven *adj.* desaseado.
slovenly *adj.* desaliñado.
sluggish *adj.* flojo, perezoso.
sluice *s.* acequia; *tr.* dar salida a.
slum *s.* barrio o calle miserable.
slumber *s.* sueño.
slump *s.* hundimiento; *intr.* hundirse; *tr.* dejar caer de golpe.
slur *s.* mancha, borrón; *tr.* manchar; *intr.* borrarse.
slut *s.* mujerzuela.
sly *adj.* astuto; travieso.
smack *s.* sabor; cachete; *intr. y tr.* chasquear el látigo.
small *adj.* pequeño; menudo.
smallpox *s.* (Med.) viruelas.
smashing *adj.* extraordinario.
smattering *s.* barniz.
smeary *adj.* graso.
smell *s.* olfato, olor; *tr.* oler.
smelt *tr.* fundir.
smile *s.* sonrisa; *intr.* sonreírse.
smite *tr.* golpear, herir; *intr.* dar golpes.
smith *s.* forjador, herrero.
smock *s.* camisa, bata.

smoke *s.* humo; *adj.* de humo.
smoking *s.* acción de fumar; *adj.* humeante; de fumar.
smooth *adj.* liso, llano; *tr.* alisar; allanar.
smother *s.* humareda; *tr.* sofocar, ahogar; *intr.* ahogarse.
smug *adj.* pulido; satisfecho.
smuggle *tr.* pasar de contrabando.
smut *s.* suciedad, mancha; *tr.* ensuciar, manchar.
snack *s.* porción, parte; sorbo.
snag *s.* nudo *(en la madera)*; tronco flotante.
snail *s.* (Zool.) caracol.
snake *s.* (Zool.) culebra, serpiente.
snappy *adj.* chispeante; vivo.
snapshot *s.* (Fot.) instantánea; *tr. e intr.* hacer una instanánea.
snare *s.* lazo, trampa; *tr.* atrapar, coger en un lazo.
snarl *s.* gruñido; regañar; gruñir.
sneeze *s.* estornudo.
snip *s.* incisión, corte; *tr.* cortar, recortar.
sniper *s.* buen tirador.
snivel *s.* moco.
snort *s.* resoplido, bufido.
snout *s.* trompa *(de elefante)*.
snow *s.* nieve.
snub *s.* repulsa, desaire; *tr.* reprender.
snuffle *s.* inspiración ruidosa por la nariz; *intr.* respirar con la nariz obstruida.
snug *adj.* cómodo, abrigado.
snuggle *intr. y tr.* arrimar.
soak *s.* remojo; *tr.* empapar, calar; *intr.* empaparse.
soap *s.* jabón; *tr.* enjabonar, dar jabón, adular.
soar *s.* vuelo, remonte; *tr.* elevarse; *intr.* elevarse.
sob *s.* sollozo; *intr.* sollozar.
sober *adj.* sobrio, moderado.

S

sock *s.* calcetín.
socket *s.* hueco en que encaja una cosa.
sodden *adj.* mojado, empapado; *tr.* mojar, empapar.
soever *adv.* por mucho, por más que sea.
soft *adj.* blando, dúctil.
soften *tr.* ablandar, reblandecer; *intr.* ablandarse, reblandecerse.
softness *s.* blandura, ductilidad.
soggy *adj.* mojado, hecho una sopa.
soil *s.* tierra, terreno, suelo; *tr.* ensuciar, manchar.
soiree *s.* reunión nocturna.
sojourn *s.* estancia; *intr.* estar, permanecer.
solace *s.* consuelo, alivio; *tr.* consolar, confortar.
solder *s.* soldadura; *tr.* soldar, estañar.
soldiery *s.* profesión o ejercicio militar.
solemnize *tr.* solemnizar.
solicit *tr.* solicitar, pedir.
solicitor *s.* (Der.) abogado; agente, corredor.
solid *adj.* sólido, macizo.
solidify *tr.* sodificar; consolidar.
solidity *s.* solidez; consistencia.
solitude *s.* soledad.
solve *tr.* resolver, aclarar.
sombre *s.* sombrío.
someone *s.* alguien.
somersault *s.* salto mortal; *intr.* dar un salto mortal.
something algo, alguna cosa.
sometime *adv.* algún día.
sometimes *adv.* algunas veces, a veces.
somewhat *s.* algo, alguna cosa, una parte; *adv.* algo.
somewhere *adv.* en alguna parte.

son *s.* hijo.
song *s.* canto; copla, poesía.
sonorous *adj.* sonoro; armonioso.
soon *adv.* pronto, presto.
soot *s.* hollín, tizne; *tr.* cubrir de hollín.
soothe *tr.* aliviar, suavizar; tranquilizar.
soothsayer *s.* adivino.
sorcerer *s.* hechicero.
sordid *adj.* interesado; bajo, vil.
sore *adj.* penoso, doloroso, delicado; *s.* úlcera, disgusto.
sorrow *s.* dolor, pesar; *intr.* disgusto.
sorrowful *adj.* afligido, pesaroso.
sorry *adj.* afligido.
sort *s.* clase, especie; *tr.* ordenar, arreglar.
soul *s.* alma, espíritu.
soup *s.* sopa.
sour *adj.* ácido, agrio; *tr e in.* agriar. avinagrar; cortarse *(la leche)*.
source *s.* origen, causa.
south *s.* sur.
southeast *adj. y s.* sudeste.
southwest *adj. y s.3* sudoeste.
souvenir *s.* recuerdo.
sovereign *adj.* soberano.
sow *tr.* sembrar, esparcir.
soy *s.* (Bot.) soja.
spa *s.* balneario.
spade *s.* pala, azada.
span *s.* palmo, extensión.
Spaniard *s.* español, hispano.
Spanish *adj.* español, hispano, hispánico; *s.* lengua española, castellano *(el idioma)*.
spare *adj.* de reserva, de recambio.
sparing *adj.* escaso, parco.
spark *s.* chispa; centella; *intr.* chispear.
sparrow *s.* (Zool.) gorrión, pardal.

sparse *adj.* esparcido, esparramado.

spasm *s.* (Med.) espasmo.

spate *s.* aguacero, chaparrón; *tr.* inundar.

spatter *s.* salpicadura; chapoteo; *tr.* salpicar, rociar.

speak *intr.* hablar; *tr.* pronunciar; proferir.

speaker *s.* orador, locutor.

spear *s.* lanza, arpón; *tr.* atravesar con arpón.

specialize *tr.* especializar; detallar.

specie *s.* efectivo, metálico; *pl.* especie.

specific, -al *adj.* específico.

specify *tr.* especificar.

specimen *s.* muestra, ejemplar.

speck, speckle *s.* manchita; *tr.* manchar.

specs *s. pl.* (fam.) gafas.

spectacle *s.* espectáculo.

spectator *s.* espectador.

speculate *intr.* especular.

speech *s.* palabra, habla; idioma, dialecto;

speechless *adj.* sin habla, mudo.

speed *s.* rapidez, prontitud; *tr.* acelerar, dar prisa.

speedy *adj.* ligero, rápido.

spell *s.* hechizo, encanto; *tr.* hechizar, encantar.

spellbind *tr.* hechizar, encantar.

spend *tr.* gastar, consumir.

spendthrift *adj.* derrochador.

spew *tr. e intr.* vomitar.

sphere *s.* esfera.

spick-and-span *adj.* nuevo, reciente.

spicy *adj.* sazonado con especias.

spider *s.* (Zool.) araña.

spike *s.* pincho, púa; *tr.* clavar.

spiky *adj.* puntiagudo.

spill *s.* vuelco; *tr e in.* verter, derramar.

spin *tr. e intr.* hilar; *tr.* tejer; *intr.* rodar.

spinach *s.* (Bot.) espinaca.

spindrift *s.* rocío.

spineless *adj.* invertebrado.

spinster *s.* solterona.

spire *s.* (Arq.) aruja.

spirit *s.* espíritu; aparición.

spirited *adj.* vivo, brioso.

spirt *s.* chorro, surtidor; *tr.* arrojar a chorro.

spit *s.* saliva; *tr.* escupir; echar.

spiteful *adj.* rencoroso, maligno.

splattered *adj.* estrellado.

splay *s.* entensión, *tr.* extender.

spleen *s.* (An.) bazo; bilis.

splendo(u)r *s.* brillo, resplandor.

splint *s.* astilla; tablilla; *tr.* entablillar.

splinter *s.* astilla, raja; cacho; *tr.* hacer astillas.

split *s.* hendedura; división, cisma; *adj.* hendido; *tr.* hender, partir.

splotch *s.* mancha; *tr.* hender, partir.

splotch *s.* mancha; *tr.* manchar, salpicar.

spokesman *s.* portavoz.

sponsor *s.* fiador, patrocinador.

spool *s.* carrette, bobina.

sporting *adj.* deportivo.

spotless *adj.* limpio, sin mancha.

spotlight *s.* reflector *(de teatros)*.

spout *s.* caño, tubo *tr.* echar, arrojar; *intr.* chorrear, borbotar.

sprain *s.* (Med.) torcedura; *tr.* (Med.) torcer, distender.

sprawl *intr.* yacer, caer; *tr.* abrir, extender.

spray *s.* líquido pulverizado; *tr.* rociar.

S

sprinkle *tr.* rociar, salpicar.
sprite *s.* duende, hada.
spud *s. pl.* patatas.
spur *s.* espuela; aguijón; *tr.* picar; aguijar.
spurn *tr. e intr.* despreciar.
spurt *s.* chorro, borbotón.
spy *s.* espía; *tr.* espiar, acechar.
squall *s.* racha, chubasco; *intr. y tr.* chillar.
squalor *s.* suciedad, miseria.
squander *tr.* malgastar, despilfarrar.
squash *s.* calabaza; pulpa; *tr.* aplastar, machacar.
squat *adj.* sentado en cuclillas; *intr.* agacharse.
squatty *adj.* regordete.
squeal *s.* chillido; *intr.* chillar.
squeamish *adj.* delicado, escrupuloso.
squeeze *s.* apretón, abrazo estrecho; *tr.* apretar, exprimir.
squire *s.* escudero; (Ingl.) hacendado; (U.S.) juez de paz.
squirm *intr.* retorcerse.
squirrel *s.* (Zool.) ardilla.
stab *s.* puñalada; *tr.* dar puñaladas.
stabilize *tr.* estabilizar.
stack *s.* pila, montón; *tr.* apilar.
staff *s.* palo, pértiga; *tr.* proveer de personal.
stag *s.* (Zool.) ciervo.
stage *s.* (Tr.) escenario, tablas; *tr.* exhibir al público.
stagger *intr.* hacer eses.
stagnate *intr.* estancarse, detenerse.
staid *adj.* grave, serio.
stainless *adj.* limpio.
stair *s.* escalón, peldaño; *pl.* escalera.
stake *s.* estaca, hoguera; *tr.* estacar; apostar, aventurar.
stale *adj.* pasado; viejo.

stalk *s.* (Bot.) tallo, caña; *tr.* cazar al acecho.
stallion *s.* semental.
stalwart *adj.* fornido.
stamina *s.* vitalidad.
stamp *s.* estampa, huella; *tr.* estampar, sellar.
stampede *s.* huída en desorden; *tr.* ahuyentar.
stanch *tr.* estancar.
stand *s.* situación, posición; *intr.* ponerse en pie, levantarse; *tr.* sufrir, tolerar; soportar; resistir.
standard *s.* norma, criterio; nivel, medida *(normales)*.
standpoint *s.* punto de vista.
standstill *s.* alto, descanso.
staple *s.* grapa; *tr.* sujetar *(papeles)* con grapa.
star *s.* estrella, lucero; *tr.* sembrar; marcar con asterisco; *intr.* brillar.
starboard *s.* (Náut.) estribor; *adj.* de estribor.
starch *s.* almidón; *tr.* almidonar.
stare *s.* mirada fija.
stark *adj.* tieso, rígido.
startle *tr.* asustar; *intr.* sobresaltarse.
starvation *s.* hambre.
starve *intr.* morir de hambre; *tr.* matar de hambre.
state *s.* estado, situación; *tr.* exponer, declarar.
stated *adj.* estblecido.
statement *s.* declaración, manifestación.
statesman *s.* estadista.
station *s.* estación; *tr.* estacionar, situar.
stationery *s.* papelería; artículos de escritorio.
statistics *s.* estadística.
statue *s.* estatua, imagen.
stature *s.* estatua, talla.
status *s.* estado legal.
statute 2s. ley decreto.
staunch *adj.* firme, constante.

stead s. sitio, servicio.
steadfast adj. firme.
steadiness s. estabilidad, seguridad.
steak s. bistec, filete.
steal s. hurto; tr. e intr. hurtar, robar.
stealth s. disimulo.
steam s. vapor; tr. evaporar.
steel s. acero; adj. de acero, siderúrgico; tr. acerar, endurecer.
steeple s. aguja, campanario.
steer s. novillo; tr. (Naut.) gobernar; dirigir; intr. navegar.
steerage s. gobierno, dirección.
steersman s. piloto, timonero.
stem s. (Bot.) tallo, tronco.
step s. paso; escalón; estribo; intr. dar un paso; correr; tr. poner, sentar, plantar.
sterile adj. estéril, infecundo.
stern adj. duro, vigoroso; s. popa (de un barco).
stew s. cocido; tr. estrofar, guisar.
steward s. mayordomo; administrador.
sticking-plaster s. esparadrapo.
sticky adj. pegajoso, tenaz.
stiff adj. rígido; duro, firme; almidonado.
stiffen tr. atiesar, dar rigidez; intr. ponerse tieso.
stiffness s. rigidez; tirantez.
stifle tr. ahogar, sofocar.
stigma s. estigma; mancha.
stillness s. quietud, inmovilidad.
stilt s. zanco; poste.
stimulate tr. estimular; incitar.
stingy adj. avaro, tacaño.
stink s. corrupción; intr. oler mal.
stipulate tr. estipular; especificar; intr. pactar.

stirrup s. estribo, pelda.o; adj. del estribo.
stitch s. puntada; intr. coser, bordar.
stockholder s. accionista.
stocking s. media, calceta.
stockist s. almacenista.
stoker s. fogonero.
stomach s. (An.) estómago; ánimo.
stonework s. obra de sillería; mampostería.
stony s. taburete.
stoop intr. agacharse; inclinarse.
stop s. alto, parada; (Gram.) punto; tr. detener, parar; intr. pararse, detenerse.
stoppage s. detención.
stopper s. tapón, estorbo.
store s. copia, abundancia; tesoro; tr. abastecer, proveer.
storehouse s. almacén.
storekeeper s. almacenero.
storey s. piso, planta.
stork s. (Zool.) cigüeña.
story (pl. -ries) historia; leyenda; (fam.) chisme.
stoup s. frasco, jarro.
stout adj. fuerte, recio, resistente.
stoutness s. fuerza, vigor.
stove s. estufa; cocina económica.
straggle intr. rodar, andar perdido.
straight adj. recto, derecho.
straighten tr. enderezar.
straightforward adj. recto; honrado.
straightway adv. inmediatemente.
strain s. tensión, torcedura; raza, linaje, descendencia; tr. extender; intr. esforzarse.
strainer s. colador, filtro.
strait adj. estrecho, angosto; s. estrecho; pasaje, canal.
straiten tr. estrechar.

S

strange *adj.* extraño, raro.
stranger *s.* extraño, extranjero.
stangle *tr.* estrangular, asfixiar.
strap *s.* correa.
stratum *s.* (Geol.) (An.) estrato; capa.
straw *s.* paja.
strawberry *s.* (Bot.) fresa.
stray *adj.* descarriado, *intr.* desviarse.
streak *s.* raya, línea; *tr.* rayar, listar; *intr.* ir como un rayo.
stream *s.* corriente; rio; *intr.* correr, fluir; *tr.* verter, derramar.
street *s.* calle, vía pública.
strength *s.* fuerza, energía.
stress *s.* fuerza; peso; *tr.* cargar, dar importancia.
stricken *adj.* golpeado, herido.
strict *adj.* estricto, absoluto.
stride *s.* paso largo, tranco; *intr.* andar a trancos.
strife *s.* disputa, contienda.
strike *s.* golpe; huelga; *tr. e in.* golpear.
striking *adj.* relevante, chocante.
string *s.* cordón, cinta.
stringent *adj.* convincente.
strip *s.* tira, lista, faja; *tr. e in.* despojar.
stripe *s.* raya, lista.
strive *intr.* esforzarse, hacer todo lo posible.
stroll *s.* paseo, vuelta; *intr.* callejear.
strong *adj.* fuerte; robusto; grande, poderoso.
struck *adj.* herido, afectado.
struggle *s.* esfuerzo, lucha; *intr.* luchar, bregar.
strumpet *s.* ramera, prostituta.
strut *s.* manera de andar; *intr.* andar con aire orgulloso.
stub *s.* cepa; persona rechoncha.
stubborn *adj.* obstinado, terco.

stuck-up *adj.* (fam.) tieso, estirado.
stud *s.* poste, montante *(de tabique)*; *tr.* tachonar, clavetear.
student *s.* estudiante.
studio *s.* estudio, taller.
study *s.* estudio; despacho, gabinete de trabajo; *tr. e intr.* estudiar; meditar.
stuffy *adj.* mal ventilado; restriado; (fam.) soso.
stumble *s.* tropiezo, tropezón.
stun *s.* aturdimiento; *tr.* aturdir.
stupefy *tr.* causar estupor; *intr.* atontarse.
stupendous *adj.* estupendo.
sturdiness *s.* robustez, fuerza.
sturdy *adj.* robusto, fornido.
stutter *s.* tartamudeo; *intr.* tartamudear.
sty *s.* pocilga.
style *s.* estilo; título; *tr.* llamar, nombrar.
stylish *adj.* elegante.
suave *adj.* suave, afable.
subdue *tr.* sojuzgar, someter.
subject *adj.* sometido, dominado; *s.* súbdito; sujeto.
subject *tr.* sujetar, someter.
subjection *s.* sometimiento.
subjugate *tr.* subyugar, dominar.
subjective *adj. y s.* (Gram.) subjuntivo.
submerge *tr.* sumergir, hundir; *intr.* sumergirse.
submit *tr.* someter, remitir; *intr. y ref.* someterse, rendirse.
subordinate *tr.* subordinar.
suborn *tr.* sobornar, cohechar.
subscribe *tr.* subsistir, firmar.
subscription *s.* firma.
subside *intr.* menguar, disminuir.
subsidence *s.* hundimiento, descenso.
subsidize *tr.* subvencionar.

subsist *intr.* subsistir; existir.
substantial *adj.* sustancia; verdadero.
substantiate *tr.* probar, establecer.
subtility *s.* sutileza.
subtle *adj.* sutil, raro, fino; apto, hábil.
subtract *tr.* sustraer; restar.
suburb *s.* suburbio; *pl.* periferia.
subway *s.* paso o conducto subterráneo; (U.S.) ferrocarril metropolitano.
succeed *intr.* suceder; tener éxito.
success *s.* éxito, fortuna.
successful *adj.* próspero, dichoso.
succor *s.* socorro, auxilio; *tr.* socorrer, asistir.
such *adj.* tal, semejante.
suchlike *adj.* tal, semejante.
suck *s.* chupada, mamada; *tr. intr.* chupar.
suckle *tr.* amamantar; *intr.* mamar.
suddenly *adv.* de repente.
suddenness *s.* precipitación.
suds *s. pl.* jabonaduras; espuma.
sue *tr. e intr.* demandar, poner pleito.
suffer *tr. e intr.* sufrir, padecer.
suffice *intr.* bastar, ser suficiente.
sufficiency *s.* suficiencia.
suffrage *s.* sufragio, voto.
suffuse *tr.* bañar, cubrir.
sugar *s.* azúcar; *tr.* azucarar, confitar.
suggest *tr.* sugerir, insinuar.
suicide *s.* suicidio.
suit *s.* solicitación, súplica; *tr. e intr.* convenir, acomodar; contener.
suitable *adj.* propio, conveniente.
suiting *s.* tela para trajes.
suitcase *s.* maleta.

suite *s.* serie, séquito, tren.
suitor *.s.* (Der.) demandante.
sullen *adj.* hosco, arisco.
sully *s.* mancha, mancilla; *tr.* manchar, ensuciar.
sulphur *s.* azufre; (poét) trueno, rayo.
sultry *adj.* bochornoso.
sum *s.* (Mat.) suma, adición; *tr.* sumar.
summarize *tr.* resumir.
summer *s.* verano, estío; *intr.* veranear.
summit *s.* cúspide, cima.
summon *tr.* llamar; requerir, convacar.
sun *s.* sol.
sunbeam *s.* rayo de sol.
sunburning *s.* quemadura del sol.
Sunday *s.* domingo; *adj.* del domingo.
sundries *s. pl.* (Com) varios, géreros diversos.
sunflower *s.* girasol.
sunny *adj.* soleado, lleno de sol.
sunrise *s.* amanecer.
sunset *s.* ocaso, puesta del sol; atardecer.
sunshade *s.* parasol, sombrilla.
sunshine *s.* sol *(luz o calor del sol).*
sup *s.* sorbo; *intr. y tr.* dar de cenar; beber.
superb *adj.* soberbio, magnífico.
superintend *tr.* vigilar, dirigir.
superior *adj. y s.* superior, rector.
superiority *s.* (*pl.* -ties) supremacía.
supersede *tr.* reemplazar.
supervise *tr.* inspeccionar, intervenir.
supervision *s.* inspección, revisión.
supervisor *s.* inspector, interventor.

S

supper s. cena; *intr.* cenar,
dar de cenar.

supplant *tr.* suplantar.

supple *adj.* suave, flexible.

supplicate *tr. e intr.* suplicar,
pedir.

supplier s. suministrador,
proveedor.

support s. soporte, apoyo,
ayuda; *tr.* soportar,
sostener.

supporter s. mantenedor,
soportador.

suppose *tr.* suponer, dar por
sentado.

suppress *tr.* suprimir; omitir.

suppression s. supresión,
omisión.

supreme *adj.* supremo, sumo.

surcharge s. sobrecarga.

sure *adj.* seguro; cierto; *adv.*
ciertamente.

surf s. marejada, resaca.

surface s. superficie; cara.

surfeit s. exceso; empacho;
tr. hartar, saciar.

surge s. ola, oleada.

surgeon s. cirujano; médico
(del ejército).

surgery s. cirugía; clinica.

surgy *adj.* agitado.

surmount *tr.* vencer; coronar.

surname s. apellido; *tr.*
apellidar.

surpass *tr.* sobrepujar,
aventajar.

surpassing *adj.* superior,
excelente.

surplus s. sobrante, exceso.

surprise s. sorpresa; *tr.*
sorprender.

surreptitious *adj.* subrepticio.

surround *tr.* rodear, cercar.

survey s. medición, estudio.

survey *tr.* medir, levantar.

survive *tr.*sobrevivir.

suspect *tr.* sospechar, recelar.

suspend *tr.* suspender, colgar.

suspense s. suspenión,
interrupción.

suspicion s. sospecha; recelo.

sustain *tr.* sostener, aguantar.

suzerain s. soberano.

swallow s. bocado, trago;
(Zool.) golondrina; *tr.* tragar.

swan s. (Zool.) cisne.

sward *c.* césped.

swarm s. enjambre; *intr.*
enjambrar.

swath s. faja, venda; *pl.*
pañales.

sway s. oscilación, vaivén;
intr. oscilar, mecerse.

swear *intr.* jurar.

sweat s. sudor; *tr. e intr.* sudar.

sweep s. barredura;
barrendero; *tr.* barrer.

sweet *adj.* dulce, azucarado;
s. dulzura; *pl.* dulces
golosinas.

sweeten *tr.* endulzar.

sweetheart s. novia,
prometida.

swift *adj.* veloz, rápido.

swim s. nadar, nado; *intr.*
nadar; flotar.

swimmer s. nadador.

swindle *tr.* estafar, timar.

swine *s sing. y pl.* (Zool.)
cerdo, marrano.

swing s. balanceo, oscilación;
tr. e in. balancear, mecer.

swirl s. remolino; *tr.* hacer
girar; *intr.* arremolinar.

switch s. vara flexible; *adj.*
agujas de cambio; *tr.* azotar.

switchboard s. cuadro de
mandos.

swollen *adj.* hinchado;
crecido *(río, etcétera).*

sword s. espada.

syllable s. sílaba.

syllabus s. sumario,
compendio.

symbol s. símbolo; signo.

symbolise *tr.* simbolizar.

sympathise *intr.* simpatizar;
compadecerse.

sympton s. síntoma.

table 117 **technique**

T

table *s.* mesa; tabla, indice; *tr.* poner sobre la mesa; dejar un asunto.

tablet *s.* tableta, pastilla, comprimido; placa, lápida.

taboo *s.* tabú.

tackle *s.* equipo, avíos; *tr.* asir, agarrar.

tact *s.* tacto, discreción.

tactful *adj.* discreto, diplomático.

tactics *s.* táctica.

tadpole *s.* (Zool.) renacuajo.

tag *s.* etiqueta; *tr.* poner membrete o etiqueta.

tail *s.* cola; fila.

tailor *s.* sastre.

taint *s.* mancha; *tr. e in.* manchar.

taking *s.* tomar, entrada en posesión; *adj.* atractivo, encantador; *s. pl.* ingresos.

tale *s.* cuento, fábula.

talk *s.* habla, charla; *tr. e intr.* hablar; decir.

tall *adj.* alto; exagerado.

tallow *s.* sebo; *tr.* ensebar.

tally *s.* cuenta; etiqueta; *tr. e in.* llevar la cuenta; marcar.

talon *s.* garra.

tambourine *s.* pandereta.

tame *adj.* manso, sumiso, dócil; *tr.* domar, domesticar.

tamer *s.* domador.

tamper *s.* apisonador; *intr.* entremeterse; sobornar.

tan *s.* casca *(para curtir)* ; color de tostado; *tr.* curtir, adobar.

tang *s.* sabor fuerte y picante.

tangle *s.* enredo, embrollo; *tr.* enredar.

tank *s.* tanque, depósito.

tankard *s.* jarro con tapa y asa.

tanker (Náut.) buque cisterna.

tantalize *tr.* atormentar.

tantamount *adj.* equivalente.

tap *s.* grifo, ca o; palmadita; *tr.* sangrar *(un árbol); abrir un agujero.*

tape *s.* cinta; *tr.* atar con cinta; medir con cinta.

taper *s.* cerilla, velilla; *tr.* disminuir, afilar.

tapestry *s.* tapiz; *tr.* tapizar.

tapeworm *s.* tenia, solitaria.

tar *s.* brea, alquitrán; *tr.* alquitranar.

tardy *adj.* tardío, lento.

target *s.* blanco, objetivo.

tarry *adj.* alquitranado, embreado; *tr.* esperar; *intr.* esperar; tardar.

tart *s.* tarta; *adj.* agrio.

task *s.* tarea, labor; *tr.* atarear; abrumar *(con trabajo)* .

tassel *s.* borla.

taste *s.* gusto, sabor; *tr.* gustar, saborear; *intr.* tener cierto sabor.

tasteful *adj.* de buen gusto.

tasteless *adj.* de mal gusto.

tattoo *s.* tatuaje; *tr.* tatuar; *intr.* tocar retreta.

taunt *s.* mofa, pulla; *tr.* provocar con insultos.

taut *adj.* tirante, tieso.

tavern *s.* taberna; mesón.

tawdry *adj.* charro, llamativo.

tax *s.* contribución, tributo; *tr.* poner impuestos; *pl.* gastos de aduana.

tea *s.* (Bot.) té.

teach *tr. e intr.* enseñar.

teacher *s.* maestro, profesor.

teaching *adj.* docente; *s.* enseñanza.

team *s.* yunta *(de bueyes)* ; equipo; *tr.* enganchar, unir.

tear *s.* lágrima.

tease *s.* aburrimiento, broma continua; *tr.* molestar, importunar.

teat *s.* pezón; teta.

technique *s.* técnica.

T

teddybear s. oso de juguete.
teddy boy s. gamberro.
teem intr. abundar; (fam.) llover a cántaros.
teen-ager s. joven de trece a diecinueve años de edad.
teeth s. pl. de **tooth** dientes.
tell tr. decir; contar; distinguir; intr. hablar; (fam.) denunciar, delatar.
temper s. temple; genio.
temporary adj. temporal, provisional, interino.
tempt tr. tentar; inducir.
ten adj. y s. diez.
tenable adj. defendible.
tenacity adj. tenacidad, tesón.
tenant s. arrendatario, inquilino.
tend tr. cuidar, vigilar; intr. tender.
tender s. oferta; adj. tierno, afable; tr. ofrecer, proponer.
tenderness s. ternura, sensibilidad.
tenement s. habitación.
tenet s. credo, dogma.
tense adj. tirante; s. (Gram.) tiempo.
tension s. tensión, esfuerzo mental.
tent s. tienda; tr. acampar bajo tiendas.
tenuous adj. tenue; raro.
tepid adj. tibio, templado.
terminate tr. e intr. terminar.
termite s. termita, hormiga.
terrace s. terraplén; terraza.
terrain s. terreno.
terrify tr. aterrorizar, espantar.
terse adj. breve.
test s. prueba, ensayo; tr. probar; examinar.
testify tr. e intr. testificar.
tether s. traba, maniobra.
than cnj. que; de.
thank tr. agradecer, dar las gracias a; s. pl. gracias.
thankful adj. agradecido.
thankless adj. ingrato.

thanksgiving s. acción de gracias.
thatch s. paja, techo de paja; tr. cubrir de paja.
thaw s. deshielo; tr. e intr. deshelar.
the art. def. el, la, los, las, lo; adv. cuanto.
theft s. hurto, robo.
their adj. pos. su, sus (de ellos, de ellas).
them pron. pers. los, las, les, ellos, ellas.
themselves pron. pers. ellos mismos; se; sí, sí mismos.
then adv. entonces; después, luego; además.
thence adv. desde allí; desde entonces.
thenceforth adv. de allí en adelante.
there adv. ahí, allí, allá; inj. ¡eso es!
thereabout adv. por ahí, por allí.
thereafter adv. después de eso, de allí en adelante.
thereby adv. con eso, con lo cual; así; por allícerca.
therefor, therefore adv. por lo tanto, por consiguiente.
theretofore adv. hasta entonces.
thereupon adv. sobre eso, encima de eso; por eso; por consiguiente; desde luego.
therewith adv. con esto.
these adj. dem. pl. **this**; estos, estas; pron. dem. éstos, éstas.
thews s.pl. músculos.
they pron. pers. ellos, ellas.
thick adj. espeso, grueso; s. espesor, grueso.
thicken tr. e intr. espesar.
thickest s. espesura, soto, matorral.
thief s. ladrón.
thigh s. (An.) muslo.
thighbone s. (An.) fémur.

thimble s. dedal.
thin adj. delgado; tr. adelgazar.
thing s. cosa.
think tr. pensar; creer, estimar; intr. pensar.
thinness s. delgadez.
third adj. tercero; s. tercero; tercera parte, tercio.
thirst s. sed; intr. tener sed.
thirsty adj. sediento.
thirteen adj. y s. trece.
thirty adj. treinta; s. (pl. -ties) treinta.
this adj. dem. (pl. these) este, esta, esto; pron. dem. éste, ésta, ésto; adv. tan.
thither adv. allá, hacia allá.
thong s. correa.
thorn s. espina, púa.
thoroughfare s. carretera.
though adv. sin embargo; cnj. aun cuando, aunque.
thought s. pensamiento.
thoughtless adj. irreflexivo.
thousand adj. y s. mil.
thrash tr. e in. trillar; azotar.
thrashing s. trilla; (vul.) paliza.
thread s. hilo, fibra, tr. enhebrar.
threaten tr. e intr. amenazar.
three adj. y s. tres.
threepence s. moneda de tres peniques.
threshold s. umbral.
thrice adv. tres veces.
thrift s. economía.
thrill s. emoción, exaltación; tr. e in. emocionar; estremecerse.
thriller s. persona o cosa emocionante.
thrive intr. prosperar, adelantar.
throat s. garganta.
throb s. latido, palpitación; intr. latir, palpitar.
throe s. dolor, congoja.
throne s. trono.

throng s. gentío, tropel; tr. e in. apretar, atestar.
throttle s. garganta; acelerador (de automóvil); tr. ahogar, sofocar.
through adj. de paso; directo; adv. a través de, un lado a otro; prep. por, a través de; mediante.
throughout adv. en todas partes; por todars partes; por todas partes; prep. en todo; durante todo.
throw s. tirada, lance; riesgo; tr. lanzar, disparar.
thrust s. empuje; acometida; pu alada; tr. e in. empujar; acometer; atravesar; hincar.
thug s. malhechor, ladrón.
thumb s. pulgar, dedo gordo.
thump s. golpazo, porrazo; tr. golpear, aporrear; intr. dar un porrazo.
thunder s. trueno; estruendo; tr. fulminar (censuras, etc.) intr. tronar.
Thursday s. jueves.
thus adv. así, tal; de este modo.
thwart s. riestra; adj. transversal; adv. de través; tr. desbaratar; frustrar.
thyme s. (Bot.) tomillo.
ticket s. billete, entrada; tr. rotular, marcar.
tickle s. cosquillas; tr. hacer cosquillas.
tidbit s. buen bocado.
tide s. (Naút.) marea; temporada; tr. llevar.
tidings s. pl. noticias, informes.
tier s. fila; tr. apilar.
tight adj. apretado, estrecho.
tighten tr. apretar; estirar; intr. apretarse.
tightness s. tensión, tirantez.
tile s. azulejo; baldosa; tr. azulejar.

T

till *s.* cajón o gaveta del dinero; *prep.* hasta; *cnj.* hasta que; *tr.* labrar.

tiller *s.* agricultor.

tilt *s.* inclinación; *tr.* inclinar, volcar.

tilth *s.* labranza.

timber *s.* madera *(de construcción)* .

timeless *adj.* eterno, infinito.

timid *adj.* tímido, temeroso.

tin *s.* estaño, hojalata; *tr.* estañar, enlatar.

tincture *s.* tinte, baño; *tr.* teñir.

tinder *s.* yesca, mecha.

tinge *s.* matiz, tinte; *tr.* colorear, teñir.

tingle *s.* comezón; *tr.* producir comezón u hormigueo a.

tinker *s.* calderero remendón; *tr.* remendar chapuceramente.

tinkle *s.* retintín; *tr. e in.* sonar.

tinwork *s.* hojalatería.

tiny *adj.* diminuto, menudo.

tipsy *adj.* cavilante; achispado.

tiptoe *s.* punta del pie; *intr.* andar de puntillas.

tiptop *s.* cumbre, cima; *adj.* (fam.) superior, excelente.

tire *s.* adorno; *tr.* cansar; *intr.* cansarse.

tireless *adj.* incansable.

tiresome *adj.* cansado, aburrido.

tithe *s.* décimo, diezmo.

title *s.* título, inscripción; *tr.* titular; roturar.

titter *s.* risita ahogada o disimulada; *intr.* reír con disimulo.

tittle-tattle *s.* charla, chismes; *intr.* chismorrear.

to *prep.* a, hacia; para; por; hasta.

toast *s.* tostada; *tr.* tostar; brindar.

today *adv. y s.* hoy.

toe *s.* dedo del pie; pezuña.

together *adv.* juntos; juntamente; a un tiempo.

toil *s.* afán, fatiga; *intr.* sudar, afanarse.

toilet *s.* tocador; utensilio de tocador.

token *s.* señal, símbolo.

tolerable *adj.* tolderable, llevadero.

tolerate *tr.* tolerar, aguantar.

toll *s.* tañido, doble de campanas; peaje; *tr.* cobrar o pagar como peaje.

tomato *s.* tomate.

tomb *s.* tumba.

tombstone *s.* lápida o piedra sepulcral.

tomcat *s.* gato.

tomorrow *adv. y s.* mañana.

ton *s.* tonelada.

tone *s.* tono; *tr.* entonar; *intr.* armonizar.

tongs *s. pl.* tenazas; pinzas.

tongue *s.* lengua, idioma.

tonight o **to-night** *adv. y s.* esta noche.

tonnage *s.* tonelaje.

tonsil *s.* amígdala.

too *adv.* también, además; demasiado.

tool *s.* utensilio, herramienta.

tooth *s.* diente, muela; *tr.* dentar; *intr.* endentar.

toothless *s.* palillo.

topic *s.* asunto, tema.

topple *tr.* derribar, volcar; *intr.* derribarse, volcarse.

torch *s.* antorcha, linterna.

torment *tr.* atormentar.

torpedo *s.* torpedo; *tr.* torpedear.

tortoise *s.* (Zool.) tortuga.

torture *s.* tortura; *tr.* torturar.

tory *s.* conservador.

toss-up *s.* cara y cruz.

total *adj. y s.* total, entero; *tr.* sumar; ascender.

totter *s.* tambaleo; *intr.* tambalearse.

touch s. toque; tacto; tr. tocar; conmover.

touching adj. conmovedor, enternecedor; prep. tocante a.

touchstone s. (Min.) y (fig.) piedra de toque.

touchwood s. yesca.

touchy adj. quisquilloso.

tough adj. duro; recio.

toughen tr. endurecer; dificultar; intr. endurecerse.

tour s. paseo, viaje largo, excursión.

touring s. turismo.

tournament s. torneo, campeonato.

tow s. remolque; estopa; tr. remolcar.

toward, towards prep. hacia; cerca de.

towel s. toalla.

tower s. torre; intr. encumbrarse, elevarse.

town s. ciudad, villa.

toy s. juguete; intr. jugar; divertirse.

trace s. rastro, pisada; tr. rastrear, seguir la pista de; atravesar.

tract s. espacio; trecho.

trade s. comercio, oficio; tr. trocar, cambiar; intr. negociar, comerciar.

trader s. comerciante, traficante.

traduce tr. calumniar, difamar.

traffic s. tráfico; intr. traficar.

trail s. huella; pista; tr. arrastrar, rastØear.

train s. tren; tr. adiestrar.

training s. instrucción, preparación.

trait s. rasgo, característrica.

tram s. trama; tranvía.

trample s. pisoteo; tr. atropellar, pisotear.

trance s. rapto, arrobamiento.

transact tr. tramitar.

transcend tr. exceder.

transfer s. traslado; transbordo.

transfix tr. traspasar.

transform tr. transformar, transfigurar.

transgress tr. violar, quebrantar.

transient adj. pasajero; s. transeúnte.

translate tr. traducir; cambiar.

translater s. traductor.

transmit tr. e intr. transmitir, traspasar.

transparency s. (pl. -cies) transparencia; dispositiva.

transport tr. transportar, deportar.

trap s. trampa; cepo; pl. equipaje; tr. atrapar.

trash s. broza; basura; tr. podar.

travel s. jiaje; intr. viajar, caminar.

traveller s. viajero.

traverse s. paso, pasaje; travesía; adj. transversal; tr. atravesar.

tray s. bandeja.

tread s. pisada; tr. pisar; pisotear; intr. andar, caminar.

treasure s. tesoro, caudal; tr. atesorar.

treble adj. triple; (Mús.) atiplado; s. (Mús.) triple; tr. triplicar.

tree s. árbol.

tremble intr. temblar.

trench s. foso, zanja; tr. excavar.

trenchant adj. agudo.

trend s. dirección, tendencia; intr. dirigirse, tender.

tress s. trenza, rizo.

trial s. ensayo, prueba.

triangle s. triángulo.

tribe s. tribu, casta.

trice s. tris, instante.

trick s. ma a, truco; *adj.*
  ingenioso; *tr.* burlar,
  engañar.
trickery s. malas mañas;
  fraude.
trickle *intr.* gotear.
tricky *adj.* tramposo.
trigger s. disparador.
trim s. adorno; aseo; *adj.*
  acicalado, compuesto; *tr.*
  ajustar, adaptar; adornar.
trimming s. guarnición,
  adorno.
trinket s. jije, joya.
tripe s.*pl.* callos.
triumph s. triunfo; *intr.* triunfar.
trolley s. tranvía; volquete.
troop s. tropa; (Mil.)
  escuadrón; *intr.* agruparse.
trooper s. soldado de
  caballería.
trot s. trote; paso vivo; *tr.*
  hacer trotar.
troth s. fe; verdad.
troublous *adj.* agitado,
  confuso.
trough s. artesa, pila.
trousers s. pl. pantalones.
trousseau s. ajuar, equipo de
  novia.
trout s. trucha.
truce s. tregua.
truck s. carro; camión; *tr.*
  tranportar.
trudge s. marcha; *intr.* viajar a
  pie.
true *adj.* verdadero; exacto.
trunk s. tronco; baul.
trustee s. administrator.
truth s. verdad, fidelidad.
try s. prueba, intento; *tr.*
  intentar, ensayar.
trying *adj.* penoso.
tube s. tubo.
tuck s. pliegue, alforza.
Tuesday s. Martes.
tuft s. copete, moño.
tumbler s. vaso, cubilete.
tun s. tonel, barril; *tr.* envasar.

tun s. tonada; armonía; *tr.*
  acordar, afinar; armonizar.
tunny s. (Zool.) atún.
turbid *adj.* turbio, borroso.
turbine s. turbina.
turkey s. (Zool.) pavo.
turmoil s. alboroto; tumulto.
turn s. vuelta; turno; *tr.* volver;
  dar vuelta a.
turning *adj.* giratorio,
  ratatorio; s. vuelta, rodeo.
turpitude s. torpeza.
turret s. torrecilla; (arq.)
  torreón.
turtle s. (Zool.) tortuga.
tusk s. colmillo *(del elefante)* ;
  tr. herir con los colmillos.
tussle s. agarrada, riña; *intr.*
  reñir.
twang s. tañido; timbre nasal;
  intr. producir un sonido
  agudo.
tweed s. mezcla de lana.
twelve *adj.* doce.
twenty *adj.* y s. veinte.
twice *adv.* dos veces; doble.
twin *adj.* y s. gemelo mellizo.
twine s. bramante; *tr.*
  enroscar.
twirl s. vuelta, giro; *tr.* torcer;
  retorcer; *intr.* torcerse;
  retorcerse.
two *adj.* y s. dos.
twofold s. doble, duplicado.
twopence s. moneda de dos
  peniques.
type s. tipo; letras impresas;
  tr. escribir a máquina.
typewriter s. máquina de
  escribir.
tyrannize *tr.* e *intr.* tiranizar.
tyre s. llanta, cubierta *(de
  ruedas de coche, etc.)* .
tyro s. novicio, novato.

U

udder *s.* ubre.
ugliness *s.* fealdad, afeamiento; (U.S.) mal genio.
ugly *adj.* feo, disforme.
ulcer *s.* (Pat.) úlcera.
umbrage *s.* sombra, umbría.
umbrella *s.* paraguas.
umpire *s.* árbitro, juez; *tr. e intr.* arbitrar.
unabashed *adj.* desvergonzado.
unable *adj.* incapaz, inhábil.
unacceptable *adj.* inaceptable.
unaccomplished *adj.* incompleto.
unaccountable *adj.* inexplicable.
unaccustomed *adj.* insólito.
unacquainted *adj.* ignorado.
unaffected *adj.* inafectado.
unanswerable *adj.* incontestable.
unarmed *adj.* desarmado.
unattached *adj.* suelto.
unauthorized *adj.* desautorizado.
unaware *adj.* inconsciente; *adv.* de improviso.
unawares *adv.* de improviso.
unbelievable *adj.* increíble.
unbending *adj.* inflexible.
unbind *tr.* desatar, desligar.
unbosom *tr.* confesar.
unbreakable *adj.* irrompible.
unbroken *adj.* intacto.
unburden *tr.* descargar.
unbutton *tr.* desabotonar.
uncanny *adj.* misterioso.
uncertain *adj.* incierto,dudoso.
uncertainty *s.* incertidumbre.
uncle *s.* tío.
unclean *adj.* sucio.
unclouded *adj.* despejado.
uncomfortable *adj.* incómodo.

uncompromising *adj.* inflexible.
unconcern *s.* indiferencia.
uncork *tr.* descorchar, destapar.
uncouple *tr.* desatraillar *(los perros)*; desconectar.
uncouth *adj.* tosco, rústico.
uncover *tr.* destapar, descubrir; *intr.* descubrirse.
unction *s.* unción; extremaunción.
uncultivated *adj.* baldío, silvestre.
undeceive *tr.* desengañar.
undecided *adj.* indeciso.
under *adj.* inferior; *adv.* debajo; *prep.* bajo; debajo de.
underclothes *s.* ropa interior.
underestimate *tr.* menospreciar.
underground *adj.* subterráneo;; secreto; *adv.* bajo tierra.
underlie *tr.* estar debajo de.
underline *tr.* subrayar.
underling *s.* inferior, subordinado.
undermine *tr.* socavar.
undermost *adj.* ínfimo; *adv.* debajo de todo.
underneath *s.* parte baja; *adj.* inferior; *adv.* debajo; *prep.* debajo de.
underpay *s.* pago insuficiente; *tr. e intr.* pagar insuficientemente.
underrate *tr.* menospreciar.
undersoil *s.* subsuelo.
understand *tr.* comprender, entender; *intr.* comprender.
undertake *tr.* emprender; compromenterse.
undertaking *s.* empresa; empeño.
undertone *s.* voz baja.
undervalue *tr.* estimar demasiado bajo.
underwater *adj.* submarino.

U

underwear s. ropa interior.
underwood s. maleza.
undeserved adj. inmerecido.
undesirable adj. y s. indeseable.
undigested adj. indigesto.
undo tr. deshacer; anular.
undoubted adj. indudable.
undress tr. desnudar.
uneasiness s. intranquilidad, desasosiego.
uneasy adj. intranquilo.
uneducated adj. ineducado, ignorante.
unending adj. inacabable.
unequal adj. desigual.
uneven adj. desnivelado.
unevennes s. desnivel.
unexpected adj. inesperado, fortuíto.
unfair adj. inicuo, injusto.
unfaithful adj. infiel.
unfesten tr. desatar, soldar.
unfeigned adj. sincero, real.
unfit adj. incapaz, inhábil; tr. inhabilitar.
unfold tr. e intr. desplegar.
unforeseen adj. imprevisto.
unfortunate adj. infeliz, desgraciado.
unfrequented adj. solitario.
unfriendly adj. enemigo.
unfurl tr. enrollar.
unhappily adv. infelizmente.
unhealthy adj. malsano; enfermizo.
unheard adj. que no se ha oído.
unholy adj. impío, malo.
unhurt adj. sin daños, ileso.
unify tr. unificar, unir.
unison s. concordancia, armonía.
unite tr. e in. unir, juntar.
unjust adj. injusto.
unkempt adj. despeinado.
unkind adj. duro, intratable.
unlace tr. desenlazar.
unlatch tr. abrir, quitar el cerrojo.

unlawful adj. ilegal.
unless cnj. a menos que.
unlike adj. desigual, distinto.
unload tr. descargar.
unlock tr. abrir (una cerradura); revelar secretos.
unloose tr. desatar, desencadenar.
unlucky adj. de mala suerte.
unmake tr. deshacer, destruir.
unmask tr. descubrir, desenmascarar.
unmixed adj. sin mezcla.
unnerve tr. acobardar.
unpack tr. desembalar.
unpleasant adj. antipático, desagradable.
unravel tr. desenredar, deshilar.
unreal adj. irreal, falso.
unrest s. intranquilidad.
unrighteous adj. injusto.
unripe adj. verde (no maduro); crudo.
unroll tr. desenrollar.
unruffled adj. tranquilo, sereno.
unscrew tr. desatornillar.
unseasonably adv. a destiempo.
unseemly adj. impropio, indecoroso.
unseen adj. invisible, oculto.
unsettle tr. desarreglar, descomponer; intr. desarreglar.
unsightly adj. feo.
unsound adj. poco firme.
unsparing adj. liberal, generoso, pródigo.
unsuspecting adj. confiado, desprevenido.
unthinking adj. irreflexivo.
unthought adj. imprevisto, inesperado.
untidy adj. sucio, desaliñado.
untie tr. desatar, desamarrar.
until prep. hasta; cnj. hasta que.

untimely *adj.* intempestivo;
  prematuro.
unto *prep.* a, en, dentro, hacia.
untold *adj.* nunca dicho.
untrained *adj.* inexperto.
untrue *adj.* falso.
unveil *tr.* descubrir.
unwary *adj.* incauto.
unwell *adj.* enfermo,
  indispuesto.
unwise *adj.* imprudente.
unwrap *tr.* desenvolver.
unyielding *adj.* implacable,
  inquebrantable.
up *adv.* arriba, en lo alto; *adj.*
  ascendente; alto, elevado.
upbraid *tr.* echar en cara,
  reprochar.
upcountry *s.* (fam.) interior;
  adj. (fam.) del interior.
uphill *adj.* ascendente;
  penoso; *adv.* cuesta arriba.
uphold *tr.* levantar en alto.
upholster *tr.* tapizar.
uplift *s.* levantamiento,
  elevación.
uplift *tr.* levantar.
upon *prep.* en, sobre, encima
  de.
upper *adj.* superior, alto.
uppermost *adj.* (el) más alto,
  más elevado.
upraise *tr.* levantar.
upright *adj.* vertical, derecho.
uproar *s.* tumulto.
uproot *tr.* desarraigar.
upset *s.* vuelco; contratiempo;
  adj. volcado; enfadado; *tr.*
  volcar; trastornar.
upside *s.* lo de arriba, parte
  superior.
upside-down *adj.* al revés,
  patas arriba.
upstairs *adv.* arriba; de arriba.
urchin *s.* chiquillo.
urge *s.* impulso, instinto; *tr.*
  urgir; impulsar; *intr.*
  apresurarse.
urinate *tr.* orinar; *intr.* orinar u
  orinarse.

urn *s.* urna.
us *pron. pers.* nos.
use *tr.* usar, emplear; *intr.*
  acostumbrar; *intr.* soler.
useful *adj.* útil.
usher *s.* acomodador; ujier;
  conserje. *tr.* acomodar.
usurp *tr.* usurpar.
utilize *tr.* utilizar, aprovechar.
utter *adj.* total, completo; *tr.*
  proferir, pronunciar.
utterly *adv.* totalmente,
  completamente.

U

V

vacancy *s.* (*pl.* -**cies**) vacío, hueco.
vacant *adj.* vacío, hueco.
vacate *tr.* dejar vacante.
vaccinate *tr.* vacunar.
vacuous *adj.* vacío, desocupado.
vague *adj.* vago, incierto.
vain *adj.* vano, vanidoso.
valediction *s.* despedida.
valet *s.* paje, camarero.
valiant *adj.* valiente, bravo.
valid *adj.* válido.
valise *s.* maleta, valija.
valley *s.* valle.
valo(u)r *s.* valor, valentía.
value *s.* valor, importe; *tr.* valorar, tasar.
valve *s.* válvula.
van *s.* carro de carga, camión de mudanzas.
vanilla *s.* (Bot.) vainilla.
vanish *intr.* desvanecerse, desaparecer.
vanquish *tr.* vencer, sujetar.
vapid *adj.* insípido; soso.
varnish *s.* barniz, charol; *tr.* barnizar; encubrir.
vary *tr. intr.* variar, cambiar; discrepar.
varying *adj.* variante.
vase *s.* florero, jarrón.
vassal *adj. y s.* vasallo, súbdito.
vast *adj.* vasto, extenso.
vaticinate *intr.* vaticinar, adivinar.
vault *s.* (arq.) bóveda, cúpula; cueva; *tr.* abovedar.
vaunt *s.* jactancia, fanfarronería; *tr. e intr.* jactarse de, ostentar.
veal *s.* carne de ternera.
veer *tr.* virar; *intr.* virar; desviarse.

vegetable *adj.* vegetal; de hortaliza; *s.* vegetal, planta.
vegetate *intr.* vegetar.
vehicle *s.* vehículo, carruaje.
veil *s.* velo; *tr.* velar, cubrir.
vein *s.* vena; veta, filón; *tr.* vetear.
vellum *s.* vitela, pergamino.
velvet *s.* terciopelo, vello.
veneer *s.* chapa, enchapado; *tr.* chapear; cubrir, ocultar.
venerate *tr.* venerar, reverenciar.
vengeful *adj.* vengativo.
venom *s.* veneno; malicia.
vent *s.* orificio, agujero; *tr.* desahogar, descargar.
ventilate *tr.* ventilar, airear.
venture *s.* aventura, riesgo; *tr.* aventurar, arriesgar; *intr.* aventurarse; emprender.
veracious *adj.* verídico.
veranda(h) *s.* terraza, galería.
verb *s.* (Gram.) verbo.
verbatim *adj.* al pie de la letra.
verdant *adj.* verde, verdoso.
verdict *s.* veredicto, dictamen.
verge *s.* borde, margen; *intr.* acercarse.
verger *s.* sacristán; alguacil de vara.
verify *tr.* verificar, comprobar, justificar.
vermicelli *s.* fideos.
vermilion *s.* bermellón; rojo.
vermin *s.pl.* sabandijas, gusanería.
vernacular *adj.* vernáculo, indígena.
versatile *adj.* flexible, hábil.
verse *s.* verso; versículo.
versed *adj.* versado, práctico.
versify *tr. e intr.* versificar.
version *s.* versión, traducción.
vertex *s.* (Mat.) y (An.) vértice.
very *adj.* mismo, mismísimo; verdadero; *adv.* muy; mucho.
vesper *s.* anochecer, tarde; *s. pl.* vísperas; *adj.* vespertino.

vessel *s.* vasija, recipiente.
vest *s.* chaleco; chaquetilla *(de mujer)*; vestido, camiseta; *tr.* vestir.
vet *s.* (fam.) veterano; veterinario; *tr.* (fam.) reconocer *(animales por un veterinario).*
veto *s.* (*pl.* -**toes**) veto, prohibición; *tr.* vetar.
vex *tr.* vejar, molestar.
via *prep.* vía, por.
viand *s.* vianda, carne; *pl.* viandas, platos selectos.
vibrate *tr. e intr.* vibrar, retemblar.
vice *s.* vicio, falta, defecto; tornillo.
vicinity *s.* vecindad; cercanía.
victor *s.* vencedor, triunfador.
victualler *s.* abastecedor, proveedor.
vie *intr.* competir, rivalizar.
view *s.* vista; panorama; *tr.* ver, mirar; contemplar.
viewer *s.* espectador; inspector.
vigour *s.* vigor; fuerza.
vile *adj.* vil; repugnante.
vilify *tr.* difamar, envilecer.
villa *s.* quinta, casa de campo.
village *s.* aldea, pueblo caserío.
villain *s.* malvado, bellaco, pícaro.
vindicate *tr.* vindicar.
vine *s.* vid, parra.
vinegar *s.* vinagre.
vineyard *s.* viña, viñedo.
vintage *s.* vendimia; cosecha.
violate *tr.* violar, violentar.
violence *s.* violencia, fuerza.
viper *s.* (Zool.) víbora.
virago *s.* marimacho.
virgin *s.* vírgen; *adj.* vírgen, inmaculado.
virtue *s.* virtud.
visa *s.* visado.
visage *s.* cara, semblante.

vis-a-vis *s.* persona que está enfrente; *adj.* enfrentado; *adv.* frente a frente; *prep.* en frente de.
visit *s.* visita; *tr. e in.* visitar; inspeccionar.
visitor *s.* visita, visitante.
visor *s.* visera.
vitiate *tr.* viciar.
vituperate *tr.* vituperar, censurar.
vivify *tr.* vivificador, avivar.
vocable *s.* voz, vocablo, palabra.
vocciferate *tr. e intr.* vocear, vociferar.
vogue *s.* boga, moda.
voice *s.* voz; *tr.* expresar; divulgar; *intr.* sonorizarse.
void *adj.* vacío; nulo, inválido; *s.* vacio; *tr.* vaciar.
volley *s.* descarga, lluvia *(de piedra, balas, etcétera)*; (Mil.) descarga; *tr.* volear *(tenis)*; lanzar una descarga.
volt *s.* (Elec.) voltio.
vomit *s.* vómito; *tr.* vomitar, provocar.
voracious *adj.* voraz, tragón.
votary *s.* partidario; monje, religioso.
vote *s.* voto; *tr. e in.* votar.
vouch *tr.* garantizar, atestiguar, certificar; *intr.* salir fiador.
voucher *s.* fiador, garante.
vouchsafe *tr. e in.* conceder, otorgar.
vow *s.* promesa solemne; voto; *tr.* prometer solemnemente, votar.
vowel *s.* vocal.
voyage *s.* viaje; *tr.* atravesar *(el mar).*
vulture *s.* (Zool.) buitre.

V

W

wad *s.* taco; guata; *tr.* colocar algodón en; acolchar.

wadding *s.* algodón.

wading *adj.* zancuda *(ave).*

wafer *s.* oblea; hostia.

waft *s.* ráfaga de aire, viento, olor; *tr.* mecer, llevar por el aire; *intr.* moverse o flotar de un sitio a otro.

wag *tr.* sacudir, menear; *intr.* menearse, oscilar; *s.* movimiento de cabeza.

wage, wages *s.* salario, pago, jornal; *tr.* emprender y continuar.

wager *s.* apuesta; *tr. e intr.* apostar.

waggery *s.* broma, chanza.

waggish *adj.* bromista.

waggon *s.* carreta, carromato, vagón.

wagon-lit *s.* coche-cama *(de ferrocarril).*

waif *s.* expósito.

wail *s.* gemido, lamento; *intr.* gemir, llorar.

waist *s.* cintura, talle.

waiscoat *s.* chaleco.

wait *s.* espera; *tr.* esperar, aguardar.

waiter *s.* camarero, mozo.

waiting *s.* espera; *adj.* que espera; que sirve.

waiting-room *s.* sala de espera.

waitress *s.* camarera, criada.

waive *tr.* renunciar a.

wake *s.* estela *(barco)*; vigilia; *tr. e intr.* velar un cadáver.

waken *tr. e intr.* despertar.

Wales *s.* Gales.

walk *s.* caminata; paseo; *intr.* andar, caminar, ir a pie.

walkie-talkie *s.* transmisor-receptor portátil.

walkout *s.* (fam.) huelga de obreros.

wall *s.* pared, muro; *tr.* emparedar; amurallar.

wallet *s.* cartera, mochila.

wallow *s.* revuelco; *intr.* revolcarse.

walnut *s.* (Bot.) nuez; nogal.

waltz *s.* vals; *adj.* de vals.

wan *adj.* pálido.

wand *s.* vara; varilla mágica.

wander *tr.* (poét.) atravesar o recorrer a la ventura; *intr.* errar, vagar.

wane *s.* mengua, disminución; *intr.* menguar.

want *s.* deseo; necesidad; *tr.* querer, desear; *intr.* faltar.

wanting *adj.* falto; defectuoso; *adv.* sin.

wanton *adj.* insensible, perverso; *s.* libertino; prostituta.

war *s.* guerra; *intr.* guerrear.

ward *s.* pupilo; tutela; *tr.* guardar, defender.

warden *s.* guardián; carcelero.

wardrobe *s.* guardarropa.

warehouse *s.* almacén, depósito; *tr.* almacenar.

warfare *s.* guerra; arte militar.

warines *s.* cautela.

warm *adj.* caliente; cálido, caluroso; *tr.* calentar; acalorar; *intr.* calentarse.

warmth *s.* calor moderado; entusiasmo, simpatía.

warn *tr.* avisar, advertir.

warning *s.* aviso, amonestación.

warrant *s.* autorización, decreto; *tr.* autorizar; justificar.

warren *s.* conejera; vivero.

wary *adj.* cauteloso, prudente.

wash *s.* lavado; jabonado; *adj.* lavable; *tr.* lavar; bañar; *intr.* lavarse; lavar la ropa.

washed-out *adj.* descolorido.

washing *s.* lavado.

washstand s. palangana.
washy adj. aguado, diluído.
wasp s. (Zool.) avispa.
wastage s. pérdida, derroche.
wasteful s. gastador, derrochador.
wasteless adj. sin desperdicio.
watch s. vigilancia; velación; tr. mirar; intr. mirar; velar.
watchful adj. vigilante, cuidadoso.
watch-maker s. relojero.
watchman s. sereno.
watchword s. santo y seña; lema.
water s. agua; adj. impermeable; acuático; tr. regar, rociar; aguar el vino; abrevar el ganado; intr. llenarse de agua.
watermelon s. sandía.
waterspout s. canalón, manga.
watertight adj. hermético, estanco.
watery adj. acuoso, mojado.
wave s. onda; ola; tr. agitar, blandir; ondear; hacer señales con (la mano o el pañuelo); intr. ondear.
waver intr. oscilar, ondear.
wax s. cera; tr. encerar; intr. hacerse, ponerse, crecer.
way s. vía, camino; manera, modo; hábito; dirección.
wayfarer s. caminante.
waylay tr. acechar.
wayside adj. junto al camino.
we pron. pers. nosotros.
weak adj. débil; flojo.
weaken tr. debilitar, enflaquecer.
weal s. bienestar, felicidad; cardenal.
wealth s. riqueza.
wean tr. destetar.
weapon s. arma.
wear s. uso (de ropa); desgaste, deterioro; tr. llevar o traer puesto; usar;

intr. desgastarse, deteriorarse; durar.
wearer s. portador.
weariness s. cansancio.
wearisome adj. aburrido.
weary adj. cansado; aburrido; tr. cansar; intr. cansarse.
weather s. tiempo; adj. meterorológico; atmosférico; tr. airear; solear; intr. curtirse a la intemperie.
weave s. tejido; tr. e intr. tejer.
web s. tela, tejido.
wedding s. boda, matrimonio.
wedge s. cuña; tr. acuñar.
wedlock s. matrimonio.
Wednesday s. miércoles.
weed s. mala hierba; s. pl. ropa de luto.
week s. semana.
weekend s. fin de semana.
ween intr. creer, pensar.
weep s. tr. llorar; derramar (lágrimas).
weigh tr. e in. pesar, medir.
weighing s. pesada, peso.
weir s. presa.
weird adj. misterioso, sobrenatural.
welcome s. bienvenida; adj. bienvenido; inj. ¡bienvenido!; tr. dar la bienvenida.
weld s. soldadura autógena; tr. soldar con autógena.
welfare s. bienestar.
well s. pozo, fuente, manantial; adv. bien, muy bien, mucho; **very** — muy bien; inj. vaya, ¡vaya!, ¡toma!, ¡vamos!, ¡bueno!.
wench s. muchacha.
wend tr. e intr. seguir su camino.
Wesleyan adj. y s. metodista.
west s. oeste, occidente.
westerly adj. occidental; adj. desde el oeste; hacia el oeste; s. viento del oeste.

W

western *adj.* occidental; *s.*
película del oeste.
wet *adj.* mojado; húmedo; *s.*
humedad; lluvia; *tr.* mojar;
intr. mojarse.
whale *s.* (Zool.) ballena.
wharf *s.* muelle, andén.
what *pron. intr.* ¿qué?,
¿cuál?; *pron. rel.* lo que;
adj. rel. el *(la, etc.)* que; *intj.*
¡qué!
whatever *pron.* lo que, todo lo
que, sea lo que sea que;
adj. cualquier que.
wheat *s.* (Bot.) trigo.
wheedle *tr.* engatusar.
wheel *s.* rueda, disco; *tr.*
proveer de ruedas; *intr.*
girar, rodar.
when *adv.* ¿cuándo?; *cnj.*
cuándo.
whence *adv.* ¿de dónde?; por
eso, por tanto.
whenever *cnj.* cuando,
cuando quiera que.
whensoever *adv.* cuando
quiera; *cnj.* cuando quiera
que.
where *adv.* dónde, adónde,
en dónde.
whereabouts *s.* paradero.
whereas *cnj.* mientras que.
whereby *adj.* por donde, por
medio del cual.
wherein *adv.* dónde, en qué,
cómo; en que, en lo cual.
whereto *adj.* adonde.
whereupon *adv.* entonces,
con lo cual.
wherever *adv.* dondequiera
que.
whet *s.* afiladura; aperitivo; *tr.*
afilar, aguzar; estimular.
whether *cnj.* si.
whey *s.* suero de leche.
which *pron. int.* ¿cuál?; *pron.
real.* que, el *(la, etc.)* que.
whichever *pron. rel.*
cualquiera; *adj.* cualquier.

whiff *s.* soplo, ráfaga; *tr. e in.*
soplar; echar bocanadas.
while *cnj.* mientras que; al
mismo tiempo que; *s.* rato;
tr. pasar el rato.
whilst *cnj.* mientras.
whim *s.* capricho, antojo.
whip *s.* látigo; azote *(golpe)*;
tr. azotar, fustigar; *intr.*
arrojarse.
whirl *s.* vuelta, giro; *tr.* hacer
girar; *intr.* dar vueltas.
whirlpool *s.* remolino.
whisk *s.* escobilla, cepillo; *tr.*
cepillar; barrer.
whisker *s.* patilla, pelo de la
barba; (fam.) bigote o
bigotes.
whisper *s.* cuchicheo; *tr.* decir
al oído; *intr.* cuchichear.
whistle *s.* silbido; *tr.* silbar.
whit *adj.* pizca.
white *adj.* blanco, pálido; *tr.*
blanquear; *intr.*
emblanquecerse.
whiten *tr.* blanquear; *intr.*
emblanquecerse.
whiter *adv.* adonde, hacia
donde; a qué parte.
whizz *s.* silbido, zumbido; *intr.*
silbar, zumbar.
who *pron.* quién, quienes.
whoever quienquiera que.
whole *adj.* entero, todo; *s.*
conjunto, todo.
wholesale *s.* venta al por
mayor.
wholesome *adj.* saludable.
whom *pron.* que, a quien.
whoop *s.* alarido, grito; *tr.*
decir a gritos; *intr.* gritar.
whooping cough *s.* tos ferina.
whop *tr.* dar una paliza a.
whopping *adj.* (fam.) enorme;
s. paliza.
whore *s.* prostituta.
whose *pron.* ¿de quién?
whosoever *pron.* quienquiera
que.

why *adv.* ¿por qué?; *cnj.* por qué; por lo que; *s.* porqué; *inj.* ¡toma!
wicker *s.* mimbre.
wicket *s.* portillo.
wide *adj.* ancho; extenso; *adv.* lejos de par en par.
widen *tr. e in.* ensanchar.
widow *s.* viuda.
width *s.* anchura.
wield *tr.* empuñar, esgrimir.
wife *s.* esposa.
wig *s.* peluca.
wild *adj.* salvaje; silvestre; *adv.* violentamente; *s.* yermo, desierto.
wildness *s.* ferocidad, fiereza.
wile *s.* ardid, engaño; *tr.* engatusar.
will *s.* voluntad; (Der.) testamento; *tr.* querer; legal; *intr.* querer; *aux.* se emplea para formar el futuro perfecto de indicativo.
willow *s.* (Bot.) sauce.
wilt *tr. e in.* marchitarse(se).
win *s.* triunfo, éxito; *tr.* ganar, triunfar.
wince *s.* sobresalto.
wind *s.* viento, aire, aliento; *tr.* husmear.
wind *tr.* enrollar; envolver; torcer; sonar; *intr.* enrollarse; dar vueltas; enroscarse; ir con rodeos.
windfall *s.* rama o fruta caída del árbol.
winding *s.* vuelta; (Elec.) bobinado; *adj.* sinuoso, tortuoso.
windmill *s.* molino de viento.
windo *s.* ventana; escaparate.
windpipe *s.* (An.) tráquea.
wine *s.* vino; *intr.* beber vino.
wing *s.* ala; paleta de hélice; *tr.* volar; *tr.* dar alas a.
wink *s.* guiño; parpadeo; *tr.* guiñar; expresar con un guiño; *intr.* guiñar, parpadear.

winner *s.* ganador.
winning *adj.* ganancioso; triunfador; *s.* triunfo; *s.pl.* ganancias.
winnow *tr.* aventar; entresacar; *intr.* aletear.
winsome *adj.* atrayente, simpático.
winter *s.* invierno; *adj.* invernal; *intr.* invernar.
winterless *adj.* sin invierno.
wipe *s.* frotadura; *tr.* enjugar, secar.
wiper *s.* limpiador; paño.
wire *s.* alambre; telégrafo; *adj.* de alambre, hecho de alambre; *tr.* proveer de alambres; atar con alambre.
wireless *s.* receptor radiofónico.
wiring *s.* (Elec.) instalación de alambres.
wisdom *s.* sabiduría.
wise *adj.* sabio, doctor, erudito.
wish *s.* deseo anhelo; *tr.* desear, querer.
wishful *adj.* deseoso.
wishy-washy *adj.* aguado, diluído.
wisp *s.* puñado; rastro.
wit *s.* ingenio; juicio.
witch *s.* bruja, hechicera; *tr.* embrujar, hechizar.
with *prep.* con; de, en compañía de.
withal *adj.* además, también; por otra parte.
withdraw *tr. e in.* retirar, quitar, separar.
wither *tr. in.* marchitar.
withhold *tr.* negar; suspender.
within *adv.* dentro, adentro; *prep.* dentro de.
without *adv.* fuera; *prep.* fuera de; sin *cnj.* sin que.
withstand *tr.* aguantar, soportar.
witness *s.* testigo; testimonio; *tr.* ver, presenciar,

W

atestiguar o testimoniar; *intr.* dar testimonio.

witty *adj.* agudo, ingenioso.

wizard *s.* brujo, hechicero.

woe *s.* dolor, pena; *inj.* ¡ay!

woeful *adj.* miserable.

wolf *s.* (Zool.) lobo.

woman *s.* mujer; *adj.* femenino.

wonder *s.* maravilla; portento; *tr.* preguntarse; *intr.* maravillarse.

wonderful *adj.* maravilloso, prodigioso.

wont *adj.* habituado; *s.* hábito, costumbre, uso.

wonted *adj.* habitual.

wood *s.* madera; bosque.

wooded *adj.* plantado de árboles.

woodland *s.* bosque, arbolado; *adj.* silvestre.

woodpecker *s.* pájaro carpintero.

woodwork *s.* ebanistería.

woodworm *s.* (Zool.) carcoma.

wool *s.* lana.

word *s.* palabra; santo y seña; *tr.* redactar; enunciar.

wordless *adj.* mudo.

work *s.* trabajo, tarea; obra; *s. pl.* **works** fábrica, taller; *tr.* trabajar, funcionar, obrar; *intr.* trabajar; funcionar.

worker *s.* trabajador, obrero.

workhouse *s.* hospicio, asilo; (U.S.) reformatorio.

working *s.* obra, trabajo.

workmanlike *adj.* esmerado.

workmanship *s.* destreza o habilidad en el trabajo.

workshop *s.* taller, fábrica.

worm *s.* gusano; lombriz; *tr.* limpiar de lombrices; conseguir por medio de artimañas; *intr.* arrastrarse.

worn *adj.* gastado, roto.

worry *s.* inquietud, preocupación; *tr.* inquietar, preocupar.

worse *adj. y adv. compar.* peor.

worsen *tr. e intr.* empeorar.

worship *s.* adoración, culto; *tr. e intr.* adorar.

worst *adj. superl.* el peor; *adv.* peor; *s.* lo peor.

worth *s.* valor; valía.

worthless *adj.* sin valor.

would *aux.* se emplea para formar el condicional.

would-be *adj.* llamado; *s.* presumido.

wound *s.* herida; *tr.* herir.

wrangle *s.* disputa, riña; *tr.* disputar; *intr.* disputar.

wrap *s.* abrigo; *tr.* envolver; *tr.* envolverse.

wrapper *s.* envoltura; funda.

wrath *s.* ira, cólera.

wreak *tr.* descargar.

wreath *s.* corona.

wreck *s.* destrucción, ruina; *tr.* destruir, arruinar; *intr.* arruinarse.

wrench *s.* llave; torcedura violenta; dolor; *tr.* retorcer, dislocar.

wrest *s.* torsión violenta; *tr.* torcer, arrancar.

wrestle *s.* luch; *intr.* luchar.

wriggle *intr.* menearse rápidamente.

wring *tr. (pret. y pp.* **wrung**) torcer; retorcer.

wrinkle *s.* arruga; *tr.* arrugar.

wrist *s.* muñeca.

writ *s.* escrito; (Der.) auto, mandato; **Holy** — la Sagrada Escritura.

writ *tr. (pret.* **wrote**; *pp.* **written**) escribir.

writing *s.* escritura.

wrong *adj.* injusto; equivocado; *tr.* agraviar, ofender.

wrongly *adj.* mal, por error.

wry *adj. (compar.* **-ier**; *superl.* **-iest**) tuerto.

X

Xmas *s.* abrev. de **Christmas** Navidad.
X-ray(s) *s.* rayos X; *tr.* radiografiar.

Y

yacht *s.* yate; *intr.* pasear en yate; **—race** regata de yates.
Yankee *adj. y s.* yanqui, norteamericano.
yard *s.* yarda *(medida = 0,91* metros); cercado, corral, patio.
yarn *s.* hilado; (fam.) cuento; *intr.* inventar y contar historietas.
yean *tr. e intr.* parir *(la cabra, la oveja)*.
year *s.* año; **every other —** cada dos años; **leap —** año bisiesto.
yearn *intr.* suspirar por.
yeast *s.* levadura.
yell *s.* grito, voz; *tr.* decir a gritos; *intr.* gritar.
yellow *adj.* amarillo.
yeoman *s.* (*pl.* **yeomen**) labrador acomodado.
yes *adv.* si, ciertamente.
yesterday *adv. y s.* ayer; **the day before —** anteayer.
yet *adv.* todavía; *cnj.* con todo, **not —** todavía no.
yield *s.* producción, rendimiento; *tr.* producir, rentar; *intr.* producir, rendir, rendirse.

yoke *s.* yugo.
yolk *s.* yema de huevo.
yon *adj. y adv.* ahí, allá.
yonder *adj.* aquel; de más allá; *adv.* allí a la vista.
you *pron. pers. sing. y pl.* tú, ti, te; vosotros; usted, ustedes; le, la les, **with —** contigo; consigo; *pron. indef.* se.
young *adj.* joven; temprano; tierno; **with —** en cinta; *s. pl.* hijuelos.
your *adj. poss. (sing. y pl.)* tu, vuestro, su, el de usted o de ustedes.
yours *pron. poss. (sing. y pl.)* tuyo, vuestro; suyo; de usted, de ustedes; el tuyo, el vuestro; el suyo; el de usted, el de ustedes.
yourself *pron. refl.* tú mismo; usted mismo; sí mismo; se; sí; **yourselves** *pl.* vosotros o ustedes mismos.
youth *s.* juventud; mozo; *s. pl.* jóvenes.

Z

zeal *s.* celo.
zelot *s.* fanático.
zenith *s.* cenit, apogeo.
zero *s.* cero; *adj.* nulo.
zest *s.* entusiasmo; gusto, sabor.
zinc *s.* cinc; *tr.* cubrir con cinc, galvanizar.
zipper *s.* cierre de cremallera.
zone *s.* zona; *tr.* dividir en zonas.
zoo *s.* parque zoológico.

SPANISH — ENGLISH DICTIONARY

A

a *pre.* to, at, on, by, in, up, to.
abad *m.* abbot.
abadejo *m.* codfish.
abadesa *f.* abbess.
abadía *f.* abbey.
abajo *adv.* down, under.
abalanzar *tr.* to balance; *int.* to rush on.
abanderado *m.* standardbearer.
abanderar *tr.* & *r.* to conscript.
abanicar *tr.* to fan.
abanico *m.* fan.
abaratar *tr.* to cheapen.
abarcar *tr.* to embrace.
abarrotar *tr.* to stow.
abastecedor *m.* & *adj.* caterer.
abastecer *tr.* & *r.* to supply.
abate *m.* priest.
abatido *adj.* dejected; spiritless.
abdicar *tr.* to abdicate, renounce.
abdomen *m.* abdomen, stomach.
abeja *f.* bee.
abejorro *m.* bumble-bee.
abertura *f.* aperture, opening; clefg.
abeto *m.* (Bot.) silver-tree, fir-tree.
abierto -ta *adj.* open, clear.
abismado *adj.* defected.
abjurar *tr.* abjure.
ablandar *tr.* & *in.* to soften, mollify.
ablución *m.* ablutions.
abobado *adj.* stupid, silly.
abocar *tr.* to take or catch with the mouth.
abofetear *tr.* to slap, to box.
abogado *m.* lawyer, advocate.
abogar *in.* to advocate.
abolengo *m.* ancestry.
abollado *adj.* curled.
abombar *tr.* to give a convex.

abominar *tr.* to abominate, to detest.
abonable *adj.* which can be subscribed to.
abono *m.* security, guarantee; subscription.
abordable *adj.* (Náut.) accessible.
abordar *tr.* (Náut.) to board a ship; *in.* to put into a port.
aborrecer *tr.* to hate, abhor; *r.* to hate each other.
aborrecible *adj.* hateful.
abortar *in.* (Med.) to miscarry, to abort.
aborto *m.* miscarriage.
abotonar *tr.* to button; *r.* to button up.
abovedar *tr.* (Arch.) to arch.
abrelatas *m.* tin-opener.
abreviar *tr.* to abridge, shorten.
abridor -ra *adj.* open; *m.* opener.
abrigar *tr.* to shelter, protect, cover.
abril *m.* April.
abrir *tr.* to open, unlock, uncover; to gain, split, inaugurate; to; *in.* to open, unfold; to extend; *r.* to open, expand, crack, yawn *(mouth)*.
abrochar *tr.* to button on, fasten.
abrumado -da *adj.* weary.
abrumar *tr.* to crush, overwhelm.
abside *m.* (Arch.) apse.
absolución *adj.* absolution.
absoluto -ta *adj.* absolute; *adv.* **en absoluto**, absolutely.
absorber *tr.* to absorb.
abstenerse . to abstain, refrain.
abstraer *tr.* to abstract; *in.* **abstraer de**, to do without; *r.* to concentrate on's mind.

abstraído -da *adj.* abstracted, absent.

absurdo -da *adj.* absurd, senseless; pointless, *m.* absurdity.

abuchear *tr.* to scoff, boo.

abuela *f.* grandmother.

abuelo *m.* grandfather.

abultado -da *adj.* big, bulky.

abultar *tr.* to enlarge.

abundar *in.* to abound, have plenty.

aburrir *tr.)* to annoy, tire, bore, weary; *r.* to grow tired.

abusar *tr.* to abuse.

abuso *m.* abuse.

acá *adv.* here.

acabado -da *adj.* perfect, complete.

acabar *tr. & in.* to finish, end; **¡acabáramos!, ¡se acabó!**, it's all up, it's all over; **acabar con**, to finish off; **acabar de**, to have just.

academia *f.* academy; school.

acalorado -da *adj.* excited.

acalorar *tr.* to warm; *r.* to grow warm.

acampar *tr., r. & in.* to (en) camp.

acantilado -da *adj.* bold, steep, *m.* cliff.

acaparar *tr.* to monopolize, buy up.

acariciar *tr.* to fondle.

acaso *m.* chance; *adv.* perhaps, may be, by chance, by accident; **por si acaso**, in case.

acatar *tr.* to respect, revere, conform.

acaudalar *tr.* to hoard up riches.

acceder *tr.* to accede.

accessorio *adj.* accessory, additional.

acción *f.* action, feat.

acechar *tr.* to waylay, lie in ambush.

aceite *m.* oil; **aceite de pescado**, train-oil; **aceite de linaza**, linseed-oil; **aceite de arder**, fuel oil.

aceituna *f.* olive.

acelerar *tr.* to accelerate, haste, hurry; to make haste.

acento *m.* accent; tone.

acentuar *tr.* to accentuate, emphasize.

acepción *f.* acceptation; (Gram.) meaning.

aceptable *adj.* acceptable.

aceptar *tr.* to accept, agree.

acequia *f.* canal, gutter.

acera *f.* pavement.

acero *m.* steel; (fig.) sword; **aceite fundido**, cast iron.

acertado -da *adj.* right, correct.

acertar *tr.* to hit *(the mark)*; to hit by chance.

acertijo *m.* riddle, puzzle.

acicate *m.* stimulant.

ácido -da *adj.* acid, sour.

acierto *m.* success, good hit.

aclamar *tr.* to shout, acclaim.

aclarar *tr.* to make clear; *in. & r.* to clear up *(weather)*.

acobardar *tr.* to daunt.

acoger *tr.* to welcome, receive; to protect.

acolchar *tr.* to quilt.

acometer *tr.* to attack, assault.

acomodado -da *adj.* convenient, fit; rich.

acomodador -ra *m. & f.* usher.

acompañar *tr.* to accompany; to lead along.

acondicionar *tr.* to dispose.

acongojar *tr.* to vex; *r.* to become vexed.

acontecer *in.* to happen.

acorazado *adj.* ironclad; *m.* armoured ship.

acordar *tr. & in.* to agree, become uniform; *r.* to remember.

acorde *adj.* agreed; *m.* (Mús.) chord.

acordonar *tr.* to make in the form of a cord of rope.

acorralar *tr.* to shut up cattle or sheep in pens.

acortar *tr.* to shorten.

acosar *tr.* to pursue closely.

acostar *tr.* to lay down; *in.* to approach; *r.* to lie down.

acostumbrar *tr.* to accustom.

acotación *f.* bounds.

acrecentar *tr.* & *r.* to increase.

acreditar *tr.* to assure, affirm; to verify; to give credit to.

acreedor -ra *adj.* deserving, *m.* creditor.

activar *tr.* to activate.

activo -va *adj.* active, quick; *m.* (Com.) assets.

acto *m.* act; event; ceremony.

actor *m.* actor, player.

actual *adj.* present.

actualidad *f.* actuality.

actuar *tr.* to put a thing in action; *in.* to digest.

acuarela *f.* water-color.

acuático *adj.* aquatic.

acuciar *tr.* to stimulate.

acuchillar *tr.* to cut.

acudir *in.* to assist, attend; to go; to come.

acuerdo *m.* resolution, determination.

acumular *tr.* to accumulate, heap together.

acurrucarse *r.* to huddle.

acusativo *m.* the accusative case.

acústica *f.* acoustics.

achacar *tr.* to impute.

achaque *m.* thene.

achatar *tr.* to flatten.

achicar *tr.* to reduce.

achicharrar *tr.* to cook crisp, roast.

adagio *m.* proverb.

adecuar *tr.* to fit, accommodate, adequate.

adelantamiento *m.* progress, advancement; growth.

adelante *adv.* ahead, forward.

adelgazado -da *adj.* made slender or thin.

adelgazamiento *m.* making slender.

ademán *m.* gesture.

además *adv.* moreover

adentro *adv.* within.

aderezar *tr.* to adorn, embellish, dress; to season.

adeudar *tr.* to owe; to be dutiable.

adherir *in.* to adhere, stick to; *r.* to hold *(see irr.* **sentir***)*.

adición *f.* addition.

adicionar *tr.* to make additions.

adiestrar *tr.* & *r.* to teach, to coach.

adiós *inj.* good-bye; (fam.) bye-bye.

adivinanza *f. con.* prediction.

adivinar *tr.* to predict.

adjetivar *tr.* (Gram.) to give adjectival value.

adjudicar *tr.* to adjudge; *r.* to appropriate.

adjunto -a *adj.* joined, annexed.

administrador *adj. m.* & *f.* administrater.

administrar *tr.* to administer.

admirado -da *adj.* astonished.

admirador -ra *m.* & *f.* admirer; fan.

admirar *tr.* to admire, marvel; *r.* to wonder.

admitir *tr.* to admit; to concede.

admonición *f.* warning.

adobar *tr.* to dress, prepare.

adoctrinar *tr.* to instruct.

adolecer *in.* to be seized with illness.

adolescencia *f.* youth, adolescence.

adónde *adv.* where; whither?

adoptar *tr.* to adopt.

adoquinar *tr.* to pave.

adquirir *tr.* to acquire, obtain.

adrede *adv.* purposely, intentionally.
aduana *f.* custom-house.
aducir *tr.* to adduce.
adulación *f.* flattery.
adular *tr.* to flatter, soothe, coax.
adúltero -ra *m.* & *f.* adulterer.
adulto *adj.* adult, grown-up.
advenedizo *adj.* & *m.* foreign, strange.
advenimiento *m.* arrive; advant.
adverbio *m.* adverb.
adversidad *f.* calamity, adversity.
advertencia *f.* warning, advice.
adviento *m.* advent.
adyacente *adj.* adjacent.
aéreo -rea *adj.* aerial; (fig.) airy.
aeronave *f.* airship.
aeroplano *m.* airplane.
aeropuerto *m.* airport.
afabilidad *f.* affability.
afamado *adj.* famous.
afanar *tr.* to try hard; *in.* to toil, labour; *r.* to toil too much.
afear *tr.* to deform, disfigure, deface.
afectar *tr.* to feign; *r.* to be moved.
afeitar *tr.* to shave.
afeminado -da *adj.* effeminate.
afeminar *tr.* to effeminate; *r.* to become weak.
aferrar *tr.* & *in.* to grasp, grapple, seize.
afianzado *adj.* guaranteed.
aficionar *tr.* to inspire affection.
afilador -ra *adj.* sharpenings.
afilar *tr.* to whet, grind; *r.* to grow thin.
afinar *tr.* to polish; to tune; *r.* to become polished.
afinidad *f.* relationship, resemblance.
afirmar *tr.* to affirm, assert, *r.* to maintain firmly.

afligir *tr.* to afflict; *r.* to grieve.
afluencia *f.* affluence.
afluente *adj.* copious; affluent; *m.* tributary.
afonía *f.* (Med.) aphonia.
afortunado -da *adj.* fortunate, happy.
aforo *m.* gauging.
afrentar *tr.* to affront, insult, *r.* to be affronted.
afrentoso -sa *adj.* outrageous.
afrontar *tr.* to confront.
afuera *adv.* away, outside.
agachar *tr.* to lower, bow down.; *rd. con.* to stoop.
agarrado *adj.* mean, close fisted.
agarrar *tr.* to grasp; *com.* to obtain; *r.* to clinch.
agasajar *tr.* to receive and treat kindly.
agencia *f.* agency.
agenciar *tr.* & *in.* to manage.
agenda *f.* notebook.
agente *m.* agent, actor.
agigantado -da *adj.* gigantic; *con.* exaggerated.
ágil *adj.* nimble.
agitanado -da *adj.* gipsy-like.
agitar *tr.* to agitate, ruffle, fret; *r.* to flutter, palpitate.
aglutinar *tr.* to glue together.
agobiar *tr.* to bend the body down.
agolpar *tr.* to heap; *r.* to crowd together.
agonía *f.* agony.
agonizar *tr. in.* to be dying.
agosto *m.* August.
agotación *m.* **agotamiento**, exhaustion, debility.
agotar *tr.* to drain off liquids; *r.* to become exhausted.
agraciar *tr.* to adorn.
agradar *in.* to please; *r.* to be pleased.
agradecer *tr.* to acknowledge *(a favor)*.
agradecimiento *m.* acknowledgement.

agrado *m.* affability.
agrandar *tr.* to enlarge.
agraviar *tr.* to wrong, offend; *v.* to be aggreived.
agravio *m.* offence, insult.
agredir *tr.* to assault, attack.
agregado -da *adj.* aggregate.
agregar *tr.* to aggregate, collect; *r.* to become united.
agresor -ra *m.* & *f.* aggressor, *adj.* aggressive, assaulting.
agriar *tr.* to make sour; *r.* to turn sour or acid.
agricultor *m.* farmer.
agrietar *tr.* & *r.* to crack.
agrio -a *adj.* sour, acid.
agrisar *tr.* to colour grey.
agrupar *tr.* to group, cluster; *r.* to gather in groups.
agua water; fluid; rain; aquadulce, fresh water; *pl.* mineral waters *(in general)*.
aguacero *m.* heavy shower.
aguafiestas *m.* & *f.* killjoy, spoilsport.
aguaniever *f.* sleet, snow-water.
aguantar *tr.* to sustain, suffer, bear; *r.* to forbear.
aguar *tr.* to dilute with water; *r.* to become inundated.
aguardar *tr.* & *r.* to wait for, expect; *in.* to wait.
aguardiente *m.* spirituous liquor.
aguarrás *m.* oil of turpentine.
agudeza *f.* acuteness, subtlety.
agüero *m.* augury.
aguijar *tr.* spur, to incite.
aguijón *m.* sting.
aguijonear *tr.* to prick.
águila *f.* eagle.
aguja *f.* needle, knitting-needle.
agujerear *tr.* to pierce.
agujero *m.* hole.
argujetas *f. pl.* pins and needles.
aguzar *tr.* to whet.

ahí *adv.* there, in that place.
ahijado *m.* godson; godchild.
ahogado -da *adj.* suffocated.
ahogar *tr.* to choke, throttle; *r.* to become suffocated.
ahora *adv.* now, at present, just now; *conj.* whether, or.
ahorcar *tr.* to hang; *rv.* to hang oneself.
ahorrar *tr.* to economize, save, spare.
ahuyentar *tr.* to drive away.
airado -da *adj.* angry.
aire *m.* air; wind; briskness.
airear *tr.* to give air, ventilate.
aislado -da *adj.* isolated; (Elec.) (Phys.) insulated.)
aislar *tr.* to insulate, to become isolated.
ajedrez *m.* chess.
ajeno -na *adj.* another's; foreign, strange.
ajetreo *m.* fatigue.
ajo *m.* (Bot.) garlic.
ajuar *f.* bridal apparel.
ajustado -da *adj.* exact, right.
ajustar *tr.* to adjust, regulate, fit; *r.* to settle matters.
ajusticiar *tr.* to execute, put to death.
al *art. (formed of a and el)* to the, at the.
alabanza *f.* praise.
alabar *tr.* to praise, extol, glorify; *r.* to praise oneself.
alacena *f.* cupboard, closet.
alacrán *m.* scorpion.
alado -da *adj.* winged.
alambicado *adj.* distilled.
alambique *m.* still.
alambre *m.* wire.
alameda *f.* poplar grove.
álamo *m.* (Bot.) poplar.
alarde *m.* ostentation.
alardear *in.* to boast, to brag.
alargar *tr.* to lengthen, extend; *r.* to become prolonged.
alarido *m.* outcry, shout.
alarma *f.* (Mil.) alarm.
alarmar *in.* to alarm.

alba *f.* dawn; alb, white vestment.
albañil *m.* mason, bricklayer.
albarda *f.* pack-saddle.
albaricoque *m.* apricot.
albedrio *m.* free-will.
albergar *tr.* to lodge, shelter, harbour; *in.* & *r.* to lodge.
albergue *m.* lodging, shelter.
alborada *f.* dawn.
albornoz *m.* burnoose.
alborotador -ra *adj.* riotous.
alborotar *tr.* to disturb; *in* & *r.* to get excited.
alcachofa *f.* (Bot.) artichoque.
alcalde *m.* mayor.
alcance *m.* pursuit; arm's length.
alcantarilla *f.* underground sewer.
alcantarillado *f.* sewerage.
alcanzar *tr.* overtake; reach; *in.* to attain.
alcázar *m.* castle; fortress.
alcoba *f.* alcove, bedroom.
alcoronoque *m.* (Bot.) corktree.
aldaba *f.* knocker, clapper.
aldea *f.* small village.
aleacion *f.* alloy.
aleccionar *tr.* to teach.
alegar *tr.* to allegate.
alegrar *tr.* to make merry, gladden; *r.* to rejoice, exult.
alejar *tr.* to remove, separate; *in.* to go away.
alentador -ra *adj.* encouraging.
alentar *in.* to breathe; *tr.* to encourage.
alero *m.* eaves.
alerta *f.* (Mil.) watchword; *adv.* vigilantly, carefully.
aleta *f.* small sing.
aletargar *tr.* to lethargize; *r.* to fall into lethargy.
alfabeto *m.* alphabet.
alfarería *f.* pottery.
alfil *m.* bishop *(chess)*.
alfiler *m.* pin, scarf-pin.

alfombra *f.* carpet.
alga *f.* seaweed.
algodón *m.* cotton.
alguacil *m.* constable.
alguien *pron.* somebody, someone, anybody.
algún *adj.* some, any; *pron.* someone.
alhaja *f.* jewel, gem.
alianza *f.* alliance, confederacy.
aliarse *r.* to become allied.
alicates *m. pl.* pincers.
aliento *m.* breath.
aligerar *tr.* to lighten; *r.* to become lighter.
alimentación *f.* feeding.
alimentar *tr.* to feed, nourish; *r.* to feed oneself.
alimento *m.* nourishment, nutriment.
alinear *tr.* to line up.
aliñar *tr.* to arrange, adorn.
alisios *m. pl.* east winds.
alistar *tr.* & *r.* to enlist.
aliviar *tr.* to lighten, help; *r.* to become lighter.
alma *f.* soul, mind, spirit; strength, vigour.
almacén *m.* warehouse, shop.
almacenar *tr.* to store, deposit.
almeja *f.* mussel.
almendra *f.* almond; kernel.
almendro *m.* almond-tree.
almibar *m.* syrup.
almidonar *tr.* to starch.
almirante *m.* admiral; commander of a fleet.
almohada *f.* pillow, bolster.
almorzar *in.* to breakfast *(or)* lunch; *tr.* to eat *(something).*
alocución *f.* allocution; speech.
alojamiento *m.* lodging.
alojar *tr.* & *in.* to oldge.
alondra *f.* (Zool.) lark.
alpiste *m.* canary-seed.
alquilar *tr.* to let, hire; *r.* to serve for wages.
alquiler *m.* wages, hire.

alquitrán *m.* tar.
alrededor *adv.* around.
altaneria *f.* hawking.
altar *m.* stone for sacrifices; altar.
altavoz *m.* loud-speaker.
alterar *tr.* to alter, change.
alteza *f.* Highness.
altibajo *m. pl.* the sinuosities of uneven ground.
altitud *f.* altitude, height.
altura *f.* height, loftiness.
alubia *f.* bean, French bean.
alud *m.* avalanche, snow-slip.
aludir *in.* to allude.
alumbrado *adj.* lighted; *m.* lighting.
alumbramiento *m.* childbirth.
alumbrar *tr.* to light, lighten.
alumno *m.* disciple, pupil.
alusivo -va *adj.* allusive.
alza *f.* (Com.) rise.
alzamiento *m.* uprising, revolt.
alzar *tr.* to raise; to heave, lift up.
allá *adv.* there, in that place, thither.
allegado -da *m. & f.* relation, intimate friend; *adj.* near.
allí *adv.* there, in that place; then.
ama *f.* mistress; landlady.
amabilidad *f.* kindliness, kindness.
amable *adj.* amiable, kind.
amado *m. & f.* beloved, loved.
amaestrar *tr.* to instruct; *r.* to train, teach oneself.
amagar *tr.* to threaten; *in.* to show a threatening attitude.
amainar *tr.* (Náut.) to lower the sails.
amanecer *in.* to dawn; to arrive at break of day.
amansar *tr.* to tame, subdue; *r.* to become tamed.
amante *m. & f.* lover; *adj.* loving.
amapola *f.* (Bot.) poppy.
amar *tr.* to love, like.

amargar *tr.* to make bitter.
amargo -ga *adj.* bitter.
amarillo -lla *adj.* yellow.
amarra *f.* (Náut.) cable; hawser.
amarrar *tr.* to tie, fasten.
amartelar *tr.* to enamour; *r.* to fall in love.
amaestrar *tr.* to knead.
amatista *f.* (Min.) amethyst.
ámbar *m.* amber.
ambicionar *tr.* to aspire to.
ambiente *adj.* surrounding; atmosphere.
ambigüedad *f.* ambiguity.
ambos -bas *adj. pl.* both.
ambulante *adj.* roving.
amenazar *tr.* to threaten, menace.
amenizar *tr.* to make pleasant or agreeable.
americana *f.* coat, jacket.
ametralladora *f.* machine-gun.
amigable *adj.* friendly.
amígdalas *f. pl.* (Med.) amygdalae; tonsils.
amigo -ga *m. & f.* friend, comrade; lover.
amistad *f.* friendship, amity.
amo *m.* master; proprietor.
amolar *tr.* to grind.
amonestar *tr.* to advise.
amor *m.* love; tenderness.
amoratado *adj.* livid, ghastly.
amordazar *tr.* to gag.
amortajar *tr.* to shroud.
amortiguar *tr.* to temper, mitigate.
amotinar *tr.* to excite to rebellion.
amparar *tr.* to shelter.
amparo *m.* favour, aid.
ampliación *f.* enlargement.
ampliar *tr.* to amplify, enlarge.
amplificador *m. & f.* amplifier.
amplio -ia *adj.* ample.
ampolla *f.* blister on the skin.
amueblar *tr.* to furnish.
analfabeto -ta *adj.m. & f.* illiterate; ignorant.

A

analizar *tr.* to analyse.
anarquía *f.* anarchy.
anciano -na *adj. m.* & *f.* old, aged; elder, senior.
anclar *tr.* & *in.* to anchor.
ancho -cha *adj.* broad, wide; *m.* width.
anchoa *f.* anchovy.
anchura *f.* breadth, width.
andada *f.* track, trail.
andamio *m.* scaffold.
andar *in.* to walk, move, to go.
andariego -ga *adj.* restless.
andén *m.* sidewalk; platform.
andrajoso -sa *adj.* ragged.
anexo -xa *adj.* annexed.
anexo *adj.* joined.
ángel *m.* angel; spiritual being.
angina *f.* (Med.) angina; *pl.* tonsils.
anglosajón -na *adj. m.* & *f.* Anglo-Saxon.
angosto -ta *adj.* narrow.
anguila *f.* eel.
angular *adj.* angular.
ángulo *m.* angle; corner, nook.
angustia *f.* anguish, afflication.
angustiar *tr.* to cause anguish, afflict.
anhelar *tr.* & *in.* to long.
anidar *in.* to nestle.
anillo *m.* ring; finger ring.
ánimo *m.* courage; thought.
aniñado -da *adj.* childish.
aniquilar *tr.* to annihilate, destroy.
anís *m.* (Bot.) anise.
aniversario *m.* anniversary.
anoche *adv.* last night.
anochecer *in.* to grow dark; *r.* to become dark.
anomalía *f.* anomaly.
anonadar *tr.* to annihilate; *r.* to humble oneself greatly.
anónimo *adj.* anonymous.
anormal *adj.* abnormal.
anotar *tr.* to annotate, to note, mark down.
anisar *tr.* to desire anxiously.

antagonista *m.* & *f.* antagonist.
antaño *adv.* formerly.
ante *m.* (Zool.) elk; buckskin.
anteanoche *adv.* the night before last.
anteayer *adv.* the day before yesterday.
antebrazo *m.* forearm.
anteceder *tr.* to precede, go before.
antedicho *adj.* aforesaid.
antelación *f.* preference.
antemano *adv.* beforehand.
antena *f.* aeiral.
anteojo *m.* spy-glass; *pl.* spectacle.s
antepecho *m.* breastwork.
anteponer *tr.* to prefer, place before.
antes *adv.* before, sooner, earlier; *adv.* beforehand; rather.
anticipado -da *adj.* premature.
anticipar *tr.* to antiicpate, forestall.
anticuario *m.* & *f.* antiquarian.
antifaz *m.* veil; mask.
antigüedad *f.* antiquity, oldness; *pl.* antiques.
antipatía *f.* antipathy, aversion.
antitesis *f.* antitheseis, contrary.
antojarse *r.* to long for, fancy.
antorcha *f.* torch.
antropófago *m.* & *f.* cannibal.
anuario *m.* year-book, trade directory.
anudar *tr.* to know; *r.* to become knotted.
anulación *f.* nullification. abrogation.
anular *tr.* to annul.
anunciar *tr.* to announce; *v.* to make oneself known.
anzuelo *m.* fishhook; bait; (fig.).
añadir *tr.* to add; join to augment.
añejo -ja *adj.* old.

A

añorar *tr.* to pine for; to feel homesickness.
apacentar *tr.* to pasture, graze.
apacible *adj.* gentle.
apaciguar *tr.* to pacify; *r.* to be appeased.
apadrinar *tr.* to sponsor, to act as godfather for a child.
apagar *tr.* to extinguish, to put out.
apaisado -da *adj.* oblong, broader.
apalabrar *tr.* to agree to something.
apalancar *tr.* to lever.
apalear *tr.* to beat; to beat down *(fruit)*.
aparto *m.* apparatus, appliance, device.
aparatoso -sa *adj.* pompous, showy.
aparcar *tr.* to park.
aparecer *in.* & *r.* to appear.
aparecido *m.* ghost, spectre.
aparejador *m.* achitect's assistant, works manager.
aparejar *tr.* to prepare, get ready; *r.* to get.
aparejo *m.* apparel, harness.
aparentar *tr.* to feign.
apartado -da *adj.* retired, aloof; Post Office (P.O.) letter box.
apasionado -da *adj.* ardent.
apasionar *tr.* to impassion, excite strongly.
apeadero *m.* horse block.
apear *tr.* to dismount, bring down.
apedrear *tr.* to throw stones at.
apelar *in.* (Law) to appeal; call upon.
apellidar *tr.* to call, name; to proclaim; *r.* to be called.
apellido *m.* surname, family name.
apenar *tr.* to pain.
apenas *adv.* scarcely, hardly.

apendicitis *f.* (Med.) appendicitis.
aperitivo *m.* aperitif.
apertura *f.* opening.
apesadumbrar *tr.* to pain, grieve.
apestar *tr.* to infect with the plague.
apetecer *tr.* to desire; to feel an appetite for.
apetecible *adj.* desirable.
apetito *m.* appetite.
apiadar *tr.* to inspire pity; *r.* to have mercy on.
apilar *tr.* to pile.
apiñar *tr.* to pack, press togehter; *r.* to crowd.
aplanar *tr.* to smooth, lever; *r.* to tumble down.
aplastar *tr.* to flatten; to crush, to quash; *r.* to flatten.
aplaudir *tr.* & *in.* to applaud.
aplazar *tr.* to adjourn, put off.
aplicar *tr.* to apply; to put; *r.* to apply *(or)* devote oneself.
apócrifo -fa *adj.* apocryphal.
apodar *tr.* to nickname.
apoderar *tr.* to empower, to grant power; *r.* seize.
apodo *m.* nickname.
apogeo *m.* (fig.) height.
apolillar *tr.* to eat.
aporrear *tr.* to cudgel, club.
aportar *tr.* to bring, furnish.
aposentar *tr.* to put up, lodge; *v.* to take lodging.
apreciar *tr.* to evaluate, appraise.
apremiante *adj.* urgent.
apremiar *tr.* to urge, press.
aprender *tr.* to learn.
apresar *tr.* to seize.
apresurar *tr.* to hasten, quicken, hurry; *v.* to hasten.
apretado -da *adj.* tight.
apretar *tr.* to squeeze, to hug; *r.* to crowd.
aprieto *m.* strait, difficulty.
aprisa *adv.* fast, quickly.
aprisionar *tr.* to imprison.

aprobación *f.* approbation.
aprobar *tr.* to approve; to pass.
aprovechable *adj.* serviceable.
approvechado -da *adj.* well spent.
aprovechar *tr.* to utilize, make use of; *in.* to be useful.
aprovisionar *tr.* to supply.
aproximación *f.* nearing.
aproximar *tr.* to bring near (*or*) nearer; *r.* to approach.
apto -pta *adj.* able.
apuesto -ta *adj.* handsome.
apuntalar *tr.* to prop.
apuntar *tr.* to aim; level, point; *in.* to break dawn.
apunte *m.* note.
apurar *tr.* to clear up; to carry to extremes; *r.* to grieve, worry.
apuro *m.* need, want.
aquejar *tr.* to ail, afflict.
aquel, aquella *adj. dem.* that.
aquellos, aquellas *adj. dem. pl.* those.
aquél, aquélla *pron. dem.* that one.
aquéllos, aquéllas *pron. dem. pl.* those ones.
aquello *pron. dem. neuter.* that, it.
aquí *adv.* here.
aquilatar *tr.* to estimate the carats of.
ara *f.* altar.
arado *m.* plough.
arancel *m.* tariff.
araña *f.* (Zool.) spider.
arañar *tr.* to scratch.
arbitrar *tr.* to arbitrate.
árbol *m.* (Bot.) tree.
arboleda *f.* grove.
arbusto *m.* (Bot.) shrub.
arca *f.* coffer, chest.
arcaico -ca *adj.* archaic.
arcilla *f.* clay.
arco *m.* arc; bow arch.

archivar *tr.* to fil; record, register.
arder *in.* to burn.
ardillar *f.* squirrel.
área *f.* area, space.
arena *f.* sand, grit.
arenal *m.* sandy ground.
argolla *f.* large ring, collar.
argüir *in.* to argue; dispute; *tr.* to infer, imply.
argumento *m.* argument.
aridez *f.* drought; barrenness.
árido -da *adj.* arid, dry.
arista *f.* (Bot.) arista; edge.
aritmética *f.* arithmetic.
arma *f.* weapon; arms.
armada *f.* navy.
armador *m.* outfitter.
armadura *f.* armour.
armar *tr.* to arm; mount; *in.* to suit; *r.* to prepare coneself.
armario *m.* cupboard; wardrobe.
armazón *f.* frame.
armonizar *tr.* to harmonize; *r.* to conform.
aro *m.* hoop.
aroma *f.* scent, fragrance.
aromatizar *tr.* to aromatize.
arpillera *f.* sackcloth.
arquear *tr.* to arch.
arquietecto *m.* architect.
arrabal *m.* suburb; *pl.* environs.
arraigar *in.* to root; *r.* to settle down.
arrancar *tr.* to extirpate, root out; *in.* to start off; *con.* to leave.
arrasar *tr.* to level; to raze, demolish.
¡arre! *inj.* gee!, get up!
arrear *tr.* to drive.
arrecife *m.* causeway.
arreglado -da *adj.* regular, moderate.
arreglar *tr.* to guide, regulate; *r.* to conform onself.
arremeter *tr.* to assail, attack.
arrendado -da *adj.* rented.

arrendador -ra *m. & f.* landlord, lessor.

arrendar *tr.* to rent, let.

arrepentido -da *m. & f.* penitent.

arrepentirse *r.* to repent, regret.

arresto *m.* detention.

arriar *tr.* (Náut.) to lower; to strike.

arriba *adv.* above, over; on high.

arribar *in.* to arrive; (Náut.) to put into a harbour.

arriendo *m.* letting, renting.

arriero *m.* muleteer.

arriesgar *tr.* to risk, hazard; *r.* to expose oneself to danger.

arrinconar *tr.* to put in a corner.

arrizar *tr.* to reef; to stow.

arroba *f.* weight of about twenty-five pounds.

arrogar *tr.* to arrogate; *r.* to appropriate to oneself.

arrojar *tr.* fling, hurl; to throw; to throw away; *r.* to launch.

arrollar *tr.* to roll up, wind.

arroyo *m.* small river.

arroz *m.* rice.

arruga *f.* wrinkle.

arrugar *tr.* to wrinkle, crumple.

arruinar *tr.* to throw, down, demolish.

arrullar *tr.* to bill.

artesa *f.* trough.

artesano *m.* artisan.

artesonado -da *adj.* (Arch.) panelled.

articular *tr.* to artiulate.

artículo *m.* article, knuckle, joint.

artificio *m.* workmanship, craft.

artillería *f.* gunnery.

artimaña *f.* trap, snare.

arzobispo *m.* archbishop.

asa *f.* handle, ear of a vase.

asador *m.* spit.

asaltar *tr.* to assial, to assault.

asar *tr.* to roast; *r.* to excessively hot.

ascendiente *m. & f.* ancestor; *m.* ascendency.

ascenso *m.* rise; promotion.

ascensor *m.* lift; U.S. elevator.

asco *m.* nausea, loathesomeness.

ascua *f.* red-hot coal.

asear *tr.* to set off, adorn; *r.* to make oneself clean.

asediar *tr.* to besiege, blockade.

asegurado -da *adj.* secured, fixed; *m. & f.* insured.

aseo *m.* cleanliness, neatness.

aserrar *tr.* to saw.

aserto *m.* assertion.

asesinar *tr.* to assassinate.

asesor -ra *m. & f.* counsellor, adviser; *adj.* advising.

asesorar *tr.* to advise, counsel, *r.* to take advice.

asfalto *m.* asphalt.

asfixiar *tr.* (Med.) to asphyxiate, suffocate.

así *adv.* so, thus, in this way, like this; also, therefore, so that.

asiento *m.* seat, chair, stool, bench.

asignar *tr.* to assign.

asignatura *f.* subject (fo study); pl curriculum.

asilo *m.* asylum, sanctuary.

asistencia *f.* attendance; actual presence.

asistenta *f.* handmaid.

asistente *m.* assistant, helper.

asistir *in.* to be present; *tr.* to accompany.

asno *m.* ass donkey.

asociación *f.* association; fellowship.

asomar *in.* to begin, to appear.

asombrar *tr.* to shade, darken; *r.* to take fright.

asombro *m.* dread, fear.

aspa *f.* cross; sail (windmill).

aspecto *m.* sight, appearance, look.
aspereza *f.* asperity, accerbity.
asperjar *tr.* to sprinkle.
áspero -ra *adj.* rough, rugged.
aspiración *adj.* aspiration, desire.
aspirar *tr.* to inspire the air, draw breath.
asquear *tr.* & *in.* to consider with disgust.
asqueroso -sa *adj.* nasty, filthy.
asta *f.* lance.
astilla1 *f.* chip, splinter.
astillero *m.* dock-yard, shipyard.
astro *m.* star, planet.
asumir *tr.* to assume, take upon.
asunto *m.* matter.
asustar *tr.* to frighten, terrify, scare; *r.* to be frightened by.
atacar *tr.* to attack.
atado -da *adj.* tied; bound; *m.* bundle.
atajo1 *m.* short-cut.
atalaya *f.* watch-tower.
atardecer *m.* dusk, sunset; *in.* to grow late.
atareado -da *adj.* busy, occupied.
atarear *tr.* to task, impose a task; *r.* to be very busy.
atascar *tr.* to stop a leak.
ataúd *m.* coffin.
ataviar *tr.* to deck out.
atemorizar *tr.* to frighten.
atención *f.* attention.
atender *tr.* & *in.* to attend, be attentive.
atenerse *r.* to depend, rely on.
atentar *tr.* to attempt, to commit a crime.
atenuar *tr.* to attenuate, extenuate.
aterrador -ra *adj.* horrible.
aterrar *tr.* to frighten.
aterrizar *tr.* to land.

atesorar *tr.* to treasure up, hoardup.
atestar *tr.* to cram, stuff.
atestiguar *tr.* to depose, witness.
atildar *tr.* to punctuate; *r.* to dress.
atinar *in.* to hit the mark.
atizar *tr.* to stir the fire.
atolondrado -da *adj.* hare-brained, giddy.
atollar *in.* & *r.* to fall into the mire.
átomo *m.* atom; mote.
atontar *tr.* to stun, stupefy; *r.* to become stupid.
atornillar *tr.* to screw.
atosigar *tr.* to poison; *r.* to become worried.
atraco *m.* highway robbery.
atraer *tr.* to attract.
atrancar *tr.* to bar a door; to block up.
atrás *adv.* backwards, behind; ¡atrás!, back!, go back!
atrasado -da *adj.* late.
atrasar *tr.* to protract, postpone.
atreverse *r.* to be too forward.
atribución *f.* attribution, conferring.
atribuir *tr.* to attribute, ascribe, impute.
atril *m.* desk, lectern, music-stand.
atrincherar *tr.* to entrench, fortify with a trench.
atropellar *tr.* to run over; to push through; to knock down; *r.* to hurry overmuch.
atroz *adj.* atrocious, cruel.
atún *m.* tunny.
aturdido, -da *adj.* dumbfounded, unnerved.
aturdir *tr.* to perturb, bewilder.
audacia *f.* boldness; audacity.
audaz *adj.* bold.
audiencia *f.* audience, hearing.
auditor *m.* judge.

auge *m.* apogee.
augurar *tr.* to augur, foretell.
aula *f.* class room.
aumentar *tr.* to augment, increase; *r.* to gather.
aún *adv.* yet, even; **aun cuando**, although.
aunque *conj.* though, although.
auricular *adj.* ear; *m.* receiver.
aurora *f.* dawn, daybreak.
auscultar *tr.* (Med.) to auscultate.
ausencia *f.* absence.
ausente *adj.* absent.
austero -ra *adj.* austere.
auto *m.* act; judicial decree *(or)* sentence.
autobús *m. (motor)* autobus; *con.* bus.
automóvil *m.* motor-car.
autoridad *f.* authority, credit.
autorizado -da *adj.* respectable.
autorizar *tr.* to authorize; legalize.
autorretrato *m.* self-portrait.
auxiliador -ra, *m. & f.* auxiliary, assistant.
auxiliar *tr.* to aid, help *m.* assistant, auxiliary.
auxilio *m.* aid, help.
aval *m.* guarantee, surety.
avalar *in.* (Com.) to guarantee by endorsement.
ave *f.* bird, fowl.
avecinar *tr. & in.* to approach; *r.* to domicile oneself.
avellana *f.* hazel-nut.
avena *f.* (Bot.) oats.
avenir *tr.* to reconcile; *r.* to settle differences in a friendly way.
aventajar *tr.* to surpass.
aventura *f.* adventure, enterprise.
avergonzar *tr.* to shame, abash; *r.* to feel shame.
avería *f.* damage.

averiguar *tr.* to inquire, investiage.
avestruz *m.* ostrich.
avidez *f.* covetousness, avidity.
ávido -da *adj.* greedy, covetous.
avinagrar *tr.* to sour, make acid; *r.* to become sour.
avión *m.* aeroplane, airplane.
avioneta *f.* light airplane.
avisar *tr.* to inform, give notice.
aviso *m.* information, intelligence.
avispa *f.* wasp.
avivar *tr.* to quicken, enliven, encourage.
avizor -ra *adj.* watchful; *m.* spy.
¡ay! *inj.* alas!
ayer *adv.* yesterday; (fig.) formerly.
ayuda *f.* help, aid.
ayudante *m.* (Mil.) adjutant; *adj.* helping, assisting.
ayudar *in.* to fast.
azada *f.* spade, hoe.
azadón *m.* mattock, hoe.
azafata *f.* air hostess.
azafrán *m.* (Bot.) saffron.
azar *m.* chance, unforeseen disaster.
azor *m.* (Zool.) goshawk.
azotar *tr.* to whip, lash, horsewhip.
azotea *f.* flat roof of a house, housetop.
azúcar *m. & f.* sugar.
azucarar *tr.* to sugar, sweeten.
azucarero -ra *m. & f.* sugar bowl.
azucena *f.* (Bot.) white lily.
azufre *m.* sulphur.
azul *adj.* blue.
azulejo *m.* glazed tile.
azuzar *tr.* to set dogs on to.

B

baba *f.* drivel, slaver.
babero *m.* bib.
babor *m.* (Náut.) port, larboad.
babucha *f.* slipper.
baca *f.* top *(of a stagecoach).*
bacalao *m.* codfish.
báculo *m.* walking-stick, staff.
bache *m.* hole; pot-hole.
bachiller *m.* & *f.* bachelor.
badajo *m.* bell clapper.
badén *m.* channel made by rainwater, rain gutter.
bagage *m.* (Mil.) baggage; (U.S.) luggage.
bahía *f.* bay.
bailar *tr. in.* to dance.
bajada *f.* descent, slope.
bajar *in.* to descend; *tr.* to lower, let down; to reduce.
bajeza *f.* meanness.
bajo -ja *adj.* short, low; *m.* deep place.
bajo *adv.* below; *prep.* under, beneath.
bala *f.* bullet.
balada *f.* ballad, song.
balance *m.* oscillation, swinging; (Náut.) rolling, rocking; (Com.) balance.
balandro *m.* (Náut.) small sloop.
balanza *f.* scale(s); balance.
balaustrada *f.* balustrade.
balbucear *in.* to stutter, stammer.
balcón *m.* balcony, open gallery.
baldar *tr.* to cripple; to trump.
balde *m.* bucket; gratis, free of charge.
baldío -día *adj.* untilled, uncultivated.
baldosa *f.* fine square tile.
balneario *m.* watering place, bathing place.
balón *m.* *(large)* ball.

balconcesto *m.* basketball.
balsa *f.* pool, pond.
ballena *f.* (Zool.) whale.
ballesta *f.* cross-bow.
bambú bamboo.
banca *f.* form, bench; washingbox.
banco *m.* bench, form, seat; (Com.) bank.
banda *f.* sash, scarf.
bandada *f.* covery, flock *(of birds).*
bandeja *f.* tray.
bandera *f.* flag, ensign, colors, banner.
banderilla *f.* small dart with a bannerol for baiting bulls.
bandido *m.* bandit, outlaw.
bando *m.* proclamation, edict.
banquete *m.* banquet.
bañar *tr.* to bathe; *r.* to bathe; to take *(or.)* to have a bath.
bañera *f.* bathtub.
baño *m.* bath.
baraja *f.* complete pack of cards; game of cards.
barajar *tr.* to shuffle *(cards); in.* to quarrel, content.
baranda *f.* railing, banister.
baratijas *f. pl.* trifles, toys.
barato -ta *adj.* cheap, low-priced.
barba *f.* chin; beard.
barbecho *m.* fallow.
barbería *f.* barber's shop *(or)* trade.
barca *f.* (Náut.) boat, barge.
barco *m.* boat, vessel, ship.
barniz *m.* varnish, glaze.
barnizar *tr.* to varnish.
barraca *f.* barrack, cabin.
barranco *m.* precipice.
barrena *f.* gimlet, borer.
barrenar *tr.* t bore, drill.
barrendero -ra *m.* & *f.* sweeper, cleaner; *m.* dust-man.
barreno *m.* large borer.
barreño earthen tub.
barrer *tr.* to sweep.

barriada f. city ward.
barriga f. abdomen, belly.
barril m. barrel, earthen jug.
barro m. clay, mud, mire.
barruntar tr. to foresee,
  conjecture.
basar tr. to base, set up.
báscula f. weighing scale.
basílica f. royal palace.
¡basta! inj. enough!, stop that!
bastante adj. sufficient,
  enough; adv. rather, quite.
bastar in. to suffice, be
  enough.
bastidor m. easel, frame.
basto -ta adj. coarse,
  homespun.
bastón m. cane, stick, staff.
basura f. sweepings, filth.
bata f. morning-gown,
  dressing-gown.
batalla f. battle, fight, combat.
batallar in. to battle, fight.
batata f. (Bot.) sweet potato.
batería f. (Mil, Elec.) battery.
batidor -ra adj. beating; m.
  beater.
batir tr. to beat, dash.
batuta f. baton.
baúl m. trunk, coffer.
bautismo m. baptism.
bautizar tr. to baptize,
  christen.
bayeta f. baise.
bayoneta f. bayonet.
bazar m. bazaar, emporium.
bazo m. spleen.
bebedor m. & f. drinker.
beber m. drinking; tr. to drink,
  swallow; in. to pledge, toast.
bebida f. drink, beverage.
beca f. scholarship or
  studentship; grant; part of
  acollegian's dress worn
  over the gown.
becerro m. young bull,
  yearling calf.
bedel m. beadle.
bélico pca adj. warlike,
  martial.

bellaco -ca adj. artful, sly.
belleza f. beauty, fairness,
  loveliness.
bello -lla adj. beautiful,
  handsome.
bellota f. acorn.
bendecir tr. praise, exalt; to
  bless.
beneficiar tr. to benefit, do
  good to. r. to make profit.
beneficio m. benefit; favor,
  kindness.
beneplácito m. good will,
  approbation.
benjamín m. youngest son.
berenjena f. (Bot.) eggplant.
berrear in. to bleat (like
  sheep).
berrinche m. con. anger,
  sulkiness of children.
berza f. (Bot.) cabbage.
besar tr. to kiss; con. to touch
  closely (objects).
bestia f. beast.
besugo m. (Zool.) seabream.
betún m. bitumen.
biberón m. feeding-bottle.
bibliófilo m. book lover.
biblioteca f. library; public
  library.
bibliotecario -ria adj. librarian.
bicho m. (general name for)
  small insect(s); grub,
  insect, vermin.
bidón m. drum.
biela f. crank.
bien m. good; well-being;
  utility, benefit; pl. property,
  fortune, land.
bienaventurado -da adj.
  blessed, happy.
bienestar m. well-being,
  comfort.
bienhechor -ra benefactor,
  benefactress.
bienvenida f. welcome.
biftec m. steak.
bifurcación f. fork.
bigote m. moustache, whisker.
bilis f. bile gall.

B

billar *m.* game of billards.
billete *m.* note; ticket; lottery ticket; brief letter.
biombo *m.* folding screen.
birria *f.* ¡qué birria!, what a thing!
bis *adv.* twice.
bisabuelo *m.* great grandfather.
bisabuela *f.* great grandmother.
bisagra *f.* hinge.
bisiesto *adj.* **año bisiesto**, a leap year.
bisturí *m.* bistoury, scalpel.
bisutería *f.* jewel(le)rey.
bizco -ca *adj.* cross-eyed; *m.* squinter.
bizcocho *m.* biscuit; hardtack.
biznieto *m.* great grandson.
biznieta *f.* great granddaughter.
blanco -ca *adj.* white; blank; light; *f.* white person.
blando -da *adj.* soft, smooth; bland; *con.* cowardly.
blanquear *tr.* to blanch, bleach, whiten, *in.* to show whiteness.
blasón *m.* heraldry, blazon.
blindar *tr.* (Mil.) & (Náutica) to protect with blindage.
bloque *m.* block.
blusa *f.* blouse.
bobada *f.* nonsense, stupidity.
bobina *f.* reel or bobbin, spool.
boca *f.* mouth; entrance, opening, hold; muzzle; taste, flavor *(of wine);* (Náut.) hatchway; *pl.* outfall *(river)*.
bocadillo *m.* sandwich.
bocado *m.* mouthful.
boceto *m.* sketch.
bocina *f.* horn, *(car)*.
bochorno *m.* hot, sultry weather.
boda *f.* marriage, nuptials, wedding.
bodega *f.* wine-vault.

bodegón *m.* eating-house.
bofetada *f.* slap, box.
boga *f.* (Zool.) kind of edible fish; (Náut.) act of rowing.
bogar *in.* to row.
boicotear *tr.* to boycott.
boina *m.* beret, flat round cap without peak.
bola *m.* ball, bowl.
boletín *m.* bulletin.
boleto *m.* ticket.
bolo *m.* skittle; (Med.) bolus; *pl.* game of nine-ins.
bolsa *f.* purse; bag.
bolsillo *m.* pocket, purse.
bolso *m.* handbag.
bollo *m.* small loaf or roll; small biscuit.
bomba *f.* pump; bomb.
bombardear *tr.* to bombard, bomb.
bombero *m.* fireman.
bombilla *f.* (Elec.) bulb.
bombón *m.* bonbon, sweet stuff.
bondad *f.* goodness, excellence.
bonificación *f.* improvement; (Com.) allowance, discount.
bonito -ta *adj.* pretty good; pretty.
boquerón *m.* (Ichth.) anchovy.
boquete *m.* gap, narrow entrance.
boquilla *f.* lower opening of breeches; cigar *(or cigarette)* holder.
borda *f.* gunwale *(ship)*.
bordar *tr.* to embroider.
borde *m.* border, outer edge.
borla *f.* tassel, tuft.
borracho -cha *adj.* drunk; *con.* inflamed by passion.
borrador *m.* blotter.
borrar *tr.* to cross out, strike out.
borrasca *f.* storm, tempest.
borrico *m.* ass; *con.* fool.
borrón *m.* blot of ink.
bosquejo *m.* sketch.

bostezar *in.* to yawn, gape.
bota *f.* boot, small leather winebag.
bote *m.* thrust *(spear)*; tin; rebound of a ball; jump; pot *(or)* jar; (Náut.) row-boat.
botella *f.* bottle; flask.
botica *f.* chemist-shop.
botijo *m.* round earthen jar *(with spout and handle)*.
botín *m.* buskin, half-boot.
botiquín *m.* First aid.
botón *m.* (Bot.) sprout, bud; button.
bóveda *f.* (Arq.) arch, vault.
bozal *m.* muzzle.
braga *f. pl.* knickers; breeches.
bragueta *f.* fly of breeches.
bramar *in.* to roar; to storm.
brasa *f.* live coal, red-hot coal *(or)* wood.
brasero *m.* brazier; fire-pan.
bravo -va *adj.* brave, valiant, strenuous, manful, fearless.
brazalete *m.* armlet, bracelet.
brazo *m.* arm; branch.
brea *f.* tar, resin, pitch.
breva *f.* early fruit of a figtree.
breve *adj.* brief, short, concise.
brevedad *f.* brevety, briefness.
bribón -na *m. & f., adj.* vagrant.
brigada *f.* (Mil.) brigade.
brillante *adj.*) brilliant, bright, shining; *m.* brilliant, diamond.
brillar *in.* to shine, sparkle.
brincar *in.* to jump, leap.
brindar *in.* to drink someone's health; *tr. & in.* to offer cheerfully, invite.
brindis *m.* health, after dinner speech.
brío *m.* strength, force.
brisca *f.* game of cards.
británico *adj.* British.
broch *f.* *(painter's)* brush.
broche *m.* clasp, brooch.
broma *f.* gaiety, jollity.

bromear *in. & r.* to joke, make fun.
bronca *f.* quarrel.
broncear *tr.* to bronze; *r.* to tan.
brotar *in.* to bud, germinate, put forth shoots.
brujo *m.* sorcerer, conjurer.
brújula *f.* compass.
bruma *f.* mist; haze.
brusco *adj.* rough, brusque.
brutal *adj.* brutal, brutish.
bruto -ta *adj.* coarse, beastly, brutish; *m.* brute, beast.
bucear *in.* (Náut.) to dive.
buenamente *adv.* freely, spontaneously.
buenaventura *f.* fortune, good luck.
bueno -na *adj.* good, kind; upright, virtuous; *adv.* very well, all right.
buey *m.* ox.
bufanda *f.* muffler; scarf.
bufete *m.* bureau.
bufón -na *adj.* funny, comical; *m.* pedlar.
buhardilla *f.* garret, attic.
buho *m.* owl; *con.* unsocial person.
buitre *m.* vulture.
bujía *f.* wax candle.
bulto *m.* bulk, anything which appears bulky.
bullir *in.* to boil, bubble up; *tr.* to move, stir; *r.* to stir.
buque *m.* (Náut.) vessel, ship.
burbujear *in.* to bubble.
burgués -sa *adj.* burgess; *m.* middle-class citizen.
burro *m.* ass, donkey.
buscar *tr.* to seek, search; to look for.
búsqueda *f.* search.
busto *m.* bust.
butaca *f.* arm-chair; easy-chair.
buzo *m.* diver.

B

C

cabal *adj.* exact.
cabalgar *tr.* to ride horseback.
caballero *m.* knight; gentleman, sir.
caballete *m.* painter's easel; ridge.
caballo *m.* horse; knight.
cabaña *f.* cabin, hut.
cabecear *in.* to nod.
cabecera *f.* beginning, head.
cabellera *f.* head of hair.
cabello *m.* hair.
caber *in.* to fit.
cabestrillo *m.* sling; bell-ox.
cabeza *f.* head, chief,leader.
cabida *f.* space, capacity.
cabildo *m.* cathedral chapter; municipal council.
cabina *f.* cabin.
cable *m.* cable, wire.
cabo *m.* end; handle; small bundle; thread.
cabotaje *m.* coasting trade.
cabra *f.* (she)-goat.
cabrito *m.* kid, small goat.
cacahuete *m.* peanut.
cacarear *in.* to cackle; to boast.
cacería *f.* hunt; hunting party.
caciquismo *(fam.)* bossism.
caco *m.* pickpocket.
cacharro *m.* crock, earthen pot.
cachear *tr.* to frisk.
cachimba *f.* tobacco-pipe.
cacho *m.* piece, slide.
cada *adj.* indef. each; every.
cadalso *m.* stand, platform.
cadáver *in.* corpse, dead body.
cadena *f.* chain.
cadera *f.* (An.) hip.
caducar *in.* to dote, to fall into disuse.
caer *in.* to fall, to fall off, to drop; *tr.* to fall, to fall down.
café *m.* coffee; café.

cafetera *f.* coffee-pot.
caída *f.* fall, downfall, drop, declination.
caja *f.* box, case; cashbox; cashiers office.
cal *f.* lime.
calabaza *f.* pumpkin, gourd.
calabozo *m.* dungeon; prison cell.
calamar *m.* squid, calamar.
calambre *m.* cramp; muscle contraction.
calar *tr.* to pierce, to permeate.
calavera *f.* skull.
calcaño *m.* heel (bone).
calcar *tr.* to trace; to copy.
calceta *f.* stocking.
calcetín *m.* sock.
calcinar *tr.* & *in.* to calcine.
calcular *tr.* & *in.* to calculate, to compute.
caldear *tr.* to heat ; *r.* to become heated.
caldera *f.* boiler, kettle.
calderilla *f.* copper coins, copper money.
caldero *m.* kettle.
caldo *m.* broth.
calefacción *f.* heat, heating.
calendario *m.* calendar.
calentador *adj.* heater.
calentar *tr.* to heat.
calibrar *tr.* to calibrate.
cálido *adj.* warm, hot.
caliente *adj.* hot; heated; fiery.
calificar *tr.* to qualify, to certify, to mark.
caligrafía *f.* calligraphy, hand writting.
calmante *adj.* soothing; *m.* (Med.) sedative.
calmar *tr.* to calm; to mitigate, to quite.
calor *m.* heat; warmth.
calva *f.* bald head.
calvo *adj.* bald; hairless.
calzada *f.* roadway, road.
calzado -da *adj.* shod, calced.
calzar *tr.* to shoe, to put on.
calzones *m.* pants, trousers.

calzoncillos *m. pl.* drawers, pants.

callar *tr.* to silence; to keep silence; *in.* to be silent, to keep slient.

calle *f.* street.

callo *m.* callus, corn. *pl.* tripe.

cama *f.* bed.

cámara *f.* hall, parlour; chamber; breech.

camarada *m.* camrade, companion.

camarero *m.* waiter.

camarote *m.* cabin.

cambiar *tr.* to change.

camelar *tr. con.* to flirt with, to trick.

camilla *f.* stretcher, litter.

caminar *tr. intr.* to walk.

camino *m.* roadway, path.

camión *m.* truck, van.

camisa *f.* shirt; slough.

camiseta *f.* vest.

camisón *m.* nightshirt.

campana *f.* bell; cloche.

campesino *adj.* rural. *m.* countryman.

campiña *f.* country, countryside.

campo *m.* field; country.

cana *f.* white (or) gray hair.

canalizar *tr.* to canalise.

canalla *m.* rascal.

canapé *m.* sofa; settee.

canasta *f.* basket.

cancelar *tr.* to annul, to cancel.

cáncer *m. (Path.)* cancer.

canciller *m.* chancellor.

canción *f.* song.

candado *m.* padlock.

candela *f.* candle, torch.

candente *adj.* candent, red-hot.

candidato -ta *m. & f.* candidate, competior.

candil *m.* oil lamp.

candilejas *f. pl.* footlights.

canela *m.* cinnamon.

cangrejo *m. (Zool.)* crab.

canijo -ja *adj.* (fam.) sickly, infirm.

canjear *tr.* to exchange.

canoa *f.* canoe; launch.

canonizar *tr.* to canonise.

cansado -da *adj.* tierd, weary.

cántaro *m.* jug.

cantera *f.* quarry.

cantidad *f.* quantity, amount.

cantina *f.* tavern, pub.

cantor *adj* singing; *m.* singer, songster.

caña *f.* cane; culm, stem; reed; glass of beer.

cáñamo *m.* (Bot.) hemp.

cañaveral *m.* canebrake.

caño *m.* tube,pipe; ditch.

cañón *m.* tube, pipe; cannon; gun; shank of key.

caoba *f.* (Bot.) mahogany.

caos *m.* chaos, confusion.

capa *f.* cape, cloak, mantle; stratum.

capacidad *f.* capacity.

capacitar *tr.* to enable, to qualify; *r.* to be come enabled.

capataz *m.* overseer, foreman.

capellán *m.* chaplian.

capilla chapel; hood, cowl.

capital *adj.* capital; main, principal.

capitalizar *tr.* to capitalize.

capitán *m.* leader; captain.

capitanear *tr.* to head, to lead.

capitel *m.* (Arch) capital; spire.

capítulo *m.* chapter.

capota *f.* (Aut.) top; hood (of carriage).

capricho *m.* caprice, whim.

cápsula *f.* (An.,Bot.,Phar. & Zool.) capsule.

captar *tr.* to catch, to attract.

capturar *tr.* to capture, arrest, seize, get.

capullo *m.* bud; cocoon.

cara *f.* face; appearance, look.

carabela *f.* (Náut.) caravel.

carabina *f.* carbine; rifle.

C

carabinero *m.* carabineer; frontier officer.

caracol *m.* (Zool.) snail.

carácter *m.* character; type.

caramba *inj.* By Jove!

caramelo *m.* carmamel; sweet, toffee.

carbón *m.* coal; charcoal.

carbonizar *tr.* & *r.* to carbonize.

carbono *m.* (Chm.) carbon.

carburador *m.* carburetor.

carburante *m.* fuel.

cárcel *f.* jail, prison.

carcomer *tr.* to bore; to gnaw away; *r.* to become undermined.

cardo *m.* (Bot. & Arch.) thistle.

carecer *tr.* to be in want; to be in need of.

carestía *f.* scarcity.

careta *f.* mask.

cargar *tr.* to load; to load up; to increase.

cargo *m.* burden, weight; job, duty, charge, post, dignity.

caricia *f.* to decay, rot.

caricia *f.* caress, pat, stroke.

caridad *f.* charity.

cariño *m.* love, affection.

cariz *m.* appearance, carmin. *m.* carmine.

carne *f.* flesh; meat.

carnero *m.* mutton, sheep.

carnet *m.* notebook.

carnicería *f.* butcher shop.

caro -ra *adj.* dear, expensive.

carpeta *f.* portfolio.

carpintería *f.* carpentry.

carraspera *f. con.* hoarseness.

carrera *f.* race; running; career; *pl.* horse racing.

carreta *f.* cart.

carrete *m.* spool, bobbin.

carretera *f.* highway; road.

carretilla *f.* wheelbarrow.

carro *m.* cart; truck; car.

carrocería *f.* coachwork.

carroza *f.* coach, carriage.

carta *f.* letter; chart.

cartear *tr.* to play low cards; *r.* to write each other.

cartel *m.* poster, placecard.

cartelera *f.* billboard.

cartero *m.* postman.

cartilla *f.* primer; short treatise.

cartón *m.* cardboard, pasteboard.

cartucho *m.* cartridge.

cartulina *f.* thin cardboard.

casa *f.* house; home; apartment.

casadero -ra *adj.* marriageable.

casamiento *m.* marriage; wedding.

casar *m.* hamlet; *tr.* to marry; *in.* to marry.

cascabel *m.* jingle bell.

cascanueces *m.* nut-cracker.

cascar *in.* to crack, burst.

cáscara *f.* rind, peel.

casco *m.* skull; hoof; potsherd.

caseta *f.* hut.

casi *adv.* almost, nearly.

casino *m.* casino; club.

caso *m.* case; chance; event.

caspa *f.* dandruff, scurf.

casquete *m.* skullcap.

casta *f.* caste, race.

castaña *f.* chestnut (fruit).

castellano -na *adj., m.* & *f.* Castilian; *m.* Castilian.

castigar *tr.* to punish, to castigate.

castizo -za *adj.* pure blooded; pure, correct (language).

casual *adj.* accidental, chance, casual.

catacumbas *f. pl.* catacombs.

cataclismo *m.* cataclysm.

catalejo *m.* telescope.

catálogo *m.* catalogue.

cataplasma *f.* poultice.

catar *tr.* to taste.

catarata *f.* cataract, waterfall.

catarro *m.* (Path.) catarrh; cold (nose).

cátedra *f.* professorship, chair (university).

catedrático *m.* professor; teacher.

catorce *adj.* fourteen.

cauce *m.* river bed.

caucho *m.* india-rubber.

causa *f.* cause; motive.

causar *tr.* to cause; to make.

cautivar *tr.* to take prisoner.

cavar *tr.* to dig.

cavidad *f.* cavity.

caza *f.* chase, hunt; game.

cazador -ra *adj.* hunting; *m.* hunter.

cazar *tr.* to chase; to hunt.

cazo *m.* ladle.

cazuela *f.* earthen casserole.

cebada *f.* barley.

cebar *tr.* to fatten up.

cebolla *f.* (Bot.) onion.

cecina *f.* dried beef.

ceder *tr.* to yield, give up.

cegar *tr.* to blind; to block.

ceguerra *f.* blindness.

ceja *f.* eyebrow.

cejar *in.* to turn back.

celar *tr.* to see to; to watch over.

celda *f.* cell.

celebérrimo -ma *adj. sp.* very or most celebrated.

celebrante *adj.* celebrating, officiating; *m.* celebrate.

celeste *adj.* celestial; heavenly.

celestina *f.* bawd, procurer.

celo *m.* zeal; distrust, envy.

célula *f.* cell.

cementerio *m.* cemetery, church yard.

cemento *m.* cement; concrete.

cena *f.* supper.

cenagoso -sa *adj.* muddy, boggy.

cenar *tr.* to have supper; *in.* to sup.

cenicero *m.* ashtray.

ceniza *f.* ash, ashes.

censo *m.* census; tax.

censurar *tr.* to censure; to blame.

centavo -va *adj.* hundredth.

centenar *m.* hundred.

centenario -ria *adj.* centennial; *m.* centenarian.

centeno -na adj. rye.

centésimo -ma *adj. m.* & *f.* hundredth.

centígrado *adj.* centigrade.

centímetro *m.* centimetre.

céntimo *adj.* hundredth; *m.* cent, centime.

centinela *m.* & *f.* sentinel, sentry, guard.

central *adj.* central; *f.* main office, headquarters.

centralizars *tr.* & *r.* to centralize.

centrar *tr.* to center; *r.* to be centered.

céntrico -ca *adj.* central.

centro *m.* center; purpose.

centuria *f.* century.

ceñir *tr.* to grid; to encircle; *r.* to tighten ones belt.

cepillo *m.* brush; plane.

cepo *m.* branch, bough.

cera *f.* wax; beeswax.

cerca *f.* fence, wall; *adv.* near, close.

cercado *m.* fence, enclosure.

cercanía *f.* nearness, proximity.

cercar *tr.* to fence; *in.* to wall in.

cerco *m.* fence, wall; hoop.

cerdo *m.* (Zool.) hog, pig; pork; dirty.

cerebro *m.* (An.) cerebrum; (fig) brain, mind.

cerezo *m.* wax chandler.

cereza f. cherry.

cifar *tr.* cipher.

cigüeña *f.* (Zool.) stork.

cigüeñal *m.* crankshaft.

cilindrada *f.* (Zool.) piston displacememt.

cilindro *m.* cylinder; roll.

cima *f.* top, summit, peak.

cimentar *tr.* to found; to lay the foundation for.

C

cinc *m.* (Chm.) zinc.
cincel *m.* chisel, cutter.
cincelar *tr.* to chisel, carve, engrave.
cinco *adj.* five; *m.* five.
cincuenta *adj.* fifty.
cinta *f.* ribbon; tape; film.
cintura *f.* waist.
circular *adj.* circular; *in.* to circulate.
círculo *m.* circle; club.
circundar *tr.* to surround.
cirio *m.* big wax candle.
ciruela *f.* plum.
cirugía *f.* surgery.
cirujano *m.* surgeon.
cisma *m.* schism.
cisne *m.* (Zool.) swan.
cita *f.* date, appointment.
citación *f.* summons.
citar *tr.* to make an appointment with.
ciudad *f.* city, town.
ciudadano -na *m. & f.* citizen, townsman; *adj.* urban, civic.
civil *adj.* civil; civilian.
civilizar *tr. & r.* to civilize.
cizaña *f.* (Bot.) darnel.
clamar *tr.* to clamour for; cry out for.
clan *m.* clan, family.
clara *f.* white of egg.
claraboya *f.* skylight.
clarear *tr.* to brighten, light up.
clarinete *m.* clarinet.
clarividencia *f.* clairvoyance.
clase *f.* class; kind; quality; rank.
clasificar *tr.* to classify, arrange.
claudicar *tr.* to limp.
clausurar *tr.* to close.
clavar *tr.* to nail; to stick.
clavel *m.* (Bot.) pink, carnation.
clavícula *f.* (An,) clavicle.
clavija *f.* pin, peg.
clavo *m.* nail; corn *(on foot)*.
clero *m.* clergy.
cliché *m.* cliché.

cliente *m. & f.* client; customer.
clima *m.* climate, weather.
clínica *f.* clinic; surgery, dispensary.
cloquear *in.* to cluck, cackle.
cloro *m.* (Chm.) chlorine.
clorofila *f.* chlorophyll.
coacción *f.* coerción, coaction.
coágulo *m.* clot.
coartada *f.* alibi.
cobarde *adj.* coward; timid.
cobertizo *m.* shed, shelter.
cobertor *m.* bedcover, bedspread, quilt.
cobijar *tr.* to cover, to lodge.
cobrador *m.* collector; conducter *(bus)*; teller *(bank)*.
cobrar *tr.* to recover; to collect; to cash.
cobre *m.* copper.
cobro *m.* cashing, collection.
cocina *f.* kitchen; cuisine.
cocinar *tr.* to cook; to do the cooking.
coche *m.* car; carriage.
cochera *f.* garage, coachhouse.
cochinada *f.* piggishness.
codiciar *tr.* to covet, to long, to have.
código *m.* code; codex.
codo *m.* elbow.
codorniz *f.* (Zool.) quail.
coexistir *in.* to coexist.
cofradía *f.* confraternity; association.
cofre *m.* coffer, trunk.
cogedor *m.* dust pan.
coger *tr.* to take, catch.
cogollo *m.* heart *(of lettuce)*.
cogote *m.* back of the neck.
cohabitar *in.* to cohabit.
cohete *m.* rocket.
cohibir *tr.* to restrain.
coincidir *in.* to coincide, fall in *(with)*.
cojear *in.* to limp, to halt.
cojín *m.* cushion.

cojo -a *adj.* crippled.
col *f.* (Bot.) cabbage.
cola *f.* tail; end seat.
colaborar *in.* to collaborate.
colada *f.* wash.
colador *m.* strainer, colander
colar *tr.* to strain, filter; *r.* to slip through.
colcha *f.* bedspread.
colchón *m.* mattress.
colchoneta *f.* quilt.
coleccionar *tr.* to collect.
colega *m.* colleague.
colegial *adj.* collegiate; *m.* collegian, schoolboy.
colegio *m.* college; school, public school.
cólera *f.* (Phyl.) bile.
coleta *f.* pigtail.
colgadura *f.* hangings, drapery.
colgante *adj.* hanging; *m.* pendant, hanging ornament.
colgar *tr.* to hang; to fix *(blame).*
cólico *m.* (Path.) colic.
coliflor *f.* (Bot.) cauliflower.
colilla *f.* butt, stump *(of cigar).*
colina *f.* hill, slope.
colmar *tr.* to fill, to heap up, satisfy completely.
colmillo *m.* eyetooth.
colmo *m.* top, plenty, fill.
colocación *f.* placing.
colacar *tr.* to place.
colonizar *tr.* to colonize, to settle.
coloquio *m.* talk, conversation.
color *m.* colour.
columpiar *tr.* to swing; *r.* to swing.
collar *m.* necklace.
comadrona *f.* midwife.
comarca *f.* region, province.
combate *m.* combat.
combatir *tr.* to combat.
combinar *tr.* to combine; *r.* to combine.
comedia *f.* comedy; play.

comedido -da *adj.* courteous, polite.
comedir *r.* to be courteous.
comedor *m.* dining room.
comensal *m. & f.* table companion.
comentar *tr.* to comment, explain, gloss.
comenzar *tr. & in.* to begin, to start, to commence.
comer *tr.* to eat; to feed on; to consume.
comerciante *adj.* trading; *m. & f.* trader, merchant.
comestible *adj.* eatable, *pl.* provisions.
cometer *tr.* to commit.
cómico -ca *adj.* comic or comical.
comida *f.* food; meal; dinner.
comienzo *m.* beginning, start.
comillas *f.pl.* quotation marks.
comisaría *f.* police headquarters.
comité *m.* committee, assembly.
comitiva *f.* retinue, suit, followers.
como *adv.* as; so; like; *cnj.* as; when, if.
cómo *adj.* how?, why?; what?
cómo así?, how so?
cómo no?, why not?
cómo no!, of course!
cómoda *f.* chest of drawers.
comodón -ona *adj. con.* comfortloving.
compadecer *tr. y r.* to pity, to feel sorry for; *r.*
compadecerse de, to pity, to feel sorry for,
compaginar *tr.* to arrange, to put in order; *r.* to fit.
compañero -ra *m. & f.* companion; school-fellow.
comparar *tr.* to compare.
comparecer *in.* (Law) to appear.
compartimiento *m.* compartment.

compartir *tr.* to divide; to share.

compás *m.* compass (Mus.) time, measure.

compatriota *m.* fellow countryman.

compendiar *tr.* to summarize, condense.

compensar *tr.* to compensate; *r.* to be compensated for.

competir *in.* to compete, strive.

complacer *tr.* to please; *r.* to be pleased.

complejiad *f.* complexity.

complementar *tr.* to complement.

completar *tr.* to complete.

completo -ta *adj.* complete.

complicar *tr.* to complicate; *r.* to become complicated.

cómplice *m. & f.* accomplice.

complot *m.* plot, conspiracy.

comportar *tr.* to bear; *r.* to behave.

compositor -ra *m. & f.* composer.

compra *f.* purchase, shopping.

comprador *adj.* buying.

comprar *tr.* to buy, to purchase.

comprender *tr.* to comprehend, understand.

compresa *f.* (Med.) compress.

comprimir *tr.* to press, squeeze.

comprobación *f.* verification.

comprobar *tr.* to verify.

compuesto *adj.* compound, composed.

comulgar *in.* to take communion; to communicate.

comunicado *m.* announcement, dispatch.

comunicar *tr., in. &r.* to communicate

con *prep.* with.

conato *m.* endeavor (Law) attempt.

concebir *tr. & in.* to conceive.

conceder *tr.* to concede, admit.

concejal *m.* councilor.

concentrar *tr.* to concentrate.

concepto *m.* concept.

conceptuar *tr.* to be of opinion, to judge.

concernir *tr.* to concern, refer to.

concertar *tr.* to concert; to arrange; *r.* to become reconciled.

concertista *m. & f.* perfoØmer.

conciencia *f.* conscience.

concierto *m.* concert.

conciliar *tr.* to conciliate; to win.

concilio *m.* council.

conciso *adj.* concise, brief.

concluir *tr.* to conclude, to finish; *tr. & in.* to conclude.

conclusión *f.* conclusion, end.

concordar *tr.* to harmonize; ro reconcile.

concretar *tr.* to concrete; *r.* to limit oneself.

concupiscencia *f.* lust.

concurrencia *f.* concurrence; crowd.

concurrir *in.* to concur; to attend, meet.

concurso *m.* crowd.

concha *f.* shell; tortoise shell.

conde *m.* earl, count.

condecorar *tr.* to decorate, confer.

condena *f.* sentence; penalty.

condenar *tr.* to condemn.

condensador *m.* condenser.

condensar *tr.* to condense.

condescender *in.* to yield, condescend.

condimentar *tr.* to season.

condiscípulo *m.* fellow student.

condoler *r.* to sympathize.

conducción *f.* conduction.

conducir *tr.* to lead, guide; *r.* to conduct oneself.

conducto *m.* conduit, pipe.
conectar *tr.* to connect.
conejo *m.* (Zool.) rabbit.
confección *m.* making, confection.
confeccionar *f.* to make.
confederar *tr. & in.* to confederate.
conferencia *f.* conference; lecture.
conferenciar *in.* to confer.
conferir *tr.* to confer, grant.
confesar *tr.* to confess; admit.
confesor *m.* confessor.
confiar *tr.* to entrust, confide.
confidencial *adj.* confidential.
configurar *tr.* to form, to shape.
confirmar *tr.* to confirm.
confiscar *tr.* to confiscate.
confite *m.* candy, bonbon.
conflicto *m.* conflict.
confluente *adj.* confluent.
confluir *in.* to flow together, to meet.
conformar *tr.* to conform; to adjust; *r.* to conform.
confortar *tr.* to comfort, console.
confuso -sa *adj.* confused.
congelar *tr.* to freeze, congeal.
congénito -ta *adj.* congenital.
conglomerado -da *adj.* comglomerate.
congoja *f.* anguish.
congregar *tr. &r.* to congregate, assemble.
congresista *m. & f.* delegate.
congrio *m.* conger.
conjeturar *tr. & in.* to conjecture, to guess.
conjugar *tr.* to conjugate.
conjunto *adj.* conjoint, conjunct; *m.* whole, groupe.
conjurar *in.* to conspire, to plot.
conmemorar *tr.* to comemorate.
conmigo with me.
conminar *tr.* to threaten.

conmovedor -ra *adj.* stirring, touching.
conmover *tr.* to stir, to move; *r.* to be moved, be touched.
conmutador *m.* (Ecl.) switch; commuter.
cono *m.* (Geom.) & (Bot.) cone.
conocedor -ra *m. & f.* connoisseur, expert.
conocer *tr.* to know; *r.* to know oneself.
conocido -da *adj.* familiar; *m. & f.* acquanted.
conocimiento *m.* knowledge.
conque *adv.* and so, so then.
conquistador -ra *adj.* conquering; *m. & f.* conqueror.
conquistar *tr.* to conquer.
consagrar *tr.* to consecrate.
consciente *adj.* conscious, aware.
consecución *f.* adquisition.
conseguir *tr.* to get, obtain.
consejero -ra *m.* counsellor; *f.* female adviser.
consejo *m.* advice, counsel.
consentimiento *m.* consent.
consentir *tr.* to allow, to tolerate, *in.* to consent.
conserje *m.* concierge.
conserjería *f.* janitorship.
conserva *f.* conserve, perserves.
conservador -ra *adj.* preservative.
conservar *tr.* to preserve; *r.* to keep, maintain.
consigna *f.* order; (Mil.) watchword.
consignar *tr.* to consign.
consigo with him, with her.
consiguiente *adj.* consequent.
consistencia *f.* consistence.
consistir *in.* to consist, be composed of.
consolar *tr.* to console, comfort.
consolidar *tr.* to consolidate.

C

consonante *f.* consonant (letter); *adj.* consistent.
consorcio *m.* consortium.
consorte *m. & f.* consort.
conspirar *in.* to conspire.
constante *adj.* constance.
constar *in.* to be clear, be certain.
consternar *tr.* to consternate.
constipar *r.* to catch cold.
constituir *tr.* to constitute.
constituyente *adj.* constituent.
constreñir *tr.* to constrain.
construir *tr.* to construct.
consulta *f.* consulting.
consultar *tr.* to consult.
consumado *adj.* consummate.
consumar *tr.* to consummate.
consumir *tr.* to consume; *con.* to harass; *r.* to consume.
consumo *m.* comsumption.
consuno in accord, together.
contabilidad *f.* accountancy, bookkeeping.
contable *adj.* countable.
contado -da *adj.* scarce.
contador *m.* counter.
contagiar *tr.* to infect; *r.* to become infected.
contaminar *tr.* to contaminate, infect.
contar *tr.* to count; to rate.
contemporizar *in.* to contemporize.
contencioso -sa *adj.* contentious, litigious.
contener *tr.* to contain; to refrain, detain; *r.* to contain oneself.
contestación *f.* answer, reply.
contestar *tr.* to answer, reply.
contextura *f.* contexture, framework.
contienda *f.* fight, dispute.
contigo with you, with thee.
contiguo -ua *adj.* contiguous, next.
continuación *f.* continuation.
continuar *tr.* to continue; *in.* to continue.

continuo -ua *adj.* endless; *m.* continuum.
contra *prep.* against; *con.* opposition.
contrabandista *adj. m. & f.* contrabandist, smuggler.
contracción *f.* contraction.
contradecir *tr.* to contradict.
contraer *tr.* to contract.
contragolpe *m.* counter coup.
contraindicar *tr.* contraindicate.
contraponer *tr.* to set in front; *r.* to be opposed.
contrariar *tr.* to oppose.
contrario -ria *adj.* contrary opposite; hostile; *m. & f* enemy; *con.* to oppose, to disagree with.
contrarrestar *tr.* to, offset, counteract.
contraseña *f.* countersign, countermark.
contrastar *tr.* to check; *in.* to contrast.
contraste *m.* resistance.
contratación *f.* trade; deal.
contratar *tr.* to contract for.
contratiempo *m.* misfortune.
contrayente *adj.* marriage-contracting; *m. & f.* contracting party.
contribuir *tr. & in.* to contribute.
control *m.* check, control.
controlar *tr.* to check, control.
controvertir *tr.* to controvert, dispute.
contundente *adj.* bruising.
conturbar *tr.* to disquiet, perturb.
convalecer *in.* to convalesce.
convecino -na *adj.* neighbouring.
convención *f.* convention.
conveniente *adj.* proper.
convenio *m.* pact, agreement.
convenir *in.* to suit; to agree.
convergir *in.* to converge.
conversar *in.* to converse.

converso -sa *adj.* converted; *m. & f.* convert.
convertir *tr.* to convert.
convidar *tr.* to invite.
convivir *in.* to live together.
convocar *tr.* to convoke, summon, call together.
conyugal *adj.* conjugal.
cónyuge *m. & f.* spouse, consort.
cooperar *in.* to cooperate, work together.
coordinar *tr.* to coordinate.
copa *f.* goblet, wineglass.
copia *f.* abundance, plenty.
copiar *tr.* to copy.
copla *f.* couplet, stanza.
cópula *f.* joining, coupling.
coquetear *in.* to flirt, to coquet.
coraje *m.* anger, spirit, courage.
coraza *f.* armor plate.
corazón *m.* heart.
corbata *f.* tie, cravat.
corcel *m.* steed.
cordel *m.* cord, string.
cordero *m.* lamb.
cordial *adj.* cordial, hearty; *m.* refreshing drink.
cordillera *f.* mountain range.
cordón *m.* lace; string.
cordura *f.* prudence, widsom.
cornada *f.* thrust with horns, goring.
cornamenta *f.* horns, antlers.
corneta *f.* (Mús.) bugle; cornet.
cornisa *f.* cornice.
coro *m.* chorus; choir.
corona *f.* crown.
coronar *tr.* to crown; to top.
coronilla *f* crown.
corpiño *m.* vest.
corpúsculo *m.* corpuscle, particle.
corral *m.* corral, stockyard.
correa *f.* leather strap.
correaje *m.* belts, belting.
corregible *adj.* corrigible, subject to correction.

corregidor -ra *adj.* correcting; *f.* wide of a corregidor; *m.* magistrate.
corregir *tr.* to correct, amend.
correo *m.* courier, mail.
correr *tr.* to run, to race; *(a risk).*
correspondencia *f.* correspondence; mail.
corresponder *in.* to correspond; to concern.
corretear *in con.* to hang around.
corrido -da *adj.* in excess *(said of a weight);* cursive.
corroborar *tr.* to strengthen.
corrupción *f.* corruption.
corsé *m.* corset, girdle.
cortado -da *adj.* cut, abrupt; *m.* cup of coffee between black and white.
cortafuego *m.* fireguard.
cortante *adj.* cutting, sharp.
cortar *tr.* cut; to trim; to clip; to cut down; *r.* to become confused.
corte *m.* cut; cutting; *f.* court; yard.
cortejar *tr.* to escort, court, woo.
cortés *adj.* courteous, polite.
cortesía *f.* courtesy, politeness.
corteza *f.* bark; peel, skin.
cortijo *m.* farmhouse, farm *(in Andalucía).*
cortina *f.* curtain.
corto -ta *adj.* short; shy; backward.
cosa *f.* thing; *con.* as if nothing had happened; *con.* something unheard of.
cosecha *f.* harvest, crop.
cosechar *tr.* to harvest.
coser *tr.* to sew; to lace *(a belt).*
cosmopolita *adj.* cosmopolitan.
cosquillas *f. pl.* tickling; *con.* to try to annoy someone.

cosquilleo *m.* tickling.
costa *f.* cost, price; coast.
costado *m.* side; (Mil.) flank.
costar *tr. & in.* to cost.
costear *tr.* to defrey the cost of; *in.* to sail along the coast; *r.* to pay for itself.
costilla *f.* rib; *f. pl.* back.
costo *m.* cost.
costoso -sa *adj.* costly, expensive.
costumbre *f.* custom, habit, practice, *pl.* habits, manners.
costura *f.* sewing, needlework; tailoring.
cotejar *tr.* to compare, confront.
cotizar *tr.* to quote *(on Stock Exchange).*
coto *m.* enclosed pasture.
coyuntura *f.* conjuncture; change.
coz *f.* kick.
cráneo *m.* (An.) skull, cranium.
crear *tr.* to create.
crecer *in.* to grow, increase; to rise, to swell *(said of stream).*
crecido -da *adj.* large, grown.
credencial *adj. & f.* credential.
crédito *m.* credit; belief.
credo *m.* creed; credo.
creer *tr. & in.* to believe.
crema *f.* cream.
cremallera *f.* rack; zipfastener.
crespón *m.* crape.
cresta *f.* crest, summit.
creyente *adj.* believing; *m. & f.* believer.
cría *f.* raising; breeding.
criadero *m.* nursery.
criado -da *adj.* bred; *m. & f.* servant; *f.* maid.
criar *tr.* to raise, rear.
criatura *f.* creature, baby.
cribar *tr.* to sieve, sift.
criollo -lla *adj. & f.* Creole; native.
cripta *f.* crypt.

crisma *m. & f.* (Ecl.) chrism; *con.* head, nut.
crisol *m.* crucible.
crispar *tr.* to twitch; *r.*
cristal *m.* crystal.
cristalizar *tr. & in.* to crystallize.
cristiandad *f.* Cristendom.
criterio *m.* criterion.
criticar *tr.* to criticize, censure.
cromo *m.* (Chm.) chromium.
crónica *f.* chronicle, news column.
cronometrar *tr.* to time.
cronónometro *f.* chronometer.
croquis *m.* sketch.
cruce *m.* crossing.
crucero *m.* cruiser.
crucigrama *m.* crossword puzzle.
crudo -da *adj.* raw, crude.
crujir *in.* to crackle.
cruz *f.* cross.
cruzada *f.* crusade.
cruzar *tr.* to cross; to cut across.
cuaderno *m.* notebook, exercise book.
cuadra *f.* stable.
cuadrante *m.* fourth part of an inheritance.
cuadrar *tr. & in.* to square.
cuadro *m.* square; picture.
cuajar *m.* (Zool.) rennet bag; *tr.* to curd, to curdle, to coagulate; *in. con.* to jell; *r.* to curd, to curdle.
cual *pr.* which.
cuál *pr.* which, what, which one.
cualquiera *pron. indef.* anyone; *pron. rel.* whichever; *m.* somebody.
cuando *conj.* when, although.
cuándo *conj.* when?
cuanto -ta *adv. & pron.* as much as, whatever.
cuaresma *f.* Lent.
cuartear *tr.* to quarter; *r.* to crack, split.

cuartel *m.* section, ward.
cuarteto *m.* quatrain.
cuartilla *f.* quarter of large sheet of paper.
cuarto -ta *adj.* fourth; quarter; *m.* fourth; quarter; room.
cuba *f.* cask, barrel.
cubeta *f.* keg, small cask or barrel.
cubicar *tr.* to determine the volume of.
cubierta *f.* cover.
cubierto *m.* knife, fork, and spoon.
cubo *m.* bucket.
cubrir *tr.* to cover; *r.* to cover oneself.
cuchara *f.* spoon; ladle.
cucharilla *f.* small spoon.
cucharón *f.* ladle.
cuchilla *f.* knife, cutting tool.
cuchillería *f.* cutlery.
cuchillo *m.* knife.
cuello *m.* neck; collar.
cuenca *f.* wooden bowl.
cuenta *f.* count, calculation; account; bill.
cuentagotas *m.* dropper.
cuento *m.* story, tale; short story; *con.* gossip.
cuerda *f.* string, rope; cord; chord.
cuerdo -da *adj.* sane.
cuerno *m.* horn; (An.) cornu; (fig.) horn.
cuero *m.* pelt, rawhide.
cuerpo *m.* body; corpus (of writings, laws, etc.).
cuervo *m.* (Zool.) raven.
cuesta *f.* hill, slope.
cuestión *f.* question; affair, matter.
cueva *f.* cave; cellar.
cuidado *m.* care; worry.
cuidadoso -sa *adj.* careful, watchful.
cuidar *tr.* to care for.
culata *f.* haunch, butt *(of gun).*
culminar *in.* to culminate.
culo *m.* seat, behind; anus.

culpa *f.* blame, guild, fault.
culpar *tr.* to blame, censure.
cultivar *tr.* to cultivate, till.
cultivo *m.* cultivating; farming.
culto -ta *adj.* cultivated, cultured; *m.* cult, worship.
cultura *f.* culture, education.
cultural *adj.* cultural.
cumbre *f.* summit.
cumpleaños *m.* birthday.
cumplidor -ra *adj.* reliable.
cumplimentar *tr.* to compliment.
cumplir *tr.* to execute, perform, fulfill.
cuna *f.* cradle.
cundir *in.* to spread.
cuneta *f.* ditch, gutter.
cuñada *f.* sister-in-law.
cuñado *m.* brother-in-law.
cuota *f.* quota.
cupón *m.* coupon.
cura *m.* priest; *f.* cure; remedy.
curación *f.* treatment.
curandero -ra *m. & f.* quack.
curar *tr.* to head; to treat.
curiosear *in. con.* to snoop, to pry around.
curioso -sa *adj.* curious.'
cursar *tr.* to haunt, to frequent, to attend.
cursillo *m.* short course.
curso *m.* course; circulation.
curtido tanned; expert.
curtir *tr.* to tan; to harden; *r.* to become tanned.
curva *f.* bend.
cúspide *f.* peak, top, summit, *(of a mountain).*
cutis *m. & f.* skin.
cuyo -ya *pr. rel.* whose, of which.

CH

chabacano *adj.* awkward, clumsy.
chacal *m.* (Zool.) jackal.
chacha *f.* (con.) lass.
chafar *tr.* to flatten.
chalado -da *adj.* (con.) addlebrained crackers.
chalar *r.* to lose one's head.
chaleco *m.* vest, waistcoat.
chalupa *f.* (Náut.) shallop, canoe.
champiñón *m.* mushroom.
champú *m.* shampoo.
chamuscar *tr.* to singe.
chanclo *m.* clog.
chantaje *m.* blackmail.
chapa *f.* plate; metal sheet.
chaparrón *m.* heavy shower.
chapista *m. & f.* tinsmith.
chapucear *tr.* to botch, bungle.
chapucero *adj.* rough, crude.
chapurrear *tr.* to jabber *(a language).*
chapuzar *tr. in. & r.* to duck, to dive, to plunge.
chaqueta *f.* jacket.
charco *m.* puddle, pool.
charla *f.* (con.) chat, chatting.
charlar *in.* (con.) to chat.
charretera *f.* epaulet; garter.
charro -rra *adj.* coarse.
chascar *tr.* to click.
chasco *m.* disappointment, frustration.
chasis *m.* chassis, body *(car).*
chatarra *f.* scrap iron.
chatarrería *f.* junk yard.
chato -ta *adj.* flat; *f.* darling, pretty girl.
chaval -la *adj.* (con.) young; *m.* (con.) lad; *f.* (con.) lass.
chaveta *f.* cotter.
chelín *m.* shilling.
chepa *f.* (con.) hunch, hump.
chicle *m.* chewing-gum.

chico -ca *adj.* small, little; *m. & f.* child; *m.* lad, little fellow.
chifla *f.* hissing.
chifladura *f.* hissing.
chiflar *tr. in* to whistle; *r.* (con.) to become unbalanced.
chillar *in.* to screech.
chillón -ona *adj.* (con.) shrieking, screaming.
chinche *m. & f.* (Zool.) bedbug.
chirigota *f.* (con.) joke.
chiripa *f.* fluke, scratch.
chirriar *in.* to sizzle.
chirrido *m.* sizzle; creak.
chisme *m.* gossip.
chispa *f.* spark.
chispazo *m.* spark.
chispear *in.* to spark.
chistar *in.* to speak.
chiste *m.* witticism; joke.
chistera *f.* basket; top hat.
chivato *m.* (Zool.) kid.
chivo -va *m. & f.* (Zool.) kid; *m.* he goat.
chocar *tr.* to shock; to collide.
chocolate *m.* chocolate.
chochear *in.* to dote, become childish.
chofer *m.* driver.
chopo *m.* (Bot.) black poplar.
choque *m.* shock; impact, collission.
chorizo *m.* (very big) sausage.
chorrear *in.* to spout; to drip.
chorro *m.* spurt, jet.
chubasco *m.* squall, shower, storm.
chufa *f.* (Bot.) tiger-nut.
chuleta *f.* chop, cutlet.
chulo -la *adj.* flashy, snappy.
chupar *tr.* to suck; to absorb; *r.* to lose strength.
chupete *m.* pacifier.
chupón -na *adj.* (con.) sucking; *m. & f.* (con.) swindler.
churruscar *tr.* to burn *(food).*
chusma *f.* galley slaves.

D

dactilógrafo -fa *m.* & *f.* typist, typewriter.
dádiva *f.* gift, present.
dado -da *adj.* given.
dador -dora *adj.* giving; *m.* & *f.* giver.
dama *f.* lady, dame.
damnificar *tr.* to damage, hurt.
danza *f.* dance; dancing.
danzar *tr.* to dance.
dañar *tr.* to hurt; to damage.
daño *m.* hurt, damaged, harm.
dar *tr.* to give; to cause; to hit, to strike.
dardo *m.* dart.
dársena *f.* inner harbor.
datar *tr.* to date; *in.* to date.
dato *m.* datum, fact.
de *pre.* of; from; by; with.
debajo *adv.* below, underneath.
debatir *tr.* to debate; *in.* to debate; *r.* to struggle.
debe *m.* (Com.) debit.
deber *m.* duty; *pl.* school work.
débil *adj.* weak; feeble.
debilitar *tr.* to debilitate; *r.* to weaken.
debutar *in.* to make one's debut.
decaer *in.* to decay; to fall, weaken.
decanato *m.* deanship.
decapitar *tr.* to decapitate, to behead.
decena *f.* ten.
decente *adj.* decent; dignified.
decepción *f.* disappointment.
decepcionar *tr.* to disappoint.
decidir *tr.* to decide; *in.* to decide.
décimo -ma *adj.* tenth.
decir *m.* saying; *tr.* to say, to tell; to speak, state, utter.
declamar *tr.* & *in.* to declaim, recite.

declarar *tr.* to declar; state; *in.* to declare; *r.* to declare oneself.
declinar *tr.* to decline, refuse; *in.* to decline.
declive *m.* declivity, slope.
decorar *tr.* to decorate.
decreciente *adj.* decreasing, diminishing.
decretar *tr.* to decree, resolve.
dedal *m.* thimble.
dedicar *tr.* to dedicate.
dedo *m.* finger; *con.* to raise one's hand.
deducir *tr.* to deduce, infer *(see irr.* **lucir***)*.
defecto *m.* defect; fault, weakness.
defender *tr.* to defend; to protect; (Law) to defend.
defensa *f.* defense; *m.* *(football)* full-back.
defensor -ra *adj.* defending; *m.* counsel for the defence.
deficiente *adj.* deficient.
déficit *m.* deficit.
definir *tr.* to define; make clear.
deformar *tr.* to deform; distort; *r.* to become deformed.
defraudar *tr.* to defraud, to cheat.
defunción *f.* death, demise.
degenerar *in.* to degenerate, decay.
degradar *tr.* to degrade.
degustar *tr.* to taste.
deificar *tr.* to deify.
dejadez *f.* laziness, negligence.
delantal *m.* apron.
delante *adv.* before; *in.* front of.
delantero -ra *adj.* front; head.
delítar *tr.* to accuse, denounce.
delator -ra *adj.* accusing; *m.* & *f.* accuser.
delegar *tr.* to delegate, depute.

D

deleitar *tr.* to delight; *r.* to delight.

delgado -da *adj.* thin, lean, slender.

deliberar *tr.* to deliberate.

delimitar *tr.* to delimit.

delincuente *adj.* guilty, delinquent; *m.* & *f.* guilty person.

delineante *adj.* delineating, drafting; *m.* & *f.* delineator.

delinear *tr.* to delineate, to outline.

delirar *in.* to be delirious.

demanda *f.* demand; petition.

demandar *tr.* to demand; (Law.) to sue.

demarcar *tr.* to demarcate.

demás *adj. indef.* the others, the rest.

demencia *f.* insanity, madness.

demoler *tr.* to demolish, tear down.

demonio *m.* demon; devil.

demorar *tr.* to delay; *in.* to retard.

demonstrar *tr.* to demonstrare, prove.

denegar *tr.* to deny, to refuse.

denigrar *tr.* to defame, revile.

denominar *tr.* to name, to denominate.

denotar *tr.* to denote, mean.

densidad *f.* density.

dentadura *f.* denture, set of teeth.

dentrífico -ca *adj.* tooth paste.

dentro *adv.* inside, within.

denunciar *tr.* to denounce.

depender *in.* to depend; to rely upon.

depilar *tr.* to depilate.

deplorar *tr.* to deplore.

deponer *tr.* to set aside.

deportar *tr.* to banish, exile.

deporte *m.* sport.

depositar *tr. to deposit.*

depósito *m.* depot, warehouse.

depravar *tr.* to deprave, vitiate.

depreciar *tr.* & *in.* to depreciate, undervalue.

deprimido -da *adj.* depressed, low-spirited.

deprimir *tr.* to depress.

depurar *tr.* to purify.

derecha *f.* right hand; right hand side; *pl.* Right Wing *(politics).*

derecho -cha *adj.* right; straight; standing; *m.* law; right.

deriva *f.* drift.

derivar *in.* & *r.* to derive; to descent from.

derogar *tr.* to abolish, derogate.

derramar *tr.* to pour out, to spill.

derretir *tr.* to melt; *r.*

derribar *tr.* to demolish, destroy; *r.* to fall down.

derrocar *tr.* to tear down.

derrotar *tr.* to rout; to defeat.

derruir *tr.* to tear down.

derrumbamiento *m.* collapse, landslide.

derrumbar *tr.* to tumble down; *r.* to collapse.

desabrochar *tr.* to unsnap; *r.* to become unfastened.

desaconsejar *tr.* to disuade.

desacreditar *tr.* to discredit.

desafiar *tr.* to challenge, dare.

desafinar *tr.* to put out of tune; *in.* to get out of tune.

desafío *m.* challenge, duel.

desagradable *adj.* disagreeable, unpleasant.

desagrado *m.* displeasure.

desaguar *tr.* to drain, empty; *m.* to flow.

desagüe *m.* drainage, sewerage.

desahogar *tr.* to relieve, give comfort to.

desahuciar *tr.* to deprive of hope.

desairar *tr.* to slight, snub.

desaire *m.* ungracefulness, slight.

desalar *tr.* to take the salt from.

desalentar *tr.* to discourage; *r.* to become discouraged.

desalquilar *tr.* to stop renting, to vacate.

desamparar *tr.* to forsake.

desamueblar *tr.* to remove the furniture from.

desangrar *tr.* to bleed copiously; *r.* to bleed to death.

desapacible *adj.* unpleasant, disagreeable.

desaparecer *tr.* to disappear; *in.* & *r.* to disappear.

desaprobar *tr.* to disapprove.

desarmar *tr.* to disarm; to dismount.

desarme *m.* disarmament.

desarrollar *tr.* to unroll, unfurl.

desarrollo *m.* unrolling, unfolding; development.

desasosegar *tr.* to disquiet, worry; *r.* to become disquieted.

desasosiego *m.* disquiet, worry.

desastre *m.* disaster.

desatento -ta *adj.* inattentive, disregardful.

desatinar *r.* to be wrong.

desatornillar *tr.* to unscrew.

desautorizar *tr.* to deprive of authority *(or) credit.*

desayunar *in.* to breakfast; *r.* to breakfast.

desbocar *tr.* to break the mouth *(or)* spout of; *r.* to break loose.

desbordamiento *m.* overflowing.

desbordar *in.* to overflow; *r.* to overflow.

descalabrar *tr.* to hit, to hurt.

descalificar *tr.* to disqualify.

descalzar *tr.* to take off; *r.* to take off *(shoes, etc.).*

descansado -da *adj.* rested; tranquil.

descansar *tr.* to stop work.

descarado -da *adj.* impudent, cheeky.

descarga *f.* unloading; discharge *(of a gun).*

descargar *tr.* to unload; to ease *(conscience).*

descargo *m.* unloading; discharge.

descarnado *adj.* lean, thin.

descaro *m.* effrontery.

descarrilar *in.* to derail.

descartar *tr.* to reject; *r.* to discard.

descendencia *f.* descent.

descender *tr.* & *in.* to descend, go down.

descentralizar *tr.* to decentralize.

descifrar *tr.* to decipher.

desclavar *tr.* to remove the nails from.

descolgar *tr.* to take down; *r.* to slip down.

descolorido -da *adj.* discolored, off color.

descomponer *tr.* to decompose; *r.* to decompose.

descomunal *adj.* extraordinary.

desconcierto *m.* disorder.

desconectar *tr.* to disconnect.

desconfiado -da *adj.* distrustful.

desconfiar *in.* to have no confidence.

descongelar *tr., in.* & *r.* to defrost, to melt.

desconocer *tr.* not to know.

desconsolado -da *adj.* disconsolate.

desconsolar *tr.* to grieve; *r.* to grieve.

desconsuelo *m.* grief.

descontar *tr.* to discount.

descorchar *tr.* remove the bar *(or) cork from.*

D

descortés *adj.* discourteous, rude.

descortezar *tr.* to strip off the bark; *con.* to polish.

descoser *tr.* to unstitch, rip.

descoyuntar *tr.* to dislocate.

descrédito *m.* discredit, disrepute.

describir *tr.* to describe, to define.

descuartizar *tr.* to quarter.

descubrir *tr.* to discover, find out; *r.* to take off one's hat.

descuento *m.* discount.

descuidado -da *adj.* careless.

descuidar *tr.* to neglect, overlook; *r.* to be distracted.

desde *prep.* since, from; after.

desdentado -da *adj.* toothless.

desdicha *f.* misfortune, unhappiness.

desdoblar *tr.* & *r.* to unfold, spread open.

desear *tr.* to desire, wish.

desembalar *tr.* to unpack.

desembarcadero *m.* wharf, pier.

desembarcar *tr.* & *in.* to disembark.

desembocadura *f.* mouth.

desembolsar *tr.* to disburse, pay out.

desembolso *m.* payment.

desempaquetar *tr.* to unpack.

desempeñar *tr.* to dedeem, to recover.

desempleo *m.* unemployment.

desenfado *m.* ease, freedom.

desenfreno *m.* unruliness, licentiousness.

desengrasar *tr.* to take the grease out of; *r. con.* to get thin.

desenmascarar *tr.* to unmask.

desenredar *tr.* to disentangle; *r.* to extricate oneself.

desentender *tr.* to take no part in.

desenterrar *tr.* to unearth.

desenvainar *tr.* to unsheathe.

desenvoltura *f.* ease, grace.

deseo *m.* desire, wish.

desequilibrado -a *adj.* unbalanced.

desestimar *in.* to underestimate.

desfallecer *tr.* to weaken, to debilitate; *in.* to fall away.

desfavorable *adj.* unfavorable.

desfiladero *m.* defile, pass.

desfile *m.* parade, march.

desgajar *tr.* to tear off, to break off.

desganado -da *adj.* not hungry.

desgañitar *r. con.* to scream.

desgarrar *tr.* to tear.

desgarro *m.* tear, rent.

desgaste *m.* wearing down.

desgracia *f.* misfortune, bad luck; disfavor.

desgraciado -da *adj.* unfortunate.

desgraciar *tr.* to spoil; *r.* to spoil.

desguazar *tr.* to roughhew.

deshabitado -da *adj.* uninhabited.

deshabitar *tr.* to move out of.

deshacer *tr.* to undo; to untie.

desharrapado -da *adj.* ragged, shabby.

deshelar *tr.* & *in.* to defrost.

desheredar *tr.* to disinherit.

deshinchar *tr.* to deflate; *r.* to get down.

deshojar *tr.* to defoliate.

deshonor *m.* dishonor.

deshonra *f.* dishonor.

deshonrar *tr.* to dishonor.

deshora *f.* inopportune time.

deshuesar *tr.* to bone.

desidia *f.* laziness, indolence.

desierto pta *adj.* desert; *m.* desert.

designar *tr.* to designare, to select.

desigual *adj.* unequal.

desilusionar *tr.* to disillusion; *r.* to be disillusioned.

desinflar *tr.* to deflate.
desintegrar *tr.* & *r.* to desintegrate.
desleal *adj.* disloyal.
desliar *tr.* to untie, unpack.
desligar *tr.* to untie, to unwind; *r.* to come loose.
desliz *m.* sliding, slipping.
deslizar *tr.* to slide, make slide; *in.* to slide; *r.* to slide.
deslucir *tr.* to tarnish.
deslumbrar *tr.* to dazzle.
desmangar *tr.* to take off the handle of *r.* to come off.
desmantelar *tr.* to dismantle.
desmayar *tr.* to dishearten; *r.* to faint.
desmayo *m.* depression; faltering.
desmentir *tr.* to contradict.
desmenuzar *tr.* to pull to pieces; *r.* to crumb.
desmoralizar *tr.* to demoralize.
desnatar *tr.* to skim.
desnudar *tr.* to strip, to undress.
desnudo -da *adj.* naked, bar; *m.* nude.
desobedecer *tr.* & *in.* to disobey.
desodorante *adj.* & *m.* deodorant.
desoir *tr.* not to hear.
desolar *tr.* to desolate.
desollar *tr.* to flay, to skin.
desordenar *tr.* to disorder, *r.* to get out of order.
desorganizar *tr.* to disorganize.
despabilar *tr.* to trim, to snuff *(candle)*; *r.* to brighten up.
despacio *adv.* slowly; *inj.* easy there!
despachar *tr.* to dispatch, to expedite.
desparpajo *m. con.* pertness.
despectivo -a *adj.* deprecitory.
despecho *m.* spite.

despedazar *tr.* to break to pieces, to tear into pieces.
despedida *f.* farewell, leave.
despedir *tr.* to throw, to hurl.
despegue *m.* take-off.
despejar *tr.* to free, to clear; *r.* to be free and easy.
despensa *f.* pantry.
desperdiciar *tr.* to waste.
despertador *m.* alarmclock.
despertar *t.* to awaken, to wake up.
despilfarro *m.* squandering, lavishness.
despintar *tr.* to take the paint off; *r.* to wash off, to fade.
depistar *tr.* to put off.
desplegar *tr.* to spread out, unfold; *r.* to spread out.
despojar *tr.* to strip, despoil; *r.* to undress.
desposar *tr.* to marry; *r.* to be betrothed.
despreciar *tr.* to despise, to scorn.
después *adv.* after, afterwards.
desquiciar *tr.* to unhinge; *r.* to come unhinged.
destacado -da *adj.* outstanding.
destacar *tr.* to emphasize; *r.* to stand out.
destajo *m.* piecework.
destapar *tr.* to uncover; *r.* to get uncovered.
destello *m.* sparkle, flash.
desteñir *tr.* to discolor.
desterrar *tr.* to exile, banish.
destierro *m.* exile, banishment.
destinar *tr.* to destine.
destituir *tr.* to deprive.
destreza *f.* skill, dexterity.
destozar *tr.* to break to pieces.
destruir *tr.* to destroy, lay waste.
desunir *tr.* & *r.* to disunite.
desuso *m.* disuse.

D

desvalijar *tr.* to steal the contents of; to rob.

desván *m.* garret, loft.

desvariar *in.* to rave, rant.

desvelar *tr.* to keep awake.

desventurado -da *adj.* unfortunate.

desvestir *tr.* & *r.* to undress.

desvío *m.* deflection, deviation.

detalle *m.* retail.

detallar *tr.* to detail.

detectar *tr.* to detect.

detener *tr.* to stop, to check.

detenidamente *adv.* carefully, thoroughly.

determinar *tr.* to determine.

detestar *tr.* to curse.

detrás *adv.* behind.

deudo -da *m.* & *f.* relative; *f.* debt.

deudor -dora *adj.* indebted; *m.* & *f.* debtor.

devastar *tr.* to devastate.

devolución *f.* return, restitution.

devolver *tr.* to return.

devorar *tr.* to devour.

día *.m.* day; daytime; daylight; *con.* when least expected.

diablo *m.* devil.

diácono *m.* deacon.

diagnosticar *tr.* to diagnose.

dialecto *m.* dialect.

dialogar *tr.* & *in.* to dialogue.

diapositiva *f.* transparency, slide.

diario -ria *adj.* daily.

dibujante *m.* & *f.* sketcher; *m.* draftsman; *f.* draftswoman.

dibujar *tr.* to draw, to design; *r.* to be outline.

dibujo *m.* drawing; sketch.

diccionario *m.* dictionary.

diciembre *m.* December.

dictaminar *in.* to pass judgment.

dictar *tr.* to dictate.

dichoso -sa *adj.* happy, lucky.

diente *m.* tooth.

diestra *f.* right hand.

diestro *adj.* right; skiful.

diez *adj.* ten.

diferir *tr.* to defer; *in.* to differ.

difícil *adj.* difficult, hard.

dificultar *tr.* to put obstacles in the way of.

difundir *tr.* to diffuse, to spread.

difunto -ta *adj.* & *m.* deceased; *m.* corpse.

difusión *f.* diffusion.

digerir *tr.* (Phyl.) & (Chm.) to digest; (fig.) to digest.

digno -na *adj.* worthy.

dilatar *tr.* to expand; *r.* to be deferred.

diluir *tr.* & *r.* to dilute.

diluvio *m.* deluge.

diminutivo -va *adj.* diminishing.

dimisión *f.* resignation.

dimitir *tr.*; *in.* to resign.

dinero *m.* money.

dintel *m.* (Arch.) lintel, doorhead.

Dios *m.* God.

diosa *f.* goddess.

diptongo *m.* diphthong.

diputado -da *m.* & *f.* representative; M.P.

dique *m.* dike, dam.

dirección *f.* direction; course; address.

directo -ta *adj.* direct.

dirigir *tr.* to direct, to manage; *r.* to go, to betake oneself to.

disciplina *f.* discipline, *pl.* studies.

discípulo -la *m.* & *f.* pupil; disciple.

disco *m.* disc; record *(of phonograph).*

discordia *f.* discord, disagreement.

discrepancia *f.* discrepancy.

disculpable *adj.* excusable.

disculpar *tr.* to excuse; *con.* to pardon; *r.* to excuse oneself.

discurrir *tr.* to invent,
contrive, *in.* to ramble.
discutir *tr.* to discuss.
disecar *tr.* to dissect; to stuff.
disentir *in.* to disent.
disertar *in.* to discourse in
detail.
disfraz *m.* disguise.
disgustar *tr.* to displease; to
upset; *r.* to be displeased.
disimular *tr.* to disimulate.
disimulo *m.* disimulation.
disipar *tr.* to dissipate.
disminuir *tr., in.* & *r.* to
diminish.
disolver *tr.* to dissolve; to
separate.
disparar *tr.* to shoot; *r.* to
dash away.
disparo *m.* shot, discharge.
disponer *tr.* to dispose,
arrange.
disponible *adj.* available.
dispuesto -ta *pp.* of disponer.
disputa *f.* dispute; quarrel.
distar *in.* to be far, be distant.
distinguir *tr.* to dintinguish,
int. to excel.
distracción *f.* distraction.
distraído -da *adj.* distracted.
distribuir *tr.* to distribute,
divide.
divagación *f.* rambling.
diversidad *f.* diversity, variety.
diversificar *tr.* to diversify.
diverso -sa *adj.* diverse,
different.
divertido -da amusing.
divertir *tr.* to amuse; *r.* to be
amused.
dividir *tr.* & *r.* to divide.
divisa *f.* emblem.
divisar *tr.* to perceive.
divorciar *tr.* to divorce.
divulgar *tr.* to divulge, to
spread.
doblar *tr.* to double, to fold.
doblegar *tr.* to fold, to bend.
doce *adj. num.* twelve.
docena *f.* dozen.

documentado -da *adj.*
documented; well-informed.
dolencia *f.* ailment, complaint.
doler *in.* to ache, to hurt; *r.* to
complain.
dolor *m.* ache, pain.
dolorido -da *adj.* sore, aching.
domar *tr.* to tame, to break.
domingo *m.* Sunday.
dominio *m.* dominion; domain.
don *m.* gift, present; talent.
donar *tr.* to give, donate.
donativo *m.* gift, donation.
doncella *f.* maiden, virgin.
donde *cnj.* where.
dónde *adv. interr.* where?
dondequiera *adv.* anywhere.
doña *f.* Mrs.
dorado -da *adj.* golden.
dormir *tr.* & *in.* to sleep; *r.* to
sleep.
dorso *m.* back.
dos *adj.* two.
dosis *f.* dose.
dotar *tr.* to endow.
dote *m.* & *f.* dowry; *f.*
endowment.
dragar *tr.* to dredge.
dramaturgo *m.* playwriter.
droga *f.* drug, medicine.
ducha *f.* shower bath.
ducho -cha *adj.* skillful.,
expert.
duda *f.* doubt.
duelo *m.* grief, sorrow.
duende *m.* elf, goblin.
dueño -ña *m.* & *f.* owner,
proprietor.
dulce *adj.* sweet; *m.* candy,
sweets.
dulzura *f.* sweetness.
dúo *m.* duet.
duplicar *tr.* to duplicate.
duracion *f.* duration, length.
durante *prep.* during.
dureza *f.* hardness.
duro -ra *adj.* hard;
hard-boiled; rough; *adv.*
hard; *m.* five peseta coin.

D

E

e *cnj.* and.
ebanista *m.* cabinetmaker.
ebrio -ebria *adj. m. & f.* drunk.
ebullición *f.* boiling.
eclipsar *tr.* to eclipse.
eco *m.* echo.
ecónomo *m.* supply priest.
edad *f.* age.
edicto *m.* edict, proclamation.
edificación *f.* building.
edificar *tr.* to building.
editar *tr.* to publish.
editor -tora *adj.* publishing; *m. & f.* publisher.
educar *tr.* to educate, to train.
efectivo -va *adj.* real, actual.
efectuar *tr.* to effect, carry out; *r.* to be carried out.
eficaz *adj.* effective.
efusión *f.* effusion.
egoísmo *m.* egoism, egotism.
eje *m.* axis, axle.
ejecutar *tr.* to execute; (Law) to distrain.
ejecutor -tora *adj.* executive; *m.&f.* executive.
ejemplar *adj.* exemplary.
ejemplo *m.* example, instance.
ejercer *tr.* to practive, exercise.
ejército *m.* army.
el *art., masc., sing.,* the
él *pron., pers., in.* he, him, it.
elaborar *tr.* to elaborate
electrizar *tr.* to electrify.
elegante *adj.* elegant; stylish.
elegir *tr.* to elect.
elevación *f.* elevation, exaltation.
elevar *tr.* to elevate; *r.* to rise.
elogiar *tr.* to praise.
elogio *m.* praise, eulogy.
ella *pron. pers. f.* she, her it.
emancipar *tr.* to emancipate; *r.* to become emancipated.
embajada *f.* embassy; message.

embalaje *m.* packing.
embalar *tr.* to pack.
embarazar *tr.* to embarrass; *r.* to be obstructed.
embarazo *m.* embarrasment.
embarrar *tr.* to splash with mud.
embaucar *tr.* to deceive.
embeber *tr.* to absorb, to soak up; *in.* to shrink; *r.* to be enchanted.
embelesar *tr.* to charm, fascinate; *r.* to be charmed.
embestir *ir.* to attack, to assail.
emblema *m.* emblem.
emboscada *f.* ambush.
embotellamiento *m.* bottling.
embotellar *tr.* to bottle.
embrión *m.* embryo.
embrollar *tr.* to embroil, confuse.
embrujar *tr.* to bewitch.
embudo *m.* funnel.
embuste *m.* lie, trick.
embutido -da *adj.* recessed; *m.* inlay, sausage.
emigrar *in.* to emigrate.
emisario -ria *m. & f.* emissary.
emisor -ra *adj.* emitting; *m.* radio transmitter.
emitir *tr.* to emit; to broadcast.
emocionar *tr.* to move, to stir.
empadronamiento *m.* census.
empadronar *tr.* to register.
empalagar *tr.* to surfeit, pall.
empalmar *tr.* to join, connect; *in.* to connect.
empañar *tr.* to get misty.
empapar *tr.* to soak, saturate; *r.* to soak.
empapelar *tr.* to wrap up in paper.
empaquetar *tr.* to pack.
empaste *m.* filling.
empatar *tr. in. & r.* to tie.
empate *m. draw.*
empedernido -da *adj.* hardened.
empeñar *tr.* to make worse; *in. & r.* to get worse.

emperador *m.* emperor.
emperatriz *f.* empress.
empezar *tr. & in.* to begin.
emplazar *tr.* to summons
emplear *tr.* to employ; to use; *r.* to be employed.
empleo *m.* employment.
empobrecer *tr.* to impoverish; *in. & r.* to become poor (or) impoverished.
empollar *tr.* to brood; *r.*
empotrar *tr.* to plant; *in. & r.* to interlock.
emprender *tr.* to undertake.
empresa *f.* enterprise, undertaking.
empujar *tr.* to push
en *prep.* in; into; at; on.
enajenar *tr.* to transport, enrapture.
enaltecer to exalt.
enamorado -da *adj.* in love; *m. & f.* sweetheart; *m.* lover.
enano -na *adj.* dwarfish; *m. & f.*
enardecer *tr.* to inflame, to fire; *r.* to get excited.
encabezar *tr.* to draw up *(a tax list).*
encadenar *tr.* to chain.
encajar *tr.* to put, to insert.
encantamiento *m.* spell; charm.
encantar *tr.* to cast a spell on; to enchant.
encarar *tr.* to aim, to point; *in. & r.* to come face to face.
encarcelar *tr.* to jail, incarcerate.
encareciminento *m.* increase.
encargar *tr.* to entrust; *r.* to take charge.
encarnar *tr.* to incarnate; *in.* to become incarnate.
encarnizado -da *adj.* bloody.
encasillar *tr.* to pigeon-hole.
encasquillar *tr.* to put a tip on; *r.* to stick.
encendedor -ra *adj.* lighting; *m.* lighter.

encender *tr.* to light, set fire to; *r.* to be stirred up.
encerado -da *adj.* waxy; *m.* blackboard.
encerar *tr.* to wax.
encerrar *tr.* to shut in, lock in.
encía *f.* (An.) gum.
encierro *m.* locking up, confinement.
enclavar *tr.* to nail; to pierce.
encoger *tr.* to shrink, contract; *r.* to shrink.
encolar *tr.* to glue; to size.
encolerizar *tr.* to anger, irritate; *r.* to become angry.
encontrar *tr.* to meet; *r.* to meet each other.
encorvar *tr.* to bend; *r.* to bend over.
encrucijada *f.* crossroads.
encuadernar *tr.* to bind.
encuadrar *tr.* to frame.
encubrir *tr.* to hide, conceal; *r.* to hide.
encuesta *f.* poll.
encumbrar *tr.* to raise, elevate; *r.* to rise.
enchufar *tr.* to switch on, plug in.
enchufe *m.* fitting; (Elec.) connector, plug and jack.
endulzar *tr.* to sweeten.
endurecer *tr.* to harden; *r.* to harden.
enemigo -ga *adj.* enemy.
enemistad *f.* enmity.
energía *f.* energy.
enero *m.* January.
enfadar *tr.* to annoy, to anger; *r.* to be annoyed.
énfasis *m. & f.* emphasis.
enfermar *in.* to sicken.
enfermedad *f.* sickness, illness.
enfermero -ra *m. & f.* nurse.
enflaquecer *tr.* to make thin; *in.* to get thin; *r.* to get thin.
enfocar *tr. & r.* to focus.
enfrentar *tr.* to confront; *r.* to meet face to face.

E

enfrente *adv.* in front, opposite, facing.

enfriamiento *m.* cooling.

enfriar *tr.* to cool, *in.* to cool off, to turn cold.

enfurecer *tr.* to infuriate, enrage; *r.* to rage.

engalanar *tr.* to adorn.

enganchar *tr.* to hook; *con.* to inveigle; *in.* to be hooked.

engañar *tr.* to deceive, cheat.

engendrar *tr.* to engender, beget.

engomar *tr.* gum, glue.

engordar *tr.* to fatten; *in.* to get fat.

engranaje *m.* gearing.

engrandecer *tr.* to enlarge, amplify.

engrasar *tr.* to grease, lubricate.

engrudo *m.* paste, glue.

enhorabuena *f.* congratulations.

enjabonar *tr.* to soap.

enjuagar *tr.* to rinse.

enjuiciar *tr.* to examine.

enlace *m.* lacing, engagement.

enlazar *tr.* to link, to connect.

enlosar *tr.* to pave with flagestone.

enmascarado -da *adj.* mask.

enmendar *tr.* to amend, to correct; *r.* to change.

enmienda *f.* emendation.

ennoblecer *tr.* to ennoble.

enojar *tr.* to anger, annoy; *r.* to become angry.

enorgullecer *tr.* to make proud; *r.* to be proud.

enorme *adj.* enormous, vast.

enrarecer *tr.* to rarefy; *in.* to become scarce.

enredar *tr.* to catch in a net; *r.* to get tangled up.

enredoso -sa *adj.* tangled.

enrejar *tr.* to put grates (*or*) grating on.

enrevesado *adj.* frisky, complicated.

enriquecer *tr.* to enrich; *in.* & *r.* to get rich.

enroscar *tr.* & *r.* to twist.

ensalada *f.* salad.

ensalzar *tr.* to extol.

ensangrentar *tr.* to stain with blood.

ensayar *tr.* to try, try on; *r.* to practice.

ensayo *m.* trying, testing.

enseñanza *f.* teaching; education.

enseñar *tr.* to teach, to train.

enseres *m. pl.* household goods.

ensillar *tr.* to saddle.

ensordecer *tr.* to deafen.

ensuciar *tr.* to dirty, stain, soil; *in.* to soil; *r.* to soil oneself.

ensueño *m.* dream.

entablar *tr.* to board, board up.

ente *m.* being.

entero -ra *adj.* whole, entire, complete.

enterrador *m.* gravedigger.

enterrar *tr.* to inter, bury; *r.* (fig.) to be buried.

entidad *f.* entity.

entonar *tr.* to intone; *r.* to sing in tune.

entonces *adv.* then; and so.

entornar *tr.* to upset.

entrante *adj.* entering; *m. & f.* entrant.

entrañable *adj.* close, intimate.

entrañar *tr.* to bury deep; *r.* to be buried deep.

entrañas *f. pl.* entrails, bowels.

entremés *m.* side dish, hors d'oeuvre.

entrenar *tr.* & *r.* (sport) to train, to coach.

entresuelo *m.* mezzanine.

entretela *f.* interlining.

entretener *tr.* to entertain, amuse.

entrever *tr.* to glimpse, descry.

entrevista *f.* interview.

entristecer *tr.* & *r.* to sadden.

entuerto *m.* wrong.

enturbiar *tr.* to stir up, to muddy; *r.* to get muddy.
enumerar *tr.* to enumerate.
enunciar *tr.* to enounce.
envasar *tr.* to pack, to package.
envase *m.* packing, bottling.
envejecer *tr.* to age, make old; *in.* to age grow old.
envenenar *tr.* to poison.
envergadura *f.* breadth.
enviar *tr.* to send.
envidia *f.* envy, grudge.
envío *m.* sending; shipment.
enviudar *in.* to become a widow or a widower.
envoltorio *m.* bundle.
envolver *tr.* to wrap, wrap up.
enyesar *tr.* to plaster.
épica *f.* epic poetry.
episodio *m.* episode, incident.
época *f.* epoch, age, time.
equilibrar *tr. & r.* to balance.
equipaje *m.* luggage; baggage.
equiparar *tr.* to compare.
erigir *tr.* to erect, build; *r.* to be elevated.
erizo *m.* (Zool.) hedgehog.
errante *adj.* wandering.
errar *tr.* to miss; *in.* to wander.
eructar *in.* to belch.
esbeltez *f.* gracefulness.
esbozo *m.* sketch.
escabeche *m.* pickle.
escabroso -sa *adj.* scabrous.
escala *f.* ladder; scale.
escalar *tr.* to escalate, to scale; *in.* to climb.
escalera *f.* staircase, stairs.
escalofrío *m.* chill.
escalón *m.* step.
escama *f.* (Zool.) & (Bot.) scale.
escandalizar *tr.* to scandalize.
escaño *m.* settle, bench.
escapar *in.* to escape, get away; *r.* to escape.
escaparate *m.* shop window.
escarabajo *m.* beetle.

escarcha *f.* frost.
escarlata *adj.* scarlet.
escarola *f.* (Bot.) endive.
escasear *tr.* to be sparing; *in.* to be scarce.
escaso -sa *adj.* short, scarce.
escena *f.* scene.
esclavitud *f.* slavery.
esclavizar *tr.* to enslave.
escoba *f.* broom.
escocer *tr.* to annoy, to displease.
escoger *tr.* to choose.
escolar *adj.* scholastic; *m.* pupil.
escolta *f.* escort.
escombro *m.* **escombros,** shambles.
esconder *tr.r.* to hide.
escondite *m.* hiding place.
escopeta *f.* shotgun.
escoria *f.* dross, refuse.
escote *m.* low neck.
escribano *m.* court clerk.
escribir *m.* writing; *tr. & in.* to write.
escritor -ra *m. & f.* writer, author.
esculpir *tr.* to carve.
escupir *tr. & in.* to spit.
escurrir *tr.* to drain; *in. & r.* to drip.
ese, esa *adj. dem.* that.
ése, ésa *pron. dem* that one.
esforzar *tr.* to stengthen; *r.* to try to.
eslabón *m.* link.
eslora *f.* (Náut.) length.
esmaltar *tr.* to enamel.
esmerar *tr.* to polish; *r.* to take pains.
eso *pron. dem. neut.* that.
espacial *adj.* spatial.
espaciar *tr.* to space; *r.* to enlarge.
espacio *m.* space; room.
espada *f.* sword.
espalda *f.* back; *con.* to have broad shoulders.
espantapájaros *m.* scarecrow.

E

espantar *tr.* to scare; *r.* to become scared.

español -la *adj.* Spanish; *m. & f.* Spaniard; *f.* Spanish woman.

esparcir *tr.* to scatter, to spread.

espárrago *m.* (Bot.) asparagus.

especializar *tr. in. & r.* to specialize.

especificar *tr.* to specify.

espectador -ra *m. & f.* spectator.

especular *tr.* to speculate about (*or*) on.

espera *f.* expectation.

esperanza *f.* hope.

esperar *tr.* to hope; to expect.

espesar *tr.* to thicken.

espeso -sa *adj.* thick, heavy.

espía *m. & f.* spy.

espiar *tr.* to spy on.

espina *f.* thorn; spine.

espinaca *f.* (Bot.) spinach.

espinilla *f.* (An.) shinbone.

espinoso -sa *adj.* thorny.

espionaje *m.* spying.

espíritu *m.* spirit.

espléndido -da *adj.* splendid.

espontaneidad *f.* spontaneity.

esposo sa *m. & f.* spouse; *m.* husband; *f.* wife.

espuela *f.* spur.

espuma *f.* foam.

espumar *tr.* to skim; *in.* to foam.

esputo *m.* sputum.

esquela *f.* note.

esqueleto *m.* skeleton.

esquiar *in.* to ski.

esquilador -dora *m. & f.* sheepshearer.

esquina *f.* corner.

estabilidad *f.* stability.

estabilizar *tr.* to stabilize; *r.* to become stabilized.

estable *adj.* stable, firm.

establecer *tr.* to establish; *r.* to take up residence.

establecimiento *m.* establishment.

estación *f.* station.

estacionar *tr.* to park; to station; *r.* to station oneself.

estadio *m.* stadium.

estadística -co *adj.* statistical; *f.* statistics.

estado *m.* state, condition.

estafa *f.* trick.

estafar *tr.* to defraud, to swindle.

estallar *in.* to burst, to explode.

estampa *f.* print, stamp.

estampar *tr.* to print, to stamp.

estancar *tr.* to staunch.

estancia *f.* stay; room.

estandarte *m.* standard, banner.

estanque *m.* reservoir.

estante *m.* shelf.

estatua *f.* statue.

estatura *f.* stature, height.

este; esta *adj. dem* this; *m.* east.

éste; ésta *pron. dem.* this one.

estantería *f.* shelving.

estaño *m.* (Chm.) tin.

estar *in.* to be; to be in.

estepa *f.* step.

estéril *adj.* sterile, barren.

estiércol *m.* dung, manure.

estimar *tr.* to esteem; to estimate.

estimular *tr. & in.* to stimulate.

estío *m.* summer.

estipulación *f.* stipulation.

estipular *tr.* to stipulate, lay down.

estirar *tr.* to stretch; to draw (metal or wite).

estirpe *f.* stock.

estival *adj.* aestival, summer.

esto *pron, dem. neut.* this.

estocada *f.* thrust, stab.

estofado -da *adj.* stew.

estofar *tr.* to stew.

estómago *m.* stomach.

estorbar *tr.* to hinder, to obstruct.

estornudar *in.* to sneeze.
estrafalario -ria *adj.* con. slovenly, sloppy.
estrangular *tr.* to estrangle.
estratagema *f.* stratagem, trick.
estrella *f.* star.
estrellar *f.* to fry *(eggs)*; *r.* (fig.) to crash.
estreno *m.* debut.
estreñir to bind, restrain.
estrépito *m.* noise.
estribillo *m.* burden, chorus.
estricto -ta *adj.* strict, severe.
estropear *tr.* to abuse; to spoil, to ruin.
estruendo *m.* crash.
estrujar *tr.* to squeeze, to crush.
estudiante *m. & f.* student; school boy.
estudiar *tr. & in.* to study.
estufa *f.* stove.
estupidez *f.* stupidity.
etapa *f.* stage.
etiqueta *f.* etiquette; formality.
evacuar *tr.* to evacuate; to empty.
evadir *tr.* to avoid; *r.* to evade.
evaluar *tr.* to evaluate.
evitable *adj.* avoidable.
evitar *tr.* to avoid.
evocar *tr.* to evoke.
exagerar *tr.* to exaggerate.
exaltar *tr.* to exalt.
examinar *tr.* to examine; *r.* to take an examination.
excedente *adj.* excessive; excess.
exceder *tr. & in.* to exceed; *r.* to exceed.
excelso -sa *adj.* lofty, elevated.
exceptuar *tr.* to except.
excitar *tr.* to excite; *r.* to become excited.
excluir *tr.* to exclude, eject.
excusa *f.* excuse, apology.
excusar *tr.* to excuse; to avoid; *r.* to send apologies.

eximir *tr.* to exempt.
existir *in.* to exist, be.
éxito *m.* outcome; success.
expansionarse *r.* (Am.) to open one's heart.
expedición *f.* expedition.
expedir *tr.* to send, to ship.
experiencia *f.* experience, trial.
experimentar *tr.* to test; to try out.
explicar *tr.* to explain, to expound.
explorador -ra *adj.* exploring; *m. & f.* explorer; *m.* boy scout.
explotar *tr.* to run, to operate; *in.* to explode.
exponer *tr.* to expose; to show; *r.* to risk; *r.* to expose oneself.
exportar *tr. & in.* to export.
expresar *tr.* to express.
expreso -sa *adj.* expressed; *m.* express.
exprimir *tr.* to express.
expropiar *tr.* to expropriate.
expulsar *tr.* to expel.
exquisito -ta *adj.* exquisite.
extender *tr.* to extend, to stretch out; *r.* to extend, to stretch out.
exteriorizar *tr.* to reveal, to make manifest.
externo -na *adj.* external; *m. & f.* day scholar.
extinguir *tr.* to extinguish, to put out; *r.* to be extinguished.
extintor -ra *adj.* extinguishing; *m.* fire extinguisher.
extraer *tr.* to extract, pull out.
extranjero -ra *adj.* foreing; *m. & f.* foreigner.
extrañar *tr.* to surprise.
extraviar *tr.* to lead astray; *r.* to go astray.
extremo -ma *adj.* extreme; *m.* end; extreme.
exuberancia *f.* exuberance.

E

F

fábrica *f.* manufacture; factory.
fabricar *tr.* to fabricate, make.
fábula *f.* fable, tale.
facilitar *tr.* to facilitate; to supply.
factor *m.* commission, merchant.
factura *f.* form; invoice, bill.
facturar *tr.* (Com.) to invoice.
facultad *f.* faculty; power; ability.
falaz *adj.* deceitful; fallacious.
falda *f.* skirt; slope.
falsear *tr.* to falsify.
falsedad *f.* falsehood.
falsificar *tr. & in.* to falsify.
falta *f.* lack, want; **echar en falta**, to miss.
faltar *tr.* to offend, to insult; *in.* to be missing; to lack; **faltar poco para**, to be near.
fallar *tr.* to ruff, to trump.
fallecer *in.* to decease, die.
familia *f.* family, household.
fanfarrón -na *adj. con.* blustering.
fango *m.* mud, slime.
fardel *m.* bag; bundle.
fardo *m.* bundle.
faro *m.* lighthouse; headlight.
farol *m.* lantern.
fastidiar *tr.* to cloy, to sicken.
fatigar *tr.* to fatigue; *r.* to tire.
favor *m.* favor.
favorecer *tr.* to favor *(see irr. nacer).*
faz *m.* face; aspect.
fe *f.* faith; certificate.
fealdad *f.* ugliness.
febrero *m.* February.
fécula *f.* starch; fecula.
fecundar *tr.* to fecundate.
fecha *f.* date.
fechar *tr.* to date.
felicidad *f.* felicity, happiness.

feligrés -sa *m. & f.* parishioner.
feliz *adj.* happy.
feo -a *adj.* ugly.
feraz *adj.* feracious, fertile.
féretro *m.* bier, coffin.
feria *f.* fair; market.
ferretería *f.* hardware shop.
ferrocarril *m.* railroad, railway.
fervor *m.* eagerness, enthusiasm, love.
festejar *tr.* to fete, entertain.
festín *m.* feast, banquet.
fiador -ra *m. & f.* bail (person).
fiambre *adj.* cold; *m.* cold lunch.
fiar *tr.* to guarantee.
ficha *f.* chip; domino *(piece).*
fichero *m.* card index.
fidedigno -na *adj.* reliable, trustworthy.
fiel *adj.* faithful; honest; exact.
fiera *f.* wild animal; fiend *(person).*
fiesta *f.* feast; holiday; festivity.
figurar *tr.* to figure; to represent.
fijar *tr.* to fix; to fasten.
fijo -ja *adj.* fixed; firm, solid, sure; **de fijo**, surely.
fila *f.* row, line; file.
filete *m.* fillet; steak.
filón *m.* vein, seam.
filtrar *tr.* to filter; to filtrate.
fin *m. & f.* end; object, aim; **a fin de**, in order to; **a fin de cuentas**, after all; **sin fin**, endless.
finca *f.* land, estate.
fingir *tr.* to feign.
firma *f.* signature.
firmar *tr.* to sign.
firme *adj.* firm, steady, solid.
fisgar *tr.* to pry, peep; to nose into.
fisgón -na *m. & f. con.* busybody.
flaco -ca *adj.* thin, skinny.
flamante *adj.* bright.
flan *m.* carmel custard.

flaquear *in.* to weaken.
fleco *m.* fringe; bangs.
flecha *f.* arrow.
fletar *tr.* (Náut.) to charter *(a ship).*
flojear *in.* to slacken, ease up; to weaken.
flor *f.* flower; (fig.) bouquet; **a flor de**, at *(or)* near the surface of.
florín *m.* florin.
flota *f.* fleet.
flotar *in.* to float.
fluir *in.* to flow.
foca *f.* (Zool.) seal.
foco *m.* focus; center *(of vice).*
fogata *f.* blaze, bonfire.
fogón *m.* cooking stove.
fogoso -sa *adj.* fiery, spirited.
follaje *m.* foliage.
fomentar *tr.* to foment; to promote.
fonda *f. in.* inn; guesthouse.
fondear *tr. in* (Náut.) to cast, anchor.
fondo *m.* bottom; *(of a house).*; **fondos**, funds *(money)*; **banjos fondos**, underworld.
fontanero -ra *adj. m.* plumber.
forastero -ra *adj.* outside.
forcejar, forcejear *in.* to struggle, struggling.
forma *f.* form; shape; format; **de forma que**, so that; **en debida forma**, in due form.
forro *m.* cover; lining.
fortalecer *tr.* to fortify, to strengthen.
forzar *tr.* to force.
forzoso -sa *adj.* inescapable; strong, husky.
foso *m.* pit; ditch.
fotómetro *m.* light meter.
fracasar *in.* to fail.
frágil *adj.* fragile; breakable.
fragor *m.* crash, din, uproar.
fraguar *tr.* to forge.
fraile *m.* friar.

franquear *tr.* to exempt; to open, to clear.
franqueo *m.* postage; franking *(of a letter).*
frasco *m.* bottle, flask.
fregar *tr.* to rub, to scrub.
freir *tr.* to fry.
freno *m.* bridle; brake; check.
frente *m.* front; *f.* brow, forehead.
fresco -ca *adj.* fresh; light *(cloth).*
friccionar *tr.* to rub; to massage.
frío -a *adj.* cold, frigid.
frito -ta *pp.* of fried.
frondoso -sa *adj.* leafy; woodsy.
frontera *f.* frontier, boundery.
frotar *tr. & r.* to rub.
frustrar *tr.* to frustrate.
fruta *f.* fruit.
fuego *m.* fire; light.
fuente *f.* fountain.
fuera *adv.* out, outside; away.
fuero *m.* law; code of laws.
fuerte *adj.* strong; intense; rough.
fuerza *f.* force; strength; power.
fugaz *adj.* brief; fugitive.
fulano -na *m. & f.* so-and-so.
fulminante *adj.* fulminant.
fulminar *tr.* to strike with lightning; to fulminate.
fumar *tr. & in.* to smoke.
funda *f.* case, sheath.
fundador -ra *adj.* founding; *m. & f.* founder.
fundamentar *tr.* to lay the foundations of.
fundar *tr.* to found; to base; *r.* to be founded.
furgón *m.* van, wagon.
furgoneta *f.* light truck.
fusible *adj.* fusible; *m.* (Elec.) fuse.
fusil *m.* gun, rifle.
fusionar *tr. & r.* to fuse.
fútbol *m.* football.

F

G

gabán *m.* overcoat.
gabardina *f.* rain coat; gabardine.
gabinete *m.* office *(of doctor, lawyer)*; studio.
gafe *m. con.* hoodoo.
gaita *f.* bagpipe.
gago *m.* branch (tree) section *(orange)*.
galán *m.* fine-looking fellow.
galardonar *tr.* to reward.
galería *f.* gallery.
galés *adj.* Welsh.
galopar *tr.* to gallop *(a horse)*; *in.* to gallop.
galvanizar *tr.* to galvanize.
gallardo -da *adj.* graceful, elegant.
galleta *f.* ship biscuit; biscuit.
gallina *f.* hen.
gallo *m.* cock.
gama *m.* buck, male fallow deer.
gamuza *f.* (Zool.) chamois.
gana *f.* desire.
ganadería *f.* cattle, stock.
ganado *m.* cattle; livestock.
ganador -ra *adj. m. & f.* winner..
ganancia *f.* gain, profit.
ganar *tr.* to earn; to gain; to win.
gancho *m.* hook.
gandul -ula *adj. m. & f. con.* loafer, idler.
ganga *f.* (Min.) gangue.
ganzúa *f.* false key.
garbato *m.* hook.
garantizar *tr.* to guarantee.
garbanzo *m.* (Bot.) chickpea.
garfio *m.* hook.
garganta *f.* throat.
garita *f.* watchtower; sentry box.
garra *f.* claw, catch.
garrafa *f.* carafe.

garrote *m.* club, cudgel.
gas *m.* gas.
gasolinera *f.* gas station.
gastar *tr.* to spend; to waste.
gata *f.* she-cat.
gatillo *m.* trigger.
gato *m.* (Zool.) cat; jack.
gavilán *m.* (Zool) sparrow hawk.
gaviota *f.* (Zool) gull, seagull.
gazpacho *m.* cold vegetable soup, gazpacho.
gemelo -la *adj. m. & f.* twin.
gemir *in.* to moan, groan.
generación *f.* generation.
género *m.* kind, sort; (Biol.) genus (Gram.) gender.
genial *adj.* inspired, genius-like; cheerful.
gentilhombre *m.* gentleman.
gentío *m.* crowd, throng.
gerente *m.* manager, director.
germen *m.* germ; source.
germinar *in.* to germinate, to bud.
gestión *f.* step; management.
gestionar *tr.* to pursue, prosecute.
gesto *m.* face; grimace.
gigante *adj.* giant, gigantic; *m.* giant.
gimnasia *f.* gymnastics.
gira *f.* tour; excursion.
girar *tr.* (Com.) to draw; *in.* to turn.
giro *adj. m.* turn; course.
gitano -na *adj.* gypsy.
global *adj.* total; global.
globo *m.* globe; balloon.
gloria *f.* glory.
glorieta *f.* square.
glosar *tr. & in.* to gloss, to comment.
glotón -na *adj. m. & f.* glutton.
gobernante *adj. m. & f.* ruler.
goce *m.* enjoyment.
gol *m.* goal.
golfo -fa *m. & f.* little scoundrel; teddy boy; *m.* gulf.

golondrina f. (Zool.) swallow.
golosina f. sweet, delicacy.
golpe m. blow, hit, beat, knock; stroke.
goma f. gum; rubber.
gordo -da adj. fat, stout, corpulent.
gorra f. cap; busby; sponging.
gota f. drop.
gotear in. to drip, lead.
gotera f. drip, dripping.
gozar tr. to enjoy.
gozo m. joy, rejoicing.
grabación f. recording.
grabado adj. engraved; stamped.
grabar tr. to record; to engrave.
gracia f. grace; joke, witticism.
gracioso-sa adj. graceful.
grada m. grade, degree.
gragea f. small colored candy; pill.
gramo m. gramme.
grande adj. big, large; great; m. grandee.
granela; granel, in bulk.
granero adj. m. granary, barn.
granizo m. hail.
granja f. farm, grange.
granjero -ra m. & f. farmer.
grano m. grain; grape.
grapa f. staple; clip.
grasa f. fat, grease.
gratificar tr. to gratify; to reward.
gratis adv. gratis, free.
gravar tr. to burden, to encumber.
grave adj. heavy; grave, serious.
gremio m. guild; union, trade union.
grey f. flock; congregation.
grieta f. crack, fissure.
grifo adj. m. faucet, tap.
grillo m. (Zool.) cricket.
gris adj. gray, m. gray.
grito m. cry, shout.

grosero -ra adj. gross, coarse, rough, rude.
grosor m. thickness, bulk.
grotesco -ca adj. gortesque.
grúa f. crane, derrick.
grueso -sa adj. thick, bulky; m. thickness.
gruñido m. grunt; growl.
grupo f. group.
gruta f. grotto, cavern.
guante m. glore.
guapo -pa .adj. con. handsome, good-looking; gallant.
guarda m. & f. guard, keeper.
guardabarros m. splashboard; (Aut.) fender.
guardapolvo m. cover, cloth.
guardar tr. to guard; to keep; to preserve.
guardarropa m. & f. wardrober.
guardería f. guard, guardship; **guardería infantil,** day nursery.
guardia f. care, protection; guard; m. guard, guardsman; m. midshipman.
guarida f. den, lair (of animals).
guarnicionería f. harness shop.
guerra f. war, conflict, struggle.
guía m.& f. guide; leader; m. (Mil.) guide; f. guide.
guiar tr. to guide, to lead; to drive; r. to be guided.
guiñar tr. to wink (an eye); in. to wink.
guión m. cross; royal standard.
guisado m. stew; meat stew.
guisante m. (Bot.) pea.
guisar tr. to stew, to cook.
guitarra f. (Mús.) guitar.
gusano m. worm.
gustar tr. to taste; to try, test; in. to please; to like.

G

H

¡ha! *inj.* ah!
habano -na *adj. m.* cigar.
habichuela *f.* (Bot.) kidney bean.
hábil *adj.* skillful, clever.
habilitar *tr.* to habilitate, qualify.
habitación *f.* dwelling; room, chamber.
habitante *m. & f.* inhabitant, dweller.
habitar *tr. & in.* to inhabit.
habituar *tr.* to habituate, accustom; *r.* to become habituated.
habla *f.* speech, speaking.
hablar *in.* to speak talk; to converse, chat; *tr.* to speak; talk; *r.* to speak to each other.
hacia *prep.* towards, toward, to, for.
hacha *f.* ax, axe.
hado *m.* fate, destiny.
halagar *tr.* to flatter; to adulate; to please.
hálito *m.* breath; vapor.
hambre *f.* hunger; starvation; **matar de hambre,** to starve; **matar el hambre,** to satisfy one's hunger.
hambriento *adj.* hungry.
harapo *m.* rag, tatter.
harina *f.* flour.
hartar *tr.* to satiate; to fill, gorge.
hastiar *tr.* to cloy, sate; to weary, bore; *r.* to weary (of).
hatajo *m.* herd, flock.
hato *m.* outfit, belongings.
haya *f.* (Bot.) beech tree.
haz *m.* bundle; beam, pencil.
hazaña *f.* deed, feat, exploit.
hazmerreír *m.* laughing-stock.
hebra *f.* needleful of thread; (meat).

hechizar *tr.* to bewitch, charm, enchant; to fascinate.
hecho -cha *ad.* made.
heder *in.* to stink.
helada *f.* freeze, freezing.
helado *adj.* frozen, *m.* ice cream.
helar *tr.* to freeze, to frostbite.
hélice *f.* (An., Arch., Geom.) helix; (Aer., Náut.) propeller.
hembra *adj.* female; *f.* female.
hendidura *adj.* cleft, crevice.
heno *m.* hay.
heredad *f.* estate.
heredero -ra *adj.* inheriting; *m. & f.* heir, heiress.
herida *f.* wound, stab.
herir *tr.* to wound, injure, hurt; to offend.
hermana *f.* sister.
hermano *m. & f.* brother.
hermoso -sa *adj.* beautiful, fair, fine.
héroe *m.* hero.
heroico -ca *adj.* heroic.
herrado *m.* horsehoeing.
herradura *f.* horseshoe.
herramienta *f.* tool, instrument.
herrumbre *f.* rust, iron rust.
hervir *in.* to boil; to hubble, effervesce.
híbrido -da *adj. & m.* hybrid.
hidrógeno *m.* to hydrogen.
hiedra *f.* (Bot.) ivy.
hiel *f.* bile gall; *fig.* gall, bitterness.
hielo *m.* ice; frost.
hierba *f.* herb, grass, weed.
hierro *m.* iron.
hígado *m.* liver; *pl.* (fig.) courage.
higiene *f.* hygiene, cleanliness.
higo *m.* fig.
hija *f.* daughter.
hijastro -tra *m. & f.* stepson, stepdaughter.
hijo *m. & f.* son, child; *m. pl.* sons, descendants.

hilar *tr.* to spin.
hilera *f.* file, line, row.
hilo *m.* thread.
hilván *m.* basting, tacking.
hilvanar *tr.* to baste, tack.
himno *m.* hymn, anthem.
hincar *tr.* to stick, introduce, drive.
hinchar *tr.* to inflate, puff up, blow up.
hinojo *m.* (Bot.) fennel.
hípico -ca *adj.* equine, horse.
hipo *m.* hiccup.
hipócrita *adj.* false; *m. & f.* hypocrite.
hipotecar *tr.* to mortgage, hypothecate.
hispano -na *adj. & m.* Hispanic, Spanish.
historia *f.* history; tale, story.
historieta *f.* story, tale.
hocio *m.* snout, muzzle.
hogar *m.* heart, fireplace; furnace; home *(family life)*.
hogaza *f.* large loaf.
hoguera *f.* bonfire, fire.
hojaldre *m. (or) f.* puff pastry.
hojear *tr.* to scan, run through *(book)*.
¡hola! *inj.* hallo!
hollín *m.* soot.
hombre *m.* man; *inj.* why! well I never.
hombro *m.* (An., Zool.) shoulder.
homenaje *m.* homage.
homenajear *tr.* to pay homage to.
homicidio *m.* homicide, manslaughter.
hondo -da *adj.* deep, profound; sincere; low *(ground); m.* depth.
hongo *m.* (Bot.) fungus, mushroom.
hora *f.* hour, time; season; *adv.* now, at this time.
horadar *tr.* to perforate, bore.
horario *adj.* hour; *m.* hour hand.

horca *f.* gallows, gibbet; pitchfork.
horchata *f.* orgeat; drink.
horma *f.* horm, mould.
hormiga *f.* ant.
hormigón *m.* concrete.
horno *m.* oven; furnace.
horror *m.* horror; atrocity.
horroroso -sa *adj.* horrible, horrid; hideous.
hortaliza *f.* vegetables.
hospedaje *m.* lodging, board.
hostal *m.* hotel.
hostia (Eccl.) Host; wafer.
hostil *adj.* hostile, adverse.
hoy *adv.* today; now, nowadays.
hoyo *m.* hole, pit; dent, indentation; pockmark.
hoz *f.* sickle; gorge.
hucha *f.* large chest *(or)* coffer; money-box.
hueco -ca *adj.* hollow; empty; vain, conceited; *m.* hollow, cavity.
huelga *f.* strike.
huelguista *m. & f.* striker.
huella *f.* track; print, footprint.
huérfano -na *adj.* fatherless; motherless; *m.* orphan.
huerta *f.* large vegetable garden *(or)* orchard.
hueso *m.* bone.
huésped *m. & f.* guest; lodger, boarder.
huevería *f.* egg shop.
huevo *m.* egg.
hulla *f.* coal.
humano -na *adj.* human.
humareda *f.* cloud of smoke; smoke.
humedad *f.* humidity, moisture.
humilde *adj.* humble; meek; plain.
humo *m.* smoke; steam, vapour; *pl.* conceit, pride.

H

I

ibero -ra *adj. & m. f.* Iberian.
ida *f.* going *(to a place)* departure.
idea *f.* idea; notion.
idear *tr.* to imagine, plan; to project.
identificar *tr.* to identify; *r.* to be identified.
idioma *m.* idiom, language.
idiota *.adj., m. & f.* idiot, silly.
idólatra *m.* idolater; *f.* idolatress.
ídolo *m.* idol.
idóneo -a *adj.* fit, suitable, appropriate.
iglesia *f.* church.
ignorado -da *adj.* unknown.
ignorancia *f.* ignorance.
ignorar *tr.* not to know, to be ignorant of.
igual *adj.* equal; level, even; equal, commensurate; *m.* (Math.) equality sign.
ilegítimo -ma *adj.* illegitimate; spurious.
ileso -sa *adj.* unhurt, unharmed.
ilógico -ca *adj.* illogical, irrational.
iluminar *tr.* illuminate, illumine; light.
iluso -sa *adj.* deluded; dreamer.
imagen *f.* image; statue.
imaginar *tr.* to imagine; conceive; *tr. & r.* to imagine; to assume.
imán *m.* magnet.
imbuir *tr.* to imbue, fill *(emotion, etcétera).*
imitar *tr.* to imitate, copy, to ape.
impacientar *tr.* to make lose patience; *r.* to lose patience.
impar *adj.* (Math.) odd.
impartir *tr.* to impart, bestow.

impedir *tr.* to impede, obstruct.
imperar *in.* to be an emperor; to rule, command.
imperdible *m.* safety pin.
imperdonable *adj.* unpardonable.
impermeabilizar *tr.* to waterproof.
ímpetu *m.* impetus, impulse.
impiedad *f.* ungodliness, lack of piety.
implantar *tr.* to implant, introduce.
implicar *tr.* to imply, involve, implicate.
implorar *tr.* to implore, beg, beseech.
imponente *adj.* imposing; impressive.
importación *f.* (Com.) importation, import.
importar *in.* to import, be important.
importe *m.* (Com.) amount.
imposible *adj.* impossible; *m.* impossible thing.
imposición *f.* imposition, charge.
impostor -ra *m.* impostor; *f.* impostress.
imprenta *f.* printing; press.
imprescindible *adj.* essential.
impresionar *tr.* to impress; to touch; to record sounds on; *r.* to be impressed.
impreso -sa *adj.* impressed, printed; *m.* print; *pl.* printed matter.
imprevisto -ta *adj.* unforeseen, unexpected.
imprimir *tr.* to impress, imprint; (Print.) to print.
improvisar *tr.* to improvise, to extemporize.
impódico -ca *adj.* immodest.
impuesto -ta imposed; informed; *m.* tax, duty.
impugnar *tr.* to impugn, oppose, contradict.
impulsar *tr.* to impel, push.

imputar *tr.* to impute, ascribe, attribute.

inadecuado -da *adj.* unsuitable.

inagotable *adja.* inexhaustible, endless.

inaguantable *.adj.* intolerable, unbearable.

inalterable *adj.* unalterable, stable, firm.

inaudito -ta *adj.* unheard of, extraordinary.

inaugurar *tr.* to inaugurate, open.

incansable *adj.* indefatigable, tireless.

incapaz *adj.* incapable, unable.

incendiar *tr.* to set on fire; *r.* to catch fire.

incensario *m.* incensory.

incertidumbre *f.* uncertainty, doubt.

incesto *m.* incest.

incidente *adj.* incidental; *m.* incident, event.

incierto -ta *adj.* not certain, untrue.

incitar *tr.* to incite, instigate, goad.

inclinado -da *adj.* inclined, slanting.

inclinar *tr.* to incline, slant; bow; *in.* to take after, to resemble; *r.* to be inclined, lean, slant, slope.

incógnito -ta *adj* unknown.

incomunicar *tr.* to isolate; to put into solitary confinement.

inconsciente *adj.* unconcious; unaware.

incontable *adj.* uncountable, countless.

inconveniente *adj.* inconvenient; *m.* obstacle, objection.

incorporar *tr.* to incorporate; *r.* to join *(regiment, etc.)*.

incorrecto -ta *adj.* incorrect, faulty.

increíble *adj.* incredible, unbelievable.

incremento *m.* increment, increase.

incrustar *tr.* to incrust, implay.

incubar *tr.* to incubate, brood, hatch.

inculcar *tr.* to inculcate, put into.

indagar *tr.* to investigate, inquire.

indeciso -sa *adj.* hesitate, irresolute.

indemnizar *tr.* to indemnify.

independizar *tr.* to free, emancipate; *r.* to make oneself independent.

indiano -na *adj. & m.* Spanish American; *m. & f.* one who returns rich from America.

indicación *f.* indication, sign; hint.

indicador -ra *adj.* indication; *m.* indicator.

indicar *tr.* to indicate, point out; to hint, suggest.

índice *m.* (An.) index; forefinger.

indignar *tr.* to irritate, make indignant; *r.* to become indignant.

indisponer *tr.* to indispose; *r.* to be indisposed, out of health.

indomable *adj.* indomitable.

inducir *tr.* to induce, persuade.

indultar *tr.* to pardon; to exempt.

indulto *m.* (Law) pardon; indult.

indumentaria *f.* clothing, dress.

industria *f.* industry.

inepto -ta *adj.* incompetent; inept; *m. & f.* incapable.

inerte *adj.* (Phys., Chim.) inert.

inevitable *adj.* inevitable, unavoidable.

I-K

inexacto -ta *adj.* inexact, inaccurate.

infamar *tr.* to defame.

infante *m.* male infant; king's son.

infantil *adj.* infantile; childlike.

infección *f.* infection, contagion.

infectar *tr.* to infect.

infeliz *adj.* unhappy; *m. & f.* unhappy person.

infestar *tr.* to infest; to infect.

infierno *m.* hell.

infinito *m.* infinite; endless; immense.

inflamar *tr. & r.* to inflame; set on fire.

inflar *tr.* to inflate; to exaggerate; *r.* to inflate.

influir *tr.* to influence *(see irr. huir).*

informar *tr.* to inform; *in.* to report.

infracción *f.* infraction, breach.

infringir *tr.* to infringe, break.

infundir *tr.* to infuse.

ingeniar *tr.* to think up, contrive.

ingenio *m.* talent, wit, talented person.

ingerir *tr.* to ingest.

ingle *f.* (An.) groin.

inglés -sa *adj.* English; *m.* Englishman; *f.* Englishwoman.

ingresar *in.* to enter; to become a member of.

inhabil *adj.* unable; unskilful; tactless.

inhabilitar *tr.* rto disable, disqualify; *r.* to become disqualified.

iniciar *tr.* to initiate, to begin, to be initiated.

injertar *tr.* to graft.

injuriar *tr.* to offend, insult; to injure.

inmiscuir *tr.* to mix; *r.* to interfere.

inmolar *tr.* to immolate; *r.* to sacrifice oneself.

inmovilizar *tr.* to immobilize; *r.* to become immobilized.

inmundicia *f.* dirt, filth, filthiness.

inmundo -da *adj.* dirty, filthy; unclean.

inmutar *tr.* to change, alter.

innovar *tr.* to innovate.

inocente *adj. & m.* innocent, not guilty.

inquietar *tr.* to disquiet, disturb; *r.* to worry, be anxious.

inquietud *f.* anxiety; worry.

inquilino -na *m. & f.* tenant.

inscribir *tr.* to inscribe; to register *(on a record)4; r..* to inscribe oneself.

insertar *tr.* to insert.

insigne *adj.* illustrious, eminent.

insinuar *tr.* to insinuate, hint, suggest.

insistir *in.* to insist.

insólito -ta *adj.* unusual.

insomnio *m.* insomnia, sleeplesness.

inspeccionar *tr.* to inspect, oversee.

inspirar *tr.* to inspire, inhale, breathe in; to inspire; *r.* to become inspired.

instalar *tr.* to install, induct; to install, lay; *r.* to install oneself.

instante *m.* instant, moment.

instaurar *tr.* to restore, re-establish.

instinto *m.* instinct.

institución *f.* institution; *pl.* institutes.

instituir *tr.* to institute, establish.

instruir *tr.* to instruct, teach; (Mil.) to drill; to instruct, inform; *r.* to learn.

insular *adj.* insular.

insultar *tr.* to insult.

intachable *adj.* blameless, faultless.

integrar *tr.* to integrate, compose form.

integridad *f.* integrity, wholeness; integrity, honesty.

íntegro -gra *adj.* integral, whole, entire; honest, upright.

inteligencia *f.* intelligence, intellect, mind.

inteligente *adj.* intelligent, clever.

intensificar *tr.* to intensify.

intentar *tr.* to try; attempt; to intend, mean.

intentona *f.* rash attempt.

interceder *in.* to intercede.

interceptar *tr.* to intercept.

interés *m.* interest.

interesante *adj.* interesting.

interesar *tr.* to interest; to concern; *in.* to be interesting; to be advantageous; to be interested.

interino -na *adj.* provisional, temporary; *m.& f.* holder of a temporary job.

intermediar *in.* to be in the middle; to mediate.

internar *tr.* to intern; *r.* to penetrate; to go deeply into.

interno -na *adj.* internal, interior; *m.& f.* boarding student; *m.* intern.

interponer *tr.* to interpose, place between; *r.* to interpose.

interrogar *tr.* to interrogate.

interrumpir *tr.* to interrupt, suspend; *r.* to be interrupted.

intimar *tr.* to intimate, notify; *in. & r.* to become intimate.

intimidar *tr.* to intimidate, daunt; *r.* to become intimidated.

intoxicar *tr.* to poison; *r.* (Med.) to be poisoned.

intrigar *in.* to intrigue, plot, scheme.

intrincado -da *adj.* intricate.

introducción *f.* introduction; preliminary step.

introducir *tr.* to introduce; to insert; *r.* to introduce oneself.

inundar *tr.* to inundate, flood, overflow; *r.* to be flooded.

inusitado -da *adja.* unusual.

inútil *adj.* useless, unserviceable.

inutilizar *tr.* to render useless; *r.* to become useless.

invadir *tr.* to invade.

invalidar *tr.* to invalidate.

inventar *tr.* to invent, contrive.

inverosímil *adj.* improbable, unbelievable.

invertir *tr.* to invert.

investigar *tr.* to investigate, inquire into.

invierno *m.* winter.

invocar *tr.* to invoke, call upon.

inyección *f.* injection.

ir *in.* to go proceed.

ira *f.* anger, wrath.

iris *m.* iris; **arco iris,** rainbow.

irreal *adj.* unreal.

irreflexión *f.* lack of reflexion.

irritar *tr.* to irritate, anger, annoy; to exasperate; *r.* to become irritated.

isla *f.* island, isle.

itinerario *adj. & m.* intinerary, route; timetable, programme.

izar *tr.* to hoist.

izquierda *f.* left hand; Left *(politics).*

izquierdo -da *adj.* left.

I-K

J

jabalí *m.* (Zool.) wild boar.
jabón *m.* soap.
jabonar *tr.* to soap.
jaca *f.* cob.
jactar *r.* to boast; to brag.
jaleo *m.* noise; trouble; work.
jamás *adv.* never, ever.
jamón *m.* ham.
jaque *m.* check.
jaqueca *f.* headache.
jarabe *m.* syrup.
jarana *f. con.* fun.
jardín *m.* garden; park.
jarra *f.* jar; jug.
jarro *m.* pitcher; jug.
jarrón *m.* vase.
jaula *f.* cage; crate.
jazmín *m.* (Bot.) jasmine.
jefatura *f.* chieftaincy; chieftainship.
jefe *m.* chief, leader.
jerarquía *f.* hierarchy.
jerez *m.* sherry.
jeringuilla *f.* syringe.
jeroglífico -ca *adj.* hieroglyphic (or) hieroglyphical; *m.* hieroglyphic.
jersey *m.* jersey, pullover, cardigan.
jilguero *m.* (Zool.) linnet.
jinete *m.* horse man; rider.
jornada *f.* day's journey; journey; workday.
jornal *m.* salary, wage.
joroba *f.* hump.
jota *f.* jota (*Spanish dance*).
joven *adj.* young; *m.* youth; *f.* girl.
jovial *adja.* jovial, cheery.
joya *f.* jewel; piece of jewelry.
jubilación *f.* retirement.
jubilar *adj.* jubilee; *tr.* to retire, to pension; *in.* to rejoice; to retire; *r.* to rejoice; to retire.
judicial *adj.* judicial, legal.

judío -a *adj.* Jewish; *m.* Jew; *f.* Jewess; (Bot.) bean, kidney bean.
juego *m.* play, playing; game; cards; set.
juerga *f. con.* carousal, spree.
jueves *m.* Thursday.
juez *m.* judge.
jugada *f.* play.
jugar *tr.* to play; to gamble; to stake; *in.* to gamble, to risk.
jugo *m.* juice; gravy.
juguete *m.* toy, plaything.
juicio *m.* judgment; opinion.
julio *m.* July.
jumento *m.* ass, donkey.
junio *m.* June.
juntar *tr.* to join, unite; to gather; *in.* to gather, to associate closely; to copulate.
jurado -da *adj.* sworn; *m.* jury; juror.
juramento *m.* oath; curse.
jurar *r. tr. & in.* to swear.
justificar *tr.* to justify.
juventud *f.* youth.
juzgado *adj.* judged; *m.* court of justice.
juzgar *tr. & in.* to judge; to give an opinion.

K

kilo *m.* kilogramme, kilo, (*about 2 lb. 3 oz.*).
kilogramo *m.* kilogram (or) kilogramme.
kilómetro *m.* kilometer.
kilovatio *m.* kilowatt.
kiosko *m.* kiosk.

L

la *art. def. f.* the; *pron. per, f.* her, it.

labio *m.* lip; (An., Bot. & Zool.) labium.

labor *f.* labour, work; farm work, farming; needlework.

laborar *tr.* to work.

laborista *adj.* Labour *(party).*

labrado -da *adj.* worked, wrought; *m.* working, carving.

labrar *tr.* to work; to carve; to plough.

laca *f.* lac.

lacra *f.* mark.

lacrar *tr.* to seal *(with wax).*

lácteo -tea *adj.* lacteous, milky.

ladera *f.* slope; hillside.

lado *m.* side, direction.

ladrar *tr. & in.* to bark.

ladrillo *m.* brick.

ladrón -na *adj. m.* thief, burgler.

lago *m.* lake.

lágrima *f.* tear; drop.

laguna *f.* lagoon, pond; gap, lacuna.

lamentar *tr. in. & r.* to lament, to mourn.

lámpara *f.* lamp, light; grease spot, oil spot.

lana *f.* wool.

lancha *f.* barge, gig (Náut.) longboat.

langosta *f.* (Zool.) locust; (Zool.) lobster.

lanza *f.* lance, pike; spear.

lanzar *tr.* to launch; to hurl, to throw; to cast *(a glance).*

lapicero *m.* pencil.

lápida *f.* tablet; tombstone.

lápiz *m.* pencil; **lápiz de labios,** lipstick.

largo -ga *adj.* long; generous; abundant; *adv.* abundantly; *m.* length.

laringe *f.* (An.) larynx.

las *def. art. pl.* the.

lástima *f.* pity.

lata *f.* tin plate; tin can.

latido *m.* beating.

latigazo *m.* lash; stroke.

latir *tr.* to beat, palpitate.

latón *m.* brass.

laurel *m.* (Bot.) laurel.

lava *f.* lava.

lavable *adj.* washable.

lavabo *m.* washstand; washroom, lavatory.

lavandera *f.* laundress, laundrywoman.

lavaplatos *m. con.* dishwasher.

lavar *tr. & r.* to wash.

lanzada *f.* bowknot.

lazo *m.* knot, bow, tie; trap; lasso; *con.* to fall into the trap.

le *prom. pers. (to)* him, *(to)* her, *(to)* it.

lección *f.* lesson.

lector -ra *adj.* reading; *m.& f.* reader; lector.

lectura *f.* reading.

lechazo *m.* sucking lamb.

leche *f.* milk.

lecho *m.* bed; couch; (Min.) floor.

lechuga *f.* (Bot.) lettuce.

leer *in.& tr.* to read.

legaña *f.* (Path.) blearieye.

legua *f.* league.

legumbre *f.* legume.

lejanía *f.* distance; remoteness.

lejía *f.* lye; bleaching.

lejos *adv.* far; **a lo lejos,** in the distance.

lencería *f.* linen goods.

lengua *f.* (An.) tongue; language.

lenguado *m.* (Zool.) sole.

lenguaje *m.* language.

lente *m. & f.* lens; *pl.* spectacles, glasses.

lenteja *f.* (Bot.) lentil.

lento -ta *adj.* slow, heavy.

leña *f.* firewood; *con.* beating.

león *m.* (Zool.) lion.

lepra *f.* (Path.) leprosy.

les *prom. pers. (to)* them, *(ta)* you.

lesionar *tr.* to hurt, injure.

letra *f.* letter; handwriting; *con.* draft.

letrado -da *adj.* learned *m.* lawyer.

letrero *m.* label; sign, placard.

levadura *f.* yeast; ferment.

levantar *tr.* to raise; to lift; to clear *(the table)*; to weigh *(anchor)*.

léxico *m.* lexicon, vocabulary.

ley *f.* law; loyalty; norm, standard.

leyenda *f.* legend; inscription.

liar *tr.* to tie, bind; to tie up; to roll *(a cigaret)*; *r.* to join together, be associated.

liberal *adj. & m.* liberal, generous.

liberar *tr.* to free.

libertad *f.* liberty, freedom.

libertar *tr.* to liberate, to set free.

libra *f.* pound.

libranza *f.* (Com.) draft, bill of exchange.

librar *tr.* to free; to save, spare; to join *(battle)*.

libre *adj.* free; vacant.

liberería *f.* bookstore, bookshop.

libreta *f.* notebook; loaf of bread.

libro *m.* book.

licenciado -da *m.* graduated; **B.A.**.

licenciar *tr.* to license; (Mil.) to discharge; *r.* to receive the master's degree.

liceo *m.* lyceum.

licor *m.* liquor, spirits.

líder *m.* leader.

lidiar *tr.* to fight *(bulls)*; to face up.

liebre *f.* (Zool.) hare.

lienzo *m.* linen; linen cloth.

ligar *tr.* to tie, bind; to alloy; to join.

ligereza *f.* lightness; fickleness.

ligero -ra *m.& f.* light; fast; slight; simply.

lijar *tr.* to sand.

lila *f.* lilac.

lima *f.* file *(tool.)*.

limar *tr.* to file; to polish.

limitar *tr.* to limit; to restrict; *int.* to borden on.

limón *m.* lemon.

limosna *f.* alms.

limpiabotas *m.* bootblak.

limpiaparabrisas *m.* windshield wiper.

limpiar *tr.* to clean; to cleanse.

limpio -pia *adj.* clean; neat; chaste; clear, free.

linaje *m.* lineage; class.

lindar *tr.* to borden on.

lindo -da *adj.* pretty, nice.

lino *m.* (Bot.) flax; flax fiber.

linterna1 *f.* lantern; torch.

lío *m.* bundle, package.

liquidar *tr. & r.* to liquefy; to liquidate.

lirio *m.* (Bot.) lily.

lisiar *tr.* to hurt, cripple; *r.* to become crippled.

liso -sa *adj.* smooth; even; plain, unadorned.

listo -ta *adj.* ready, prepared.

listón *m.* tape, ribbon; strip *(of wood)*.

litera *f.* litter; berth *(in train)*.

litigio *m.* lawsuit, litigation.

litro *m.* litre.

lívido -da *adj.* livid.

lo *art. def. neut.* the; him, it.

loba *f.* she-wolf.

lobo *m.* (Zool.) wolf.

local *adj.* local; *m.* rooms, quarters.

localidad f. locality; seat (in cinema).

localizar tr. to localize; to locate; r. to locate; r. to be (or) become localized.

loción f. wash; lotion.

loco -ca adja. mad; crazy; insane; wild; loose (pulley).

locura f. madness, insanity.

locutor -tora m.& f. announcer; speaker.

lodo m. mud.

logar tr. to get, obtain; to produce.

loma f. down, hillock.

lombriz f. (Zool.) worm; earthworm.

lomo m. back.

lona f. canvas.

loncha f. slab; slice.

longaniza f. pork sausage.

longitud f. length; longitude.

lonja f. exchange, market.

loro m. (Zool.) parrot.

losa f. slab, flagstone.

lote m. lot, share.

lotería f. lottery.

loza f. earthenware; crockery.

lubricar tr. to lubricate.

lucidez f. lucidity, clarity.

lucir tr. to illuminate, light up; to show; to plaster; in. to shine; r. to dress up; to come off well.

lucrar r. to profit, to get money.

lucha f. fight; struggle; quarrel.

luchar in. to fight; to struggle, to quarrel.

luego adv. soon; at once; **desde luego,** of course; right away; **hasta luego,** see you.

lugar m. place, position; spot; seat.

lógubre adj. dismal, gloomy, dark.

lujo m. luxury.

lumbre f. fire, light.

luna f. moon; mirror.

lunar adj. lunar; m. mole.

lunes m. Monday.

lupa f. magnifying glass.

lópulo m. (Bot.) hop.

luto m. mourning; sorrow.

luz f. light; opening; pl. enlightenment.

LL

llaga f. ulcer; sore.

llama f. flame, blaze.

llamada f. call; sign, signal.

llamar tr. to call; to summon; in. to knock, to ring; r. to be called.

llano -na adj. smooth, even, level; plain; clear, evident.

llanto m. weeping, crying.

llanura f. smoothness, evenness; plain.

llave f. key; wrench; tap; faucet.

llavero m. keeper of the keys; key ring.

llavín m. latchkey.

llegada f. arrival, coming

llegar in. to arrive; to happen; to reach; to amount to.

llenar tr. to fill; to fulfill; to satisfy; fill up, become full.

llevadero -ra adj. bearable, tolerable.

llevar tr. to carry, to take, to lead; to yield; to keep (accounts); to be in charge of; to lead (a certain life); to bear, to suffer (punishment); to take off; in. to lead; r. to carry away; to seize.

llorar tr. to weep; in. to weep, cry.

lloro m. weeping.

L

M

macabro -bra *adj.* macabre.
macarrón *m.* macaroni; macaroon.
maceta *f.* plant pot.
machacar *tr.* to pound, crush, bruise, drum; *in.* to importune.
machete *m.* cutlass.
madeja *f.* hank *(or) skein; lock of hair.*
madera *f.* wood, timber.
madrastra *f.* step-mother.
madre *f.* mother; generatrix; nun.
madrina *f.* godmother; sponsor.
madrugada *f.* dawn, prime.
madrugar *in.* to rise early, to get up early.
madurar *tr.* to ripen, mature; to season.
maestra *f.* teacher, instructress.
maestro -tra *adj.* masterly, main; *m.* master, teacher.
magnetofón *m.* tape recorder.
magno -na *adj.* great.
mago -ga *m.* magician.
magulladura *f.* bruising; contusion.
magullar *tr.* to bruise, to mangle.
mayonesa *f.* mayonnaise.
maicena *f.* corn starch.
maíz *m.* (Bot.) maize.
majo *adj.* showy; *m.* dandy.
mal *adj. m.* evil, harm, wrong, injury, sickness, ache.
maldecir *tr.* to damn, curse, accurse.
malear *tr.* to pervert, corrupt, to forge.
malestar *m.* uneasiness, discomfort.
maleta *f.* valise, suit-case.

malgastar *tr.* to misspend, waste, squander.
maligno -na *adj.* malign *(ant.)* perverse, ill-minded.
malograr *tr.* to lose, waste, miss; *r.* to fall through.
malparado -da *adj.* damaged.
malsonante *adj.* ill-sounding.
maltratar *tr.* to mishandle, abuse; to spoil.
malva *f.* (Bot.) mallow.
mamá *f.* mother, ma(m)ma.
mamar *tr.* to suck(le).
manada *f.* flock, herd, pack.
manantial *adj.* flowing; *m.* waterspring, fountain.
manar *in.* to spring from, flow.
mancha *f.* stain, spot.
manchar *tr.* to stain, spot, dirty.
mandar *tr. & in.* to command; to govern, boss, dictate; lead.
mandíbula *f.* jawbone.
mandil *m.* apron.
manga *f.* sleeve; waterspout; breath of ship's beam.
manía *f.* mania, frenzy.
manicomio *m.* madhouse.
manifestación *f.* demonstration; declaration.
maniobra *f.* handiwork; stratagem.
manipular *tr.* to manipulate, handle.
manivela *f.* crank-handle, lever.
manojo *m.* handful; parcel.
mansión *f.* residence.
manso -sa *adj.* tame; domestic.
manta *f.* blanket.
mantel *m. (table)* cloth.
mantequilla *f.* butter.
manutención *f.* maintaining; maintenance.
manzana *f.* (Bot.) apple, block.
mañana *f.* morning; tomorrow; **pasado mañana,** the day after tomorrow.

mapa *m.* map, chart.
mar *m. & f.* sea, ocean.
maravilla *f.* wonder, marvel.
maravillar *tr.* to admire; *tr.* to wonder *(at).*
marca *f.* mark, stamp; sign; character.
marchar *in.& r.* to go; get away, walk away, depart, leave; (Mil.) to march.
marchitar *tr.* to wither, fade.
marea *f.* tide.
marear *tr.* to navigate a ship; to turn; *r.* to be seasick.
marejada *f.* swell.
marfil *m.* ivory.
margen *m. & f.* margin *(river)* side; border; edge.
María *f.* Mary.
marido *m.* husband.
marioneta *f.* puppet.
mariposa *f.* butterfly.
marisco *m.* shell-fish.
mármol *m.* marble.
marrón *adj.* brown.
martes *m.* Tuesday.
martillo *m.* hammer; (An.) hammer, malleus.
marzo *m.* March.
más *adv.* more; most; plus; longer; rather.
mas *cnj.* but.
masa *f.* mass; dough.
masaje *m.* massage.
mascar *tr.* to chew; *con.* to mumble, to mutter.
masilla *f.* putty.
matador *m.* killer; matador.
materia *f.* matter; stuff, material; subject.
maternidad *f.* maternity; hospital for expectant mothers.
matinal *adj.* morning.
matiz *m.* hue; shade.
matrícula *f.* register, roll; matriculation.
matrimonio *m.* matrimony; marriage.

matriz *adj.* main, mother; *f.* womb.
mayo *m.* May.
mazmorra *f.* dungeon.
mazo *m.* mallet, maul; bunch.
mear *tr.* to urinate on; *in. & r.* to urinate.
mecanizar *tr.* to merchandise.
mecanografía *f.* typewriting.
mecer *tr.* to stir, to shake; to swing, to rock; *r.* to swing, to rock.
mecha *f.* wick; fuse; match; tinder.
mechero *m.* burner; lighter.
medalla *m.* medal.
media *f.* stocking.
medianoche *f.* midnight.
mediar *in.* to be or get halfway; to be half over; to mediate.
medicina *f.* medicine.
medición *f.* measuring, measurement.
médico -ca *adj.* medical; *m.* doctor.
medida *f.* measurement; measure; step.
medio -dia *adj.* half; middle; medium; mean average; *m.* middle; medium; step, measure; means; *con.* to get out.
mediodía *m.* noon, mid-day; south.
medir *tr.* to measure; to scan *(verse); in.* to be moderate.
médula *f.* marrow.
mejilla *f.* check.
mejor *adj.* better; best; *adv.* better; best; rather.
mejorar *tr.* to make better, to improve; to mend; *in. & r.* to get better, to recover.
melena *f.* long lock of hair; long hair; loose hair.
melocotón *m.* (Bot.) peach.
mella *f.* nick; dent; gap, hollow; harm.
mellizo -za *adj.& m. f.* twin.

M

membrete *m.* letterhead; heading.
membrillo *m.* (Bot.) quince.
mencionar *tr.* to mention.
menear *tr.* to stir; to shake; to wage; *r.* to shake; to wag; to wiggle.
menguar *tr.* to lessen, diminish, to wane; to fall.
menor *adj.* less; smaller; younger; least; smallest; youngest.
menos *adv.* less; fewer;; least; lowest.
mensaje *m.* message.
mensual *adj.* monthly.
menta *f.* (Bot.) mint.
mente *f.* mind.
mentir *in.* to lie; to be false.
mentira *f.* lie.
mentiroso -sa *adj.* lying; *m.&* *f.* liar.
menudillo *m. pl.* giblets.
menudo -da *adj.* small, slight; minute.
meñique *adj.* little; *m.* little finger.
meollo *m.* marrow, essence.
mercancía *f.* trade, dealing; merchandise; *pl.* goods, merchandise.
merecer *tr.* to deserve, to merit; to be worth.
merendar *tr.* to lunch, to have afternoon tea; *in.* to lunch.
merienda *f.* lunch,snack, afternoon tea, picnic.
merluza *f.* (Zool.) hake; *con.* drunkeness.
mermelada *f.* marmalade, jam.
mero -ra *adj.* mere.
mes. *m.* month.
mesa *f.* table; desk.
meta *f.* goal, limit, purpose.
metal *m.* metal; brass, latten.
método *m.* method; system.
metralla *f.* grapeshot; shrapnel balls.
mezclar *tr.* to mix; *r.* to mix; to mingle.

mezquita *f.* mosque.
mi *adj.* my; *m.* mi.
mí *pron. per.* me, myself.
miedo *m.* fear; dread.
miedoso -sa *adj. con.* afraid; fearful.
miel *f.* honey.
miembro *m.* member; limb.
mientras *adj. & cnj.* while.
miércoles *m.* Wednesday.
mies *f.* grain, cereal; harvest time.
miga *f.* bit; crumb.
milla *f.* mile.
millar *m.* thousand.
millón *m.* million.
mimar *tr.* to pet, fondle.
mimbre *m. & f.* wicker.
minar *tr.* to mine; to undermine; to consume; *in.* to mine.
minimizar *tr.* to diminish.
mínimo *adj.* least, slightest *m.* minimum; tiny bit.
minuto *m.* minute.
mío, mí)a *adj. poss.* mine, of mine; *pron. poss.* mine.
miope *adj.* myopic, shortsighted; *m.* myope.
mirar *tr.* to look at; to watch; to contemplate; to consider carefully.
misa *f.* (Ecl.) mass.
miserable *adj.* wretched; vile; wicked; wretch.
misericordia *f.* mercy, compassion.
mísero -ra *adj.* wretched, vile.
mismo -ma *adj. & pron. indef.* same; own, very; self.
mitad *f.* half; middle.
mitigar *tr. & r.* to mitigate.
mito *m.* myth.
mobiliario -ria *m. & f.* set of furniture.
moco *m.* mocus; snuff *(of candlewick)*.
mochila *f.* (Mil.) knapsak, haversack.
moda *f.* fashion, style.

modelar *tr.* to model; to form, shape; *r.* to model.

modificar *tr. & r.* to modify, alter.

modismo *m.* idiom.

modista *f.* dressmaker, modiste.

modo *m.* mode, manner, way, method.

mofar *in. & r.* to scoff, jeer, mock.

mojado -da *adj.* wet; *m. & f.* wetting.

mojar *tr.* to wet; to drench; to moisten.

moldear *tr.* to mould, to cast.

moler *tr.* to grind, to mill; to tire out.

molido -da *adj.* worn out, exhausted; milled.

molino *m.* mill.

molleja *f.* gizzard; sweetbread.

momia *f.* mummy.

mondar *tr.* to clean; to prune; to peel, to hull.

moneda *f.* money; coin.

monedero *m.* moneybag.

monja *f.* nun.

monje *m.* monk; anchorite.

montacargas *m.* freight elevator, lift.

montaje *m.* mounting, assembly.

montaña *f.* mountain.

montar *tr.* to mount; to get on; to ride; to set up, establish; to set; to cover; (Mil.) to mount *(guard)*; *in.* to mount; to get on top; to ride; *r.* to mount; to get on top.

monte *m.* mount, mountain.

montón *m.* pile, heap; crowd.

monumento *m.* monument.

morado -a *adj.* mauve, dark violet.

moral *adj.* moral; morals.

morar *in.* to live, dwell.

morder *tr.* to bite; to eat away; to gossip about; *in.* to bite.

moreno -na *adj.* brown.

morfinómano -a *m.* drug addict.

morir *in.* to die; *r.* to die; to be dying.

morro *m.* know.

mortadela *f.* luncheon meat.

mortero *m.* mortar.

mosca *f.* (Zool.) fly; *con.* money.

mostaza *f.* (Bot.) mustard.

mosto *m.* grape juice.

mostrador -ra *adj.* showing, pointing.

mostrar *tr. & r.* to show, prove.

mote *m.* nickname.

motivar *tr.* to motivate, cause.

moto *m.* motorcycle.

motor *m.* motor; engine.

mover *tr.* to move; to stir.

movilizar *tr. in. & r.* to mobilize.

mozo -za *adj.* young, youthful; single; *m.* youth, lad; *f.* girl.

muchacha *f.* girl, wench.

muda *f.* change of clothes.

mudo *adj.* dumb, silent.

mueble *m.* piece of furniture; *pl.* furniture.

muela *f.* millstone; grindstone; back tooth.

muelle *adj.* soft; easy; *m.* spring; pier.

muerte *f.* death; murder.

muestra *f.* sample; specimen.

mujer *f.* woman; wife.

mula *f.* mule, she-mule.

muleta *f.* cruth; red cloth.

mulo *m.* mule *(or)* jinny.

multa *f.* fine.

mundo *m.* world.

muñeco -a *m.* (An.) wrist; doll; puppet; *m. (fig)* puppet.

muralla *f.* wall, rampart.

muro *m.* wall.

músculo *m.* (An.) muscle.

museo *m.* museum.

muslo *m.* (An.) thigh.

mutilar *tr.* to mutilate; to cripple.

muy *adv.* very; very much.

M

N

nácar *m.* nacre.
nacer *in.* to be born; to arise.
nacimiento *m.* birth; origin;
  crib.
nación *.f.* nation, country.
nada *f.* nothingness; *pron.*
  indef. nothing.
nadar *in.* to swim.
nadie *m.* nobody.
nalga *f.* buttock, rump.
nana *f.* lullaby.
naranja *f.* orange.
nariz *f.* nose.
narrar *tr.* to narrate, tell.
nata *f.* cream; élite.
natillas *f. pl.* custard.
natividad *f.* birth, nativity.
naturaleza *f.* nature,
  disposition.
naufragar *in.* to be wrecked to
  sink, to be shipwrecked.
navaja *f.* folding knife; **navaja
  de afeitar**, razor.
nave *f.* ship; vessel; (Arch.)
  nave.
navegar *tr.* to navigate; to sail.
Navidad *f.* Christmas.
navío *m.* ship, vessel.
neblina *f.* mist, haze.
necesitar *tr.* to require; to
  need.
nefasto -ta *adj.* ominous, fatal.
negación *f.* negation, denial.
negar *tr.* to deny; to refuse; *in.*
  to deny.
negociado *m.* department,
  bureau.
negociar *tr.* to negotiate; to
  trade.
negro -gra *adj.* black; dark,
  negro.
nena *f con.* baby, child.
nene *m. con.* baby, child.
nervio *m.* nerve; vigour,
  strength.
neto -ta *adj.* pure, neat.
neumático -ca *adj.* pneumatic.
neutralizar *tr.* to neutralize.

nevado -da *adj.*
  snow-covered; *f.* snow fall.
nevar *in.* to snow.
nevera *f.* refrigerator, ice box.
ni *conj.* neither, nor.
nido *m.* nest; home.
niebla *f.* fog, mist.
nieto -ta *m. & f.* grandchild; *m.*
  grandson; *f.* granddaughter.
nieve *f.* snow.
ninguno -na *adj. indef.* no not
  any.
niño -ña *adj. m. & f.* child.
niquelar *tr.* to nickel-plate.
nitidez *f.* brightness,
  clearness, brilliance.
nivel *m.* level.
noche *f.* night, nighttime;
  buenas noches, good
  evening; good night.
nochebuena *f.* Christmas Eve.
nómada *adj. m. & f.* nomad.
nombrar *tr.* to name; to
  appoint, to mention.
nombre *m.* name; reputation;
  (Gram.) noun; **nombre y
  apellido**, full name.
nómina *f.* list; pay roll.
nono -na *adj. & m.* ninth.
noria *f.* chain pump,
  water-wheel.
norma *f.* norm, standard.
norte *m.* north.
nosotros -tras *pron. pers.* we;
  us.
nota *f.* note; mark; bill.
notar *tr.* to note, to notice; to
  criticize.
notaría *f.* notary's office.
noticia *f.* news; notion.
notificar *tr.* to notify, inform.
novato -ta *adj. m. & f.*
  beginner.
novedad *f.* novelty.
novela *f.* novel.
novia *f.* fiancée; bride; girl
  friend.
noviembre *m.* November.
nublar, *to* cloud; to wither.
nudo *m.* knot; tie.

nuera *f.* daughter-inlaw.
numeral *adj.* numeral.
nunca *adv.* never.
nupcias *f. pl.* nuptials, marriage.
nutrir *tr.* to nourish, to feed; *r.* to be enriched.

O

o *cnj.* either, or.
obedecer *tr. & in.* to obey.
obelisco *m.* obelisk.
obertura *f.* (Mós.) overture.
obispada *m.* bishopric.
obispo *m.* bishop.
objeto *m.* object, purpose, aim.
obligar *tr.* to obligate; to oblige; to force; to compel.
obra *f.* work, building.
obrar *tr.* to build; to work; *in.* to behave.
obsequiar *tr.* to give presents, flatter; to present; to court.
observar *tr.* to observe; to notice; to obey.
obsesionar *tr.* to obsess.
obstruir *tr.* to obstruct, block.
obtener *tr.* to obtain, get acquire.
oca *f.* (Zool.) goose.
ocasión *f.* opportunity, occasion, chance.
ocasionar *tr.* to cause, arouse.
ocho *adj.* eight.
ocio *m.* idleness.
octubre *m.* October.
ocular *adja.* ocular.
ocultar *tr.* to hide, conceal; *r.* to hide.
ocupar *tr.* to occupy; to busy; to employ; *r.* to become occupied; to be busy.

ocurrir *in.* to occur, to happen.
odiar *tr.* to hate, detest.
oeste *m.* west.
ofender *tr. & in.* to offend; *r.* to take offense.
oferta *f.* offer.
oficina *f.* office.
oficio *m.* office, occupation.
ofrecer *tr. in. & r.* to offer, promise.
oído *m.* hearing *(sense)*; (An.) ear.
ojear *tr.* to eye, stare at.
ojival *adj.* ogival, gothic.
ojo *m.* (An.) eye; key-hole; span, bay *(of bridge)*.
ola *f.* wave.
óleo *m.* holy oil; oil painting.
oler *tr.* to smell; to sniff; *in.* to smell.
oliva *f.* (Bot.) olive.
olmo *m.* (Bot.) elm tree.
olor *m.* odour, smell.
olvidar *tr.* to forget.
olla *f.* pot, kettle; stew.
ombligo *m.* umbilicus; (fig.) center.
omitir *tr.* to omit.
once *adj.* eleven.
onda *f.* wave.
ondear *tr.* to wage; to ripple; *r.* to wave, to sway.
ondular *tr.* to wage; *in.* to undulate.
onza *f.* ounce.
operar *tr.* to operate on; *in.* to cause.
opinar *in.* to opine; to judge, consider.
oponer *tr.* to oppose, resist.
oposición *f.* opposition; examination *(for professorship, etc.)*.
oprimir *tr.* to oppress; to press.
opuesto -ta *pp.* of opener; *adj.* adverse.
oración *f.* oration; speech; prayer; (Gram.) sentence.
orar *in.* to pray.

N-O

P

paciencia f. patience.
pacificar tr. to pacify.
pactar tr. to pact, stipulate.
padecer tr. to suffer, to endure.
padrastro m. stepfather.
padre m. father; **padres,** m. pl. parents; **padre político,** father-in-law.
padrino m. godfather.
padrón m. poll, census.
pagar tr. to pay; to pay for.
página f. page.
país m. country, land, nation.
paisaje m. landscape, countryside.
paja f. straw; padding (in writing).
pájaro m. bird; crafty fellow.
pala f. shovel; racket.
palabra f. word.
paladear tr. to taste, to relish.
palanca f. lever; pole, bar.
palancana f. washbowl.
palco m. box (theatre).
paleta f. small shovel; fire shovel.
paliar tr. to palliate.
pálido -da adj. pale.
palillo m. toothpick.
paliza f. beating.
palmada f. slap.
palmo m. span, palm.
palo m. stick; (Náut.) mast.
paloma f. (Zool.) pigeon.
palpar tr. to touch, to feel.
palpitar in. to palpitate.
pamplina f. con. nonsense, trifle.
pan m. bread.
panadería f. bakery; baker's shop.
panal m. honeycomb.
panera f. granary; bread basket.
pantalón m. trousers.

pantalla f. lamp shade; screen.
pantano m. dam.
pantorrilla f. calf.
panza f. paunch; belly.
pañal, pañales, m. pl. swaddling clothes.
paño m. cloth.
pañuelo m. handkerchief, kerchief.
papel m. paper; part, role; pl. documents.
papeleo m. red tape.
papeleta f. slip of paper; pawn ticket.
paquete -ta m. parcel, packet.
para prep. to, for; towards.
parabien m. congratulation.
parabrisa m. windshield.
parachoques m. bumper.
paradero m. end; whereabouts.
paraguas m. umbrella.
paralizar tr. to paralyze.
páramo m. high barren plain, moor.
parangón m. comparison.
paraninfo m. assembly hall, auditorium.
parar tr. to stop; to fix (attention).
pararrayo m. lightning rod.
parcela f. plot, piece of ground, lot.
parco -ca adj. frugal, sparing.
pardal adj. m. sparrow.
pardo -da adj. brown; dark; cloudy.
parecer m. opinion; look.
parecido -da adj. like, similar; **parecidos -das,** adj. pl. alike.
pared f. wall.
pareja f. pair, couple.
parentela f. kinsfolk, relations.
parir tr. to give birth.
parlamentar in. to talk, chat.
parlanchín -na adj. con. chattering.
paro m. shutdown, work stoppage.

parpadear *in.* to blink, to wink.
párpado *m.* eyelid.
parrafada *f. con.* talk, chat.
parrilla *f.* grill; grate, grating.
parroquia *f.* parish; clientele, customers.
parte *f.* part; share; side.
participante *adj. m. & f.* notifier.
participar *tr.* to communicate; to inform; *in.* to participate.
partícula *f.* particle.
partidario -ria *adj. m. & f.* partisan, follower.
partido -da *adj.* broken; *m.* party; decision.
partir *tr.* to divide; to distribute; *in.* to start, depart.
partitura *f.* (Mós.) score.
parto *adj. m. & f.* child-birth.
párvulo *adj. m. & f.* child.
pasa *adj.* dried.
pasaje *m.* passage.
pasaporte *m.* passport.
pasarela *f.* footbridge catwalk.
pascua *f.* Easter; **Felices Pascuas!**, Merry Christmas!
pase *m.* pass.
pasear *tr.* to walk; *in. & r.* to take a walk.
paseo *m.* walk, stroll.
pasillo *m.* passage, corridor.
pasmo *m.* astonishment; wonder.
paso *m.* step, pace; passing, measure.
pasta *f.* paste, dough, pie crust.
pastel *m.* cake.
pastelería *f.* cake-shop.
pastilla *f.* tablet.
pasto *m.* pasture; grass.
pastor *m.* shepherd.
pata *f.* foot, leg; (Zool.) duck.
patada *f.* hick.
patalear *in.* to hick, to stamp.
patán *adj. m. con.* churlish, simpleton.
patata *f.* (Bot.) potato.

patear *tr. con.* to trample on, tread on.
patente *adj.* patent, clear.
paternidad *f.* paternity.
patíbulo *m.* scaffold.
patinar *in.* to skate; to skil.
patio *m.* patio, court, yard; pit.
pato *m.* (Zool.) duck, drake; **pagar el pato,** *con.* to be the goat.
patria *f.* country; mother country, fatherland.
patrocinar *tr.* to sponsor, patronise.
patrón -na *m. & f.* sponsor, protector; patron saint; *m.* patron.
patronato *m.* employers' association; patronage.
patrono -na *m. & f.* sponsor, protector; landlord.
pausa *f.* pause, slowness.
pauta *f.* guide lines.
pavimentar *tr.* to pave.
pavo *m.* (Zool.) turkey.
pavor *m.* fear, terror
paz *f.* peace; **dejar en paz**, to leave alone; **estar en paz,** to be even.
peaje *m.* toll.
peatón *m.* pedestrian.
pecar *in.* to sin.
pecera *f.* fish globe, fish bowl.
pecuario -a *adj.* pertaining to cattle.
pecho *m.* (An.) chest; breast; **tomar a pecho**, to take to heart.
pedal *m.* pedal, treadle.
pedernal *m.* flint.
pedrada *f.* stoning; hit (or) blow with a stone.
pedregal *m.* stony ground.
pedrisco *m.* shower of stones; hailstones; hailstorm.
peinar *tr.* to comb; *r.* to comb one's hair.
pelado -da *adj.* bare; bald; barren.

peldaño m. step.

pelear in. to fight; to quarrel; to struggle.

peletería f. furrier.

peliagudo -da adj. con. arduous, ticklish.

peligro m. danger, risk; **correr peligro**, to be in danger.

pelirroja -ja adj. redhaired, redheaded.

pelma m. & f. con. lump, poke, sluggard.

pelota f. ball; **ne pelota**, stripped naked; **pelotas**, con. person who butters-up.

pelotera f. con. brawl, row.

pelotón m. (Mil.) platoon; main body

peluca f. wig.

pelusa f. down; con. jealousy.

pellejo m. skin; hide; **hallarse en el pellejo de otro**, to be in somebody else's shoes.

pellizcar tr. to pinch; to nip.

pena f. pity, grief; fine, punishment; **vale la pena**, it iw worthwhile.

penar tr. to punish; in. to suffer.

pendencia f. dispute, quarrel.

penetrar tr. to penetrate; to break into; to see through (someone's intentions).

penitenciaría f. penitentiary, prison.

penoso -sa adj. arduous, difficult.

pensar tr. to think; to think over; in. to think (see irr. **acertar**).

pensativo -va adj. thoughtful.

pensionista m. & f. pensioner; boarder; **medio pensionista**, day boarder.

penúltimo -ma adj. penultimate, last but one.

penumbra f. penumbra, shade.

peón m. worker, laborer, pawn (chess).

peor adj. & adv. worse; worst.

pepita f. pip; melon seed.

pequeño -ña1 adj. little, small.

percance m. mischance.

percatar in. & r. to think, to be aware of.

perchero m. rack.

perdonar tr. to pardon, forgive; to excuse.

perdurar in. to last a long time.

perecer in. to perish (see irr. **nacer**).

peregrino -na adj. rare, strange; singular; m. & f. pilgrim.

pereza f. laziness; sloth.

perfeccionar tr. to perfect, improve.

perfilar tr. to profile, to outline.

preforar tr. to perforate, drill.

perfume m. perfume.

pericia f. skill, expertness.

perillán -llana adj. rascally; m.

periodista m. & f. journalist.

perito -ta adj. skilled, skillful; m. expert.

perjudicar tr. to harm, damage.

perjurar in. to commit perjury; to swear.

perla f. pearl; **de perlas**, pat.

permanecer in. to stay, remain; to last.

permiso m. permission; **permiso de conducir**, driver's license.

permitir tr. to permit, to allow; r. to be permitted; to allow oneself.

permutar tr. to interchange; to barter; to permute.

pernera f. leg (of trousers).

pernoctar in. to spend the night.

pero conj. but.

perro -rra m. dog; **a otro perro con ese hueso**, tell that to the marines.

perseguir *tr.* to pursue; to persecute.

perseverar *in.* to persevere; to insist.

persiana *f.* window blinds.

persignar *r.* to cross oneself, make the sign of the cross.

persistir *in.* to persist.

persona *f.* person.

perspectivo -va *adj.* perspective; *f.* perspective; outlook.

persuadir *tr.* to persuade; *r.* to become persuaded, to get convinced.

pertenecer *in.* to belong; to pertain.

perturbar *tr.* to perturb; to disturb; to confuse.

pervertir *tr.* to pervert; *r.* to become perverted (*see irr. sentir*).

pesa *f.* weight.

pesadilla *f.* nightmare.

pesado -da *adj.* heavy; clumsy.

pésame *m.* condolence.

pescado *m.* fish.

pescador -ra *adj. m. & fm.* fisher.

pescar *tr.* to fish; to catch; to angle.

pescuezo *m.* neck.

pésimo -ma *adj.* super, very bad.

peso *m.* weight; burden, load; **caerse de su peso**, to be self-evident.

pesquisa *f.* inquiry, search.

pestaña *f.* eyelash.

pestañear *in.* to wink; **sin pestañear**, without batting an eye.

pestillo *m.* bolt; door latch.

petardo *m.* bomb; fraud.

peto *m.* breastplate.

petrificar *tr. & r.* to petrify.

petrolero *m.* oil tanker.

pez *m.* fish; **pez espada**, swordfish.

pezuña *f.* hoof.

piar *in.* to peep.

pica *f.* pike.

picante *adj.* biting, pricking; hot; *m.* piquancy.

picardía *f.* knavery, crookedness.

picazón *m.* itch, itching.

pico *m.* beak; **cerrar el pico**, *con.* to shut up.

picudo -da *adj.* beaked; pointed.

piedra *f.* stone; rock; **piedra angular**, cornerstone; keystone; **piedra de afilar**, grindstone.

piel *f.skin, pelt; leather.*

pienso *m.* feed.

pierna *f.* leg.

pijama *m.* pyjamas.

pila *f.* basin; trough; sink; pile; heap.

pilar *m.* basin, bowl; pillar.

píldora *f.* pill.

pillaje *m.* pillage, plunder.

pillar *tr.* to pillage, plunder.

pimentón *m.* red pepper powder; paprika.

pimiento (Bot.) red-pepper

pinar *m.* pine wood.

pincel *m.* brush.

pinchar *tr.* to prick; puncture; to stir up, provoke.

pingüe *adj.* oily, greasy; rich, abundant.

pino -na *adj. m.* (Bot.) pine-tree.

pintar *tr.* to paint; to picture, depict; *in.* to paint; to paint oneself, make-up.

pintor -ra *m. & f.* painter.

piña *f.* pine cone; (Bot.) pineapple.

piojo *m.* (Zool.) louse.

pipa *f.* pipe; wine cask.

piquete *m.* sharp jab; stake, picket; (Mil.) picket.

piragua *f.* canoe.

pirámide *f.* pyramid.

P-Q

piropo *m. con.* compliment, flattering sentence.

pisapapeles *m.* paperweight.

pisar *tr.* tread on; step on; to press with the feet; *fig.* to abuse.

piscina *f.* swimming pool.

piso *m.* floor, story; flat, apartment.

pisotón *m.* heavy tread on someone's foot.

pista *f.* track; trace; clue.

pistola *f.* pistol; gun.

pitillo *m.* cigarette.

pito *m.* whistle; horn.

pizarra *f.* slate; blackboard.

placa *f.* plate, insignia.

placer *m.* pleasure; *tr.* to please.

plaga *f.* plague; pest.

plagar *tr.* to plague, infest; *r.* to become plagued.

plan *m.* plan; scheme.

planchar *tr.* to iron, to press.

planeta *m.* planet.

plano -na *adj.* plane; level; *m.* plan; map.

planta *f.* (Bot.) plant; sole; floor.

plantar *tr.* to plant; *con.* to throw (*into the street); r.* to stand.

plata *f.* (Chm.) silver; wealth; money.

plátano *m.* banana.

plática *f.* talk, chat, homily.

plato *m.* dish; plate; course (*at meals).*

playa *f.* beach, shore.

plaza *f.* square; market; office, employment.

plazo *m.* term; time; limit.

plegar *tr.* to fold; to plait; to fold over.

pliego *m.* sheet; folder.

plomo *m.* lead.

pluma *f.* feather; pen, nib; fountain pen.

población *f.* population; village town.

poblar *tr.* to people, populate; to found, settle; *in.* to settle, colonize.

pobre *adj.* poor; *m. & f.* beggar.

poco -ca *adj.* little; *adj. pl.* few; a few.

podar *tr.* to prune, to trim.

poder *m.* power; might; proxy.

poderoso -sa *adj.* powerful, mighty; wealthy.

poema *m.* poem.

poesía *f.* poetry; poem.

policía *f.* police.

polilla *f.* (Zool.) moth; (Zool.) carpet moth.

póliza *f.* check, draft; constract; tax stamp.

polo *m.* support; pole.

polvo *m.* dust; powder; *m. pl.* dust.

pólvora *f.* powder, gunpowder.

pollo *m.* children.

pómulo *m.* (Am.) cheekbone.

ponderar *tr.* to weigh; to ponder; to exaggerate.

ponencia *f.* paper, report.

popularizar *tr.* to popularize; *r.* to become popular.

por *prep.* by; through; for the sake of; in place of; out of.

porcelana *f.* porcelain.

porcentaje *m.* percentage.

pordiosero -ra *m. & f.* beggar.

porque *cnj.* because.

porqué *m. con.* why, reason.

porrazo *m.* blow.

portaaviones *m.* aircraft carrier.

portada *f.* front, facade; titlepage.

portaequipajes *m.* baggage rack.

portal *m.* vestibule, entrance hall; porch.

portalámparas *m.* socket.

portamonedas *m.* purse.

portavoz *m.* spokesman.

pórtico *m.* portico, porch.

porvenir *m.* future.

pos after, behind.
posada *f.* inn; boarding house.
poseer *tr.* to own, to possess, to hold.
poso *m.* sediment; dregs.
postal *adj.* postal, *f.* postcard.
poste *m.* post, pole, pillar.
posterior *adj.* posterior, back, rear.
postigo *m.* wicket, shutter.
postizo -za *adja.* false, artificial; *m.* switch.
postrar *tr.* to postrate; *r.* to postrate oneself.
postre *adj.* last, final; *m.* dessert; *m. pl.* dessert.
póstumo -ma *adj.* posthumous.
potable *adj.* potable, drinkable.
potage *m.* stew, medley.
potestad *f.* power; dominion.
potro -tra *m. & f.* colt; young horse; rack.
pozo *m.* well; pool (Min.) shaft.
practicar *tr. in. & r.* to practice, perform, exorcise.
pradera *f.* meadow; prairie; field.
precaver *tr.* to try, to prevent; to be on one's guard.
preceder *tr. & in.* to precede, go before.
preces *f. pl.* prayers.
precio *m.* price; value; cost.
preciosidad *f.* preciousness; beauty.
precipitar *tr.* to precipitate; to rush; *r.* to rush.
precisar *tr.* to state precisely, to specify; to need; *in.* to be necessary.
precoz *adj.* precocious, premature.
predecir *tr.* to predict, foretell.
predicado *m.* predicate.
predicador -ra *adj.* preaching; *m. & f.* preacher.
predicar *tr. & in.* to preach; to predicate.

predominar *tr.* to predominate; to over-rule.
prefabricar *tr.* to prefabricate.
preferir *tr.* to prefer, like.
pregonar *tr.* to proclaim; to bring to public notice.
preguntar *tr.* to ask; *in.* to ask, to inquire; *r.* to wonder.
prematuro -ra *adj.* premature.
premiar *tr.* to reward.
prender *tr.* to seize, grasp; to catch; *in.* to catch; to take root, to set fire.
preocupar *tr.* to preoccupy; *r.* to become preoccupied, to take interest.
preparar *tr.* to prepare.
presa *f.* dike, dam; seizure.
prescribir *tr. & in.* to prescribe.
presencia *f.* presence.
presenciar *tr.* to witness; to be present at.
presentar *tr.* to present; to introduce; to display; *in.* to present oneself; to appear.
preservar *tr.* to preserve, keep.
presidente *m.* president; chairman.
presidiario *m.* convict.
presidir *tr.* to preside over; *in.* to preside.
presión *f.* pressure.
préstamo *m.* loan.
presumir *tr.* to presume; *in.* to be conceited; to boast.
presupuesto -ta *adj.* presupposed; *m.* reason; supposition; budget.
pretender *tr.* to pretend to; to try; to aspire.
prevalecer *in.* to prevail.
prevenir *tr.* to prepare; to forestall, prevent; *r.* to get prepared.
prever *tr.* to foresee.
primario -ria *adja.* primary; chief.
primavera *f.* spring.
primer *adj.* form of primero.

P-C

primero -ra *adj.* first; former.
primosa -ma *m. & f.* cousin.
primogénito -ta *adj. M. & f.* firstborn.
principio *m.* star, beginning; source; (Chm.) principle.
prior *m.* prior.
prisa *f.* hurry, haste; urgency.
privar *tr.* to deprive; *in* to be in vogue; to be in favour.
privilegio *m.* privilege.
pro *m. & f.* profit, advantage.
proa *f.* (Náut.) prow.
probar *tr.* to prove; to test; to try; to taste; to fit; to try.
problema *m.* problem.
procedencia *f.* origin, source.
procesar *tr.* to sue; to indict.
procrear *tr.* to procreate, breed.
procurador *m.* solicitor, attorney.
procurar *tr.* to try; to get.
pródigo -ga *adj. m. & f.* prodigal.
producir *tr.* to produce; to yield; to cause.
proferir *tr.* to utter, to say, to express.
profesar *tr. & in.* to profess, to take religious vows.
profesor -ra *m. & f.* teacher; professor.
profetizar *tr. & in.* to prophecy, foretell.
prófugo -ga *adj. m. & f.* fugitive; *m.* (Mil.) slacker.
profundizar *tr.* to deepen; *in.* to go deep into.
prohibir *tr.* to prohibit, to forbid.
prójimo *m.* fellow man; *con.* fellow.
proletario - ria *adj. & m.* proletarian.
prolongar *tr.* to prolong, to extend; *r.* to extend.
promesa *f.* promise.
promotor -ra *adj. m. & f.* promoter.

promover *tr.* to promote, raise, cause.
promulgar *tr.* to promulgate issue.
pronto -ta *adj.* quick; prompt; ready.
pronunciar *tr.* to pronounce; *r.* to rebel, revolt.
propaganda *f.* advertisement; propaganda.
propagar *tr.* to propagate; to spread.
propiedad *f.* property; ownership; **propiedad literaria**, copyright.
propina *f.* tip, fee.
propio -pia *adj.* proper, suitable; peculiar; himself, herself, etc.
proporcionar *tr.* to proportion; to provide, supply.
prorrogar *tr.* to prorogue.
prosa *f.* prose.
prosperar *tr. to prospect.*
protagonista *m. & f.* protagonist.
protector -ra *adj.* protective; *m.* protector; *f.* protectress.
proteger *tr.* to protect; to shelter.
protestar *tr. & in.* to protest.
provecho *m.* advantage, benefit; profit, gain.
proveedor -ra *m. & f.* supplier; provider, purveyor.
proveer *tr.* to provide, furnish; *r.* to provide oneself, make provisions.
provenir *in.* to come, originate.
provocar *tr.* to provoke; to incite, to tempt.
próximo -ma *adj.* next; near.
proyectar *tr.* to project; to plan.
prueba *f.* proof; trial; test, examination.
póa *f.* sharp point, barb; quill.
publicar *tr.* to publish.
público -ca *adj.* public; *m.* public.

puchero *m.* pot, kettle.
pudrir *tr.* to rot, putrefy.
pueblo *m.* town, village.
puente *m.* bridge; (Náut.) deck.
puerta *f.* door; gate.
puerto *m.* port, harbour, pass; (fig.) haven.
pues *adv.* then, well; yes.
pujar *tr.* to push; to raise; *in.* to struggle.
pulga *f.* flea.
pulgada *f.* inch.
pulgar *m.* thumb.
pulido -da *adj.* pretty; neat.
pulpo *m.* (Zool.) octopus.
pulsar *tr.* to feel *(or)* take the pulse of.
pulsera *f.* bracelet.
puntería *f.* aim.
puntilla *f.* brad, finishing nail.
punto *m.* point, dot; loop; jot, mote; *fig.* point.
puntual *adj.* punctual.
puntualizar *tr.* to fix in the memory; to enumerate.
puñado *m.* handful.
puñal *m.* dagger.
puñetazo *m.* punch.
puño *m.* fist; blow; cuff; handle *(of umbrella)*.
pupitre *m.* desk.
purgar *tr.* to purge; to purify, refine; to expiate; *r.* to take a purge.
pus *m.* pus.

Q

que *adj. & pron. rel.* that, which; who; *adv.* than; *conj.* that; for, because.
qué *adj. & pron. interr.* what, which; what a!

quebrantar *tr.* to break; to twist; to crush; *in.* to fail.
quebrar *tr.* to break; to twist; to crush; *in.* to fail.
quedar *in.* to remain; to stay; to be left; agree on.
quehacer *m.* work, task.
quejar *tr.* to complain, lament; to whine.
quema *f.* fire, burning.
quemadura *f.* burn, scald.
quemar *tr.* to burn; to scald; to parch; *in.* to burn, be hot. *r.* to burn; to be burning up.
querella *f.* complaint; quarrel, dispute.
querer *m.* love, affection; will; *tr.* to wish, want; desire; to like; to love.
querido -da *adj.* dear; beloved; mistress; *m.* lover.
queso *m.* cheese.
quicio *m.* pivot hole; hinge.
quien *pron. rel.* who; whom.
quién *pron. int. & rel.* who; whom.
quienquiera *pron. indef.* anyone, anybody; *pron. ref.* whoever, whichever.
quilate *m.* carat.
quilla *f.* (Náut. & Bot.) keel.
químico -ca *adj.* chemical; *m.* chemist; *f.* chemistry.
quincalla *f.* hardware; costume jewelry.
quince *adj.* fifteen.
quincena *f.* fortnight.
quinqué *m.* oil lamp.
quinto -ta *adj.* fifth; *f.* villa, country house.
quiosco *m.* kiosk.
quirófano *m.* operating room, operating theatre.
quitanieve *m.* snowplow.
quitasol *m.* parasol.
quizá *(or)* **quizás** *adv.* maybe, perhaps.

P-Q

R

rábano *m.* (Bot.) radish.
rabí *m.* rabbi.
rabia *f.* anger, rage.
rabiar *in.* to rage, to get mad.
rabo *m.* tail.
racimo *m.* bunch; cluster.
raciocinio *m.* argument, reasoning.
racha *f.* squall; *con.* streak.
radiador -ra *adj.* radiating, *m.* radiator.
radiar *tr.a* to radio; to broadcast; *in.* to radiate.
radio *m.* edge, outskirt; spoke, rung *(of wheel)*; radium; *f.* radio, wireless.
radiodifusión *f.* broadcasting.
ráfaga *f.* gust, puff; burst.
raíl *m.* rail.
raíz *f.* root; origin.
rajar *tr.* to split, to cleave; to crack; to slice; *con.* give up.
rallar *tr.* to grate; *con.* to grate on.
rama *f.* branch, department.
ramal *m.* strand; branch line.
rambla *f.* dry ravine; tenter; boulevard.
ramera *f.* whore, strumpet.
ramificar *tr. & r.* to ramify, to spread out.
ramo *m.* branch; cluster, bough; bouquet.
rampa *f.* ramp, gradient.
rana *f.* (Zool.) frog.
rancio *adj.* rank, rancid, old-fashioned.
rancho *m.* mess; ranch.
ranura *f.* groove; slot.
rape *m.* **al rape**, crew cut.
rapidez *f.* rapidity, speed.
raposo *m.* male fox; *con.* fox.
raptar *tr.* to abduct; to kidnap.
raqueta *f.* racket.
raro -ra *adja.* rare; odd; uncommon; querer.
ras, a ras de, *m.* even with.
rascacielos *m.* skyscraper.

rascar *tr.* to scrape; to scuff; to scratch.
rasgar *tr.* to tear; to rip; *r.* to become torn.
rasguño *m.* scratch.
raspar *tr.* to scrape, scrape off; to scratch.
rastrear *tr.* to trail, to track, to trace; *in.* to rake, to drag.
rastrillo *m.* rake.
rasurar *tr. & r.* to shave.
rata *f.* (Zool.) rat.
ratificar *tr.* to ratify.
ratón (Zool.) mouse.
raya *f.* stripe; stroke; dash; parting *(hair)*; rayfish; boundary.
rayar *tr.* to rule, to line; to stripe; to scratch, score; *in.* to border; to begin, arise.
rayo *m.* ray, beam; lightning (fig.) thunderbolt.
raza *f.* race; breed; quality.
razón *f.* reason; right; account, story.
razonable *adj.* reasonable, fair.
razonar *tr. & in.* to reason, to think.
reaccionar *in.* to react.
reacio-cia *adj.* obstinate, stubborn.
reactor *m.* (Elec. & Phys.) reactor; jet plane.
realce *m.* splendor.
realizar *tr.* to fulfill; to perform; to make; *r.* to become fulfilled.
realzar *tr.* to raise, elevate; to emboss; to heighten, set off.
reanimar *tr. & r.* to reanimate, revive.
rebaja *f.* rebate, reduction.
rebajar *tr.* to lower; to diminish, reduce; to rebate; to deflate; *r.* to stoop; to humble oneself; to become deflated.
rebanada *f.* slice, piece.
rebaño *m.* flock, herd.

rebosar *in.* to overflow, run over; to overflow with, burst with.

rebozar *tr.* to muffle up; to cover with batter; *r.* to muffle up.

rebuznar *in.* to bray.

recadero -ra *m.* messenger; *m.* errand boy; errand girl.

recaer *in.* to fall again; to relapse.

recalentar *tr.* to heat up; to warm up.

recambio *tr.* spare part.

recargar *tr.* to overload; to overcharge; to increase; to overwork.

recaudación *f.* tax collecting; sum collected.

recaudar *tr.* to gather, collect.

recepción *f.* reception admission.

receptor -ra *adj.* receiving; *m.* receiver, radio set.

recetar *tr. & in.* to prescribe.

recibir *tr.* to receive; to welcome; *r.* to be received, be admitted.

recibo *m.* receipt.

recién *adv.* recently, just, newly.

recipiente *m.* container, vessel.

recitar *tr.* to recite, declaim.

reclamar *tr.* to claim, demand; to complaint.

reclinar *tr. & r.* to recline, to lean.

recluir *tr.* to seclude, shut in; to imprison; *r.* to go into seclusion.

recluta *f.* recruiting; levy *m.* recruit.

recobrar *tr. & r.* to recover.

recoger *tr.* to pick up; to gather; to harvest; to collect, fetch; *r.* to take shelter, take refuge; to go home.

recomendar *tr.* to recommend.

recompensar *tr.* to recompense, reward.

reconciliar *tr.* to reconcile.

reconocer *tr.* to recognize; to admit; to inspect.

reconstruir *tr.* to rebuild, to reconstruct.

recopilar *tr.* to compile.

record *m.* record.

recordar *tr.* to remember; to remind.

recordatorio *m.* reminder.

recorrer *tr.* to cross, to traverse, to go over *(or)* through; to run over.

recortar *tr.* to trim, cut off, to cut out.

recostar *tr. & r.* to recline, to lean against.

recrear *tr. & r.* to amuse, enjoy.

rectificación *f.* rectification, correction.

rectificar *tr.* to rectify, amend.

recto -ta *adj.* straight, right.

rector -ra *adj.* governing; managing; *m.* principal, superior; director; Vice-Chancellor.

recubrir *tr.* to cover.

recuento *m.* recount.

recuerdo *m.* memory, remembrance; souvenir.

recuperar *tr. & r.* to recuperate, recover, regain.

recurrir *in.* to resort, have recourse.

rechazar *tr.* to repel, repulse, reject, refuse.

red *f.* net.

redacción *f.* writing; editing.

redactar *tr.* to write up, to word; to edit.

redada *f.* catch.

redil *m.* sheepfold.

redimir *tr.* to redeem.

redondel *m. con.* circle; arena.

redondo -da *adj.* round.

reducir *tr. & r.* to reduce, abridge, confine.

R

reembolso *m.* reimbursement; **contra reembolso,** cash on delivery.

reemplazar *tr.* to replace, to act as substitute.

referir *tr. & r.* to refer.

refinar *tr.* to refine, purify.

reflexionar *tr.* to reflect; to think over.

reformar *tr.* to reform.

reforzar *tr.* to reinforce; to strengthen.

refrán *m.* proverb, saying.

refrenar *tr.* to rein; curb; to check; to restrain.

refrescar *tr.* to refresh; to cool; *in.* to cool off, get cooler.

refrigerador -ra *adj.* refrigerating; *m.* refrigerator.

refrigerar *tr.* to cool; to refrigerate, to refresh; *r.* to cool off.

refugiar *tr.* to shelter; *r.* to take refuge.

refutar *tr.* to refute.

regadío *m.* irrigated land.

regalar *tr.* to give, to present; to regale.

regalo *m.* gift, present; joy.

regar *tr.* to water, sprinkle; to irrigate.

regata *f.* regatta, boat race.

regenerar *tr. & in.* to regenerate; to revive.

regentar *tr.* to direct, to manage.

regir *tr.* to rule, govern; to control; *in.* to prevail, be in force.

registrar *tr.* to examine, to inspect; to register.

regla *f.* rule; ruler.

reglamento *m.* regulation; constitution.

regocijar *tr.* to cheer; *r.* to rejoice.

regresar *in.* to return.

rehén *m.* hostage.

rehuir *tr.* to shrink from; *in.* to avoid.

rehusar *tr.* to refuse; turn down.

reina *f.* queen; queen bee.

reino *m.* kingdom, reign.

reintegrar *tr.* to restore; *r.* to redintegrate; to recover.

reír *tr.* to laugh at *(or)* over; *in.* to laugh; *r.* to laugh at.

reja *f.* grate, grating; plowshare; rail.

relacionar *tr. & r.* to relate; to connect.

rebajar *tr.* to relax; to become relaxed.

relatar *tr.* to relate; (Law) to report.

relevo *m.* (Mil.) relief; *pl.* relay race.

relicario *m.* reliquary, shrien.

relieve *m.* relief; prominence.

reliquia *f.* relic; trace, vestige.

reloj *m.* watch; clock.

relucir *in.* to shine, glow.

relumbrar *in.* to shine brightly, sparkle.

rellenar *tr.* to refill, to fill up *(bricks);* to stuff.

remar *in.* to row.

remedio *m.* remedy; help; recourse.

remendar *tr.* to mend, patch.

remesa *f.* remittance; shipment.

remisión *f.* remission; pardon.

remitente *adj.* remittent; *m.* sender.

remitir *tr.* to remit; to forward.

remo *m.* oar.

remojar *tr.* to soak, to steep.

remolacha *f.* (Bot.) beet.

remolcar *tr.* to tow.

remolque *m.* towing.

remover *tr.* to remove; to disturb; move away.

renacer *in.* to be reborn; to bloom again.

rendir *tr.* to conquer; to subdue; to exhaust, wear

out; to return; *in.* to yield; *r.*
to surrender.
renglón *m.* line.
renovar *tr.* to renovate; *r.* to
renew.
renta *f.* rent; annuity; income.
renunciar *tr.* to renounce; to
resign.
reñir *tr.* to scold; *in* quarrel;
wrangle.
reorganizar *tr. & r.* to
reorganize.
reparar *tr.* to repair, to mend;
to notice.
repasar *tr.* to repass; to
retrace; to revise; to mend.
repeler *tr.* to repel.
repercusión repercussion.
repercutir *in.* to rebound.
repetir *tr. & in.* to repeat.
repleto -ta *adj.* replete, full.
replicar *tr.* to argue against;
in. to argue back.
repoblar *tr.* to repopulate; to
afforest.
reportaje *m.* reporting; report.
representar *tr.* to represent;
to appear to be; to perform.
reprobar *tr.* to reprove.
reproducir *tr. & r.* to
reproduce.
repuesto *m.* stock, supply.
repugnar *tr.* to conflict with; to
loathe; *in.* to be repugnant.
requemar *tr.* to burn again; to
parch; to overcook; *r.* to
become tanned *(or)*
sunburned.
res *f.* head of cattle; beat.
resbalar *in.* to slide; to slip.
rescatar *tr.* to ransom; to
rescue.
resentir *r.* to become
weakened; to be resentful.
reservar *tr.* to reserve; to put
aside; to conceal.
resfriado *m.* cold.
resfriar *r.* to catch cold.
resguardo *m.* defense;
protection; voucher.

residir *in.* to reside.
resignar *tr.* to resign; to
submit.
resistir *tr.* to resist; to bear, to
stand; *in.* to resist.
resolver *tr.* to resolve; to
solve; *int.* to determine,
decide.
resorte *m.* spring; means.
respaldar *tr.* to endorse, to
back.
respetar *tr.* to respect,
reverence.
respirar *tr. & in.* to breathe.
resplandor *m.* brilliance,
radiance; glare; glow.
resta *f.* (Math.) subtraction.
restablecer *tr.* to reestablish;
r. to recover; to get better.
restar *tr.* to subtract; to
reduce.
restauración *f.* restoration.
restaurante *m.* restaurant.
restregar *tr.* to rub.
restringir *tr.* to restrict.
resumen *m.* summary,
recapitulation.
resumir *tr.* to sum up,
summarize; to resume.
retablo *m.* altarpiece, retable.
retal *m.* remnant, piece.
retener *tr.* to retain, keep,
withhold.
retina *f.* (An.) retina.
retirar *tr.* to retire, to
withdraw; to take away.
reto *m.* challenge.
retorcer *tr.* to twist; *r.* to twist;
to writhe.
retornar *tr.* to return, give
back; *tr. & r.* to return, go
back.
retractar *tr.* to retract,
withdraw.
retrasar *tr.* to delay, retard; to
put off; to set *(or) turn back
(a watch); in.* to be too
slow; *r.* to delay, be late, be
slow.

R

retratar *tr.* to portray; to make a portrait *(or)* photograph; *r.* to have a photograph taken.

retrete *m.* toilet, water closet.

retroceder *in.* to recede; to go back.

reunir *tr.* to join, unite; to assemble; gather together; to have possess.

revelar *tr.* to reveal; to develop.

reventón *adj.* bursting; *m.* burst.

reverso *m.* back side; reverse.

revés *m.* back, reverse.

revisar *tr.* to revise, review, check.

revista *f.* review; inspection.

revolcar *tr.* to knock down, to roll over; *r.* to wallow.

revolver *tr.* to stir; to turn upside down; to disturb; upset; *r.* to turn around.

revólver *m.* revolver, pistol.

rey *m.* king.

rezar *tr.* to pray; to say.

rezumar *tr. r. & in.* to ooze.

ría *f.* estuary; ria; inlet.

ribera *f.* bank, shore, riverside.

rico -ca *adj.* rich; delicious, *m.* rich person.

riego *m.* irrigation; watering.

rienda *f.* rein.

riesgo *m.* risk, danger.

rifa *f.* raffle; fight.

rifle *m.* rifle.

rigor *m.* rigour, severity, harshness, strictness.

rimar *tr. & in.* to rhyme.

riña *f.* right, schuffle, quarrel, dispute.

río *m.* river.

risa *f.* laugh; laughter.

rival *adj. & m.* rival.

rivera *f.* creek.

robar *tr.* to rob, to steal.

roble *m.* oak tree.

robustecer *tr.* to make strong; *r.* to become strong.

roca *f.* rock.

rociar *tr.* to sprinkle; to spray.

rocío *m.* dew; sprinkling.

rodaja *f.* disk, small wheel; slice.

rodar *tr.* to roll; to film; to screen; *in.* to roll, to run.

rodear *tr.* to surround, go around; *in.* to go around; *r.* to turn, twist.

rodilla *f.* (An.) knee.

rodillo *m.* roller.

roedor *m.* (Zool.) rodent.

roer *tr.* to gnaw.

rojo -ja *adj.* red; *m.* Red; red.

rollo *m.* roll; roller.

romería *f.* pilgrimage; gathering at a shrine.

rompecabezas *m.* riddle, puzzle.

rompeolas *m.* breakwater.

romper *tr.* to break; to tear; to smash; to burst open.

ron *m.* rum.

roncar *in.* to snore; to roar.

rondar *tr.* to go around, fly around; to patrol by night; to serenade.

roñoso -sa *adj.* scabby; mangy; dirty; *con.* stingy.

ropa *m.* clothing; clothes.

ropero *m.* wardrobe.

rosa *f.* rose; pink.

rostro *m.* beak; face.

roto -ta *adj.* broken; torn; ragged.

rotular *adj.* rotular; *tr.* to label, to title.

rozar *tr.* to grub; *in.* to graze; to brush *(rub)* against, to chafe.

rubí *m.* ruby.

rubio -bia *adja.* golden; blonde; fair hair.

rubricar *tr.* to sign, to indorse one's flourish.

rueda *f.* wheel; ring.

rugir *m.* to roar; to bellow.

ruin *adj.* base, mean, vile; puny; *m.* scoundrel.

ruina *f.* ruin.

S

sábado *m.* Saturday.
sábana *f.* sheet.
saber *m.* knowledge, learning; *tr.* to know; to be able to, in to taste.
sabiduría *f.* wisdom.
sabio -bia *adj.* wise; *m. & f.* wise man, scientist.
sable *m.* saber.
sabor *m.* taste, flavor.
sabroso -sa *adj.* tasty, delicious.
sacapuntas *m.* pencil sharpener.
sacerdote *m.* priest.
saciar *tr.* to stiate, get enough, satisfy.
saco *m.* sack, bag.
sacrificar *tr.* to sacrifice.
sacro -cra *adj.* sacred; holy.
sacudir *tr.* to shake; to jar; to beat; *r.* to shake.
sagaz *adj.* sagacioues, clever.
sal *f.* salt; charm, grace.
sala *f.* hall; drawing room, living room; parlor.
salar *tr.* to salt; to season.
salario *m.* wages, salary.
salchicha *f.* sausage.
saldo *m.* settlement, liquidation.
salero *m.* saltcellar; *con.* charm, grace, wit.
saliva *f.* saliva.
salmo *m.* psalm.
salón *m.* lounge, saloon.
salpicar *tr.* to splash.
salsa *f.* sauce.
saltar *tr.* to jump, jump over, leap; to spring; to come off.
saltear *tr.* to attack, to hold up.
salto *m.* jump, leap, bound.
salud *f.* health; welfare.
saludable *adj.* healthy.
saludar *tr.* to greet, salute.

salvador -ra *adj.* saving; *m. & f.* saviour; *m.* Saviour.
salvaguardia *f.* safeguard; protection; *m.* bodyguard.
salvo -va *adj.* safe.
sancionar *tr.* to sanction, ratify; to fine.
sandalia *f.* sandal.
sandía *f.* (Bot.) watermelon.
sanear *tr.* to guarantee; to make sanitary.
sangrar *tr.* to bleed; to tap.
sangre *f.* blood.
sanidad *f.* health.
sano -na *adj.* healthy; healthful, salutary; right, sane.
santificar *tr.* to sanctify, to consecrate.
santo -ta *adj.* saint, holy, blessed; *m. & f.* saint; *con.* picture.
sapo *m.* (Zool.) toad.
saquear *tr.* to sack, to plunder.
sarampión *m.* (Path.) measles.
sartén *f.* frying pan.
sastre *m.* tailor.
satirizar *tr. & in.* satirize.
satisfacer *tr. & in.* to satisfy.
saturar *tr.* to saturate; to fill.
savia *f.* sap.
sazonar *tr.* to ripen, to mature; to season, flavor.
secador -ra *adj.* drying; *m.* dryer; *f.* clothes dryer.
secar *tr.* to dry, *r.* to dry, to get dry.
secretario -ria *adj. m. & f.* secretary.
secreto -ta *adj. secret; m.* secret.
secta *f.* sect.
secuestrar *tr.* to kidnap; to sequestrate.
sed *f.* thirst.
seda *f.* silk.
seducir *tr.* to tempt; to seduce; to captivate.

S

segador -ra *adj.* harvesting;
m. harvester; *f.* harvester.
segar *tr. & in.* to reap, to mow,
to harvest.
seguido -da *adj.* continued,
succesive; straight; in a row.
segundo -da *adj.* second.
seguridad *f.* security; surety.
seleccionar *tr.* to select.
selva *f.* forest, woods.
sellar *tt.* to seal; to stamp.
sello *m.* seal; stamp.
semáforo *m.* traffic lights.
sembrar *tr.* to sow; to plant.
semejante *adj.* like, similar.
semilla *f.* seed.
sencillez *f.* simplicity
simpleness.
senda *f.* path, foolpath.
seno *m.* bosom, breast;
womb; asylum, refuge.
sensual *adj.* sensual; *m. & f.*
sensualist.
sentado -da *adj.* seated;
established.
sentar *tr.* to seat; to suit, fit; *r.*
to sit, to sit down; to settle
down.
sentenciar *tr.* to sentence; to
condemn.
sentir *m.* feeling; opinion,
judgment; *tr.* to feel; to
regret, to be *(or)* feel sorry;
to hear.
señal *f.* sign, mark; landmark;
bookmark; trace, vestige;
signal; traffic light.
señalar *tr.* to mark; to show,
indicate; to signal; *r.* to
distringuish oneself.
señor -ra *adj.* ruling, master;
m. sir, mister; gentleman;
lord, master, owner.
señorita *f.* young lady; miss.
separar *tr.* to separate; to
dismiss; to detach.
sepelio *m.* burial.
septiembre *m.* September.
séptimo -ma *adj. & m.*
seventh.

sepulcro *m.* sepulcher, grave.
sepultar *tr.* to bury; *r.* to be
buried.
sequía *f.* drought.
ser *m.* being; essence; *in.* to
be.
serenata *f.* serenade.
serie *f.* series.
serpiente *f.* serpent; (fig.)
snake.
serrín *m.* sawdust.
servilleta *f.* napkin *(table)* .
servir *tr.* to serve; *in.* to serve;
to be useful.
sesenta *adj.* sixty.
seso *m.* brain.
seta *f.* mushroom.
seto *m.* fence, hedge.
sexo *m.* sex.
sexto -ta *adj.* sixth; *m.* sixth.
si *conj.* if; whether.
sí *adv.* yes; indeed; *m.* yes;
pron. reflex. himself,
herself, itself, themselves;
yourself, yourselves;
oneself.
sidra *f.* cider.
siembra *f.* sowing.
siempre *adv.* always.
sien *f.* (An.) temple.
siervo -va *m. & f.* slave;
humble servant.
siesta *f.* siesta.
siete *adj.* seven.
sigla *f.* initial.
siglo *m.* century.
significado *m.* meaning.
signo *m.* sign; mark.
siguiente *adj.* following, next.
sílaba *f.* syllable.
silbar *tr.* to whistle; to blow *(a
whistle)*; to hiss.
silencio *m.* silence.
silueta *f.* silhouette, profile.
silla *f.* chair.
sillón *m.* armchair.
símbolo *m.* symbol.
simiente *f.* seed.
simpatía *f.* sympathy;
congeniality.

simpatizar *in.* to be congenial, to get on well together.

simplificar *tr.* to simplify.

simular *tr.* to simulate, to feign.

sin *prep.* without.

sincero -ra *adj.* sincere, frank, true.

singular *adj.* singular; unique, peculiar.

siniestro -tra *adj.* sinister; *m.* disaster; *f.* left hand.

sinónimo -ma *adj.* synoymous; *m.* synonym.

sintaxis *f.* syntax.

sintonizar *tr.* to tune.

siquiera *adv.* at least; *cnj.* although, even though.

sirena *f.* mermaid; siren.

sitiar *tr.* to surround, besiege.

situar *tr.* to situate; to place, locate; *r.* to take a position.

sobaco *m.* (An.) armpit.

sobornar *tr.* to bribe, to suborn.

sobrar *tr.* to exceed, supass; *in.* to be more than enough.

sobre *prep.* on, upon, above; about; *m.* envelope.

sobrecargar *tr.* to overload; to overcharge.

sobrepasar *tr.* to excel; *r.* to go too far.

sobresalir *in.* to project; to stand out, excel.

sobresaltar *tr.* to assail, to rush upon; to frighten; *r.* to be frightened, be startled.

sobrevivir *in.* to survive.

sobrina *f.* niece.

sobrino *m.* nephew.

socarrón *f.* sly, cunning, shrewd.

socavar *tr.* to dig under, to undermine.

socio -cia *m. & f.* partner; member; shareholder.

socorrer *tr.* to succour, help, aid.

sofá *m.* sofa.

sofocar *tr.* choke, suffocate; to extinguish; *r.* to choke; to get out of breath.

sol *m.* sun.

solamente *adv.* only.

solapa *f.* lapel.

solar *adj.* solar; *m.* lot, plot, ground.

soldar *tr.* to solder.

soler *in.* to be accustomed to.

solfear *tr.* (Mús.) to solfa.

solicitar *tr.* to solicit; to woo, to court, to apply.

solidaridad *f.* solidarity.

solista *m. & f.* (Mús.) solist.

solo -a *adj.* only; along, on one's own.

sólo *adv.* only.

solomillo *m.* sirloin.

soltero -ra *adj.* single; *m.* bachelor; *f.* spinster.

sollozar *in.* to sob.

sollozo *m.* sob.

sombra *f.* shade, shadow; grace, charm, wit; *con.* in jail.

sombrero *m.* hat.

sombrilla *f.* parasol, sunshade.

someter *tr.* to force, to yield, to subdue; to submit; *r.* to yield, submit.

somier *m.* spring mattress.

sonado -da *adj.* noted, famous.

sonajero *m.* child's rattle.

sonido *m.* sound.

sonreír *in. & r.* to smile.

so ar *tr.* to dream.

sopa *f.* soup.

soplar *tr.* to blow; to whisper; to tip; *in.* to blow.

soportar *tr.* to support, bear; to suffer.

sordo -da *adj.* deaf.

sorprender *tr.* to surprise.

sortear *tr.* to raffle, to cast lots for.

sortija *f.* ring; curl.

S

soso -sa *adj.* insipid, tasteless; dull, flat.

sospechar *tr. & in.* to suspect.

sostén *m.* support, brass.

sostener *tr.* to support, hold up, sustain.

sótano *m.* basement.

suave *adj.* smooth, soft, gentle.

suavizar to smooth, to soften.

subastar *tr.* to auction.

súbdito -ta *adj. m. & f.* subject.

subir *tr.* to raise; to lift up; to carry up; to climb; *in.* to go up; to rise; increase; to amount to.

sublevar *tr.* to incite to rebellion; *r.* to revolt; to disgust.

submarino -na *adj. m.* submarine.

subordinar *tr.* to subordinate.

subrayar *tr.* to underline; to emphasize.

subscribir *tr.* to subscribe.

substituir *tr. & in.* to substitute, replace.

substraer *tr.* to subtract; deduct; *r.* to elude, evade.

subsuelo *m.* subsoil.

suburbio *m.* suburb.

suceder *in.* to happen, occur, to inherit, to go after, follow.

suceso *m.* event, happening.

suciedad *f.* dirtiness, rubbish.

sucursal *adj.* branch; *f.* branch.

sudar *tr.* to sweat.

sudor *m.* sweat

suegra *f.* mother-in-law.

suegro *m.* father-in-law.

suela *f.* sole.

sueldo *m.* salary, pay.

suelo *m.* ground, soil; floor; pavement.

sueño *m.* sleep, dream.

suerte *f.* luck, fortune, chance; kind, sort; way.

sufragar *tr.* to help, support.

sufrir *tr.* to suffer; to undergo.

sugerir *tr.* to suggest.

suicidarse *r.* to commit suicide.

sujetador *m.* fastener; brass.

sujetar *tr.* to subject; to fasten; *r.* to subject oneself, to submit.

suma *f.* addition, amount.

sumar *tr.* to add, to sum; *in.* to add.

sumergir *tr. & r.* to submerge.

sumiso -sa *adj.* submissive, humble.

sumo -ma *adj.* high, great; supreme.

superabundar *in.* to superabound, overflow.

superar *tr.* to surpass, excel, overcome.

superficie *f.* surface; area.

superfluo -ua *adj.* superfluous.

superviviente *adj. m. & f.* survivor.

suplicar *tr. & in.* to supplicate; implore, beg, play.

suplir *tr.* to supply, provide.

suprimir *tr.* to suppress, cut out.

sur *m.* south.

surcar *tr.* to furrow; to plough, to plough through.

surgir *in.* to sprout, spurt; to come forth; to arise.

surtir *tr.* to provide, furnish; to produce.

suspender *tr.* to hang; to adjourn, to fail.

suspirar *in.* to sigh; to long for.

sustentar *tr.* to sustain, support.

susto *m.* scare, fright.

susurrar *in.* to whisper, murmure, hum; *r.* to be whispered about.

sutil *adj.* subtle, keen.

suyo -ya *adj. & pron. poss.* his, hers, yours, theirs, its, one's.

T

tabaco *m.* tobacco; **tabaco de polvo**, snuff.

taberna *f.* tavern, pub.

tabique *m.* thin wall.

tabla *f.* board; table; butcher shop.

tablero *m.* board; panel.

tableta *f.* tablet.

taburete *m.* stool.

tacaño -ña *adj.* stingy; cunning.

taco *m.* bung, plug; cue; swearword.

tacto *m. (sense of)* touch; tact.

tachar *tr.* to erase; to strike out; to censure.

tajada *f.* cut, slice.

tajo *m.* cut; trench.

tal *adj. indef.* such; *pron. indef.* so-and-so; *adv.* so.

taladrar *tr.* to bore, drill.

talar *adj.* long; *tr.* to fell.

talega *f.* bag, sack.

talón *m.* (An.) heel; heel; counterfoil.

talonario *m.* receipt book.

talla *f.* cut; carving; height, stature; size.

tallar *tr.* to carve; to engrave; to cut.

talle *m.* shape, figure.

taller *m.* shop, workshop; atelier, studio.

tallo *m.* sterm, stalk.

tamaño -ña *adj.* such a big; *m.* size.

también *adv.* also, too.

tambor *m.* drum.

tamizar *tr.* to sieve.

tampoco *adv.* neither, not either, nor.

tan *adv.* so; **tan siquiera**, at least.

tanque *m.* tank.

tantear *tr.* to compare; to size up; to test; to keep the score of; *in.* to keep score.

tapadera *f.* lid, cover, cap.

tapar *tr.* to cover up; to conceal *(a fugitive)*; *r.* to cover oneself.

tapete *m.* rug; cardtable.

tapicería *f.* tapestry; upholstery.

tapón *m.* cork; plug.

taquigrafía *f.* shorthand.

taquilla *f.* file; ticket office.

tara *f.* tare; defect.

tardar *in.* to be long; to be late; **a más tardar**, at the latest.

tarde *adv.* late; too late.

tarifa *f.* tariff; price list; rate; fare.

tarima *f.* stand; platform.

tarjeta *f.* card.

tarro *m.* jar.

tarta *f.* tart; pan.

tartamudo -da *adj.* stuttering, stammering; *m. & f.* stutterer, stammerer.

tasa *f.* measure; estimate.

tasar *tr.* to appraise; to regulate.

tatuaje *m.* tattoo, tattooing.

tauromaquia *f.* bullfighting.

taxi *m.* taxi, cab.

taza *f.* cup.

tazón *m.* bowl.

té *m.* tea; drink.

teatro *m.* theathe.

tecla *f.* key.

techo *m.* ceiling; roof, shelter.

teja *f.* roofing tile; shovel hat.

tejer *tr.* to weave.

tejido *m.* weave, texture.

tela *f.* cloth, fabric.

telar *m.* loom; frame *con.* thing.

telaraña *f.* spider web, cobweb.

telefonear *tr. & in.* to telephone, ring up.

T-U

telegrafiar *tr. & in.* to telegraph, wire, cable.

telegrama *m.* telegram wire.

telón *m.* curtain.

tema *m.* theme, subject; (Gram.) stem; ida.

temblar *in.* to tremble, quiver; to shiver.

temer *tr. & in.* to fear, dread.

temor *m.* fear, dread.

tempestad *f.* storm, tempest.

templar *tr.* to temper; to soften; *in.* to warm up; *r.* to temper; to moderate.

templo *m.* temple, church.

temporada *f.* season; period.

temprano -na *adj.* early.

tender *tr.* to spread, spread out, stretch out.

tendero -ra *m. & f.* storekeeper, shopkeeper.

tenedor *m.* fork; holder.

tener *tr.* to have; to keep; to own, possess; to esteem; *r.* to keep from falling.

tenis *m.* (sport) tennis.

tenorio *m.* lady-killer.

tenso -sa *adj.* tense, tight, stiff.

tentar *tr.* to touch; to try; to tempt, to attempt.

teñir *tr.* to dye; to stain; to tinger.

tercero -ra *adj.* third; *m. & f.* third; mediator.

tercio -cia *adj.* third; *m.* third, corps, troop.

terciopelo *m.* velvet.

tergiversar *tr.* to twist; *in.* to distort.

terminar *tr.* to terminate, to end; to finish; *in.* to terminate; *r.* to terminate, to end.

término *m.* end, limit; term.

termo *m.* thermos bottle, flask.

termómetro *m.* thermometer.

ternera *f.* calf; veal.

terraplén *m.* rampart, bank.

terraza *f.* terrace.

terremoto *m.* earthquake.

terreno -na *adj.* terrestrial; mundane; *m.* land, ground; field; (fig.) field, sphere.

terrón *m.* lump.

terruño *m.* homeland, little country.

tertulia *f.* party, cirde.

tesis *f.* thesis, theme.

tesorería *f.* treasury.

tesoro *m.* treasure; treasury.

testamento *m.* testament, will.

testificar *tr. & in.* to testify, witness.

testimoniar *tr.* to attest, to testify to.

teta *f.* breast, nipple.

tetera *f.* teapot, teakettle.

texto *m.* text.

tez *f.* complexion, skin.

tía *f.* aunt; *con.* bawd.

tibio -bia *adj.* tepid, lukewarm; *f.* (An.) tibia shinbone.

tiburón *m.* shark.

tiempo *m.* time; occasion; opportunity; weather; (Gram.) tense; (Mús.) tempo.

tienda *f.* shop.

tierno -na *adj.* tender; soft; delicate.

tierra *f.* earth; ground; land; country.

tieso -sa *adj.* stiff; tight; tense.

tiesto *m.* flowerpot.

tijera *f.* scissors, shears.

tila *f.* (Bot.) linden tree.

timar *tr.* to cheat, trick.

timbre *m.* seal, stamp; tax stamp; bell, electric bell; timbre.

timo *m. con.* theft, swindle; *con.* lie.

timón *m.* beam, helm.

tímpano *m.* eardrum; (An.) tympanum.

tinaja *f.* large earthen jar.

tinieblas *f. pl.* darkness.

tinta *f.* ink.

tinto *adj.* red *(wine)*.

tío *m.* uncle; *con.* old man.

tira *f.* strip.

tirabuzón *m.* corkscrew; curl.

tirador -ra *m. & f.* thrower; drawer; *m.* knob; (Elec.) pull cord.

tirante *adj.* tense; (fig.) tense; **tirantes**, *m. pl.* suspenders (U.S.A.) braces.

tirar *tr.* to throw, cast; to shoot, fire *(a gun)*; to draw, pull *(wire)*; to print; to tear down; to knock down.

tiritar *in.* to shiver.

tiro *m.* shot; range; draft; team; pull cord; sport drive, shot.

titubear *in.* to stagger, totter; to stammer.

titular *adj.* titular official; *m.* bearer, holder *(of a passport)*; *f.* capital letter; *tr.* to title, to entitle.

título *m.* title; headline.

tiza *f.* chalk.

toalla *f.* towel.

tobillo *m.* ankle.

tobogán *m.* slide.

tocadiscos *m.* record player.

tocador *m.* boudoir; dressing table.

tocar *tr.* to feel; to touch; to ring; (Mús.) to play; *ni.* to pertain to, to concern; to be one's turn; to fall; to one's lot.

tocino *m.* the white of the bacon; bacon.

todavía *adv.* still, yet.

todo -da *adj.* all, whole, every; full *(speed)*; *m.* whole; *m. pl.* all, everybody.

toga *f.* gown.

toldo *m.* awning.

tolerar *tr.* to tolerate; to bear, suffer, endure.

tomar *tr.* to take; to get; to seize; to catch *(cold)*; to have *(breakfast)*.

tomate *m.* (Bot.) tomato.

tomillo *m.* (Bot.) thyme.

tomo *m.* volume.

tonel *m.* cask, barrel.

tonelada *f.* ton.

tonelaje *m.* tonnage.

tono *m.* tone.

tonto -ta *adj.* foolish, stupid; silly.

topo *m.* (Zool.) mole.

toque *m.* touch; knock; beat.

taquilla *f.* triangular kerchief.

torcer *tr.* to twist; to turn; to twist up; *in.* to turn; *r.* to sprain, dislocate.

torear *tr.* to fight; *in.* to fight bulls.

torero -ra *m.* bull fighter, matador.

tormenta *f.* storm, tempest.

tornillo *m.* screw, vice.

torno *m.* lathe; vice.

toro *m.* bull.

torre *f.* tower; watchtower; (Nav.) turret; castle *(chess)*.

torrente *m.* torrent.

torta *f.* cake; *con.* slap.

tortilla *f.* omelet.

tortuga *f.* (Zool.) tortoise, turtle.

torturar *tr.* to torture, to torment.

tos *f.* cough.

toser *in.* to cough.

tostar *tr. & r.* to toast; to roast; to tan.

total *adj. & m.* total; entire, whole.

trabajar *tr.* to work; to till *(the soil)*.

trabajo *tr.* to join, unite; to join *(battle)*; *in.* to take hold; *r.* to become entangled.

traca *f.* string of firecrackers.

traducción *f.* translation.

traducir *tr.* to translate.

traer *tr.* to bring; to carry; to cause.

traficar *in.* to traffic, deal, trade.

tragaluz *m.* skylight, bull's eye.

T-U

tragaperras *m. con.* slot machine.

tragar *tr.* to swallow; to gulp, *r.* to swallow up; (fig.) to swallow.

trago *m.* swallow; gulp; *con.* misfortune.

traición *f.* treachery; treason.

traicionar *tr.* to betray.

traído -da *adj.* threadbare.

traidor -ra *adj. m. & f.* traitor betrayer.

traje *m.* dress, costume; suit; gown.

trajín *m.* carrying; going and coming.

tramar *tr.* to weave; to plot, to scheme.

tramo *m.* tract, stretch; flight.

trampa *f.* trap; snare, pitfall; foul play.

trampolín *m.* spring board.

tranquilizar *tr. in. & r.* to tranquilize, calm down.

transcurrir *in.* to pass, elapse.

transeúnte *adj.* transient; *m. & f.* transient; passer-by.

transferir *tr.* to transfer.

transformar *tr.* to transform; to change; *r.* to transform, to turn into.

transigir *tr. & in.* to settle, to compromise.

transitar *in.* to travel, journey; to pass by.

transmitir *tr. & in.* to transmit, forward.

transpirar *tr. & in.* to transpire.

transportar *tr.* to transport; to transfer; *r.* to be carried away.

trapo *m.* rag.

trasero -ra *adj.* back; *m.* buttock, rump, bottom.

trasladar *tr.* to transfer, *r.* to move.

trasnochar *tr.* to be up all night, *in.* to spend the night.

traspasar *tr.* to cross, cross over; to pierce, to

transgress *(a law); r.* to go too far.

transplantar *tr.* to transplant; *r.* to transplant.

traste *m.* fret.

trastienda *f.* back shop.

tratar *tr.* to handle; to deal with.

través *m.* reverse.

travesaño *m.* crosspiece, crosstimber.

travieso -sa *adj.* cross, transverse; keen; restless, naught; *f.* crosstie.

trayecto *m.* journey, passage.

trazar *tr.* to plan, design; to outline; to trace; to draw *(a line).*

trébol *m.* (Bot.) clover, trefoil, shamrock.

trece *adj.* thirteen.

trecho *m.* strech.

tregua *f.* truce; letup.

treinta *adj.* thrity.

tren *m.* train; outfit.

trenza *f.* braid, plait.

trepar *tr.* to climb.

tres *adj.* three; *m.* three.

tresillo *m.* ombre; three piece suit.

tribunal *m.* court, bar.

tributar *tr.* to pay.

trigo *m.* (Bot.) wheat.

trillar *tr.* to thresh.

trimestre *m.* term.

trinchar *tr.* to carve, to slice.

trino *adj.* trinal, three fold *m.* rill, warble.

tripa *f.* gut, intestine.

triple *adj. & m.* triple.

tripulación *f.* crew.

tripular *tr.* to man *(ship).*

triste *adj.* sad; sorrowful.

triturar *tr.* to triturate; to mash, grind.

trofeo *m.* trophy.

tromba *f.* column; avalanche; water-sport.

trompo *m.* top.

tronco *m.* trunk; stalk.

tronchar *tr.* to chop off; to break off.

tropa *f.* troop, flock; (Mil.) troops.

tropezar *tr.* to hit; to strike; *in.* to stumble.

trozo *m.* piece, bit, fragment.

trucha *f.* trout.

trueno *m.* thunder.

tú *pron. pers.* you.

tubería *f.* piping, pipes.

tubo *m.* tube; pipe.

tuerca *f.* (Mach.) nut.

tuerto -ta *adj.* one-eyed person.

tufo *m.* fume, vapor.

tullir *tr.* to cripple, paralyze; *r.* to become crippled or paralyzed.

tumba *f.* grave, tomb.

tumbar *tr.* to knock down; *r. con.* to lie down.

tuna *f.* group of students that play guitars.

tundir *tr.* to shear *(cloth)*; *con.* to beat.

túnel *m.* tunnel.

turbar *tr.* to distrub, upset, trouble.

turnar *in.* to alternate.

turno *m.* turn, shift.

turrón *m.* nougat, almond sweetmeat.

tutor -ra *m. & f.* guardian, protector, tuter.

tuyo -ya *adj. pron. poss.* yours.

U

u *cn.* (used instead of o before words beginning by o).

ubicación *f.* location, situation.

ubicar *tr.* (Am.) to place, locate; *in. & r.* to be located.

úlcera *f.* ulcer.

ultimar *tr.* to end, finish.

último -ma *adj.* last, latest.

ultrajar *tr.* to outrage.

ultramar *m.* country overseas.

ultranza; a ultranza, to the death.

umbral *m.* threshold.

un, una *art. indef.* a, an; *adj.* one *(numeral)*.

unción *f.* unction.

ungir *tr.* to annoint, consacrate.

único -ca *adj.* only, sole, unique.

unidad *f.* unit, unity.

unificar *tr.* to unify.

uniforme *adj. & m.* uniform.

unir *tr. & r.* to unite, join.

universo -sa *adj.* universal; *m.* univers, earth.

uno -una *adj. & pron. indef.* one, someone; *m.* one *(numeral)*.

untar *tr.* to annoint; to smear, grease; *con.* to slap; *r.* to get smeared.

unto *m.* grease, fat.

uña *f.* nail, fingernail, toenail.

uralita *f.* asbestos.

uranio *in.* (Chm.) uranium.

urbano -na *adj.* urban, urbane.

urbe *f.* big city, metropolis.

urgencia *f.* urgency; emergency.

urgir *in.* to be urgent.

urinario toilet; public conveniencies.

urna *f.* urn; ballot box.

usado -da *adj.* used.

usar *tr.* to use, make use of.

uso *m.* use; custom; habit; practice.

usted *prom. pers.* you.

usurpar *tr.* usurp.

útil *adj.* useful; *m.* use.

utilizar *tr.* to utilize, use.

uva *f.* grape.

T - U

V

vaca f. cow; beef.
vacación f. vacation, holidays.
vaciar tr. to drain, to empty.
vacilar in. to vacillate.
vacuna f. vaccination.
vacunar tr. to vaccinate.
vado m. ford.
vagabundear in. to wander.
vagón m. wagon.
vaguedad f. vagueness, ambiguity.
vaho m. vapor, fume.
vaivén m. coming and going.
vajilla f. set of dishes.
vale m. bond; receipt.
valer m. worth, merit.
validez f. validity.
válido -da adj. valid; strong.
valija f. valise, bag.
valor m. value, worth.
valoración f. valuation.
valorar tr. to value.
válvula f. valve.
valla f. fence, barricade.
valle m. valley, vale.
vanagloriar r. to boast.
vanidoso -sa vain, conceited.
vapor m. steam, vapour.
vaquero m. cowboy.
vara f. twig, stick.
variable adj. variable.
variar tr. & in. to vary, to change.
varilla f. rod, twig; wand.
varón m. man, male.
vasija f. vessel, container.
vaso m. glass; vessel.
vaticinar tr. to prophesy.
vatio m. (Elec.) watt.
vecindad f. neighbourhood.
vecindario m. inhabitants.
vecino -na adj. neighboring, near; m. & f. neighbor.
veda f. prohibition.
vedar tr. to forbid, prohibit.
vega f. fertile plain.

vegetal adj. vegetal; m. plant.
vehículo m. vehicle.
veinte adj. twenty.
vejez f. old age.
vejiga f. bladder.
vela f. wakefulness; candle.
velar tr. to watch; in. to stay awake.
velero m. sailmaker.
veleta f. weathercock; m. & f. fickle person.
velo m. veil; humeral veil.
velocidad f. velocity; speed.
vello m. down.
vena f. vein.
venablo m. javelin, dart.
vencedor -ra adj., m. & f. conqueror; winner.
vendaje m. bandage.
vendar tr. to bandage; to blind.
vendaval m. strong wind.
vender tr. to sell; in. to sell; r. to sell oneself.
vendimia f. vintage.
vendimiar tr. to gather (grapes).
veneno m. poison.
vengar tr. to avenge; r. to take revenge.
venidero -ra adj. coming, future.
venir in. to come.
venta f. sale; inn.
ventaja f. advantage, profit.
ventana f. window.
ventilador m. ventilator.
ventilar tr. to ventilate; to do.
ventoso -sa adj. windy.
ventura f. happiness; luck.
veraneo m. summer holidays.
verano m. summer.
veras f. pl. truth; **de veras**, in truth.
verbena f. (Bot.) verbena; night festival.
verbo m. (Gram.) verb; the word.
verdad f. truth.
verdadero -ra adj. true.
verde adj. green; unripe.

voltaje *m.* (Elec.) voltage.
voltear *tr.* to upset, to roll over.
voltio *m.* (Elec.) volt.
volumen *m.* volume, bulk, amount.
voluntad *f.* will; determination.
volver *tr.* to turn; to turn over.
vomitar *tr.* to vomit, throw up.
vos *pron. pers.* you.
vosotros -tras *pron. pers.* you.
votación *f.* voting.
votante *adj.* voting; *m. & f.* voter.
votar *tr.* to vow; to vote.
voz *f.* voice; word; *f. pl.* outcry.
vuelco *m.* upset, overturning.
vuelo *m.* flight, flying.
vuelto -ta *pp.* of **volver**; turn, rotation; change.
vulcanizar *tr.* to vulcanize.
vulgar *adj.* vernacular; common.
vulnerar *tr.* to harm, injure.

Y

yacer *in.* to lie; to rest.
yacimiento *m.* bed,
yanqui *adj., m. & f.* Yankee.
yarda *f.* yard.
yate *m.* yacht.
yegua *f.* mare.
yelmo *m.* helmet.
yema *f.* yolk *(of egg); bud.*
yerno *m.* son-in-law.
yerro *m.* error, mistake.
yesca *f.* tinder.
yeso *m.* gypsum.
yo *pron. pers.* I.
yunque *m.* anvil.

Z

zafiro *m.* sapphire.
zagal *m.* youth; shepherd's helper.
zagala *f.* shepherdess.
zaguán *m.* vestibule, entrance.
zalamero -ra *adj., m. & f.* flatterer.
zamarra *f.* shepherd's sheepskin jacket.
zanahoria *f.* (Bot.) carrot.
zanca *f.* long leg.
zanco *m.* stilt.
zángano *m.* (Zool.) drone.
zanja *f.* ditch, trench.
zanjar *tr.* to dig a ditch *(or)* ditches in.
zapata *f.* half boot.
zapatería *f.* shoe's shop.
zapatilla *f.* slipper.
zarandear *tr.* to sift, to screen.
zarpar *tr.* to weigh.
zarza *f.* (Bot.) blackberry bush.
zarzal *m.* blackberry patch.
zarzuela *f.* zarzuela, musical comedy.
zócalo *m.* (Arch.) socle, pediment.
zona *f.* zone.
zoológico -ca *adj.* zoological.
zoquete *m.* block, chunk.
zorro *m.* (Zool.) male fox.
zozobrar *tr.* to sink; *in.* to capsize, founder.
zueco *m.* wooden shoe.
zumbar *in.* to buzz, to hum.
zumbido *m.* buzz, hum.
zumbón *adj.* waggish; *m. & f.* wag.
zuma *m.* juice.
zurcir *tr.* to darn.
zurrar *tr.* to curry; *con.* to drub, to thrash.
zurrón *m.* shepherd's leather bag.

V-Z

SPECIAL OFFER
Reference Library

WEBSTER'S
FRENCH-ENGLISH
ENGLISH-FRENCH
DICTIONARY

$5.95

NEW
WEBSTER'S
LARGE PRINT
DICTIONARY

$5.95

NEW
WEBSTER'S
EXPANDED
DICTIONARY

$6.95

HOME
MEDICAL
DICTIONARY

$5.95

NEW
WEBSTER'S
SPANISH-ENGLISH
ENGLISH-SPANISH
DICTIONARY

$5.95

NEW
WEBSTER'S
DICTIONARY

$5.95

Special: Purchase any first book at regular price and choose any second book for $2.95 plus $1.50 for postage and handling for each book.

Please send me the following books:

____ Home Medical Dictionary ____ New Webster's Large Print Dictionary
____ Webster's Spanish/English Dictionary ____ New Webster's Dictionary
____ Webster's French/English Dictionary ____ New Webster's Expanded Dictionary

Name_____

Address _____

City_____ State_____ ZIP _____

I have enclosed $_____ for ____ books which includes all postage and handling costs. (No C.O.D.)

Send to: Paradise Press, Inc.
12956 S.W. 133rd Ct.
Miami, FL 33186